ISEE Lower Level
2500+ Practice Questions

ISEE Lower Level: 2500+ Practice Questions

For any questions about this book or any of our other ISEE resources, you can contact us at info@elevateprep.com or visit us at www.elevateprep.com.

Table of Contents

Elevate Prep's Other Books and Educational Resources

Visit us at www.elevateprep.com to learn more about our test prep books, math workbooks, and math game.

Test Prep Books: Our ISEE Middle Level prep book, ISEE Upper Level prep book, and HSPT prep book each come with over 2500 practice questions and three full-length practice tests.

Math Workbooks: Our elementary and middle school workbooks are great for mastering fundamental math concepts. Each workbook comes with over 3000 practice problems and over 150 practice drills.

Games: Looking for a fun way to practice math with your children? Try Target! Target is a fast-paced mental math game that helps students practice their addition, subtraction, multiplication, and division facts in a fun and engaging way.

We'd love to hear from you after using our book!

At Elevate Prep, it's our mission to create educational resources that help students succeed. We are constantly revising our materials to make sure that they meet the needs of our students. If you have any feedback after using this book, we'd love it if you left us a review!

Introduction

Welcome

Dear Students, Parents, and Educators,

At Elevate Prep, we believe that the key to scoring well on the ISEE is going into the test with confidence. From our experience working with hundreds of students, we've found that the key to feeling confident on test day is to practice, practice, and practice some more! While test taking strategies are helpful, students cannot feel fully confident on test day if they don't have a solid foundation of the core concepts that are being tested.

That's why our workbook contains over 2500 practice problems. We've thoroughly researched the test and identified the core concepts that are tested in each section. Our questions are comprehensive and cover a wide range of topics that show up on the test. Our questions range in difficulty, so students can learn the fundamentals of a concept before diving into challenging, test-like questions.

We want our students to have the resources they need to be successful during their test prep process. To help, we have created detailed answer explanations for every multiple-choice question in this book. We have also put together a free list of online videos that cover all of the math topics in this book. You can find the explanations and video list at www.elevateprep.com/isee-lower-level

If you have any questions while working through this book, don't hesitate to reach out to us! We are here to help. Send us an email at info@elevateprep.com, or visit our website for free resources and information about the ISEE, other admissions tests, and the private school admissions process.

Happy studying!

Lisa James – Founder of Elevate Prep

How to Use This Book

Overview

The purpose of this practice book is to provide students with comprehensive practice material for the ISEE Lower Level. While the book gives a brief overview of the ISEE, students should have some prior knowledge about the test before using this practice book. You can learn more about the ISEE by visiting www.erblearn.org.

How the Book is Organized

The book is broken up into six main chapters: Verbal, Math Fundamentals, Math Multiple Choice, Reading, Essay, and Practice Tests.

Verbal: This chapter covers the Verbal Reasoning section of the ISEE Lower Level. In consists of practice sets for each type of question that shows up on the Verbal Reasoning section.

Math Fundamentals: This chapter covers fundamental topics that are necessary for answering question in the Quantitative Reasoning and Mathematics Achievement sections of the ISEE Lower Level. It covers over 20 topics ranging from addition and subtraction to multiplication and division of fractions and includes two practice sets for each topic. The purpose of this chapter is to provide students with material that will allow them to master the math fundamentals needed to answer more challenging test questions, so the practice sets consist of non-multiple choice, straightforward computation questions.

Math Multiple Choice: This chapter covers multiple choice questions that show up in the Quantitative Reasoning and Mathematics Achievement sections of the ISEE Lower Level. It covers 40 topics and includes two practice sets for each topic. The purpose of this chapter is to provide students with practice questions that mirror the style and difficulty of questions on the actual test.

Reading: This chapter covers the Reading Comprehension section of the ISEE Lower Level. It consists of 40 reading comprehension passages, each followed by five multiple-choice questions.

Essay: This chapter covers the Essay section of the ISEE Lower Level. It includes an overview of the Essay section, tips on how to approach the essay, and 10 practice essay prompts.

Practice Tests: This chapter includes three full-length practice tests for the ISEE Lower level.

At the beginning of each of the above chapters, there are more details about how to use that chapter. It's important that students carefully read the directions at the beginning of each chapter to ensure they get the most out of this book.

Tips for Using this Book

1. **Use one of the practice tests as a diagnostic.** It is helpful to understand your areas of weakness before working through this book. To do this, you can use one of the three practice tests at the end of the book as a diagnostic test. Once you finish the test and grade it, determine which types of questions you are struggling with, and focus on those areas first.

2. **Write your answers in a separate notebook**. If you want to have the ability to redo practice sets, write your answers and show your work in a separate notebook. This will allow you to go back and redo practice sets that you struggled with.

3. **Save two practice tests for the end.** While we suggest using one of the practice tests as a diagnostic test, we highly recommend saving the other two practice tests for the end of your prep process. Once you've worked through the topics in this book, use the practice tests to make sure you feel confident with all of the concepts. We recommend taking the last two practice tests during the month before your official exam. After taking these two practice tests, review any concepts that you are still struggling with.

4. **Start early and study in small chunks**. The ISEE prep process can be long, so it's important to start early. We suggest giving yourself four to eight months to prepare, depending on your starting scores. As you're working through the book, be sure to pace yourself. Studying for one or two hours each week for a few months is better than studying for five hours each day for a week.

ISEE Lower Level Overview

The ISEE (Independent School Entrance Exam) is an admissions test used by many independent schools throughout the United States and abroad. The lower level of the test is used for students applying for admissions to 5th and 6th grade. The test is broken up into five different sections:

Section 1: Verbal Reasoning

The Verbal Reasoning section is made up of 34 questions, and students are given 20 minutes to complete the section. The section is broken up into synonym questions and sentence completion questions. Synonym questions consist of an abstract, grade-level appropriate word followed by four answer choices. Sentence completion questions consist of a sentence missing a single word or a phrase followed by four answer choices. Students must choose the answer choice that best completes the sentence.

Section 2: Quantitative Reasoning

The Quantitative Reasoning section is made up of 38 questions, and students are given 35 minutes to complete the section. The section consists of word problems that are somewhat different than what most students have seen in school, and some require very little or no calculation. The purpose of this section is to test students' mathematical reasoning skills.

Section 3: Reading Comprehension

The Reading Comprehension section is made up of 25 questions, and students are given 25 minutes to complete the section. The section is made up of five reading passages covering a variety of topics including history, science, literature, and contemporary life. Each passage is accompanied by five multiple-choice questions.

Section 4: Mathematics Achievement

The Mathematics Achievement section is made up of 30 questions, and students are given 30 minutes to complete the section. The questions in this section cover topics that students have learned throughout their math career and are more straightforward than the word problems found in the Quantitative Reasoning section.

Section 5: Essay

The essay section asks students to respond to a prompt, and students are given 30 minutes to complete the section. The essay section is not graded, but it is sent to private schools along with the rest of the test scores.

Verbal

How to Use the Verbal Chapter

Chapter Overview

This chapter of the book covers the Verbal Reasoning section. The purpose of this chapter is to present students with test-like questions so they can become familiar with the style and difficulty of questions that show up on the ISEE Lower Level.

Using the Practice Passages

The chapter contains 10 practice sets for synonym questions and 10 practice sets for sentence completion questions. Work through each practice set one at a time and review your answers before moving on to the next practice set.

Tips for Working Through this Chapter

1. **Study vocabulary words before working through the practice sets**. Before working through all of the practice sets, we suggest studying vocabulary words. While no one knows exactly which words will show up on the test, there are many great vocabulary lists online. You can find ISEE Lower Level vocabulary lists online by searching for "ISEE Lower Level Vocabulary List." Once you've studied vocabulary words, use the practice sets to test yourself.

2. **Write down any words that you don't know.** Since no one knows exactly which words will show up on the test, it's important to learn as many words as possible. While you're working through these sets, keep a list of any words that you don't know and study this list throughout your prep process. Look up a short definition for each word and write it down next to the word in your list. We also suggest writing a sentence for each word. Try to make up a sentence that relates to you and shows the meaning of the word. For example, if the word is *aggravating* which means *annoying or irritating*, you can make a sentence that says, "It's very **aggravating** when my little brother turns the TV off while I'm in the middle of playing Fortnite."

3. **Break up your practice.** Remember to break up your practice into small chunks. Don't try and cram all of the practice sets into a short amount of time. Studying vocabulary can take months, so be sure to give yourself enough time to not only complete the practice sets, but to also study any vocabulary words that you don't know.

Synonyms Practice Set 1

1. ABANDON

   (A) desert
   (B) forgive
   (C) dislike
   (D) punish

2. REGRETFUL

   (A) embarrassed
   (B) apologetic
   (C) appreciative
   (D) confused

3. SYMPATHETIC

   (A) regretful
   (B) apathetic
   (C) supportive
   (D) understandable

4. ENGAGING

   (A) annoying
   (B) popular
   (C) timid
   (D) charming

5. SUPERB

   (A) average
   (B) excellent
   (C) thrilling
   (D) intriguing

6. DESPAIR

   (A) worry
   (B) hopelessness
   (C) outrage
   (D) uncertainty

7. TRIVIAL

   (A) inconsequential
   (B) questioning
   (C) crucial
   (D) intelligent

8. TEDIOUS

   (A) disastrous
   (B) risky
   (C) simple
   (D) boring

9. ARROGANT

   (A) humble
   (B) attacking
   (C) cocky
   (D) respectful

10. ASSUMPTION

   (A) rumor
   (B) guess
   (C) insult
   (D) statement

11. APPRENTICE

   (A) master
   (B) peer
   (C) trainee
   (D) teacher

12. STERN

   (A) foolish
   (B) hurtful
   (C) influential
   (D) serious

13. FLEXIBLE

   (A) weak
   (B) bouncy
   (C) adaptable
   (D) sturdy

14. OPTIMISTIC

   (A) worried
   (B) hopeful
   (C) energized
   (D) relaxed

15. EXILE

   (A) kill
   (B) imprison
   (C) reject
   (D) banish

16. FATIGUED

   (A) tired
   (B) refreshed
   (C) lazy
   (D) sickly

17. INDIFFERENT

   (A) unconcerned
   (B) emotional
   (C) similar
   (D) ignorant

18. BIZARRE

   (A) unsettling
   (B) odd
   (C) expected
   (D) lonely

Synonyms Practice Set 2

1. DELIBERATE

   (A) accidental
   (B) malicious
   (C) intentional
   (D) compassionate

2. CONFORM

   (A) adapt
   (B) verify
   (C) reject
   (D) observe

3. AROMA

   (A) flower
   (B) taste
   (C) smell
   (D) sensation

4. ARID

   (A) deserted
   (B) awful
   (C) rough
   (D) dry

5. BLATANT

   (A) intentional
   (B) obvious
   (C) intense
   (D) offensive

6. ABNORMAL

   (A) unfriendly
   (B) strange
   (C) common
   (D) impossible

7. IMPULSIVE

   (A) spontaneous
   (B) aggressive
   (C) precise
   (D) foolish

8. ATROCIOUS

   (A) amazing
   (B) mournful
   (C) violent
   (D) horrible

9. CATASTROPHE

   (A) disaster
   (B) injury
   (C) situation
   (D) coincidence

10. MODEST

    (A) bold
    (B) humble
    (C) kind
    (D) interesting

11. ABSURD

    (A) confident
    (B) loud
    (C) ridiculous
    (D) incorrect

12. SUBJECTIVE

    (A) disinterested
    (B) neutral
    (C) abusive
    (D) biased

13. PEDESTRIAN

    (A) professional
    (B) exciting
    (C) unusual
    (D) commonplace

14. PRESERVE

    (A) maintain
    (B) persist
    (C) steal
    (D) withstand

15. JUVENILE

    (A) criminal
    (B) mature
    (C) humorous
    (D) youthful

16. IMMENSE

    (A) unbearable
    (B) huge
    (C) intense
    (D) challenging

17. JUBILEE

    (A) celebration
    (B) invitation
    (C) expectation
    (D) excitement

18. COMPREHENSIVE

    (A) complete
    (B) confusing
    (C) selective
    (D) overwhelming

Synonyms Practice Set 3

1. VAGUE

   (A) consistent
   (B) incorrect
   (C) unclear
   (D) obvious

2. QUAINT

   (A) quiet
   (B) charming
   (C) modern
   (D) small

3. MEANDERING

   (A) long
   (B) narrow
   (C) confusing
   (D) winding

4. NAÏVE

   (A) sophisticated
   (B) disobedient
   (C) inexperienced
   (D) irresponsible

5. NONCHALANT

   (A) serious
   (B) unconcerned
   (C) passionate
   (D) lazy

6. WEALTHY

   (A) arrogant
   (B) destitute
   (C) charitable
   (D) rich

7. FRUGAL

   (A) poor
   (B) thrifty
   (C) tasty
   (D) selfish

8. INFECTIOUS

   (A) kindhearted
   (B) dangerous
   (C) sickly
   (D) contagious

9. COMPROMISE

   (A) understanding
   (B) triumph
   (C) disagreement
   (D) decision

10. ACCELERATE

   (A) speed
   (B) halt
   (C) incline
   (D) elaborate

11. APPROXIMATE

   (A) estimated
   (B) precise
   (C) incorrect
   (D) optional

12. CONFINE

   (A) release
   (B) restrict
   (C) reveal
   (D) penalize

13. AGGRAVATE

   (A) intimidate
   (B) disrespect
   (C) irritate
   (D) meditate

14. MANDATORY

   (A) optional
   (B) stressful
   (C) unpleasant
   (D) required

15. INTERRUPT

   (A) interfere
   (B) continue
   (C) prank
   (D) speak

16. FORBID

   (A) permit
   (B) suggest
   (C) discipline
   (D) ban

17. IMMATURE

   (A) developed
   (B) unintelligent
   (C) childish
   (D) goofy

18. LENIENT

   (A) strict
   (B) funny
   (C) unbalanced
   (D) forgiving

Synonyms Practice Set 4

1. SINCERE

   (A) tricky
   (B) genuine
   (C) gentle
   (D) affectionate

2. ABBREVIATE

   (A) shorten
   (B) whisper
   (C) expand
   (D) discontinue

3. DILIGENT

   (A) hardworking
   (B) admirable
   (C) creative
   (D) punctual

4. THRILLED

   (A) late
   (B) content
   (C) agreeable
   (D) excited

5. SKILLED

   (A) adjusted
   (B) intellectual
   (C) talented
   (D) inferior

6. ILLUMINATE

   (A) realize
   (B) invent
   (C) encourage
   (D) brighten

7. FLOURISH

   (A) decorate
   (B) maintain
   (C) thrive
   (D) strive

8. SUFFOCATE

   (A) suffer
   (B) smother
   (C) trap
   (D) kill

9. PECULIAR

   (A) rejected
   (B) evil
   (C) familiar
   (D) atypical

10. ANONYMOUS

    (A) unimportant
    (B) unknown
    (C) famous
    (D) insignificant

11. COMPEL

    (A) force
    (B) obey
    (C) suggest
    (D) require

12. CELEBRATE

    (A) graduate
    (B) dance
    (C) honor
    (D) laugh

13. QUENCH

    (A) drink
    (B) destroy
    (C) increase
    (D) satisfy

14. SOLITARY

    (A) alone
    (B) disliked
    (C) surrounded
    (D) depressed

15. AGENDA

    (A) schedule
    (B) task
    (C) meeting
    (D) information

16. OPPORTUNE

    (A) lucky
    (B) inconvenient
    (C) enjoyable
    (D) consistent

17. CONTENT

    (A) excited
    (B) satisfied
    (C) unbothered
    (D) forgiving

18. ABIDE

    (A) reject
    (B) assist
    (C) obey
    (D) understand

Synonyms Practice Set 5

1. CHORE

   (A) task
   (B) cleaning
   (C) requirement
   (D) career

2. CONQUER

   (A) compete
   (B) brag
   (C) attempt
   (D) defeat

3. SLUGGISH

   (A) slimy
   (B) relaxed
   (C) lazy
   (D) busy

4. CREATE

   (A) adapt
   (B) trick
   (C) instruct
   (D) invent

5. OBVIOUS

   (A) unconcerned
   (B) evident
   (C) simple
   (D) irrelevant

6. ABSTRACT

   (A) concrete
   (B) artistic
   (C) theoretical
   (D) incorrect

7. INGENIOUS

   (A) unintelligent
   (B) abnormal
   (C) shy
   (D) imaginative

8. VIGOROUS

   (A) overwhelming
   (B) lively
   (C) joyous
   (D) delicate

9. THRIFTY

   (A) prudent
   (B) creative
   (C) rich
   (D) greedy

10. OBSTRUCT

   (A) initiate
   (B) block
   (C) break
   (D) instruct

11. PRETENTIOUS

   (A) wealthy
   (B) impolite
   (C) showy
   (D) stubborn

12. INTRIGUE

   (A) question
   (B) fascinate
   (C) bore
   (D) terrify

13. MEDIOCRE

   (A) extraordinary
   (B) disgusting
   (C) weird
   (D) average

14. CUNNING

   (A) sensitive
   (B) criminal
   (C) crafty
   (D) honest

15. REFLECTIVE

   (A) happy
   (B) bitter
   (C) thoughtful
   (D) dangerous

16. DISGRACE

   (A) sadness
   (B) honor
   (C) dishonesty
   (D) shame

17. OBLIVIOUS

   (A) unaware
   (B) clear
   (C) unintelligent
   (D) unemotional

18. IMMACULATE

   (A) messy
   (B) spotless
   (C) decorated
   (D) genius

Synonyms Practice Set 6

1. NOURISHING

   (A) delicious
   (B) tasteless
   (C) nutritious
   (D) vegetarian

2. OBSTACLE

   (A) advantage
   (B) hurdle
   (C) situation
   (D) protest

3. DESTRUCTIVE

   (A) damaging
   (B) intense
   (C) unexpected
   (D) jumbled

4. REFRAIN

   (A) withhold
   (B) reframe
   (C) forbid
   (D) continue

5. LAVISH

   (A) cheap
   (B) luxurious
   (C) perfect
   (D) passionate

6. CONCEITED

   (A) egotistical
   (B) defeated
   (C) nervous
   (D) brilliant

7. APPREHENSIVE

   (A) saddened
   (B) attacking
   (C) lazy
   (D) worried

8. PENETRATE

   (A) accelerate
   (B) pierce
   (C) skim
   (D) enrage

9. HARSH

   (A) sarcastic
   (B) mild
   (C) uncomfortable
   (D) rough

10. PRUDENT

    (A) reckless
    (B) afraid
    (C) careful
    (D) extravagant

11. VOW

    (A) pledge
    (B) understand
    (C) trust
    (D) breach

12. SARCASTIC

    (A) vengeful
    (B) untruthful
    (C) ironic
    (D) hilarious

13. PASSIVE

    (A) athletic
    (B) unresisting
    (C) kindhearted
    (D) argumentative

14. WAGER

    (A) bet
    (B) wobble
    (C) purchase
    (D) play

15. EXPAND

    (A) enlarge
    (B) trap
    (C) shrink
    (D) purchase

16. DEPLETE

    (A) conserve
    (B) drain
    (C) determine
    (D) depress

17. TAUNT

    (A) insult
    (B) disrupt
    (C) uplift
    (D) strike

18. FEUD

    (A) conversation
    (B) agreement
    (C) divorce
    (D) conflict

Synonyms Practice Set 7

1. APATHETIC

   (A) empathetic
   (B) mean
   (C) unsure
   (D) disinterested

2. ABUNDANT

   (A) delicious
   (B) heavy
   (C) plentiful
   (D) average

3. UNPREDICTABLE

   (A) expected
   (B) impossible
   (C) unstable
   (D) inflexible

4. INSIGNIFICANT

   (A) understated
   (B) unimportant
   (C) obedient
   (D) relevant

5. OVERWHELMING

   (A) negative
   (B) overpowering
   (C) stimulating
   (D) dull

6. HYSTERICAL

   (A) hilarious
   (B) unordinary
   (C) corny
   (D) offensive

7. CONTROVERSIAL

   (A) offensive
   (B) unanimous
   (C) unthinkable
   (D) disputed

8. DECEITFUL

   (A) sincere
   (B) humorous
   (C) dishonest
   (D) destructive

9. VIGILANT

   (A) heroic
   (B) stressful
   (C) combative
   (D) observant

10. PRIMITIVE

    (A) complex
    (B) developed
    (C) ancient
    (D) useless

11. SUBTLE

    (A) incorrect
    (B) unsure
    (C) understated
    (D) evident

12. MEDDLE

    (A) interfere
    (B) iron
    (C) observe
    (D) mishandle

13. JUSTIFY

    (A) revenge
    (B) prove
    (C) question
    (D) reject

14. KEEN

    (A) sharp
    (B) kind
    (C) sneaky
    (D) likeable

15. DISCREET

    (A) subtle
    (B) unfair
    (C) intentional
    (D) reliable

16. ELEGANT

    (A) wealthy
    (B) dramatic
    (C) inspiring
    (D) graceful

17. CANDID

    (A) guarded
    (B) honest
    (C) expected
    (D) artistic

18. ABRUPT

    (A) gradual
    (B) sudden
    (C) invasive
    (D) unlucky

Synonyms Practice Set 8

1. REBEL

   (A) conform
   (B) disobey
   (C) agitate
   (D) terrorize

2. CONTRADICT

   (A) contract
   (B) prove
   (C) misunderstand
   (D) oppose

3. HAZARDOUS

   (A) hurtful
   (B) deadly
   (C) dangerous
   (D) unfortunate

4. DEVOTED

   (A) studious
   (B) inconsistent
   (C) loyal
   (D) repetitive

5. EMPATHETIC

   (A) compassionate
   (B) arrogant
   (C) content
   (D) personable

6. REPRIMAND

   (A) praise
   (B) injure
   (C) scold
   (D) apologize

7. IMPOVERISHED

   (A) poor
   (B) incompetent
   (C) dirty
   (D) negligent

8. ECCENTRIC

   (A) varied
   (B) amused
   (C) energetic
   (D) odd

9. WARY

   (A) tired
   (B) cautious
   (C) stylish
   (D) terrified

10. MIMIC

    (A) quiet
    (B) act
    (C) imitate
    (D) appreciate

11. TERMINATE

    (A) destroy
    (B) commence
    (C) interrupt
    (D) finish

12. IMPARTIAL

    (A) biased
    (B) fair
    (C) infrequent
    (D) practical

13. DEFICIENT

    (A) unknowledgeable
    (B) lacking
    (C) unacceptable
    (D) immature

14. SCOLD

    (A) gasp
    (B) trick
    (C) apologize
    (D) reprimand

15. HIDEOUS

    (A) unique
    (B) ugly
    (C) mean
    (D) violent

16. SCOUR

    (A) tart
    (B) search
    (C) observe
    (D) scream

17. SKEPTICAL

    (A) distressed
    (B) dishonest
    (C) doubtful
    (D) convincing

18. NUMEROUS

    (A) many
    (B) mathematical
    (C) complicated
    (D) similar

Synonyms Practice Set 9

1. SENTIMENTAL

   (A) emotional
   (B) likeable
   (C) cautious
   (D) exaggerated

2. GRACEFUL

   (A) wealthy
   (B) pleasant
   (C) elegant
   (D) intriguing

3. PERPLEX

   (A) prank
   (B) confuse
   (C) deceive
   (D) manipulate

4. SELDOM

   (A) sneakily
   (B) infrequently
   (C) unwillingly
   (D) cautiously

5. SOCIABLE

   (A) popular
   (B) charitable
   (C) outgoing
   (D) introspective

6. RECEDE

   (A) decrease
   (B) halt
   (C) advance
   (D) relax

7. SANCTUARY

   (A) ceremony
   (B) building
   (C) acceptance
   (D) protection

8. ABHOR

   (A) respect
   (B) wound
   (C) hate
   (D) criticize

9. MANIPULATIVE

   (A) calculating
   (B) compassionate
   (C) unpopular
   (D) insane

10. PERIL

    (A) danger
    (B) desire
    (C) security
    (D) misfortune

11. SOMBER

    (A) stern
    (B) gloomy
    (C) wicked
    (D) bitter

12. SPECIFIC

    (A) ordinary
    (B) interesting
    (C) smart
    (D) particular

13. ELEMENTARY

    (A) educational
    (B) basic
    (C) abstract
    (D) artistic

14. REFORM

    (A) improve
    (B) imprison
    (C) inspire
    (D) lecture

15. BETRAY

    (A) damage
    (B) befriend
    (C) deceive
    (D) punish

16. REMOTE

    (A) electronic
    (B) tiny
    (C) decayed
    (D) distant

17. ERUPT

    (A) break
    (B) fracture
    (C) eject
    (D) heat

18. UNITED

    (A) passionate
    (B) friendly
    (C) courageous
    (D) joined

Synonyms Practice Set 10

1. ACCOMPLISH

   (A) attempt
   (B) aid
   (C) hire
   (D) achieve

2. SUSPENSE

   (A) anticipation
   (B) composure
   (C) surprise
   (D) fear

3. CONDESCENDING

   (A) inconsiderate
   (B) unaware
   (C) patronizing
   (D) respectful

4. CHAOTIC

   (A) weird
   (B) noisy
   (C) disturbing
   (D) disordered

5. OBSCURE

   (A) unclear
   (B) scary
   (C) obvious
   (D) challenging

6. CONTEMPLATING

   (A) thinking
   (B) bothering
   (C) inventing
   (D) tricking

7. OBJECTIVE

   (A) purposeful
   (B) fair
   (C) deceitful
   (D) sincere

8. INTRICATE

   (A) simplified
   (B) complex
   (C) unique
   (D) beautiful

9. PRONE

   (A) likely
   (B) hesitant
   (C) unwilling
   (D) eager

10. UNIFORM

    (A) changeable
    (B) fashionable
    (C) constant
    (D) effortless

11. PREVIOUS

    (A) following
    (B) prior
    (C) superior
    (D) initial

12. BELITTLE

    (A) discount
    (B) trim
    (C) withdraw
    (D) criticize

13. FEASIBLE

    (A) practical
    (B) unreasonable
    (C) affordable
    (D) relevant

14. TRAGEDY

    (A) obstacle
    (B) hate
    (C) misfortune
    (D) positivity

15. ACCURATE

    (A) approximate
    (B) correct
    (C) excellent
    (D) interesting

16. ORIGINAL

    (A) flawless
    (B) used
    (C) interesting
    (D) novel

17. INEPT

    (A) capable
    (B) unskilled
    (C) satisfactory
    (D) irresponsible

18. ASSERT

    (A) advise
    (B) impose
    (C) declare
    (D) surrender

Sentence Completion Practice Set 1

1. Even though Sam believed his laptop's features were ------- to those of his classmates, he did not think their laptops were worth the expensive cost.

   (A) parallel
   (B) inferior
   (C) better
   (D) similar

2. Although Sara wanted to go to the movies with her friends, studying for her exam took ------- over her social life.

   (A) enjoyment
   (B) domination
   (C) respect
   (D) priority

3. Mrs. Johnson wanted her son to stop throwing temper tantrums, but it is likely difficult to change behaviors of children without continuous -------.

   (A) reinforcement
   (B) anger
   (C) meditation
   (D) obedience

4. After having surgery on her hip, Cindy's grandmother remained ------- after returning home from the hospital, despite the doctor giving her permission to be discharged.

   (A) healthy
   (B) unhappy
   (C) feeble
   (D) painful

5. Due to his ability to be easily distracted and his lack of focus, if Josiah spends hours on social media after school, he will ------- forget to do his homework.

   (A) apologetically
   (B) intentionally
   (C) likely
   (D) unusually

6. As Sasha performed her ballet routine, all of the other dancers envied her ability to remain ------- throughout the entire audition, despite her nerves.

   (A) motionless
   (B) eccentric
   (C) clumsy
   (D) graceful

7. Though the young woman was hungry and without money, she refused to ------- the law by stealing bread from the local bakery.

   (A) follow
   (B) violate
   (C) question
   (D) mock

8. Over the years, as industrial practices continue to contribute to -------, the air has become significantly more unhealthy.

   (A) pollution
   (B) production
   (C) dangers
   (D) radiation

9. Catie, who always did the right thing, refused to sneak out with her friends because it was against her -------.

   (A) morals
   (B) imagination
   (C) desires
   (D) intentions

10. In an effort to create order, provide structure, and keep people safe, one leader was selected to ------- the community and enforce the laws.

    (A) respect
    (B) encourage
    (C) save
    (D) govern

11. The many types of animals in Africa, such as zebras, elephants, lions and gazelles, demonstrate the extraordinary ------- of wildlife.

    (A) beauty
    (B) diversity
    (C) dangers
    (D) habitats

12. In light of Ellie losing her job, she decided to -------.

    (A) quit her second job.
    (B) buy expensive jewelry.
    (C) hold off on buying a new car.
    (D) see if any of her friends had lost their jobs.

13. In spite of Tim's teacher informing the class there would be a quiz tomorrow, he decided -------.

    (A) that studying would be a good idea because his grade was low.
    (B) to play video games all night instead of studying.
    (C) to ask his friend what material would be on the quiz.
    (D) to look over his notes from the past week.

14. Since Niko's cat had gone missing from his yard, he decided to -------.

    (A) put up flyers around the neighborhood.
    (B) go to the park with his friends.
    (C) purchase brand new cat toys.
    (D) clean his cat's litter box.

15. Recently, the summers have felt extra hot in Phoenix, but yesterday -------.

    (A) it was especially hot outside.
    (B) it was over 100 degrees Fahrenheit.
    (C) it almost rained for part of the day.
    (D) it was pleasant outside with a slight breeze.

16. Due to her bad knee, Aunt Sue -------.

    (A) enjoys jogging along the beach.
    (B) is turning 93 this year.
    (C) uses her cane when she leaves the house.
    (D) is often frustrated with her husband.

Sentence Completion Practice Set 2

1. After taking a bite into his chicken and realizing it was slightly undercooked, the food critic wrote a very ------- review.

   (A) intense
   (B) negative
   (C) uplifting
   (D) impartial

2. In 2019, The United States ------- approximately 5.3 million bags of coffee from countries such as Brazil and Colombia.

   (A) created
   (B) extracted
   (C) imported
   (D) immigrated

3. After Mark lost his wife in a terrible car accident, his relatives were constantly checking up on him, sending him food, and keeping him company during his period of -------.

   (A) nostalgia
   (B) inactivity
   (C) chaos
   (D) grief

4. Although Mrs. James was feeling better, the doctors felt it would be ------- to her health to move her from the hospital.

   (A) detrimental
   (B) beneficial
   (C) influential
   (D) important

5. Since Charlie had only recently started learning to speak French, it was surprising how ------- he was while giving his presentation to the class.

   (A) energetic
   (B) articulate
   (C) uncomfortable
   (D) concise

6. Since Kelly had only recently cut out sweets from her diet, she would often ------- sugar and found it hard to resist eating a candy bar.

   (A) despise
   (B) enjoy
   (C) crave
   (D) resist

7. Eleanor Roosevelt was a committed ------- for social justice and fought for the rights of women and African Americans.

   (A) advocate
   (B) president
   (C) vocalist
   (D) detractor

8. Liam had been feeling very lazy lately and could not find the ------- to complete his science project, even though he knew it was worth half of his grade.

   (A) instructions
   (B) intelligence
   (C) procrastination
   (D) motivation

9. On my 12-hour plane ride home from France, I had the ------- experience of sitting next to an incredibly loud and obnoxious woman who talked my ear off for hours.

   (A) unique
   (B) entertaining
   (C) terrifying
   (D) miserable

10. If you do not wash and clean an open wound, it is likely to cause -------.

    (A) death
    (B) hallucinations
    (C) infection
    (D) anxiety

11. Harry could not understand how someone could just ------- a cat on the side of the road, so he decided to rescue the cat and take her to an animal shelter.

    (A) retrieve
    (B) abandon
    (C) punish
    (D) adopt

12. Some people think New Mexico is the best state to live in while others -------.

    (A) argue that Arizona is better.
    (B) think that New Mexico has great weather.
    (C) say that living near New Mexico would be nice.
    (D) say that the people in Wisconsin aren't nice.

13. Due to Virginia's extreme fear of heights, -------.

    (A) she doesn't like to go into caves.
    (B) her sister doesn't fly on planes.
    (C) she does not want to go rock climbing.
    (D) she is terrified of spiders.

14. Since Paula broke her wrist playing soccer -------.

    (A) her teammates will wear their white jerseys tonight.
    (B) her coach is having her play every game.
    (C) she is very angry at her parents.
    (D) she will likely miss the rest of the season.

15. Erik has never been outside of the US, so his parents -------.

    (A) bought him a plane ticket to Canada for his graduation present.
    (B) decided to move to New York City in the fall.
    (C) asked his sister from London to come visit.
    (D) are travelling to Europe this summer for their anniversary.

16. Jeffrey wants his son to clear the snow from the driveway, but unfortunately -------.

    (A) his son has already started shoveling.
    (B) he cannot remember where he put the shovel.
    (C) Jeffrey hurt his back last night.
    (D) it is supposed to be sunny next week.

Sentence Completion Practice Set 3

1. Since the pandemic caused people to panic and stock up on supplies, grocery stores were worried that they would not have a(n) ------- amount of food for people in the coming weeks.

   (A) meager
   (B) attractive
   (C) sufficient
   (D) lavish

2. After accidentally leaving his dirty dishes in the sink for over a week, Ben noticed a ------- odor wafting through his apartment.

   (A) subtle
   (B) comforting
   (C) fragrant
   (D) foul

3. Rich planned to ------- next year and move to Florida, but because of the recent economic crash, he will likely have to stay at his job for at least three more years.

   (A) invest
   (B) retire
   (C) divorce
   (D) travel

4. During a wedding ceremony, couples will often write their own vows to express their ------- to each other.

   (A) commitment
   (B) inspiration
   (C) intelligence
   (D) admiration

5. I had the pleasure of working with Barack Obama on his presidential campaign and am very ------- that I had the opportunity to be part of such a significant historical event.

   (A) appalled
   (B) grateful
   (C) content
   (D) baffled

6. Having moved around the country three times this year, Jenna had to ------- to another new school, new town, and new group of friends.

   (A) retreat
   (B) establish
   (C) adapt
   (D) engage

7. After receiving a perfect score on her SAT test, Linda had a(n) ------- when applying to top colleges in the country.

   (A) guarantee
   (B) bias
   (C) limitation
   (D) advantage

8. Candace had lived a very ------- life, filled with poverty, disappointment, and constant hardships that she had to overcome.

   (A) eventful
   (B) vibrant
   (C) tragic
   (D) dangerous

9. Although the roads were ------- after the snowstorm, Lydia was determined to drive to her family's house for Christmas Eve.

(A) treacherous
(B) meandering
(C) reliable
(D) crowded

10. In the middle of the night, Kenya would often sleepwalk in a trance, ------- wandering through the house without being conscious.

(A) intentionally
(B) hastily
(C) precisely
(D) aimlessly

11. Because the chandelier was so -------, the decorators had wrapped it in soft padding before carrying it into the home, trying their best not to break it.

(A) intricate
(B) delicate
(C) gorgeous
(D) extravagant

12. As I was walking home in the winter storm, I realized that my hat barely covered my ears, and I feared that -------.

(A) my friends would throw snowballs at me as we walked.
(B) my ears might be frostbitten by the time I arrived home.
(C) the hat was more stylish than I had previously thought.
(D) my backpack would get wet from the heavy snow that was falling.

13. The weather had been very nice lately, but unfortunately, the forecast for Thursday called for -------.

(A) heavy rain and wind.
(B) sunshine and clear skies.
(C) mild temperatures with few clouds.
(D) more beautiful weather.

14. The choir teacher thought all of his students were ready to begin class, but as he glanced around the room -------.

(A) he was unable to locate one of his star singers, Lawanda.
(B) he noticed that his students had rearranged the chairs.
(C) all his students stared back at him with anticipation.
(D) he realized that the window was open.

15. Antoinette was gazing at the last piece of carrot cake when Amy selfishly -------.

(A) asked Antoinette if she would like to split the last piece.
(B) commented on how tasty the cake looked.
(C) ate the entire piece without asking Antoinette if she would like some.
(D) offered to let Antoinette have the rest of the cake.

16. Thomas had already done the dinner shopping, so he called his wife, Freda, to tell her that -------.

(A) she would need to pick up bread for dinner.
(B) she didn't need to stop at the grocery store on her way home.
(C) he would be home late from work.
(D) he was going for a run.

Sentence Completion Practice Set 4

1. Because many Americans are frustrated by the number of immigrants in the country, many immigrants often experience ------- when looking for housing, jobs, healthcare, and education options.

   (A) favoritism
   (B) delays
   (C) violence
   (D) discrimination

2. Snake rely on their ability to ------- with their environment to protect and hide themselves from dangerous predators.

   (A) camouflage
   (B) accelerate
   (C) burrow
   (D) enhance

3. With her ------- attitude, Giselle fearlessly strut down the runway and made it look as if she had been modeling for years.

   (A) confident
   (B) stylish
   (C) timid
   (D) playful

4. The performance by the comedian caused a(n) ------- outburst of laughter that spread like wildfire throughout the entire audience.

   (A) roaring
   (B) prolonged
   (C) contagious
   (D) obnoxious

5. Anne argued, "If he does not do the work that is asked of him, then it is only fair that I ------- his employment at my company."

   (A) extend
   (B) terminate
   (C) discipline
   (D) demolish

6. The Harry Potter Series, written by J.K. Rowling, falls within the ------- of fantasy fiction because it is full of witchcraft, wizardry, and magic.

   (A) genre
   (B) popularity
   (C) idea
   (D) narrative

7. The child lacked manners and was extremely ------- and disrespectful to his teachers, coaches, and parents.

   (A) obedient
   (B) dangerous
   (C) impolite
   (D) deceptive

8. While most penguins live in ------- habitats in the Southern Hemisphere, the Galapagos penguin is actually found on tropical islands near the equator.

   (A) warm
   (B) frigid
   (C) humid
   (D) dangerous

9. Although Ray and Teresa had only been dating for three weeks, the couple made a ------- dash to the altar because they were madly in love.

(A) calculated
(B) thoughtful
(C) loving
(D) hasty

10. William used a bow-drill to start his fire, which works by rotating a wooden spindle against a fireboard, producing friction that ------- an ember.

(A) decreases
(B) replicates
(C) maintains
(D) ignites

11. Paige, who didn't do well in school or sports, felt ------- to her older sister who was an honor student, captain of the volleyball team, and student-body president.

(A) comparable
(B) related
(C) inferior
(D) superior

12. Ismael hardly ever rode his bike, so yesterday his cousin was surprised when -------.

(A) the garage door was left open.
(B) Ismael bought a brand new bike.
(C) there was a tricycle in the front yard.
(D) Ismael said he was going to run a marathon.

13. Never having looked underneath her couch before, Gilda -------.

(A) was grossed out by how dirty the floor was.
(B) decided to buy a new couch.
(C) looked underneath her chair.
(D) contemplated purchasing a new TV.

14. Before committing to buying a new car, Jerry was sure to -------.

(A) move into a new apartment.
(B) ask his friends when they bought their first car.
(C) buy a motorcycle.
(D) research different brands and models.

15. Altogether, the play was a great performance, but -------.

(A) Daryl brought his cousins to see the show a second time.
(B) the cost of a ticket was too high for Terry's liking.
(C) next year the theater would be putting on *The Lion King*.
(D) the actors worked very well together on stage.

16. Regardless of the status of her broken arm, Maria was determined to -------.

(A) speak with her mother.
(B) continue to rest her arm.
(C) learn to play pool.
(D) get an A on her math test.

Sentence Completion Practice Set 5

1. Sebastian, who often experienced stage fright, forgot all of his lines during the opening night of the school play and was forced to ------- on the spot.

   (A) improvise
   (B) audition
   (C) recite
   (D) compromise

2. Because Diana had an allergic reaction the last time she ate seafood, she was ------- to try octopus on her date.

   (A) excited
   (B) content
   (C) reluctant
   (D) persuaded

3. Since Carl's assistant ------- to inform him that the board meeting had been moved from Thursday to Tuesday, Carl ended up missing the meeting.

   (A) failed
   (B) decided
   (C) remembered
   (D) hesitated

4. During the pandemic, some stores tried to ------- the prices of essential items like toilet paper and dish soap, forcing customers to pay more money than they normally would.

   (A) improve
   (B) decrease
   (C) predict
   (D) inflate

5. As a child, Johnny believed that his parents were -------: unable to be hurt or defeated by anything, just like his favorite superheroes.

   (A) unique
   (B) invincible
   (C) courageous
   (D) amazing

6. Having no responsibilities, Shayna was able to live a life of ------- and would relax by the pool everyday.

   (A) hardship
   (B) ignorance
   (C) leisure
   (D) purpose

7. The beauty store had a ------- selection of hair products, including shampoos, conditioners, hair creams, and many other types of products.

   (A) limited
   (B) unique
   (C) expensive
   (D) varied

8. Millicent Fawcett was a women's right ------- who formed the International Woman Suffrage Alliance and played an influential role in fighting for women's rights during the 19th century.

   (A) critic
   (B) employee
   (C) activist
   (D) contributor

9. Kenya had recently started a business and wasn't making any profit, so she was ------- on her parents for housing and food.

   (A) dependant
   (B) insistent
   (C) preying
   (D) thriving

10. China is (a)n ------- country, having the capability to mass produced almost anything in the world.

   (A) unique
   (B) industrial
   (C) significant
   (D) inventive

11. Kevin ------- his boss because of her achievements and wealth, and he hoped to one day be as successful as her.

   (A) hated
   (B) researched
   (C) inspired
   (D) envied

12. Clifton was sure that the bird was a robin, yet Elsie insisted that -------.

   (A) Clifton was correct.
   (B) the bird was sitting on a branch.
   (C) the squirrel next to the bird was angry.
   (D) it was in fact a sparrow.

13. As Louie walked to the backyard to unlock the shed, he unfortunately realized that -------.

   (A) he had forgotten the key.
   (B) his lawnmower was inside the shed.
   (C) his wife had just repainted the shed.
   (D) he forgot to make dinner.

14. If one is curious about how to use different kinds of power tools, they can -------.

   (A) borrow power tools from their friends.
   (B) ask their family for money to buy tools for Christmas.
   (C) look online for classes to learn those skills.
   (D) buy lumber at a hardware store.

15. Orval was terrified of the dark, so he would never dream of -------.

   (A) purchasing a flashlight.
   (B) riding his bike at sunrise.
   (C) going to a movie theater.
   (D) walking in the woods at night.

16. Unaware of the impending rain, Maria decided to -------.

   (A) pack a jacket for her hike.
   (B) go for a long jog.
   (C) stay in and watch a movie.
   (D) finish her homework.

Sentence Completion Practice Set 6

1. Ashley really wanted a puppy, so she wrote an essay to her parents explaining the benefits of owning a pet in an effort to ------- them.

   (A) threaten
   (B) confuse
   (C) manipulate
   (D) persuade

2. Cassandra came prepared for her job interview with two copies of her resume and a professional portfolio showcasing her work because she wanted to ------- the potential employer.

   (A) deceive
   (B) impress
   (C) question
   (D) intimidate

3. Zachary was an extremely ------- person who cared deeply about other people and always tried to help those in need.

   (A) sociable
   (B) submissive
   (C) charismatic
   (D) compassionate

4. To my surprise, my husband's ------- on whether or not our daughter should be allowed go to the school dance changed once he learned she was going with her friends and not a date.

   (A) regulation
   (B) issue
   (C) opinion
   (D) conversation

5. When the storeowner checked his ------- and realized his supply of toilet paper was low, he placed a very larger order for more.

   (A) inventory
   (B) cashier
   (C) production
   (D) prescription

6. Since the burglar knew that the family was very rich, he felt no ------- when he stole from them and did not feel the need to apologize.

   (A) remorse
   (B) emotion
   (C) anger
   (D) indifference

7. There had been growing ------- between the two countries for decades, so many citizens were worried that a war would soon break out.

   (A) cooperation
   (B) tension
   (C) regulations
   (D) indifference

8. Hundreds of people living in Greensville began to feel ill after the town's local water supply was ------- with bacteria.

   (A) healed
   (B) purified
   (C) contaminated
   (D) fabricated

9. Without ------- sunlight and water, many plants will lose their green color and eventually die.

(A) minimal
(B) healthy
(C) adequate
(D) excessive

10. Because Sade's grandparents are from an older generation that didn't grow up using technology, they found the process of setting up their new computer to be -------.

(A) unrealistic
(B) manageable
(C) complicated
(D) entertaining

11. Due to her commitment to volunteering and donating to local causes, Haley received the award for the most ------- student in the senior class.

(A) popular
(B) enthusiastic
(C) accomplished
(D) charitable

12. After two hours of writing, Quentin had hardly -------.

(A) made much progress on his essay.
(B) considered what his dad would make for dinner.
(C) even touched the bowl of cereal he had poured.
(D) emailed his teacher with questions.

13. Louis was grounded for failing to complete his chores when he -------.

(A) finished his homework on time.
(B) argued with his sister over the TV.
(C) refused to go on a bike ride with his friend, David.
(D) didn't take the trash out by Sunday night.

14. Phyllis was glad she went on the field trip to the art museum after she saw -------.

(A) her teacher instructing the class on proper museum etiquette.
(B) a beautiful painting of a mountain.
(C) a long line to get into the private gallery.
(D) her friends Joaquin and Marcie getting along.

15. Acting swiftly, Ines was able to -----.

(A) catch the glass before it fell on the floor.
(B) call her grandpa on his birthday.
(C) finish her chores on Thursday.
(D) cook the steaks perfectly on the grill.

16. Daniel is gluten-free, meaning that he cannot eat bread, so when he buys groceries he excludes -------.

(A) buying milk products like cheese.
(B) walking down the bread aisle.
(C) buying bagels and donuts.
(D) buying yogurt and apples.

Sentence Completion Practice Set 7

1. Andre's parents were extremely strict and set ------- expectations for him that were often impossible for him to live up to.

   (A) unpredictable
   (B) unreasonable
   (C) academic
   (D) realistic

2. Kim was very ------- and would always find a way to overcome any obstacle or problem she faced.

   (A) lazy
   (B) sophisticated
   (C) resilient
   (D) stubborn

3. Although the defendant still maintains his innocence, the jury agreed that he was -------, and he was sentenced to three years in jail.

   (A) capable
   (B) vicious
   (C) framed
   (D) guilty

4. The encouragement of his friends convinced Damien to ------- in the track competition, despite his fear of being the slowest runner.

   (A) participate
   (B) triumph
   (C) lose
   (D) observe

5. The gray wolf has a wooly fur coat that provides ------- and keeps it warm during the cold winters.

   (A) disguise
   (B) insulation
   (C) shelter
   (D) isolation

6. Greg hated ------- when it came to his schoolwork and would often start his assignments days, if not weeks, ahead of time.

   (A) succeeding
   (B) failing
   (C) studying
   (D) procrastinating

7. Joe often had a hard time ------- to set his alarm clock, and his first period teacher was getting frustrated that he was constantly late to class.

   (A) preparing
   (B) asking
   (C) remembering
   (D) forgetting

8. Jennifer found it ------- that her salary was not equivalent to that of her male co-worker Tommy, especially since they had the same exact title and responsibilities.

   (A) necessary
   (B) discriminatory
   (C) harmful
   (D) reasonable

9. Carl became ------- in Spanish because he lived abroad in Spain for three years and practiced speaking the language regularly.

    (A) proficient
    (B) inept
    (C) persistent
    (D) mediocre

10. The newlywed ------- her wedding day to her children, telling them about the beautiful vows their father had written, the wedding decorations, and other details that made the day so memorable.

    (A) envisioned
    (B) fabricated
    (C) characterized
    (D) recounted

11. Corinne was very well versed in European ------- and could locate every country and capital on a map.

    (A) geography
    (B) sociology
    (C) culture
    (D) history

12. Santo is very scared of insects, so he -------.

    (A) signed up for a class to learn more about them.
    (B) decided to ask his parents if he could get a pet lizard.
    (C) ran away when Jeremy brought a grasshopper over.
    (D) volunteered to pet-sit his cousin's tarantula.

13. Melvin knew that he wanted to join the Navy after graduating, so -------.

    (A) his parents bought him a new car.
    (B) he worked extra hard in his math and science courses.
    (C) he decided to learn to play the trumpet.
    (D) he enlisted in the military as soon as he turned 18.

14. Ike always like the tea his sister made him, but -------.

    (A) he also thought Coca-cola was good.
    (B) tonight she paired it with a well-done steak.
    (C) the herbal tea she made today was rather disgusting.
    (D) sometimes the cup was the perfect temperature.

15. It is Mary's wedding, so she gets to decide -------.

    (A) what the weather will be like on that day.
    (B) what will be served for dessert.
    (C) the exact temperature during the ceremony.
    (D) whether or not people cry during the ceremony.

16. Although the company had already hired Andrea's replacement, they allowed her to -------.

    (A) quit her job early.
    (B) clean her office out.
    (C) ask who her replacement was.
    (D) keep working for three more weeks.

Sentence Completion Practice Set 8

1. Some animals that live in Antarctica are ------- on the sea for food, while other animals migrate to other regions during the winter to find food.

   (A) attracted
   (B) self-sufficient
   (C) dependent
   (D) crowded

2. The minute Tom saw the kitchen go up in flames, his ------- told him to grab his dog and run for the door.

   (A) instincts
   (B) memory
   (C) demeanor
   (D) character

3. As a(n) ------- tennis player, Chance was able to skip the beginner course, but could not participate in the advanced tournament.

   (A) novice
   (B) intermediate
   (C) professional
   (D) dedicated

4. When the girl was caught making offensive comments on social media, the University had no choice but to ------- her acceptance.

   (A) revoke
   (B) punish
   (C) celebrate
   (D) grant

5. Since it was her first time flying on a plane and she was very scared of heights, Deidra felt ------- as the plane began to take off.

   (A) peaceful
   (B) uneasy
   (C) excited
   (D) disgusted

6. In order for a new rule to be created, all of the members of the club had to be in agreement and come to a(n) ------- decision.

   (A) proven
   (B) practical
   (C) divided
   (D) unanimous

7. Even though they had opened all of their windows and sprayed perfume in the room, the horrible stench still ------- throughout their apartment.

   (A) decreased
   (B) precipitated
   (C) sheltered
   (D) lingered

8. Having dreamt about her wedding day since she was a little girl, Kayla was ------- after hearing that Chauncey might propose to her this weekend.

   (A) elated
   (B) stressed
   (C) confused
   (D) apathetic

9. When scientists conduct experiments they must make small changes and ------ certain variables to see if the changes will cause an effect in something they observe.

   (A) research
   (B) comprehend
   (C) manipulate
   (D) stabilize

10. If you choose to use content from an article without direct quotes, you must instead ------- the article to avoid plagiarizing.

    (A) steal
    (B) paraphrase
    (C) imitate
    (D) disguise

11. After suffering from depression for years, Daniel's ------- on life became more positive when he met his fiancé Madeline.

    (A) sadness
    (B) rendition
    (C) outlook
    (D) hypothesis

12. Typically, Caroline would play the bass guitar during concerts, but this month she -------.

    (A) wasn't sure who would play the drums.
    (B) played the bass at every show.
    (C) decided to play the electric guitar.
    (D) invited her cousins to see the show.

13. Ben wished his grandma would visit him in New Orleans, but -------.

    (A) she has too much free time.
    (B) the weather is very nice.
    (C) the flight is too cheap.
    (D) she is too sick right now.

14. Even with his earplugs, Kirk thought that -------.

    (A) the jet engine was still very loud.
    (B) it was very hard to hear his sister whispering.
    (C) it still might rain today.
    (D) the paintings in the museum looked very nice.

15. While it was nice that Dianna's coworkers threw her a surprise party, she -------.

    (A) thanked each and every one of them.
    (B) wasn't in the mood to celebrate.
    (C) decided to go out to celebrate with them.
    (D) didn't like spending so much time at work.

16. It hardly ever rains in Phoenix, so it's not necessary to ------.

    (A) carry an umbrella in your car.
    (B) buy a pair of shorts.
    (C) think that it gets too hot.
    (D) worry about the heat.

Sentence Completion Practice Set 9

1. There are many conflicting theories about the ------- of soccer, with some people arguing that it was created as far back as 2500 B.C.

   (A) origins
   (B) admiration
   (C) findings
   (D) rules

2. When it comes to fashion, footwear is worn to protect the feet, but jewelry is almost always -------, serving no practical purpose as a part of the outfit.

   (A) intentional
   (B) protective
   (C) unattractive
   (D) decorative

3. Since the rain prevented the boys from playing in their tree fort, they used the couch cushions and bed sheets to create a ------- fort in their bedroom that they could use until the rain stopped.

   (A) dangerous
   (B) permanent
   (C) intricate
   (D) makeshift

4. Although Dennis was expected to win the election by a landslide, it was only a ------- twenty votes that put him ahead of the other candidates.

   (A) whopping
   (B) mere
   (C) inconclusive
   (D) substantial

5. Clarence preferred to eat trail mix for his afternoon snack over potato chips because he enjoyed the ------- of different nuts, dried fruit, and chocolate.

   (A) confusion
   (B) vibrancy
   (C) medley
   (D) expectation

6. Even though the family had lost their house to the fire, they remained ------- that they would find a new home that was just as nice as their old one.

   (A) terrified
   (B) cautious
   (C) optimistic
   (D) nostalgic

7. The number of deer in the North East has started to ------- because too many people have been hunting them.

   (A) balance
   (B) plummet
   (C) improve
   (D) disappear

8. My mother is very ------- when baking her banana bread and counts out exactly 100 chocolate chips to bake into each loaf.

   (A) creative
   (B) relaxed
   (C) aggressive
   (D) precise

9. Many U.S. companies have their products ------- oversees because the production costs are less expensive.

(A) manufactured
(B) sold
(C) invented
(D) distributed

10. Since the acceptance rate at Harvard is a mere 5%, a ------- of applicants will be rejected.

(A) variety
(B) priority
(C) majority
(D) median

11. Clara had no problem making new friends; her welcoming smile and ------- personality made her an attractive person to be around.

(A) intelligent
(B) charismatic
(C) sarcastic
(D) impolite

12. Despite all the work that Luz needed to finish yesterday, he still -------.

(A) went out to eat with his friends.
(B) decided to get as much done as possible.
(C) spent four hours working.
(D) thought that it was a lot of work.

13. It had been a while since Melissa had sung in front of people, so -------.

(A) she was very nervous.
(B) the stage was lit up, ready for her performance.
(C) in spite of the weather, she made it to the theater.
(D) her parents decided not to come see her perform.

14. Some people think that black cats are bad luck, while others think -------.

(A) parrots make good pets.
(B) that grey dogs are very cute.
(C) that superstitions are not real.
(D) about what it takes to raise a horse.

15. Before he knew it, Kurtis was a published poet because -------.

(A) he called his aunt to tell her about his latest poem.
(B) he thought of a very good poem idea.
(C) he intends to put together 15 of his poems next month.
(D) *The Examiner* put one of his poems in their publication.

16. Frieda has been complaining of a toothache for a week now, so I think we should -------.

(A) tell her to brush her teeth less.
(B) bring her to the dentist.
(C) try giving her more sugar.
(D) ask if her tooth hurts tonight.

Sentence Completion Practice Set 10

1. If the house cannot ------- ten people at a time, I have no choice but to find a larger home to rent for my family vacation.

   (A) stabilize
   (B) reserve
   (C) hinder
   (D) accommodate

2. Kevin's ------- tone was frightening to his children, so his wife asked him to speak in a softer, calmer voice.

   (A) stern
   (B) gentle
   (C) comedic
   (D) deceptive

3. During her valedictorian speech, Jenna's nerves took over as she ------- her words, forgetting what to say.

   (A) improvised
   (B) screamed
   (C) personified
   (D) jumbled

4. When Chloe spilled her tea all over her research paper, the ink began to bleed causing the writing to become -------.

   (A) illegible
   (B) comprehensible
   (C) demolished
   (D) evident

5. Trina's new apartment was more ------- than her previous one, so she was excited to purchase new furniture to fill the space.

   (A) modest
   (B) spacious
   (C) comfortable
   (D) extravagant

6. The author often used ------- in her writing in an attempt to help readers create a visual representation of the story in their minds.

   (A) synonyms
   (B) symbolism
   (C) imagery
   (D) hyperbole

7. Due to the ------- amount of trauma that Kara experienced in her childhood, her therapist strongly suggested that she keep a journal to write down her feelings and emotions in an attempt to reflect on her difficult past.

   (A) mediocre
   (B) minor
   (C) significant
   (D) reasonable

8. Since the couple had not paid their rent in three months, their landlord asked that they ------ the apartment and find a new place to live.

   (A) confiscate
   (B) vacate
   (C) sanitize
   (D) purchase

9. Although he was not sure who stole his bike, he ------- that it was a boy named Carl who had been bullying him the entire year.

    (A) doubted
    (B) knew
    (C) suspected
    (D) realized

10. If my mother is not winning a game, her interest in playing begins to -------, and she will usually quit before the game is finished.

    (A) wane
    (B) grow
    (C) continue
    (D) interrupt

11. Because the musician did not have a good sense of humor, he was ------- by the parody that someone made of his song.

    (A) amused
    (B) frightened
    (C) moved
    (D) offended

12. Francine forgot to save her essay before turning the computer off and thus -------.

    (A) decided to skip parts of her assignment.
    (B) her mom asked her why she didn't save.
    (C) decided to buy a new computer.
    (D) had to rewrite parts of her assignment.

13. Antonio always listened to his parents, so when they asked him to be home by 11 PM, he -------.

    (A) screamed at his parents.
    (B) arrived home at 12:00 AM.
    (C) arrived home at 10:45 to avoid getting into trouble.
    (D) didn't leave his friend's house until 11:45 PM.

14. Although the sign said to only take one sample per customer, I decided to ------.

    (A) not try the sample.
    (B) take a few for myself.
    (C) ask my brother if he also wanted one.
    (D) remove the sign.

15. Emerson had every intention of arriving to the party on time, but somehow he -------.

    (A) invited three friend to the party.
    (B) arrived just on time.
    (C) ended up being 30 minutes late.
    (D) took a taxi to the party.

16. Reluctantly, Darcy handed over the keys to her old apartment while thinking about ------.

    (A) the good times she had spent there.
    (B) if she would like to get a dog in her next apartment.
    (C) how long it would take for her to get her oil changed.
    (D) how much she needed to spend on groceries that month.

Verbal Chapter Answer Key

Synonyms Practice Set 1

1. A
2. B
3. C
4. D
5. B
6. B
7. A
8. D
9. C
10. B
11. C
12. D
13. C
14. B
15. D
16. A
17. A
18. B

Synonyms Practice Set 2

1. C
2. A
3. C
4. D
5. B
6. B
7. A
8. D
9. A
10. B
11. C
12. D
13. D
14. A
15. D
16. B
17. A
18. A

Synonyms Practice Set 3

1. C
2. B
3. D
4. C
5. B
6. D

7. B
8. D
9. A
10. A
11. A
12. B
13. C
14. D
15. A
16. D
17. C
18. D

Synonyms Practice Set 4

1. B
2. A
3. A
4. D
5. C
6. D
7. C
8. B
9. D
10. B
11. A
12. C
13. D
14. A
15. A
16. A
17. B
18. C

Synonyms Practice Set 5

1. A
2. D
3. C
4. D
5. B
6. C
7. D
8. B
9. A
10. B
11. C
12. B
13. D
14. C
15. C

16. D
17. A
18. B

Synonyms Practice Set 6

1. C
2. B
3. A
4. A
5. B
6. A
7. D
8. B
9. D
10. C
11. A
12. C
13. B
14. A
15. A
16. B
17. A
18. D

Synonyms Practice Set 7

1. D
2. C
3. C
4. B
5. B
6. A
7. D
8. C
9. D
10. C
11. C
12. A
13. B
14. A
15. A
16. D
17. B
18. B

Synonyms Practice Set 8

1. B
2. D

3. C
4. C
5. A
6. C
7. A
8. D
9. B
10. C
11. D
12. B
13. B
14. D
15. B
16. B
17. C
18. A

Synonyms Practice Set 9

1. A
2. C
3. B
4. B
5. C
6. A
7. D
8. C
9. A
10. A
11. B
12. D
13. B
14. A
15. C
16. D
17. C
18. D

Synonyms Practice Set 10

1. D
2. A
3. C
4. D
5. A
6. A
7. B
8. B
9. A
10. C
11. B

12. D
13. A
14. C
15. B
16. D
17. B
18. C

**Sentence Completion
Practice Set 1**

1. B
2. D
3. A
4. C
5. C
6. D
7. B
8. A
9. A
10. D
11. B
12. C
13. B
14. A
15. D
16. C

**Sentence Completion
Practice Set 2**

1. B
2. C
3. D
4. A
5. B
6. C
7. A
8. D
9. D
10. C
11. B
12. A
13. C
14. D
15. A
16. B

**Sentence Completion
Practice Set 3**

1. C

2. D
3. B
4. A
5. B
6. C
7. D
8. C
9. A
10. D
11. B
12. B
13. A
14. A
15. C
16. B

**Sentence Completion
Practice Set 4**

1. D
2. A
3. A
4. C
5. B
6. A
7. C
8. B
9. D
10. D
11. C
12. B
13. A
14. D
15. B
16. C

**Sentence Completion
Practice Set 5**

1. A
2. C
3. A
4. D
5. B
6. C
7. D
8. C
9. A
10. B
11. D
12. D
13. A

14. C
15. D
16. B

**Sentence Completion
Practice Set 6**

1. D
2. B
3. D
4. C
5. A
6. A
7. B
8. C
9. C
10. C
11. D
12. A
13. D
14. B
15. A
16. C

**Sentence Completion
Practice Set 7**

1. B
2. C
3. D
4. A
5. B
6. D
7. C
8. B
9. A
10. D
11. A
12. C
13. D
14. C
15. B
16. D

**Sentence Completion
Practice Set 8**

1. C
2. A
3. B
4. A
5. B

6. D
7. D
8. A
9. C
10. B
11. C
12. C
13. D
14. A
15. B
16. A

**Sentence Completion
Practice Set 9**

1. A
2. D
3. D
4. B
5. C
6. C
7. B
8. D
9. A
10. C
11. B
12. A
13. A
14. C
15. D
16. B

**Sentence Completion
Practice Set 10**

1. D
2. A
3. D
4. A
5. B
6. C
7. C
8. B
9. C
10. A
11. D
12. D
13. C
14. B
15. C
16. A

Math Fundamentals

How to Use the Math Fundamentals Chapter

Chapter Overview

This chapter of the book covers over 25 fundamental math topics that are necessary for answering questions in the Quantitative Reasoning and Mathematics Achievement sections. The purpose of this chapter is to master basic math skills, so the questions are not multiple-choice questions. Instead, the chapter consists of two sets of math "drills" for each fundamental topic.

Using the Practice Sets

Each topic in this chapter comes with two practice sets, each with 20 practice questions. Complete practice set 1 for a topic, and grade your answers using the answer key at the end of this chapter. If you don't do well on practice set 1, review your answers and the concepts; then complete practice set 2 for that topic.

Tips for Working Through this Chapter

1. **Write your answers in a separate notebook.** We strongly suggest showing your work in a separate notebook. This will allow you to keep your work organized and neat. It will also allow you to redo practice problems later in your prep process if you need to review any topics.

2. **Understand your areas of weakness.** Before diving into this chapter, make sure you have an idea of what topics you struggle with. If you are not sure which topics you struggle with, try a few problems from each topic and check your answers. Focus on the topics where you answered some of the questions incorrectly.

3. **Do not use a calculator.** A calculator is NOT allowed on the ISEE, so do not use a calculator for any of the problems in this chapter.

4. **Complete the topics in order.** Some topics covered in this chapter build off of previous topics, so we suggest going through the topics in order.

5. **Break up your practice.** Remember to break up your practice into small chunks. Don't try and cram all of the practice sets into a short amount of time. You are less likely to fully master the concepts if you cram, and you are more likely to feel stressed out during the prep process.

Addition Practice Set 1

1.	29 + 10	6.	37 + 37	11.	467 + 528	16.	7584 + 8374
2.	30 + 43	7.	25 + 49	12.	198 + 913	17.	7482 + 2048
3.	123 + 45	8.	108 + 76	13.	645 + 2048	18.	936 + 2649 + 648
4.	287 + 112	9.	675 + 55	14.	2938 + 736	19.	1047 + 7849 + 76
5.	762 + 137	10.	238 + 398	15.	6384 + 3748	20.	4629 + 8778 + 1079

Addition Practice Set 2

1.	53 + 16	6.	89 + 59	11.	654 + 456	16.	7284 + 2738
2.	72 + 34	7.	94 + 48	12.	803 + 487	17.	1938 + 2849
3.	506 + 23	8.	116 + 76	13.	1736 + 927	18.	7463 + 64 + 2847
4.	113 + 75	9.	43 + 275	14.	834 + 4608	19.	104 + 999 + 2749
5.	807 + 172	10.	888 + 343	15.	9274 + 8471	20.	3068 + 8741 + 67

Subtraction Practice Set 1

1.	78 − 32	6.	366 − 44	11.	708 − 79	16.	4602 − 2894
2.	99 − 44	7.	36 − 18	12.	654 − 367	17.	4004 − 326
3.	97 − 83	8.	55 − 28	13.	780 − 292	18.	5008 − 3379
4.	256 − 32	9.	223 − 67	14.	2138 − 288	19.	2008 − 568 − 173
5.	278 − 56	10.	304 − 67	15.	7058 − 4469	20.	3004 − 368 − 1059

Subtraction Practice Set 2

1.	45 − 34	6.	84 − 67	11.	521 − 275	16.	8005 − 827
2.	76 − 45	7.	64 − 29	12.	407 − 368	17.	9001 − 3647
3.	840 − 30	8.	984 − 99	13.	9218 − 765	18.	8206 − 3360 − 946
4.	638 − 36	9.	203 − 58	14.	8032 − 2785	19.	7008 − 1985 − 4736
5.	74 − 48	10.	945 − 868	15.	7003 − 675	20.	9002 − 3994 − 1549

Multiplication Practice Set 1

1.	14×4	**6.**	56×62	**11.**	234×45	**16.**	134×176
2.	7×33	**7.**	93×14	**12.**	443×53	**17.**	804×154
3.	3×76	**8.**	36×37	**13.**	432×64	**18.**	567×809
4.	31×13	**9.**	543×4	**14.**	732×32	**19.**	934×657
5.	12×34	**10.**	6×450	**15.**	239×45	**20.**	546×654

Multiplication Practice Set 2

1.	23×3	**6.**	83×37	**11.**	67×273	**16.**	235×165
2.	82×5	**7.**	27×48	**12.**	87×356	**17.**	439×382
3.	39×5	**8.**	46×85	**13.**	982×33	**18.**	258×376
4.	22×33	**9.**	7×294	**14.**	209×99	**19.**	684×843
5.	43×12	**10.**	289×3	**15.**	97×678	**20.**	928×945

Division Practice Set 1

1.	$39 \div 3$	**6.**	$258 \div 2$	**11.**	$546 \div 2$	**16.**	$7072 \div 4$
2.	$72 \div 6$	**7.**	$258 \div 6$	**12.**	$705 \div 3$	**17.**	$624 \div 13$
3.	$72 \div 4$	**8.**	$702 \div 9$	**13.**	$6895 \div 7$	**18.**	$8100 \div 15$
4.	$42 \div 3$	**9.**	$549 \div 3$	**14.**	$6390 \div 9$	**19.**	$884 \div 52$
5.	$91 \div 7$	**10.**	$472 \div 4$	**15.**	$1552 \div 8$	**20.**	$2080 \div 65$

Division Practice Set 2

1.	$48 \div 2$	**6.**	$119 \div 7$	**11.**	$477 \div 3$	**16.**	$7308 \div 3$
2.	$77 \div 7$	**7.**	$264 \div 3$	**12.**	$984 \div 8$	**17.**	$696 \div 12$
3.	$65 \div 5$	**8.**	$148 \div 2$	**13.**	$4785 \div 5$	**18.**	$5520 \div 12$
4.	$56 \div 4$	**9.**	$635 \div 5$	**14.**	$9873 \div 9$	**19.**	$945 \div 45$
5.	$99 \div 9$	**10.**	$892 \div 4$	**15.**	$9056 \div 8$	**20.**	$1428 \div 14$

Division with Remainders Practice Set 1

1. $29 \div 3$	**6.** $268 \div 3$	**11.** $1731 \div 7$	**16.** $691 \div 12$
2. $47 \div 2$	**7.** $131 \div 2$	**12.** $3705 \div 4$	**17.** $817 \div 15$
3. $67 \div 7$	**8.** $367 \div 6$	**13.** $5491 \div 9$	**18.** $3956 \div 87$
4. $89 \div 5$	**9.** $461 \div 9$	**14.** $3896 \div 7$	**19.** $4384 \div 126$
5. $74 \div 6$	**10.** $824 \div 6$	**15.** $2607 \div 5$	**20.** $6804 \div 1033$

Division with Remainders Practice Set 2

1. $57 \div 4$	**6.** $118 \div 7$	**11.** $5708 \div 6$	**16.** $3048 \div 11$
2. $94 \div 9$	**7.** $934 \div 4$	**12.** $1652 \div 8$	**17.** $9039 \div 37$
3. $68 \div 3$	**8.** $512 \div 9$	**13.** $5299 \div 9$	**18.** $5428 \div 42$
4. $94 \div 4$	**9.** $697 \div 2$	**14.** $539 \div 14$	**19.** $8904 \div 548$
5. $73 \div 2$	**10.** $785 \div 8$	**15.** $7523 \div 12$	**20.** $3564 \div 2307$

Order of Operations Practice Set 1

1. $5 + 8 - 3$	**11.** $8(13 + 7)$
2. $20 + 4 - 2 + 7$	**12.** $43 + 4(18 - 16)$
3. $29 - 14 - 3 + 13$	**13.** $55 - 2(29 - 27)$
4. $25 \div 5 + 7 - 3$	**14.** $25 - 10(8 - 6) + 4 \times 3$
5. $7 \times 4 + 3$	**15.** $86 - 2(10 + 10) - 5 \times 6$
6. $18 - 4 + 3 \times 2$	**16.** $17 + 2(3 + 4) - 2 \times 2$
7. $54 \div 6 - 3 \times 3$	**17.** $15 + 2(2 + 5) - 66 \div 6$
8. $15 + 4 \times 2 - 18 \div 9$	**18.** $3(10 - 7) + 5(6 - 6)$
9. $67 - (13 - 3)$	**19.** $90 \div (5 + 2 \times 2) + 3(60 \div 3 - 4 \times 3)$
10. $78 - (15 + 3)$	**20.** $(2)32 \div (28 \div 4 + 1) - 2(2 + 4 \times 3 - 6 \times 2)$

Order of Operations Practice Set 2

1. $12 - 6 + 4$
2. $29 - 9 + 10 - 3$
3. $67 + 8 + 2 - 20$
4. $56 + 14 - 18 - 7 + 6$
5. $7 \times 2 - 4 + 1$
6. $18 \div 3 - 1$
7. $45 \div 5 - 18 \div 6$
8. $5 \times 6 + 3 \times 7$
9. $50 - 24 \div 3 + 5 \times 3$
10. $8 + 2(7)$

11. $8 + (5 - 3)$
12. $52 - (20 + 4)$
13. $4(8 - 6)$
14. $66 - 3(6 + 14)$
15. $7 + 2(8 + 3)$
16. $65 + 4 - 2(20 - 17) + 6 \times 2$
17. $100 - 4(10 - 4 - 3) - 2 \times 4$
18. $15 \div 3 + 2(2 + 5 - 1) - 48 \div 6$
19. $4(4 \times 2) + 3(16 \div 4)$
20. $3(17 - 2) \div 5 + 5(20 \div 5 - 1)$

Negative Number Addition and Subtraction Practice Set 1

1. $-3 - 7$
2. $-8 + 5$
3. $5 + (-6)$
4. $20 - (-9)$
5. $-26 + 15$

6. $-36 - 12$
7. $-18 - 12$
8. $-32 + 10$
9. $7 + (-16)$
10. $50 - (-7)$

11. $-16 + 43$
12. $-38 + 40$
13. $12 - 26$
14. $-24 - (-5)$
15. $-29 + (-3)$

16. $2 - (-46)$
17. $13 - 18$
18. $-36 + 16$
19. $24 - 11$
20. $-13 + 20$

Negative Number Addition and Subtraction Practice Set 2

1. $10 - (-9)$
2. $-11 + 7$
3. $13 - 5$
4. $-15 - 2$
5. $-22 + 33$

6. $50 + (-2)$
7. $4 - 12$
8. $-5 - 17$
9. $-19 - (-9)$
10. $37 + (-6)$

11. $-24 + 13$
12. $15 - 35$
13. $7 - (-24)$
14. $-25 + 15$
15. $17 - 20$

16. $-22 + 12$
17. $-9 - 26$
18. $8 - 34$
19. $-18 + 7$
20. $-29 - (-40)$

Negative Number Multiplication and Division Practice Set 1

State if each answer will be positive or negative.

1. -8×5

2. $-18 \div 2$

3. $96 \div -6$

4. 9×-7

5. -12×-11

6. $-132 \div -11$

7. 13×-2

8. $-648 \div -4$

9. $-66 \div 11$

10. $-87 \times -56 \times -3$

11. $44 \times -33 \times 15$

12. $29 \times -33 \times -17$

13. $-72 \times 15 \times -98$

14. $16 \times -20 \times 34$

15. $-18 \times -41 \times -14$

16. $144 \div (-12) \times 3$

17. $81 \times (-9) \div (-3)$

18. $900 \times (-10) \div (-2) \times (-4)$

19. $15 \times (-8) \times 5 \div (-3)$

20. $-130 \div (-13) \times (-8) \div (-4)$

Negative Number Multiplication and Division Practice Set 2

State if each answer will be positive or negative.

1. -9×-9

2. $-27 \div -3$

3. $-84 \div 4$

4. 4×-7

5. -17×19

6. $-240 \div 12$

7. -23×-5

8. $-348 \div 4$

9. $-99 \div -9$

10. $-17 \times 57 \times -43$

11. $14 \times -53 \times -17$

12. $-33 \times -56 \times -14$

13. $-42 \times -25 \times 75$

14. $160 \times -20 \times 34$

15. $-70 \times 13 \times 56$

16. $-196 \div (-14) \times 2$

17. $64 \times (-6) \div 4$

18. $784 \times (-7) \div 4 \times (-8)$

19. $42 \times (-2) \times (-15) \div (-4)$

20. $-50 \div (-5) \times (-6) \div (-3)$

Multiplication with Zeros Practice Set 1

1. 10×8
2. $9 \times 1{,}000$
3. 70×20
4. 80×8
5. 100×30

6. 600×60
7. 500×4
8. 110×20
9. 13×300
10. 50×50

11. 860×100
12. 600×70
13. $80 \times 5{,}000$
14. $4 \times 15{,}000$
15. $1{,}300 \times 20$

16. 900×900
17. $11{,}000 \times 7$
18. 330×200
19. $1{,}200 \times 120$
20. 70×110

Multiplication with Zeros Practice Set 2

1. 10×6
2. 90×3
3. 3×30
4. 300×20
5. 500×600

6. 52×10
7. 70×90
8. 8×60
9. 100×90
10. 70×300

11. $8{,}000 \times 8$
12. 300×250
13. $1{,}000 \times 30$
14. $16 \times 2{,}000$
15. 120×300

16. 110×11
17. 310×20
18. 40×25
19. $1{,}100 \times 12$
20. 800×250

Division with Zeros Practice Set 1

1. $800 \div 4$
2. $60 \div 2$
3. $90 \div 3$
4. $2{,}400 \div 6$
5. $400 \div 20$

6. $8{,}000 \div 40$
7. $1{,}800 \div 300$
8. $800 \div 20$
9. $2{,}500 \div 50$
10. $160 \div 4$

11. $7{,}200 \div 80$
12. $320 \div 4$
13. $6{,}000 \div 30$
14. $36{,}000 \div 300$
15. $49{,}000 \div 70$

16. $4{,}500 \div 1{,}500$
17. $5{,}500 \div 110$
18. $6{,}000 \div 60$
19. $63{,}000 \div 7{,}000$
20. $10{,}800 \div 90$

Division with Zeros Practice Set 2

1. $40 \div 2$
2. $5{,}000 \div 5$
3. $16{,}000 \div 400$
4. $180 \div 60$
5. $1{,}500 \div 300$

6. $800 \div 80$
7. $36{,}000 \div 90$
8. $250 \div 50$
9. $1{,}600 \div 80$
10. $3{,}000 \div 300$

11. $24{,}000 \div 80$
12. $18{,}000 \div 9$
13. $350 \div 7$
14. $4{,}500 \div 500$
15. $160 \div 2$

16. $810 \div 9$
17. $360 \div 40$
18. $4{,}200 \div 70$
19. $84{,}000 \div 1{,}200$
20. $7{,}500 \div 50$

Simplifying Fractions Practice Set 1

Simplify each fraction completely.

1. $\dfrac{2}{4}$

2. $\dfrac{4}{16}$

3. $\dfrac{3}{18}$

4. $\dfrac{8}{24}$

5. $\dfrac{2}{18}$

6. $\dfrac{8}{36}$

7. $\dfrac{18}{45}$

8. $\dfrac{21}{35}$

9. $\dfrac{22}{66}$

10. $\dfrac{12}{21}$

11. $\dfrac{8}{22}$

12. $\dfrac{24}{27}$

13. $\dfrac{30}{40}$

14. $\dfrac{12}{42}$

15. $\dfrac{14}{21}$

16. $\dfrac{16}{40}$

17. $\dfrac{21}{30}$

18. $\dfrac{18}{63}$

19. $\dfrac{54}{60}$

20. $\dfrac{24}{33}$

Simplifying Fractions Practice Set 2

Simplify each fraction completely.

1. $\dfrac{3}{9}$

2. $\dfrac{2}{8}$

3. $\dfrac{5}{15}$

4. $\dfrac{6}{42}$

5. $\dfrac{7}{14}$

6. $\dfrac{9}{21}$

7. $\dfrac{10}{15}$

8. $\dfrac{12}{18}$

9. $\dfrac{6}{20}$

10. $\dfrac{35}{45}$

11. $\dfrac{14}{49}$

12. $\dfrac{24}{32}$

13. $\dfrac{32}{56}$

14. $\dfrac{26}{39}$

15. $\dfrac{27}{36}$

16. $\dfrac{55}{66}$

17. $\dfrac{49}{63}$

18. $\dfrac{24}{64}$

19. $\dfrac{24}{60}$

20. $\dfrac{34}{38}$

Mixed Numbers to Improper Fractions Practice Set 1

Convert each mixed number into a simplified improper fraction.

1. $1\dfrac{1}{2}$

2. $2\dfrac{1}{3}$

3. $6\dfrac{1}{3}$

4. $4\dfrac{1}{5}$

5. $1\dfrac{1}{8}$

6. $2\dfrac{2}{5}$

7. $1\dfrac{2}{3}$

8. $2\dfrac{3}{4}$

9. $4\dfrac{5}{6}$

10. $2\dfrac{3}{8}$

11. $1\dfrac{4}{20}$

12. $2\dfrac{8}{32}$

13. $2\dfrac{12}{15}$

14. $3\dfrac{12}{42}$

15. $5\dfrac{14}{21}$

16. $7\dfrac{16}{40}$

17. $5\dfrac{49}{63}$

18. $9\dfrac{24}{64}$

19. $6\dfrac{21}{30}$

20. $10\dfrac{30}{45}$

Mixed Numbers to Improper Fractions Practice Set 2

Convert each mixed number into a simplified improper fraction.

1. $1\dfrac{1}{4}$

2. $3\dfrac{1}{2}$

3. $2\dfrac{1}{5}$

4. $4\dfrac{1}{3}$

5. $2\dfrac{1}{7}$

6. $2\dfrac{3}{5}$

7. $3\dfrac{2}{3}$

8. $3\dfrac{3}{7}$

9. $2\dfrac{4}{9}$

10. $5\dfrac{7}{10}$

11. $4\dfrac{11}{22}$

12. $2\dfrac{9}{21}$

13. $4\dfrac{10}{15}$

14. $4\dfrac{18}{63}$

15. $5\dfrac{26}{39}$

16. $8\dfrac{24}{36}$

17. $9\dfrac{55}{66}$

18. $6\dfrac{20}{30}$

19. $7\dfrac{54}{60}$

20. $10\dfrac{24}{33}$

Improper Fractions to Mixed Numbers Practice Set 1

Convert each improper fraction into a simplified mixed number.

1. $\dfrac{5}{4}$

2. $\dfrac{7}{6}$

3. $\dfrac{8}{5}$

4. $\dfrac{18}{7}$

5. $\dfrac{19}{5}$

6. $\dfrac{29}{4}$

7. $\dfrac{56}{6}$

8. $\dfrac{58}{5}$

9. $\dfrac{25}{3}$

10. $\dfrac{37}{3}$

11. $\dfrac{72}{7}$

12. $\dfrac{51}{4}$

13. $\dfrac{39}{7}$

14. $\dfrac{100}{80}$

15. $\dfrac{56}{32}$

16. $\dfrac{63}{14}$

17. $\dfrac{66}{24}$

18. $\dfrac{150}{14}$

19. $\dfrac{400}{48}$

20. $\dfrac{450}{36}$

Improper Fractions to Mixed Numbers Practice Set 2

Convert each improper fraction into a simplified mixed number.

1. $\dfrac{3}{2}$

2. $\dfrac{6}{5}$

3. $\dfrac{9}{4}$

4. $\dfrac{13}{9}$

5. $\dfrac{15}{2}$

6. $\dfrac{20}{3}$

7. $\dfrac{17}{5}$

8. $\dfrac{32}{7}$

9. $\dfrac{61}{5}$

10. $\dfrac{35}{3}$

11. $\dfrac{49}{5}$

12. $\dfrac{63}{6}$

13. $\dfrac{47}{4}$

14. $\dfrac{51}{6}$

15. $\dfrac{27}{18}$

16. $\dfrac{88}{33}$

17. $\dfrac{35}{12}$

18. $\dfrac{68}{14}$

19. $\dfrac{720}{30}$

20. $\dfrac{370}{150}$

Adding and Subtracting Fractions Practice Set 1

Write all answers as simplified fractions or mixed numbers where applicable.

1. $\dfrac{1}{3}+\dfrac{1}{6}$

2. $\dfrac{1}{4}-\dfrac{1}{8}$

3. $\dfrac{1}{2}-\dfrac{1}{6}$

4. $\dfrac{1}{2}+\dfrac{1}{3}$

5. $\dfrac{1}{7}-\dfrac{1}{9}$

6. $\dfrac{2}{5}+\dfrac{1}{2}$

7. $\dfrac{2}{4}+\dfrac{1}{8}$

8. $\dfrac{8}{12}-\dfrac{3}{6}$

9. $\dfrac{3}{4}-\dfrac{1}{2}$

10. $\dfrac{5}{7}+\dfrac{1}{8}$

11. $\dfrac{4}{12}+\dfrac{1}{3}$

12. $\dfrac{3}{4}-\dfrac{2}{3}$

13. $\dfrac{8}{16}+\dfrac{4}{6}$

14. $\dfrac{3}{9}+\dfrac{1}{7}$

15. $\dfrac{3}{9}-\dfrac{3}{12}$

16. $\dfrac{6}{18}-\dfrac{7}{42}$

17. $\dfrac{5}{15}-\dfrac{9}{27}$

18. $\dfrac{18}{45}-\dfrac{14}{49}$

19. $\dfrac{30}{35}-\dfrac{18}{30}$

20. $\dfrac{32}{72}+\dfrac{8}{24}$

Adding and Subtracting Fractions Practice Set 2

Write all answers as simplified fractions or mixed numbers where applicable.

1. $\dfrac{1}{2}+\dfrac{1}{4}$

2. $\dfrac{1}{4}-\dfrac{1}{5}$

3. $\dfrac{1}{3}+\dfrac{1}{5}$

4. $\dfrac{1}{3}-\dfrac{1}{6}$

5. $\dfrac{1}{6}+\dfrac{1}{8}$

6. $\dfrac{8}{10}-\dfrac{2}{5}$

7. $\dfrac{2}{3}+\dfrac{2}{6}$

8. $\dfrac{2}{9}-\dfrac{1}{6}$

9. $\dfrac{3}{8}+\dfrac{2}{7}$

10. $\dfrac{5}{10}-\dfrac{5}{11}$

11. $\dfrac{5}{8}+\dfrac{4}{10}$

12. $\dfrac{5}{6}-\dfrac{2}{3}$

13. $\dfrac{5}{12}+\dfrac{1}{8}$

14. $\dfrac{3}{7}-\dfrac{2}{8}$

15. $\dfrac{3}{5}+\dfrac{3}{10}$

16. $\dfrac{4}{8}-\dfrac{2}{9}$

17. $\dfrac{10}{40}+\dfrac{18}{48}$

18. $\dfrac{21}{42}+\dfrac{15}{40}$

19. $\dfrac{12}{36}-\dfrac{11}{55}$

20. $\dfrac{36}{48}-\dfrac{9}{81}$

Adding and Subtracting Mixed Fractions Practice Set 1

Write all answers as simplified fractions or mixed numbers where applicable.

1. $2\frac{1}{7}+1\frac{4}{7}$

2. $6\frac{2}{5}-3\frac{4}{5}$

3. $\frac{10}{7}+\frac{8}{5}$

4. $3\frac{1}{4}+1\frac{1}{3}$

5. $3\frac{5}{6}-2\frac{2}{3}$

6. $\frac{11}{3}-\frac{5}{2}$

7. $1\frac{6}{7}+2\frac{4}{5}$

8. $2\frac{3}{8}-\frac{3}{4}$

9. $\frac{12}{5}+\frac{2}{3}$

10. $\frac{6}{7}+\frac{18}{8}$

11. $6\frac{1}{2}-2\frac{3}{4}$

12. $4\frac{4}{10}+2\frac{4}{6}$

13. $2\frac{8}{9}+5\frac{1}{3}$

14. $2\frac{5}{6}-2\frac{2}{4}$

15. $4+\frac{21}{8}$

16. $3\frac{2}{8}-\frac{12}{9}$

17. $8-3\frac{2}{3}$

18. $\frac{24}{6}-1\frac{5}{9}$

19. $5-\frac{13}{9}$

20. $2\frac{10}{25}+\frac{12}{8}$

Adding and Subtracting Mixed Fractions Practice Set 2

Write all answers as simplified fractions or mixed numbers where applicable.

1. $2\frac{1}{6}+1\frac{3}{6}$

2. $5\frac{1}{4}-1\frac{3}{4}$

3. $\frac{11}{9}+\frac{7}{3}$

4. $2\frac{1}{5}+2\frac{1}{4}$

5. $4\frac{1}{7}-3\frac{2}{4}$

6. $\frac{12}{8}-\frac{7}{6}$

7. $2\frac{3}{5}+1\frac{7}{10}$

8. $4\frac{6}{8}-\frac{5}{10}$

9. $\frac{14}{5}+\frac{5}{6}$

10. $1\frac{2}{9}+\frac{8}{6}$

11. $4\frac{1}{3}-3\frac{3}{4}$

12. $5\frac{4}{12}-1\frac{3}{6}$

13. $2\frac{9}{15}+5\frac{2}{10}$

14. $4\frac{10}{16}-2\frac{6}{8}$

15. $3+\frac{26}{8}$

16. $2\frac{15}{20}-\frac{15}{9}$

17. $4-2\frac{18}{27}$

18. $\frac{28}{4}-5\frac{4}{9}$

19. $4-\frac{18}{8}$

20. $3\frac{12}{36}+\frac{16}{6}$

Multiplying Fractions Practice Set 1

Write all answers as simplified fractions or mixed numbers where applicable.

1. $\dfrac{1}{3} \times \dfrac{1}{9}$

2. $\dfrac{1}{5} \times \dfrac{1}{8}$

3. $\dfrac{1}{6} \times \dfrac{1}{5}$

4. $\dfrac{1}{4} \times 3$

5. $\dfrac{1}{7} \times \dfrac{5}{6}$

6. $\dfrac{2}{3} \times \dfrac{7}{9}$

7. $\dfrac{2}{7} \times \dfrac{1}{2}$

8. $\dfrac{5}{8} \times \dfrac{3}{5}$

9. $\dfrac{1}{8} \times \dfrac{4}{6}$

10. $\dfrac{4}{8} \times 4$

11. $\dfrac{5}{12} \times \dfrac{7}{10}$

12. $\dfrac{3}{8} \times \dfrac{12}{13}$

13. $\dfrac{9}{10} \times \dfrac{15}{18}$

14. $\dfrac{7}{9} \times \dfrac{18}{35}$

15. $\dfrac{15}{18} \times \dfrac{12}{25}$

16. $\dfrac{11}{18} \times 30$

17. $\dfrac{21}{25} \times \dfrac{20}{33}$

18. $\dfrac{11}{54} \times 24$

19. $\dfrac{15}{28} \times \dfrac{7}{20}$

20. $\dfrac{36}{60} \times \dfrac{16}{54}$

Multiplying Fractions Practice Set 2

Write all answers as simplified fractions or mixed numbers where applicable.

1. $\dfrac{1}{3} \times \dfrac{1}{4}$

2. $\dfrac{1}{3} \times \dfrac{1}{5}$

3. $\dfrac{1}{7} \times \dfrac{1}{8}$

4. $\dfrac{5}{8} \times \dfrac{1}{9}$

5. $\dfrac{2}{3} \times \dfrac{3}{9}$

6. $\dfrac{4}{9} \times \dfrac{2}{4}$

7. $\dfrac{3}{16} \times \dfrac{4}{7}$

8. $\dfrac{3}{4} \times 2$

9. $\dfrac{2}{9} \times \dfrac{3}{8}$

10. $\dfrac{4}{15} \times \dfrac{3}{10}$

11. $\dfrac{7}{12} \times \dfrac{4}{21}$

12. $\dfrac{5}{8} \times 20$

13. $\dfrac{3}{12} \times \dfrac{8}{27}$

14. $\dfrac{6}{16} \times \dfrac{4}{15}$

15. $\dfrac{16}{72} \times \dfrac{32}{40}$

16. $\dfrac{12}{40} \times \dfrac{12}{48}$

17. $\dfrac{7}{45} \times 27$

18. $\dfrac{27}{42} \times \dfrac{14}{30}$

19. $\dfrac{12}{42} \times \dfrac{9}{72}$

20. $\dfrac{30}{70} \times \dfrac{7}{21}$

Dividing Fractions Practice Set 1

Write all answers as simplified fractions or mixed numbers where applicable.

1. $\dfrac{1}{4} \div \dfrac{1}{3}$

2. $\dfrac{1}{5} \div \dfrac{1}{6}$

3. $\dfrac{1}{9} \div \dfrac{1}{3}$

4. $\dfrac{1}{8} \div \dfrac{2}{5}$

5. $\dfrac{5}{6} \div \dfrac{1}{5}$

6. $\dfrac{2}{7} \div 2$

7. $\dfrac{5}{8} \div \dfrac{5}{7}$

8. $\dfrac{2}{3} \div \dfrac{3}{9}$

9. $\dfrac{4}{9} \div \dfrac{8}{11}$

10. $\dfrac{3}{4} \div \dfrac{9}{16}$

11. $\dfrac{2}{19} \div \dfrac{2}{19}$

12. $\dfrac{4}{6} \div \dfrac{8}{18}$

13. $\dfrac{7}{12} \div \dfrac{21}{24}$

14. $\dfrac{15}{24} \div \dfrac{4}{10}$

15. $\dfrac{6}{24} \div 9$

16. $\dfrac{9}{22} \div 18$

17. $\dfrac{16}{27} \div \dfrac{40}{72}$

18. $\dfrac{12}{40} \div \dfrac{48}{50}$

19. $\dfrac{35}{40} \div 14$

20. $\dfrac{27}{42} \div \dfrac{9}{14}$

Dividing Fractions Practice Set 2

Write all answers as simplified fractions or mixed numbers where applicable.

1. $\dfrac{1}{6} \div \dfrac{1}{5}$

2. $\dfrac{1}{7} \div \dfrac{1}{3}$

3. $\dfrac{1}{9} \div \dfrac{1}{6}$

4. $\dfrac{1}{6} \div \dfrac{3}{8}$

5. $\dfrac{5}{8} \div \dfrac{3}{5}$

6. $\dfrac{1}{8} \div \dfrac{3}{4}$

7. $\dfrac{4}{8} \div \dfrac{8}{10}$

8. $\dfrac{5}{12} \div \dfrac{5}{6}$

9. $\dfrac{3}{8} \div \dfrac{9}{14}$

10. $\dfrac{6}{11} \div 4$

11. $\dfrac{3}{16} \div \dfrac{9}{16}$

12. $\dfrac{3}{10} \div \dfrac{18}{25}$

13. $\dfrac{7}{9} \div \dfrac{35}{54}$

14. $\dfrac{15}{18} \div \dfrac{12}{27}$

15. $\dfrac{10}{15} \div \dfrac{12}{50}$

16. $\dfrac{12}{27} \div \dfrac{9}{72}$

17. $\dfrac{30}{70} \div \dfrac{7}{21}$

18. $\dfrac{18}{54} \div \dfrac{18}{24}$

19. $\dfrac{15}{27} \div 10$

20. $\dfrac{36}{60} \div \dfrac{16}{48}$

Multiplying and Dividing Mixed Fractions Practice Set 1

Write all answers as simplified fractions or mixed numbers where applicable.

1. $\dfrac{5}{2} \times \dfrac{14}{13}$

2. $\dfrac{7}{6} \times \dfrac{18}{5}$

3. $7\dfrac{1}{2} \div \dfrac{9}{6}$

4. $2\dfrac{2}{3} \times 1\dfrac{3}{4}$

5. $\dfrac{56}{9} \div \dfrac{14}{5}$

6. $3\dfrac{3}{4} \div 3\dfrac{3}{7}$

7. $4\dfrac{1}{3} \div \dfrac{26}{24}$

8. $\dfrac{19}{2} \times \dfrac{4}{3}$

9. $\dfrac{8}{7} \div 2\dfrac{3}{5}$

10. $1\dfrac{2}{3} \times \dfrac{12}{7}$

11. $\dfrac{48}{14} \div \dfrac{15}{4}$

12. $\dfrac{9}{5} \div \dfrac{15}{7}$

13. $4\dfrac{2}{5} \times 2\dfrac{1}{7}$

14. $3\dfrac{3}{4} \div 2\dfrac{5}{8}$

15. $1\dfrac{3}{7} \div 2\dfrac{1}{5}$

16. $2\dfrac{1}{6} \div 3\dfrac{2}{3}$

17. $5\dfrac{5}{10} \times 1\dfrac{6}{14}$

18. $1\dfrac{4}{16} \times 2\dfrac{36}{45}$

19. $3\dfrac{6}{9} \times 2\dfrac{12}{16}$

20. $4\dfrac{15}{40} \div 3\dfrac{6}{8}$

Multiplying and Dividing Mixed Fractions Practice Set 2

Write all answers as simplified fractions or mixed numbers where applicable.

1. $\dfrac{10}{6} \div \dfrac{12}{5}$

2. $\dfrac{10}{9} \times \dfrac{16}{15}$

3. $\dfrac{18}{5} \times 2\dfrac{3}{9}$

4. $\dfrac{12}{4} \times \dfrac{9}{7}$

5. $\dfrac{12}{7} \div \dfrac{3}{2}$

6. $2\dfrac{1}{4} \times \dfrac{16}{15}$

7. $\dfrac{11}{3} \times \dfrac{9}{4}$

8. $3\dfrac{3}{5} \times \dfrac{20}{9}$

9. $\dfrac{32}{3} \div \dfrac{24}{11}$

10. $1\dfrac{3}{4} \div \dfrac{5}{3}$

11. $\dfrac{16}{5} \times 4\dfrac{1}{6}$

12. $\dfrac{18}{12} \div 3\dfrac{3}{5}$

13. $1\dfrac{2}{9} \times \dfrac{21}{22}$

14. $4\dfrac{2}{3} \div 5\dfrac{3}{5}$

15. $1\dfrac{4}{7} \times 1\dfrac{3}{18}$

16. $3\dfrac{2}{6} \times 2\dfrac{1}{5}$

17. $1\dfrac{21}{24} \times 2\dfrac{4}{6}$

18. $1\dfrac{9}{21} \div 2\dfrac{7}{49}$

19. $3\dfrac{8}{14} \times 2\dfrac{40}{50}$

20. $1\dfrac{21}{28} \div 4\dfrac{26}{39}$

Rounding Decimals Practice Set 1

1. Round 4.926 to the nearest tenth.
2. Round 4,993.0283 to the nearest thousandth.
3. Round 37.096 to the nearest hundredth.
4. Round 99.905 to the nearest whole number.
5. Round 106.995 to the nearest hundredth.
6. Round 2,046.5234 to the nearest thousandth.
7. Round 5.93622 to the nearest ten thousandth.
8. Round 40.874 to the nearest tenth.
9. Round 3.07899 to the nearest ten thousandth.
10. Round 3.4862 to the nearest unit.
11. Round 313.349 to the nearest tenth.
12. Round 107.33487 to the nearest ten thousandth.
13. Round 52.867 to the nearest tenth.
14. Round 96.9973 to the nearest hundredth.
15. Round 15,224.9995 to the nearest thousandth.
16. Round 36.4741 to the nearest hundredth.
17. Round 12.502 to the nearest unit.
18. Round 14.97 to the nearest whole number.
19. Round 12.83291 to the nearest ten thousandth.
20. Round 6.23482 to the nearest thousandth.

Rounding Decimals Practice Set 2

1. Round 5.0079 to the nearest thousandth.
2. Round 130.5278 to the nearest unit.
3. Round 403.223 to the nearest hundredth.
4. Round 15.05 to the nearest tenth.
5. Round 39.962 to the nearest tenth.
6. Round 8.8948 to the nearest hundredth.
7. Round 14.87601 to the nearest ten thousandth.
8. Round 5.478 to the nearest whole number.
9. Round 15.18897 to the nearest ten thousandth.
10. Round 46.4499 to the nearest thousandth.
11. Round 79.6 to the nearest whole number.
12. Round 7.0849 to the nearest hundredth.
13. Round 28.4952 to the nearest thousandth.
14. Round 5.973 to the nearest tenth.
15. Round 192.246 to the nearest hundredth.
16. Round 5.498 to the nearest unit.
17. Round 129.5489 to the nearest tenth.
18. Round 1.00789 to the nearest ten thousandth.
19. Round 2.03402 to the nearest ten thousandth.
20. Round 348.8999 to the nearest thousandth.

Adding Decimals Practice Set 1

1. $3.2 + 12$	6. $1.9 + 5.9$	11. $1.02 + 10.99$	16. $84.65 + 3.595$
2. $15 + 5.8$	7. $9.9 + 4.8$	12. $1.42 + 11.09$	17. $90.07 + 122.768$
3. $5.6 + 3.2$	8. $5.4 + 8.8$	13. $6.47 + 11.35$	18. $1,089.7 + 675.58$
4. $9.1 + 5.6$	9. $3.45 + 8.67$	14. $12.77 + 13.09$	19. $487.07 + 76.049$
5. $7.8 + 4.2$	10. $9.04 + 3.84$	15. $14.6 + 39.84$	20. $69.98 + 156.073$

Adding Decimals Practice Set 2

1. $10 + 3.4$	6. $8.7 + 0.6$	11. $7.11 + 5.89$	16. $22.043 + 16.2$
2. $6.5 + 4$	7. $3.3 + 6.6$	12. $1.04 + 19.4$	17. $786.22 + 54.092$
3. $1.8 + 4.5$	8. $8.37 + 5.36$	13. $17.5 + 5.46$	18. $18.31 + 88.9$
4. $5.1 + 3.9$	9. $12.38 + 19.89$	14. $78.96 + 16.6$	19. $385.3 + 29.824$
5. $2.3 + 3.2$	10. $5.73 + 9.04$	15. $184.5 + 6.98$	20. $1,234.56 + 78.9$

Subtracting Decimals Practice Set 1

1. $13.4 - 10$	6. $16.4 - 5.4$	11. $64.47 - 9.8$	16. $90.01 - 58.9$
2. $6.5 - 4$	7. $19.8 - 14.4$	12. $42.7 - 13.09$	17. $202.768 - 81.42$
3. $25.6 - 13$	8. $25.4 - 18.8$	13. $17.5 - 5.46$	18. $831.84 - 743.083$
4. $31.8 - 24$	9. $23.32 - 10.9$	14. $78.9 - 16.56$	19. $4,853 - 37.712$
5. $8.1 - 4.2$	10. $83.87 - 5.6$	15. $184.5 - 16.98$	20. $583 - 46.05$

Subtracting Decimals Practice Set 2

1. $14.2 - 3$	6. $38.2 - 14.6$	11. $54.75 - 49.4$	16. $122.4 - 16.25$
2. $15.8 - 5$	7. $46.3 - 32.6$	12. $27.01 - 15.8$	17. $84.6 - 3.59$
3. $52.1 - 36$	8. $31.4 - 28.6$	13. $16.42 - 7.9$	18. $1,234.56 - 69.8$
4. $27.3 - 18$	9. $19.04 - 3.8$	14. $54.6 - 39.84$	19. $1,036 - 773.59$
5. $9.6 - 5.1$	10. $82.38 - 19.8$	15. $61.4 - 19.09$	20. $206 - 49.78$

Multiplying Decimals Practice Set 1

1. 0.3×4	**6.** 0.9×0.6	**11.** 0.32×4	**16.** 0.98×5.8
2. 5×0.1	**7.** 0.4×0.5	**12.** 0.16×0.2	**17.** 5.76×4
3. 3×0.7	**8.** 0.3×0.6	**13.** 0.47×0.5	**18.** 3.1×4.07
4. 0.8×8	**9.** 0.8×0.7	**14.** 0.86×2	**19.** 16.12×123
5. 0.6×10	**10.** 0.6×0.7	**15.** 0.73×0.4	**20.** 63.725×0.43

Multiplying Decimals Practice Set 2

1. 0.9×6	**6.** 0.7×0.3	**11.** 0.2×0.53	**16.** 8.7×0.31
2. 5×0.4	**7.** 0.8×0.8	**12.** 0.9×0.41	**17.** 29×3.7
3. 0.3×6	**8.** 0.1×0.6	**13.** 0.87×0.8	**18.** 0.32×0.57
4. 0.8×7	**9.** 0.3×0.5	**14.** 0.91×7	**19.** 87.6×2.4
5. 7×0.6	**10.** 0.1×0.9	**15.** 0.7×0.63	**20.** 0.57×5.031

Dividing Decimals Practice Set 1

1. $4.8 \div 4$	**6.** $26.4 \div 0.3$	**11.** $0.28 \div 0.08$	**16.** $63.3 \div 0.6$
2. $10.8 \div 9$	**7.** $73.8 \div 0.9$	**12.** $7.2 \div 0.36$	**17.** $0.59 \div 0.04$
3. $16.2 \div 3$	**8.** $16 \div 0.4$	**13.** $0.371 \div 2$	**18.** $0.369 \div 0.03$
4. $3.2 \div 32$	**9.** $24 \div 0.04$	**14.** $5 \div 0.8$	**19.** $672 \div 0.004$
5. $3.9 \div 0.3$	**10.** $0.18 \div 1.2$	**15.** $7.59 \div 1.1$	**20.** $0.483 \div 2.3$

Dividing Decimals Practice Set 2

1. $3.6 \div 3$	**6.** $5.2 \div 0.4$	**11.** $0.455 \div 0.2$	**16.** $56.4 \div 0.004$
2. $27.3 \div 3$	**7.** $1.7 \div 0.5$	**12.** $0.1 \div 0.4$	**17.** $0.58 \div 0.8$
3. $7.2 \div 72$	**8.** $0.81 \div 0.03$	**13.** $65 \div 0.05$	**18.** $47.7 \div 0.3$
4. $6.4 \div 0.4$	**9.** $17.5 \div 0.7$	**14.** $3.52 \div 1.6$	**19.** $3.58 \div 0.08$
5. $16.8 \div 0.6$	**10.** $54.7 \div 0.02$	**15.** $9.4 \div 4$	**20.** $0.0602 \div 0.007$

Converting Decimals to Fractions Practice Set 1

Change each decimal into a simplified fraction.

1.	0.1	**5.**	0.9	**9.**	0.11	**13.**	0.25	**17.**	2.04
2.	3.4	**6.**	7.3	**10.**	0.08	**14.**	4.09	**18.**	0.054
3.	0.7	**7.**	0.2	**11.**	18.45	**15.**	0.86	**19.**	4.008
4.	5.6	**8.**	0.5	**12.**	0.34	**16.**	9.88	**20.**	62.625

Converting Decimals to Fractions Practice Set 2

Change each decimal into a simplified fraction.

1.	9.9	**5.**	17.2	**9.**	4.4	**13.**	0.52	**17.**	0.05
2.	0.8	**6.**	0.4	**10.**	0.04	**14.**	90.67	**18.**	3.004
3.	3.7	**7.**	11.9	**11.**	0.75	**15.**	8.65	**19.**	4.075
4.	0.3	**8.**	6.5	**12.**	13.02	**16.**	0.92	**20.**	0.006

Converting Decimals to Percents Practice Set 1

Change each decimal into a percent.

1.	0.2	**5.**	0.08	**9.**	0.11	**13.**	0.25	**17.**	0.008
2.	4.1	**6.**	9.9	**10.**	0.06	**14.**	5.12	**18.**	0.0054
3.	0.6	**7.**	0.4	**11.**	18.03	**15.**	0.0682	**19.**	4.0003
4.	2.7	**8.**	0.05	**12.**	0.78	**16.**	4.018	**20.**	62.625

Converting Decimals to Percents Practice Set 2

Change each decimal into a percent.

1.	5.5	**5.**	39.2	**9.**	2.08	**13.**	0.59	**17.**	21.25
2.	0.09	**6.**	0.07	**10.**	0.05	**14.**	60.72	**18.**	8.004
3.	0.1	**7.**	20.9	**11.**	0.75	**15.**	4.35	**19.**	5.0075
4.	0.3	**8.**	1.5	**12.**	31.18	**16.**	0.43	**20.**	0.007

Converting Percents to Fractions Practice Set 1

Change each percent into a simplified fraction or mixed number.

1.	50%	**5.**	72%	**9.**	425%	**13.**	28%	**17.**	99%
2.	25%	**6.**	9%	**10.**	120%	**14.**	4%	**18.**	70%
3.	34%	**7.**	2%	**11.**	350%	**15.**	4.5%	**19.**	40.8%
4.	66%	**8.**	200%	**12.**	17%	**16.**	8.2%	**20.**	0.6%

Converting Percents to Fractions Practice Set 2

Change each percent into a simplified fraction or mixed number.

1.	30%	**5.**	33%	**9.**	750%	**13.**	15%	**17.**	77%
2.	65%	**6.**	3%	**10.**	240%	**14.**	6%	**18.**	150%
3.	12%	**7.**	7%	**11.**	6000%	**15.**	9.5%	**19.**	20.3%
4.	20%	**8.**	100%	**12.**	40%	**16.**	2.4%	**20.**	0.2%

Converting Percents to Decimals Practice Set 1

Change each percent into a decimal.

1.	10%	**5.**	7%	**9.**	143%	**13.**	45.6%	**17.**	0.06%
2.	4%	**6.**	100%	**10.**	783%	**14.**	100.8%	**18.**	300.5%
3.	34%	**7.**	230%	**11.**	1.5%	**15.**	0.37%	**19.**	180.45%
4.	25%	**8.**	8000%	**12.**	850.2%	**16.**	4.05%	**20.**	0.005%

Converting Percents to Decimals Practice Set 2

Change each percent into a decimal.

1.	20%	**5.**	1%	**9.**	650%	**13.**	99.9%	**17.**	450.6%
2.	8%	**6.**	200%	**10.**	102%	**14.**	190.3%	**18.**	0.08%
3.	22%	**7.**	3450%	**11.**	60.5%	**15.**	0.32%	**19.**	1.0052%
4.	50%	**8.**	4000%	**12.**	7.8%	**16.**	2.25%	**20.**	0.004%

Converting Fractions to Decimals Practice Set 1

Change each fraction into a decimal.

1. $\dfrac{3}{4}$

2. $\dfrac{1}{2}$

3. $\dfrac{2}{3}$

4. $\dfrac{4}{5}$

5. $\dfrac{1}{10}$

6. $\dfrac{28}{40}$

7. $\dfrac{5}{8}$

8. $\dfrac{8}{100}$

9. $\dfrac{53}{100}$

10. $5\dfrac{2}{5}$

11. $2\dfrac{3}{10}$

12. $1\dfrac{18}{20}$

13. $4\dfrac{3}{8}$

14. $\dfrac{43}{50}$

15. $\dfrac{6}{25}$

16. $\dfrac{128}{1000}$

17. $\dfrac{28}{500}$

18. $\dfrac{37}{5}$

19. $\dfrac{15}{4}$

20. $\dfrac{23}{10}$

Converting Fractions to Decimals Practice Set 2

Change each fraction into a decimal.

1. $\dfrac{1}{4}$

2. $\dfrac{3}{10}$

3. $\dfrac{2}{5}$

4. $\dfrac{9}{30}$

5. $\dfrac{3}{8}$

6. $\dfrac{1}{100}$

7. $\dfrac{82}{100}$

8. $8\dfrac{2}{3}$

9. $2\dfrac{1}{5}$

10. $1\dfrac{7}{10}$

11. $4\dfrac{2}{10}$

12. $2\dfrac{5}{8}$

13. $\dfrac{7}{50}$

14. $\dfrac{24}{25}$

15. $\dfrac{512}{1000}$

16. $\dfrac{231}{500}$

17. $\dfrac{9}{2}$

18. $\dfrac{9}{8}$

19. $\dfrac{24}{5}$

20. $5\dfrac{6}{20}$

Converting Fractions to Percents Practice Set 1

Change each fraction into a percent.

1. $\dfrac{1}{2}$ 5. $\dfrac{7}{10}$ 9. $\dfrac{3}{25}$ 13. $1\dfrac{4}{5}$ 17. $5\dfrac{9}{1000}$

2. $\dfrac{3}{4}$ 6. $\dfrac{1}{5}$ 10. $\dfrac{10}{16}$ 14. $6\dfrac{5}{9}$ 18. $1\dfrac{16}{36}$

3. $\dfrac{5}{10}$ 7. $\dfrac{2}{3}$ 11. $\dfrac{82}{100}$ 15. $3\dfrac{8}{9}$ 19. $2\dfrac{3}{20}$

4. $\dfrac{3}{5}$ 8. $\dfrac{1}{8}$ 12. $\dfrac{21}{1000}$ 16. $4\dfrac{6}{50}$ 20. $5\dfrac{14}{21}$

Converting Fractions to Percents Practice Set 2

Change each fraction into a percent.

1. $\dfrac{1}{3}$ 5. $\dfrac{2}{5}$ 9. $\dfrac{5}{6}$ 13. $1\dfrac{8}{24}$ 17. $2\dfrac{33}{500}$

2. $\dfrac{1}{4}$ 6. $\dfrac{2}{8}$ 10. $\dfrac{13}{100}$ 14. $3\dfrac{14}{50}$ 18. $1\dfrac{11}{250}$

3. $\dfrac{4}{5}$ 7. $\dfrac{1}{10}$ 11. $\dfrac{17}{20}$ 15. $5\dfrac{3}{1000}$ 19. $2\dfrac{6}{16}$

4. $\dfrac{9}{10}$ 8. $\dfrac{3}{9}$ 12. $\dfrac{7}{8}$ 16. $2\dfrac{22}{25}$ 20. $3\dfrac{8}{72}$

Math Fundamentals Chapter Answer Key

Addition Practice Set 1

1. 39
2. 73
3. 168
4. 399
5. 899
6. 74
7. 74
8. 184
9. 730
10. 636
11. 995
12. 1,111
13. 2,693
14. 3,674
15. 10,132
16. 15,958
17. 9,530
18. 4,233
19. 8,972
20. 14,486

Subtraction Practice Set 1

1. 46
2. 55
3. 14
4. 224
5. 222
6. 322
7. 18
8. 27
9. 156
10. 237
11. 629
12. 287
13. 488
14. 1,850
15. 2,589
16. 1,708
17. 3,678
18. 1,629
19. 1,267
20. 1,577

Multiplication Practice Set 1

1. 56
2. 231
3. 228
4. 403
5. 408
6. 3,472
7. 1,302
8. 1,332
9. 2,172
10. 2,700
11. 10,530
12. 23,479
13. 27,648
14. 23,424
15. 10,755
16. 23,584
17. 123,816
18. 458,703
19. 613,638
20. 357,084

Division Practice Set 1

1. 13
2. 12
3. 18
4. 14
5. 13
6. 129
7. 43
8. 78
9. 183
10. 118
11. 273
12. 235
13. 985
14. 710
15. 194
16. 1,768
17. 48
18. 540
19. 17
20. 32

Addition Practice Set 2

1. 69
2. 106
3. 529
4. 188
5. 979
6. 148
7. 142
8. 192
9. 318
10. 1,231
11. 1,110
12. 1,290
13. 2,663
14. 5,442
15. 17,745
16. 10,022
17. 4,787
18. 10,374
19. 3,852
20. 11,876

Subtraction Practice Set 2

1. 11
2. 31
3. 810
4. 602
5. 26
6. 17
7. 35
8. 885
9. 145
10. 77
11. 246
12. 39
13. 8,453
14. 5,247
15. 6,328
16. 7,178
17. 5,354
18. 3,900
19. 287
20. 3,459

Multiplication Practice Set 2

1. 69
2. 410
3. 195
4. 726
5. 516
6. 3,071
7. 1,296
8. 3,910
9. 2,058
10. 867
11. 18,291
12. 30,972
13. 32,406
14. 20,691
15. 65,766
16. 38,775
17. 167,698
18. 97,008
19. 576,612
20. 876,960

Division Practice Set 2

1. 24
2. 11
3. 13
4. 14
5. 11
6. 17
7. 88
8. 74
9. 127
10. 223
11. 159
12. 123
13. 957
14. 1,097
15. 1,132
16. 2,436
17. 58
18. 460
19. 21
20. 102

Division with Remainders Practice Set 1

1. 9 R 2
2. 23 R 1
3. 9 R 4
4. 17 R 4
5. 12 R 2
6. 89 R 1
7. 65 R 1
8. 61 R 1
9. 51 R 2
10. 137 R 2
11. 247 R 2
12. 926 R 1
13. 610 R 1
14. 556 R 4
15. 521 R 2
16. 57 R 7
17. 54 R 7
18. 45 R 41
19. 34 R 100
20. 6 R 606

Division with Remainders Practice Set 2

1. 14 R 1
2. 10 R 4
3. 22 R 2
4. 23 R 2
5. 36 R 1
6. 16 R 6
7. 233 R 2
8. 56 R 8
9. 348 R 1
10. 98 R 1
11. 951 R 2
12. 206 R 4
13. 588 R 7
14. 38 R 7
15. 626 R 11
16. 277 R 1
17. 244 R 11
18. 129 R 10
19. 16 R 136
20. 1 R 1,257

Order of Operations Practice Set 1

1. 10
2. 29
3. 25
4. 9
5. 31
6. 20
7. 0
8. 21
9. 57
10. 60
11. 160
12. 51
13. 51
14. 17
15. 16
16. 27
17. 18
18. 9
19. 34
20. 4

Order of Operations Practice Set 2

1. 10
2. 27
3. 57
4. 51
5. 11
6. 5
7. 6
8. 51
9. 57
10. 22
11. 10
12. 28
13. 8
14. 6
15. 29
16. 75
17. 80
18. 9
19. 44
20. 24

Negative Number Addition and Subtraction Practice Set 1

1. -10
2. -3
3. -1
4. 29
5. -11
6. -48
7. -30
8. -22
9. -9
10. 57
11. 27
12. 2
13. -14
14. -19
15. -32
16. 48
17. -5
18. -20
19. 13
20. 7

Negative Number Addition and Subtraction Practice Set 2

1. 19
2. -4
3. -12
4. -17
5. 11
6. 48
7. -8
8. -22
9. -10
10. 31
11. -11
12. -20
13. 31
14. -10
15. -3
16. -10
17. -35
18. -26
19. -11
20. 11

Negative Number Multiplication and Division Practice Set 1

1. negative
2. negative
3. negative
4. negative
5. positive
6. positive
7. negative
8. positive
9. negative
10. negative
11. negative
12. positive
13. positive
14. negative
15. negative
16. negative
17. positive
18. negative
19. positive
20. positive

Negative Number Multiplication and Division Practice Set 2

1. positive
2. positive
3. negative
4. negative
5. negative
6. negative
7. positive
8. negative
9. positive
10. positive
11. positive
12. negative
13. positive
14. negative
15. negative
16. positive
17. negative
18. positive
19. negative
20. positive

Multiplication with Zeros Practice Set 1

1. 80
2. 9,000
3. 1,400
4. 640
5. 3,000
6. 36,000
7. 2,000
8. 2,200
9. 3,900
10. 2,500
11. 86,000
12. 42,000
13. 400,000
14. 60,000
15. 26,000
16. 810,000
17. 77,000
18. 66,000
19. 144,000
20. 7,700

Multiplication with Zeros Practice Set 2

1. 60
2. 270
3. 90
4. 6,000
5. 300,000
6. 520
7. 6,300
8. 480
9. 9,000
10. 21,000
11. 64,000
12. 75,000
13. 30,000
14. 32,000
15. 36,000
16. 1,210
17. 6,200
18. 1,000
19. 13,200
20. 200,000

Division with Zeros Practice Set 1

1. 200
2. 30
3. 30
4. 400
5. 20
6. 200
7. 6
8. 40
9. 50
10. 40
11. 90
12. 80
13. 200
14. 120
15. 700
16. 3
17. 50
18. 100
19. 9
20. 120

Division with Zeros Practice Set 2

1. 20
2. 1,000
3. 40
4. 3
5. 5
6. 10
7. 400
8. 5
9. 20
10. 10
11. 300
12. 2,000
13. 50
14. 9
15. 80
16. 90
17. 9
18. 60
19. 70
20. 150

Simplifying Fractions Practice Set 1

1. $\dfrac{1}{2}$
2. $\dfrac{1}{4}$
3. $\dfrac{1}{6}$
4. $\dfrac{1}{3}$
5. $\dfrac{1}{9}$
6. $\dfrac{2}{9}$
7. $\dfrac{2}{5}$
8. $\dfrac{3}{5}$
9. $\dfrac{1}{3}$
10. $\dfrac{4}{7}$
11. $\dfrac{4}{11}$
12. $\dfrac{8}{9}$
13. $\dfrac{3}{4}$
14. $\dfrac{2}{7}$
15. $\dfrac{2}{3}$
16. $\dfrac{2}{5}$
17. $\dfrac{7}{10}$
18. $\dfrac{2}{7}$
19. $\dfrac{9}{10}$
20. $\dfrac{8}{11}$

Simplifying Fractions Practice Set 2

1. $\dfrac{1}{3}$
2. $\dfrac{1}{4}$
3. $\dfrac{1}{3}$
4. $\dfrac{1}{7}$
5. $\dfrac{1}{2}$
6. $\dfrac{3}{7}$
7. $\dfrac{2}{3}$
8. $\dfrac{2}{3}$
9. $\dfrac{3}{10}$
10. $\dfrac{7}{9}$
11. $\dfrac{2}{7}$
12. $\dfrac{3}{4}$
13. $\dfrac{4}{7}$
14. $\dfrac{2}{3}$
15. $\dfrac{3}{4}$
16. $\dfrac{5}{6}$
17. $\dfrac{7}{9}$
18. $\dfrac{3}{8}$
19. $\dfrac{2}{5}$
20. $\dfrac{17}{19}$

Mixed Numbers to Improper Fractions Practice Set 1	**Mixed Numbers to Improper Fractions Practice Set 2**	**Improper Fractions to Mixed Numbers Practice Set 1**	**Improper Fractions to Mixed Numbers Practice Set 2**
1. $\dfrac{3}{2}$	1. $\dfrac{5}{4}$	1. $1\dfrac{1}{4}$	1. $1\dfrac{1}{2}$
2. $\dfrac{7}{3}$	2. $\dfrac{7}{2}$	2. $1\dfrac{1}{6}$	2. $1\dfrac{1}{5}$
3. $\dfrac{19}{3}$	3. $\dfrac{11}{5}$	3. $1\dfrac{3}{5}$	3. $2\dfrac{1}{4}$
4. $\dfrac{21}{5}$	4. $\dfrac{13}{3}$	4. $2\dfrac{4}{7}$	4. $1\dfrac{4}{9}$
5. $\dfrac{9}{8}$	5. $\dfrac{15}{7}$	5. $3\dfrac{4}{5}$	5. $7\dfrac{1}{2}$
6. $\dfrac{12}{5}$	6. $\dfrac{13}{5}$	6. $7\dfrac{1}{4}$	6. $6\dfrac{2}{3}$
7. $\dfrac{5}{3}$	7. $\dfrac{11}{3}$	7. $9\dfrac{1}{3}$	7. $3\dfrac{2}{5}$
8. $\dfrac{11}{4}$	8. $\dfrac{24}{7}$	8. $11\dfrac{3}{5}$	8. $4\dfrac{4}{7}$
9. $\dfrac{29}{6}$	9. $\dfrac{22}{9}$	9. $8\dfrac{1}{3}$	9. $12\dfrac{1}{5}$
10. $\dfrac{19}{8}$	10. $\dfrac{57}{10}$	10. $12\dfrac{1}{3}$	10. $11\dfrac{2}{3}$
11. $\dfrac{6}{5}$	11. $\dfrac{9}{2}$	11. $10\dfrac{2}{7}$	11. $9\dfrac{4}{5}$
12. $\dfrac{9}{4}$	12. $\dfrac{17}{7}$	12. $12\dfrac{3}{4}$	12. $10\dfrac{1}{2}$
13. $\dfrac{14}{5}$	13. $\dfrac{14}{3}$	13. $5\dfrac{4}{7}$	13. $11\dfrac{3}{4}$
14. $\dfrac{23}{7}$	14. $\dfrac{30}{7}$	14. $1\dfrac{1}{4}$	14. $8\dfrac{1}{2}$
15. $\dfrac{17}{3}$	15. $\dfrac{17}{3}$	15. $1\dfrac{3}{4}$	15. $1\dfrac{1}{2}$
16. $\dfrac{37}{5}$	16. $\dfrac{26}{3}$	16. $4\dfrac{1}{2}$	16. $2\dfrac{2}{3}$
17. $\dfrac{52}{9}$	17. $\dfrac{59}{6}$	17. $2\dfrac{3}{4}$	17. $2\dfrac{11}{12}$
18. $\dfrac{75}{8}$	18. $\dfrac{20}{3}$	18. $10\dfrac{5}{7}$	18. $4\dfrac{6}{7}$
19. $\dfrac{67}{10}$	19. $\dfrac{79}{10}$	19. $8\dfrac{1}{3}$	19. 24
20. $\dfrac{32}{3}$	20. $\dfrac{118}{11}$	20. $12\dfrac{1}{2}$	20. $2\dfrac{7}{15}$

Adding and Subtracting Fractions Practice Set 1

1. $\frac{1}{2}$

2. $\frac{1}{8}$

3. $\frac{1}{3}$

4. $\frac{5}{6}$

5. $\frac{2}{63}$

6. $\frac{9}{10}$

7. $\frac{5}{8}$

8. $\frac{1}{6}$

9. $\frac{1}{4}$

10. $\frac{47}{56}$

11. $\frac{2}{3}$

12. $\frac{1}{12}$

13. $1\frac{1}{6}$

14. $\frac{10}{21}$

15. $\frac{1}{12}$

16. $\frac{1}{6}$

17. 0

18. $\frac{4}{35}$

19. $\frac{9}{35}$

20. $\frac{7}{9}$

Adding and Subtracting Fractions Practice Set 2

1. $\frac{3}{4}$

2. $\frac{1}{20}$

3. $\frac{8}{15}$

4. $\frac{1}{6}$

5. $\frac{7}{24}$

6. $\frac{2}{5}$

7. 1

8. $\frac{1}{18}$

9. $\frac{37}{56}$

10. $\frac{1}{22}$

11. $1\frac{1}{40}$

12. $\frac{1}{6}$

13. $\frac{13}{24}$

14. $\frac{5}{28}$

15. $\frac{9}{10}$

16. $\frac{5}{18}$

17. $\frac{5}{8}$

18. $\frac{7}{8}$

19. $\frac{2}{15}$

20. $\frac{23}{36}$

Adding and Subtracting Mixed Fractions Practice Set 1

1. $3\frac{5}{7}$

2. $2\frac{3}{5}$

3. $3\frac{1}{35}$

4. $4\frac{7}{12}$

5. $1\frac{1}{6}$

6. $1\frac{1}{6}$

7. $4\frac{23}{35}$

8. $1\frac{5}{8}$

9. $3\frac{1}{15}$

10. $3\frac{3}{28}$

11. $3\frac{3}{4}$

12. $7\frac{1}{15}$

13. $8\frac{2}{9}$

14. $\frac{1}{3}$

15. $6\frac{5}{8}$

16. $1\frac{11}{12}$

17. $4\frac{1}{3}$

18. $2\frac{4}{9}$

19. $3\frac{5}{9}$

20. $3\frac{9}{10}$

Adding and Subtracting Mixed Fractions Practice Set 2

1. $3\frac{2}{3}$

2. $3\frac{1}{2}$

3. $3\frac{5}{9}$

4. $4\frac{9}{20}$

5. $\frac{9}{14}$

6. $\frac{1}{3}$

7. $4\frac{3}{10}$

8. $4\frac{1}{4}$

9. $3\frac{19}{30}$

10. $2\frac{5}{9}$

11. $\frac{7}{12}$

12. $3\frac{5}{6}$

13. $7\frac{4}{5}$

14. $1\frac{7}{8}$

15. $6\frac{1}{4}$

16. $1\frac{1}{12}$

17. $1\frac{1}{3}$

18. $1\frac{5}{9}$

19. $1\frac{3}{4}$

20. 6

Multiplying Fractions Practice Set 1

1. $\frac{1}{27}$
2. $\frac{1}{40}$
3. $\frac{1}{30}$
4. $\frac{3}{4}$
5. $\frac{5}{42}$
6. $\frac{14}{27}$
7. $\frac{1}{7}$
8. $\frac{3}{8}$
9. $\frac{1}{12}$
10. 2
11. $\frac{7}{24}$
12. $\frac{9}{26}$
13. $\frac{3}{4}$
14. $\frac{2}{5}$
15. $\frac{2}{5}$
16. $18\frac{1}{3}$
17. $\frac{28}{55}$
18. $4\frac{8}{9}$
19. $\frac{3}{16}$
20. $\frac{8}{45}$

Multiplying Fractions Practice Set 2

1. $\frac{1}{12}$
2. $\frac{1}{15}$
3. $\frac{1}{56}$
4. $\frac{5}{72}$
5. $\frac{2}{9}$
6. $\frac{2}{9}$
7. $\frac{3}{28}$
8. $1\frac{1}{2}$
9. $\frac{1}{12}$
10. $\frac{2}{25}$
11. $\frac{1}{9}$
12. $12\frac{1}{2}$
13. $\frac{2}{27}$
14. $\frac{1}{10}$
15. $\frac{8}{45}$
16. $\frac{3}{40}$
17. $4\frac{1}{5}$
18. $\frac{3}{10}$
19. $\frac{1}{28}$
20. $\frac{1}{7}$

Dividing Fractions Practice Set 1

1. $\frac{3}{4}$
2. $1\frac{1}{5}$
3. $\frac{1}{3}$
4. $\frac{5}{16}$
5. $\frac{25}{6}$
6. $\frac{1}{7}$
7. $\frac{7}{8}$
8. 2
9. $\frac{11}{18}$
10. $1\frac{1}{3}$
11. 1
12. $1\frac{1}{2}$
13. $\frac{2}{3}$
14. $1\frac{9}{16}$
15. $\frac{1}{36}$
16. $\frac{1}{44}$
17. $1\frac{1}{15}$
18. $\frac{5}{16}$
19. $\frac{1}{16}$
20. 1

Dividing Fractions Practice Set 2

1. $\frac{5}{6}$
2. $\frac{3}{7}$
3. $\frac{2}{3}$
4. $\frac{4}{9}$
5. $1\frac{1}{24}$
6. $\frac{1}{6}$
7. $\frac{5}{8}$
8. $\frac{1}{2}$
9. $\frac{7}{12}$
10. $\frac{3}{22}$
11. $\frac{1}{3}$
12. $\frac{5}{12}$
13. $1\frac{1}{5}$
14. $1\frac{7}{8}$
15. $2\frac{7}{9}$
16. $3\frac{5}{9}$
17. $1\frac{2}{7}$
18. $\frac{4}{9}$
19. $\frac{1}{18}$
20. $1\frac{4}{5}$

Multiplying and Dividing Mixed Fractions Practice Set 1

1. $2\frac{9}{13}$

2. $4\frac{1}{5}$

3. 5

4. $4\frac{2}{3}$

5. $2\frac{2}{9}$

6. $1\frac{3}{32}$

7. 4

8. $12\frac{2}{3}$

9. $\frac{40}{91}$

10. $2\frac{6}{7}$

11. $\frac{32}{35}$

12. $\frac{21}{25}$

13. $9\frac{3}{7}$

14. $1\frac{3}{7}$

15. $\frac{50}{77}$

16. $\frac{13}{22}$

17. $7\frac{6}{7}$

18. $3\frac{1}{2}$

19. $10\frac{1}{12}$

20. $1\frac{1}{6}$

Multiplying and Dividing Mixed Fractions Practice Set 2

1. $\frac{25}{36}$

2. $1\frac{5}{27}$

3. $8\frac{2}{5}$

4. $3\frac{6}{7}$

5. $1\frac{1}{7}$

6. $2\frac{2}{5}$

7. $8\frac{1}{4}$

8. 8

9. $4\frac{8}{9}$

10. $1\frac{1}{20}$

11. $13\frac{1}{3}$

12. $\frac{5}{12}$

13. $1\frac{1}{6}$

14. $\frac{5}{6}$

15. $1\frac{5}{6}$

16. $7\frac{1}{3}$

17. 5

18. $\frac{2}{3}$

19. 10

20. $\frac{3}{8}$

Rounding Decimals Practice Set 1

1. 4.9
2. 4,993.028
3. 37.10
4. 100
5. 107.00
6. 2,046.523
7. 5.9362
8. 40.9
9. 3.0790
10. 3
11. 313.3
12. 107.3349
13. 52.9
14. 97.00
15. 15,225.000
16. 36.47
17. 13
18. 15
19. 12.8329
20. 6.235

Rounding Decimals Practice Set 2

1. 5.008
2. 131
3. 403.22
4. 15.1
5. 40.0
6. 8.89
7. 14.8760
8. 5
9. 15.1890
10. 46.450
11. 80
12. 7.08
13. 28.495
14. 6.0
15. 192.25
16. 5
17. 129.5
18. 1.0079
19. 2.0340
20. 348.900

Adding Decimals Practice Set 1

1. 15.2
2. 20.8
3. 8.8
4. 14.7
5. 12
6. 7.8
7. 14.7
8. 14.2
9. 12.12
10. 12.88
11. 12.01
12. 12.51
13. 17.82
14. 25.86
15. 54.44
16. 88.245
17. 212.838
18. 1,765.28
19. 563.119
20. 226.053

Adding Decimals Practice Set 2

1. 13.4
2. 10.5
3. 6.3
4. 9
5. 5.5
6. 9.3
7. 9.9
8. 13.73
9. 32.27
10. 14.77
11. 13
12. 20.44
13. 22.96
14. 95.56
15. 191.48
16. 38.243
17. 840.312
18. 107.21
19. 415.124
20. 1,313.46

Subtracting Decimals Practice Set 1

1. 3.4
2. 2.5
3. 12.6
4. 7.8
5. 3.9
6. 11
7. 5.4
8. 6.6
9. 12.42
10. 78.27
11. 54.67
12. 29.61
13. 12.04
14. 62.34
15. 167.52
16. 31.11
17. 121.348
18. 88.757
19. 4,815.288
20. 536.95

Subtracting Decimals Practice Set 2

1. 11.2
2. 10.8
3. 16.1
4. 9.3
5. 4.5
6. 23.6
7. 13.7
8. 2.8
9. 15.24
10. 62.58
11. 5.35
12. 11.21
13. 8.52
14. 14.76
15. 42.31
16. 106.15
17. 81.01
18. 1,164.76
19. 262.41
20. 156.22

Multiplying Decimals Practice Set 1

1. 1.2
2. 0.5
3. 2.1
4. 6.4
5. 6
6. 0.54
7. 0.2
8. 0.18
9. 0.56
10. 0.42
11. 1.28
12. 0.032
13. 0.235
14. 1.72
15. 0.292
16. 5.684
17. 23.04
18. 12.617
19. 1,982.76
20. 27.40175

Multiplying Decimals Practice Set 2

1. 5.4
2. 2
3. 1.8
4. 5.6
5. 4.2
6. 0.21
7. 0.64
8. 0.06
9. 0.15
10. 0.09
11. 0.106
12. 0.369
13. 0.696
14. 6.37
15. 0.441
16. 2.697
17. 107.3
18. 0.1824
19. 210.24
20. 2.86767

Dividing Decimals Practice Set 1

1. 1.2
2. 1.2
3. 5.4
4. 0.1
5. 13
6. 88
7. 82
8. 40
9. 600
10. 0.15
11. 3.5
12. 20
13. 0.1855
14. 6.25
15. 6.9
16. 105.5
17. 14.75
18. 12.3
19. 168,000
20. 0.21

Dividing Decimals Practice Set 2

1. 1.2
2. 9.1
3. 0.1
4. 16
5. 28
6. 13
7. 3.4
8. 27
9. 25
10. 2,735
11. 2.275
12. 0.25
13. 1,300
14. 2.2
15. 2.35
16. 14,100
17. 0.725
18. 159
19. 44.75
20. 8.6

Decimals to Fractions Practice Set 1

1. $\frac{1}{10}$
2. $3\frac{2}{5}$
3. $\frac{7}{10}$
4. $5\frac{3}{5}$
5. $\frac{9}{10}$
6. $7\frac{3}{10}$
7. $\frac{1}{5}$
8. $\frac{1}{2}$
9. $\frac{11}{100}$
10. $\frac{2}{25}$
11. $18\frac{9}{20}$
12. $\frac{17}{50}$
13. $\frac{1}{4}$
14. $4\frac{9}{100}$
15. $\frac{43}{50}$
16. $9\frac{22}{25}$
17. $2\frac{1}{25}$
18. $\frac{27}{500}$
19. $4\frac{1}{125}$
20. $62\frac{5}{8}$

Decimals to Fractions Practice Set 2

1. $9\frac{9}{10}$
2. $\frac{4}{5}$
3. $3\frac{7}{10}$
4. $\frac{3}{10}$
5. $17\frac{1}{5}$
6. $\frac{2}{5}$
7. $11\frac{9}{10}$
8. $6\frac{1}{2}$
9. $4\frac{2}{5}$
10. $\frac{1}{25}$
11. $\frac{3}{4}$
12. $13\frac{1}{50}$
13. $\frac{13}{25}$
14. $90\frac{67}{100}$
15. $8\frac{13}{20}$
16. $\frac{23}{25}$
17. $\frac{1}{20}$
18. $3\frac{1}{250}$
19. $4\frac{3}{40}$
20. $\frac{3}{500}$

Decimals to Percents Practice Set 1

1. 20%
2. 410%
3. 60%
4. 270%
5. 8%
6. 990%
7. 40%
8. 5%
9. 11%
10. 6%
11. 1,803%
12. 78%
13. 25%
14. 512%
15. 6.82%
16. 401.8%
17. 0.8%
18. 0.54%
19. 400.03%
20. 6,262.5%

Decimals to Percents Practice Set 2

1. 550%
2. 9%
3. 10%
4. 30%
5. 3,920%
6. 7%
7. 2,090%
8. 150%
9. 208%
10. 5%
11. 75%
12. 3,118%
13. 59%
14. 6,072%
15. 435%
16. 43%
17. 2,125%
18. 800.4%
19. 500.75%
20. 0.7%

Percents to Fractions Practice Set 1

1. $\frac{1}{2}$
2. $\frac{1}{4}$
3. $\frac{17}{50}$
4. $\frac{33}{50}$
5. $\frac{18}{25}$
6. $\frac{9}{100}$
7. $\frac{1}{50}$
8. 2
9. $4\frac{1}{4}$
10. $1\frac{1}{5}$
11. $3\frac{1}{2}$
12. $\frac{17}{100}$
13. $\frac{7}{25}$
14. $\frac{1}{25}$
15. $\frac{9}{200}$
16. $\frac{41}{500}$
17. $\frac{99}{100}$
18. $\frac{7}{10}$
19. $\frac{51}{125}$
20. $\frac{3}{500}$

Percents to Fractions Practice Set 2

1. $\frac{3}{10}$
2. $\frac{13}{20}$
3. $\frac{3}{25}$
4. $\frac{1}{5}$
5. $\frac{33}{100}$
6. $\frac{3}{100}$
7. $\frac{7}{100}$
8. 1
9. $7\frac{1}{2}$
10. $2\frac{2}{5}$
11. 60
12. $\frac{2}{5}$
13. $\frac{3}{20}$
14. $\frac{3}{50}$
15. $\frac{19}{200}$
16. $\frac{3}{125}$
17. $\frac{77}{100}$
18. $1\frac{1}{2}$
19. $\frac{203}{1,000}$
20. $\frac{1}{500}$

Percents to Decimals Practice Set 1

1. 0.1
2. 0.04
3. 0.34
4. 0.25
5. 0.07
6. 1
7. 2.3
8. 80
9. 1.43
10. 7.83
11. 0.015
12. 8.502
13. 0.456
14. 1.008
15. 0.0037
16. 0.0405
17. 0.0006
18. 3.005
19. 1.8045
20. 0.00005

Percents to Decimals Practice Set 2

1. 0.2
2. 0.08
3. 0.22
4. 0.5
5. 0.01
6. 2
7. 34.5
8. 40
9. 6.5
10. 1.02
11. 0.605
12. 0.078
13. 0.999
14. 1.903
15. 0.0032
16. 0.0225
17. 4.506
18. 0.0008
19. 0.010052
20. 0.00004

Fractions to Decimals Practice Set 1

1. 0.75
2. 0.5
3. $0.\overline{6}$
4. 0.8
5. 0.1
6. 0.7
7. 0.625
8. 0.08
9. 0.53
10. 5.4
11. 2.3
12. 1.9
13. 4.375
14. 0.86
15. 0.24
16. 0.128
17. 0.056
18. 7.4
19. 3.75
20. 2.3

Fractions to Decimals Practice Set 2

1. 0.25
2. 0.3
3. 0.4
4. 0.3
5. 0.375
6. 0.01
7. 0.82
8. $8.\overline{6}$
9. 2.2
10. 1.7
11. 4.2
12. 2.625
13. 0.14
14. 0.96
15. 0.512
16. 0.462
17. 4.5
18. 1.125
19. 4.8
20. 5.3

Fractions to Percents Practice Set 1

1. 50%
2. 75%
3. 50%
4. 60%
5. 70%
6. 20%
7. $66.\overline{6}\%$
8. 12.5%
9. 12%
10. 62.5%
11. 82%
12. 2.1%
13. 180%
14. $655.\overline{5}\%$
15. $388.\overline{8}\%$
16. 412%
17. 500.9%
18. $144.\overline{4}\%$
19. 215%
20. $566.\overline{6}\%$

Fractions to Percents Practice Set 2

1. $33.\overline{3}\%$
2. 25%
3. 80%
4. 90%
5. 40%
6. 25%
7. 10%
8. $33.\overline{3}\%$
9. $83.\overline{3}\%$
10. 13%
11. 85%
12. 87.5%
13. $133.\overline{3}\%$
14. 328%
15. 500.3%
16. 288%
17. 206.6%
18. 104.4%
19. 237.5%
20. $311.\overline{1}\%$

Math Multiple Choice

How to Use the Math Multiple Choice Chapter

Chapter Overview

This chapter of the book covers 40 math topics that show up in the Quantitative Reasoning and Mathematics Achievement sections. The purpose of this chapter is to present students with test-like, multiple-choice questions, so they can become familiar with the style and difficulty of questions that show up on the ISEE Lower Level.

Using the Practice Sets

Each topic in this chapter comes with two practice sets, each with 10 practice questions. Complete practice set 1 for a topic, and grade your answers using the answer key at the end of this chapter. If you don't do well on practice set 1, review your answers and the concepts; then complete practice set 2 for that topic.

Tips for Working Through this Chapter

1. **Write your answers in a separate notebook.** We strongly suggest showing your work in a separate notebook. This will allow you to keep your work organized and neat. It will also allow you to redo practice problems later in your prep process if you need to review any topics.

2. **Understand your areas of weakness**. Before diving into this chapter, make sure you have an idea of what topics you struggle with. If you are not sure which topics you struggle with, try a few problems from each topic and check your answers. Focus on the topics where you answered some of the questions incorrectly.

3. **Do not use a calculator.** A calculator is NOT allowed on the ISEE, so do not use a calculator for any of the problems in this chapter.

4. **Complete the topics in order.** Some topics covered in this chapter build off of previous topics, so we suggest going through the topics in order.

5. **Break up your practice.** Remember to break up your practice into small chunks. Don't try and cram all of the practice sets into a short amount of time. You are less likely to fully master the concepts if you cram, and you are more likely to feel stressed out during the prep process.

Fundamentals Practice Set 1

1. What is the value of the expression 4,878 + 3,296?

   (A) 7,174
   (B) 8,164
   (C) 8,174
   (D) 8,274

2. What is the value of the expression 728 ÷ 13?

   (A) 46
   (B) 49
   (C) 55
   (D) 56

3. What is the value of the expression 905 + 47,358?

   (A) 48,263
   (B) 48,273
   (C) 48,308
   (D) 56,363

4. What is the value of the expression 1,203 × 7?

   (A) 7,401
   (B) 8,421
   (C) 8,491
   (D) 8,521

5. What is the value of the expression 8,004 − 367?

   (A) 5,334
   (B) 7,637
   (C) 7,743
   (D) 7,937

6. What is the value of the expression 3,328 ÷ 104?

   (A) 21
   (B) 22
   (C) 31
   (D) 32

7. What is the value of the expression 48 × 29?

   (A) 528
   (B) 1,352
   (C) 1,392
   (D) 1,394

8. What is the value of the expression 20,542 − 19,658?

   (A) 774
   (B) 884
   (C) 1,116
   (D) 1,884

9. What is the value of the expression 17 × 912?

   (A) 15,504
   (B) 15,506
   (C) 16,404
   (D) 16,504

10. What is the value of the expression 5,632 ÷ 8?

    (A) 74
    (B) 704
    (C) 740
    (D) 804

Fundamentals Practice Set 2

1. What is the value of the expression
    834 − 576?

    (A) 242
    (B) 256
    (C) 258
    (D) 342

2. What is the value of the expression
    32,409 + 872?

    (A) 32,281
    (B) 33,271
    (C) 33,281
    (D) 119,609

3. What is the value of the expression
    336 ÷ 16?

    (A) 21
    (B) 22
    (C) 31
    (D) 32

4. What is the value of the expression
    786 + 2,375?

    (A) 3,151
    (B) 3,161
    (C) 3,171
    (D) 10,235

5. What is the value of the expression
    45 × 82?

    (A) 3,397
    (B) 3,660
    (C) 3,687
    (D) 3,690

6. What is the value of the expression
    23,604 ÷ 4?

    (A) 591
    (B) 681
    (C) 5,901
    (D) 6,801

7. What is the value of the expression
    209 × 8?

    (A) 1,552
    (B) 1,617
    (C) 1,664
    (D) 1,672

8. What is the value of the expression
    6,072 − 2,838?

    (A) 3,234
    (B) 3,246
    (C) 3,834
    (D) 4,834

9. What is the value of the expression
    13 × 486?

    (A) 1,944
    (B) 6,312
    (C) 6,318
    (D) 6,348

10. What is the value of the expression
    3,451 ÷ 17?

    (A) 23
    (B) 203
    (C) 230
    (D) 303

Writing Numbers as Words Practice Set 1

1. What is the standard form for four hundred ten?

    (A) 410
    (B) 4,010
    (C) 400,010
    (D) 400,100

2. What is the standard form for three thousand fifty-seven?

    (A) 357
    (B) 3,057
    (C) 3,570
    (D) 3,507

3. What is the standard form for ninety-one thousand five hundred six?

    (A) 910,560
    (B) 910,506
    (C) 91,560
    (D) 91,506

4. What is the standard form for two hundred eighty thousand fifty-seven?

    (A) 28,057
    (B) 280,057
    (C) 280,570
    (D) 2,857,000

5. What is the standard form for eleven thousand three hundred ninety-four?

    (A) 1,394
    (B) 11,349
    (C) 11,394
    (D) 110,394

6. What is the standard form for nine and one tenth?

    (A) 9.001
    (B) 9.01
    (C) 9.1
    (D) 90.1

7. What is the standard form for nineteen thousandths?

    (A) 19,000
    (B) 1,900
    (C) 0.19
    (D) 0.019

8. What is the standard form for eighteen and five hundredths?

    (A) 18.005
    (B) 18.05
    (C) 18.5
    (D) 18,500

9. What is the standard form for twenty-seven and six thousandths?

    (A) 27.006
    (B) 27.06
    (C) 27,600
    (D) 276,000

10. What is the standard form for five hundred and seventy-nine hundredths?

    (A) 5.79
    (B) 500.079
    (C) 500.79
    (D) 57,900

Writing Numbers as Words Practice Set 2

1. What is the standard form for fifty-four thousand twenty-one?

    (A) 54,012
    (B) 54,021
    (C) 54,210
    (D) 540,210

2. What is the standard form for seven thousand four hundred eighty-seven?

    (A) 7,478
    (B) 7,487
    (C) 70,487
    (D) 7,400,087

3. What is the standard form for nine hundred seven?

    (A) 907
    (B) 970
    (C) 9,007
    (D) 900,007

4. What is the standard form for eight thousand thirty-two?

    (A) 80,032
    (B) 8,320
    (C) 8,032
    (D) 8,023

5. What is the standard form for six hundred thousand seven hundred two?

    (A) 607,702
    (B) 607,200
    (C) 600,720
    (D) 600,702

6. What is the standard form for six and three tenths?

    (A) 6.003
    (B) 6.03
    (C) 6.3
    (D) 60.3

7. What is the standard form for seventy-two and nine hundredths?

    (A) 72.009
    (B) 72.09
    (C) 72.9
    (D) 72,900

8. What is the standard form for fifty-seven thousandths?

    (A) 0.057
    (B) 0.57
    (C) 5,700
    (D) 57,000

9. What is the standard form for five and eleven thousandths?

    (A) 511,000
    (B) 500,011
    (C) 5.11
    (D) 5.011

10. What is the standard form for forty and thirty-six hundredths?

    (A) 40.0036
    (B) 40.036
    (C) 40.36
    (D) 40,360

Place Value Practice Set 1

1. What value does the digit 4 represent in the number 54,687?

   (A) 4
   (B) 40
   (C) 400
   (D) 4,000

2. Which number is in the thousandths place in the number 5,609.4283?

   (A) 2
   (B) 3
   (C) 5
   (D) 8

3. Which number is in the hundreds place in the number 347.092?

   (A) 2
   (B) 3
   (C) 4
   (D) 9

4. What value does the digit 2 represent in the number 3.821?

   (A) 2
   (B) $\dfrac{2}{10}$
   (C) $\dfrac{2}{100}$
   (D) $\dfrac{2}{1,000}$

5. What value does the digit 7 represent in 3,710,925?

   (A) 7,000
   (B) 70,000
   (C) 700,000
   (D) 7,000,000

6. Which number is in the tenths place in the number 24.957?

   (A) 4
   (B) 5
   (C) 7
   (D) 9

7. What value does the digit 1 represent in the number 43,718?

   (A) 0.1
   (B) 1
   (C) 10
   (D) 100

8. What value does the digit 1 represent in the number 45.0821?

   (A) 1
   (B) $\dfrac{1}{1,000}$
   (C) $\dfrac{1}{10,000}$
   (D) $\dfrac{1}{100,000}$

9. Which number is in the ones place in the number 9,726?

   (A) 2
   (B) 6
   (C) 7
   (D) 9

10. Which number is in the hundredths place in the number 745.3289?

    (A) 2
    (B) 7
    (C) 8
    (D) 9

Place Value Practice Set 2

1. Which number is in the thousands place in the number 452,809?

   (A) 2
   (B) 4
   (C) 5
   (D) 8

2. What value does the digit 3 represent in the number 88.4236?

   (A) 30
   (B) $\dfrac{3}{100}$
   (C) $\dfrac{3}{1,000}$
   (D) $\dfrac{3}{10,000}$

3. Which number is in the tens place in the number 19,402?

   (A) 0
   (B) 1
   (C) 2
   (D) 4

4. What value does the digit 1 represent in the number 81,523?

   (A) 10
   (B) 100
   (C) 1,000
   (D) 10,000

5. Which number is in the ten-thousandths place in the number 3.59478?

   (A) 4
   (B) 7
   (C) 8
   (D) 9

6. Which number is in the ten thousands place in the number 34,925,006?

   (A) 2
   (B) 3
   (C) 4
   (D) 9

7. What value does the digit 9 represent in the number 0.984?

   (A) 90
   (B) 9
   (C) $\dfrac{9}{10}$
   (D) $\dfrac{9}{100}$

8. Which number is in the hundredths place in the number 601.7942?

   (A) 2
   (B) 4
   (C) 6
   (D) 9

9. What value does the digit 6 represent in the number 34,056?

   (A) 0.6
   (B) 6
   (C) 60
   (D) 600

10. Which digit is in the thousandths place in the number 4.2053?

    (A) 0
    (B) 2
    (C) 3
    (D) 5

Divisibility and Remainders Practice Set 1

1. Which of the following numbers has a remainder of 6 when divided by 8?

   (A) 13
   (B) 30
   (C) 48
   (D) 68

2. A number is divisible by 3. Which of the following could be the number?

   (A) 136
   (B) 233
   (C) 515
   (D) 690

3. Which of the following numbers has a remainder of 2 when divided by 9?

   (A) 18
   (B) 21
   (C) 31
   (D) 83

4. The quotient of a number and 5 leaves a remainder of 4. Which of the following could NOT be the number?

   (A) 34
   (B) 59
   (C) 129
   (D) 136

5. When 153 is divided by a number, the remainder is 3. Which of the following could be the number?

   (A) 3
   (B) 4
   (C) 6
   (D) 9

6. When a number is divided by 7, there is no remainder. Which of the following could NOT be the number?

   (A) 69
   (B) 70
   (C) 84
   (D) 98

7. A number is divisible by 2 and 5. Which of the following could be the number?

   (A) 18
   (B) 80
   (C) 96
   (D) 105

8. If z is an integer that can be divided by 4 and 5 without leaving a remainder, then z can also be divided by which number without leaving a remainder?

   (A) 9
   (B) 15
   (C) 20
   (D) 24

9. A number is divisible by 2. Which of the following could NOT be the number?

   (A) 48
   (B) 530
   (C) 6,784
   (D) 45,801

10. If x is an integer that can be divided by 3 and 7 without leaving a remainder, then x can also be divided by which number without leaving a remainder?

    (A) 4
    (B) 10
    (C) 14
    (D) 21

Divisibility and Remainders Practice Set 2

1. Which of the following numbers has a remainder of 1 when divided by 2?

   (A) 341
   (B) 430
   (C) 574
   (D) 786

2. Which of the following numbers has a remainder of 3 when divided by 4?

   (A) 12
   (B) 42
   (C) 65
   (D) 83

3. If a is an integer that is divisible by 9, which of the following could be equal to a?

   (A) 186
   (B) 273
   (C) 690
   (D) 945

4. If y is an integer that is divisible by 3 and 10, which of the following could NOT be equal to y?

   (A) 60
   (B) 430
   (C) 540
   (D) 2,400

5. If a is an integer that can be divided by 5 and 7 without leaving a remainder, then a can also be divided by which number without leaving a remainder?

   (A) 10
   (B) 14
   (C) 25
   (D) 35

6. The quotient of 57 and some number leaves a remainder of 1. Which of the following could be the number?

   (A) 3
   (B) 5
   (C) 6
   (D) 7

7. The quotient of a number and 8 leaves a remainder of 2. Which of the following could NOT be the number?

   (A) 18
   (B) 34
   (C) 46
   (D) 82

8. If b is an integer that can be divided by 6 and 8 without leaving a remainder, then b can also be divided by which number without leaving a remainder?

   (A) 24
   (B) 30
   (C) 32
   (D) 48

9. A number is divisible by 6. Which of the following could be the number?

   (A) 246
   (B) 292
   (C) 340
   (D) 357

10. When a number is divided by 4, the remainder is 1. Which of the following could be the number?

    (A) 6
    (B) 35
    (C) 61
    (D) 67

Multiples and Factors Practice Set 1

1. What is the LCM of 4 and 6?

    (A) 2
    (B) 8
    (C) 12
    (D) 24

2. What is the GCF of 12 and 18?

    (A) 2
    (B) 4
    (C) 6
    (D) 9

3. Which of the following is NOT a factor of 24?

    (A) 3
    (B) 4
    (C) 8
    (D) 9

4. What is the LCM of 5, 10 and 15?

    (A) 5
    (B) 15
    (C) 30
    (D) 60

5. What is the GCF of 90, 45, and 25?

    (A) 5
    (B) 9
    (C) 15
    (D) 25

6. Which of the following is a multiple of 16?

    (A) 4
    (B) 12
    (C) 28
    (D) 32

7. What is the LCM of 9, 6, and 4?

    (A) 12
    (B) 18
    (C) 36
    (D) 72

8. Which of the following is a factor of 27?

    (A) 5
    (B) 7
    (C) 27
    (D) 54

9. What is the GCF of 14, 42, and 28?

    (A) 7
    (B) 14
    (C) 42
    (D) 84

10. What of the following is NOT a multiple of 12?

    (A) 6
    (B) 12
    (C) 24
    (D) 60

Multiples and Factors Practice Set 2

1. What is the GCF of 20 and 15?

   (A) 5
   (B) 10
   (C) 15
   (D) 60

2. Which of the following is NOT a factor of 50?

   (A) 5
   (B) 15
   (C) 25
   (D) 50

3. What is the LCM of 12 and 8?

   (A) 4
   (B) 24
   (C) 36
   (D) 48

4. What is the LCM of 3, 6 and 5?

   (A) 15
   (B) 18
   (C) 30
   (D) 60

5. Which of the following is NOT a multiple of 18?

   (A) 9
   (B) 18
   (C) 36
   (D) 180

6. What is the GCF of 36, 18, and 45?

   (A) 5
   (B) 6
   (C) 9
   (D) 18

7. Which of the following is a factor of 36?

   (A) 8
   (B) 12
   (C) 24
   (D) 72

8. Which of the following is a multiple of 15?

   (A) 3
   (B) 5
   (C) 25
   (D) 75

9. What is the GCF of 22, 55, and 33?

   (A) 1
   (B) 3
   (C) 5
   (D) 11

10. What is the LCM of 10, 4, and 8?

   (A) 2
   (B) 20
   (C) 40
   (D) 80

Prime Factorization Practice Set 1

1. What is the prime factorization of 12?

   (A) $2^2 \times 3$
   (B) 2×3
   (C) 3×4
   (D) 2×3^2

2. What is the prime factorization of 18?

   (A) $2^2 \times 3$
   (B) 2×3^2
   (C) 2×9
   (D) 3×6

3. What is the prime factorization of 24?

   (A) $2^2 \times 6$
   (B) $2^3 \times 3$
   (C) $3^2 \times 2^2$
   (D) 3×2^4

4. What is the prime factorization of 30?

   (A) 5×6
   (B) $3^2 \times 5$
   (C) $2 \times 3 \times 5$
   (D) 3×10

5. What is the prime factorization of 40?

   (A) $2 \times 4 \times 5$
   (B) $3^2 \times 5$
   (C) $2^4 \times 5$
   (D) $2^3 \times 5$

6. What is the prime factorization of 45?

   (A) $3^2 \times 5$
   (B) 5×9
   (C) 3×15
   (D) $3^3 \times 5$

7. What is the prime factorization of 56?

   (A) 7×8
   (B) $4^2 \times 7$
   (C) $2^4 \times 7$
   (D) $2^3 \times 7$

8. What is the prime factorization of 21?

   (A) 3×7
   (B) 3^3
   (C) $3^2 \times 7$
   (D) 1×21

9. What is the prime factorization of 60?

   (A) $2^2 \times 15$
   (B) $2^2 \times 3 \times 5$
   (C) $2 \times 5 \times 6$
   (D) $2 \times 3^2 \times 5$

10. What is the prime factorization of 49?

   (A) 7^2
   (B) $3^2 \times 7$
   (C) 3^4
   (D) 7^3

Prime Factorization Practice Set 2

1. What is the prime factorization of 15?

    (A) $3^2 \times 5$
    (B) 1×15
    (C) 2×5
    (D) 3×5

2. What is the prime factorization of 81?

    (A) 9^2
    (B) $3^2 \times 9$
    (C) 3^3
    (D) 3^4

3. What is the prime factorization of 10?

    (A) 2×5
    (B) 1×10
    (C) 3×5
    (D) $2^2 \times 5$

4. What is the prime factorization of 25?

    (A) 25×1
    (B) 5^2
    (C) $5^2 \times 2$
    (D) 5×2^2

5. What is the prime factorization of 27?

    (A) 9×3
    (B) 3^2
    (C) 3^3
    (D) $2^3 \times 3$

6. What is the prime factorization of 20?

    (A) 2×10
    (B) $2^2 \times 5$
    (C) 2×5^2
    (D) 4×5

7. What is the prime factorization of 50?

    (A) $5^2 \times 2$
    (B) 5^2
    (C) 5×2^2
    (D) 25×2

8. What is the prime factorization of 36?

    (A) 9×2^2
    (B) 6^2
    (C) 3×2^3
    (D) $2^2 \times 3^2$

9. What is the prime factorization of 35?

    (A) 7×5
    (B) 5×5
    (C) 7×5^2
    (D) 35×1

10. What is the prime factorization of 16?

    (A) 4×2^2
    (B) 2^3
    (C) 4^2
    (D) 2^4

Order of Operations Practice Set 1

1. What is the value of the expression $55 - 40 \div 5$?

   (A) 3
   (B) 47
   (C) 48
   (D) 63

2. What is the value of the expression $64 \div 4 \times 8$?

   (A) 2
   (B) 32
   (C) 96
   (D) 128

3. What is the value of the expression $80 + 20 \times 5$?

   (A) 90
   (B) 160
   (C) 180
   (D) 500

4. What is the value of the expression $\dfrac{50(40 - 20)}{25}$?

   (A) 4
   (B) 40
   (C) 50
   (D) 400

5. Which expression is equal to 31?

   (A) $36 - 18 \div 6 - 5 + 3$
   (B) $(36 - 18) \div 6 - 5 + 3$
   (C) $36 - 18 \div (6 - 5) + 3$
   (D) $36 - 18 \div 6 - (5 + 3)$

6. What is the value of the expression $16 + 4(45 - 15)$?

   (A) 96
   (B) 136
   (C) 600
   (D) 885

7. What is the value of the expression $\dfrac{20(35 + 55)}{6}$?

   (A) 300
   (B) 600
   (C) 900
   (D) 1800

8. Which expression is equal to 9?

   (A) $6 - 3(14 - 7)$
   (B) $30 - 3 \times 14 - 7$
   (C) $30 - 3(14 - 7)$
   (D) $(6 - 3) \times 14 - 7$

9. What is the value of the expression $6 + 3(89 - 87) + 7 \times 3$?

   (A) 33
   (B) 39
   (C) 57
   (D) 75

10. Which expression is equal to 40?

    (A) $6 \times 3 + 5 - 8$
    (B) $6 \times (3 + 5 - 8)$
    (C) $6 \times 3 + (5 - 8)$
    (D) $6 \times (3 + 5) - 8$

Order of Operations Practice Set 2

1. What is the value of the expression
   $32 + 8 \times 3$?

   (A) 56
   (B) 64
   (C) 80
   (D) 120

2. What is the value of the expression
   $64 - 16 \div 8 + 4$?

   (A) 4
   (B) 10
   (C) 58
   (D) 66

3. What is the value of the expression
   $\dfrac{6(120 - 40)}{30}$?

   (A) 12
   (B) 16
   (C) 160
   (D) 480

4. What is the value of the expression
   $7 + 5(6 + 4)$?

   (A) 57
   (B) 62
   (C) 120
   (D) 130

5. Which expression is equal to 7?

   (A) $10 + 20 \div 5 - 3 + 4$
   (B) $10 + (20 \div 5) - 3 + 4$
   (C) $(10 + 20) \div 5 - 3 + 4$
   (D) $10 + 20 \div (5 - 3) + 4$

6. What is the value of the expression
   $54 - 14 + 10 - 7 - 2$?

   (A) 21
   (B) 31
   (C) 41
   (D) 69

7. What is the value of the expression
   $\dfrac{140(5 + 95)}{7}$?

   (A) 200
   (B) 2,000
   (C) 3,000
   (D) 14,000

8. What is the value of the expression
   $12 \times 6 - 24 \div 8$?

   (A) 6
   (B) 68
   (C) 69
   (D) 81

9. Which expression is equal to 14?

   (A) $(5 + 2) \times 10 - 8$
   (B) $(5 + 2) \times (10 - 8)$
   (C) $5 + 2 \times (10 - 8)$
   (D) $5 + 2 \times 10 - 8$

10. Which expression is equal to 10?

   (A) $12 - (4 + 8 \div 4)$
   (B) $(12 - 4 + 8) \div 4$
   (C) $12 - (4 + 8) \div 4$
   (D) $12 - 4 + 8 \div 4$

Story Word Problems Practice Set 1

1. Vivian has 28 pieces of candy. If she wants to eat the same amount of candy each day for one week, how should she figure out how many pieces, p, to eat each day?

   (A) $28 \div 7 = p$
   (B) $28 \times 7 = p$
   (C) $28 + 7 = p$
   (D) $28 - 7 = p$

2. Which story best fits the expression $28 + 14$?

   (A) Butch bought 28 pencils in June and 14 pencils in July. How many more pencils did Butch buy in June than July?
   (B) Butch bought 28 pencils each day for 14 days. How many pencils did Butch buy?
   (C) Butch bought 28 pencils and split them into 14 groups. How many pencils were in each group?
   (D) Butch bought 28 pencils on Monday and 14 pencils on Tuesday. How many total pencils did Butch buy?

3. Justin is 37 years old. Justin is 26 years younger than Anthony. Which equation can be used to determine Anthony's age, a?

   (A) $26 - 37 = a$
   (B) $37 \times 26 = a$
   (C) $37 + 26 = a$
   (D) $37 - 26 = a$

4. Which story best fits the expression $43 - 27$?

   (A) Gwen had $27 in her bank account. If Gwen spent $43, how much money does she have left in her bank account?
   (B) Last week, Gwen made $43 babysitting. This was $27 more than she made last week. How much money did Gwen make last week?
   (C) Last week, Gwen made $43 babysitting. This was $27 less than she made last week. How much money did Gwen make last week?
   (D) Gwen had $27 in her bank account. If she deposited $43 more into her bank account, how much money does she have in total?

5. Greg needs to read for his English class. He knows how many pages he needs to read by the end of the week, and he knows how many pages he has read so far. How would he determine how many more pages, p, he needs to read this week?

   (A) p = the number of pages he needs to read by the end of the week − the number of pages he has read so far
   (B) p = the number of pages he needs to read by the end of the week × the number of pages he has read so far
   (C) p = the number of pages he needs to read by the end of the week + the number of pages he has read so far
   (D) p = the number of pages he needs to read by the end of the week ÷ the number of pages he has read so far

6. Which story best fits the equation $35 \times 7 = 245$?

    (A) Brenda is selling boxes of cookies for \$7 each. How many boxes does she need to sell to make \$245?
    (B) Brenda has 245 cookies that she wants to split between her 42 friends. How many cookies does each friend get?
    (C) Brenda had 245 boxes of cookies and her friend had 35 boxes of cookies. How many more boxes does Brenda have than her friend?
    (D) Brenda had 35 boxes of cookies and sells 7 boxes. How many boxes does Brenda have left?

7. Which story best fits the equation $96 \div 12 = 8$?

    (A) Henry drank 96 ounces of water on Wednesday. He drank 12 fewer ounces of water on Thursday. How many ounces of water did Henry drink on Thursday?
    (B) Henry drank 96 ounces of water over 12 days. If he drank the same amount of water each day, how many ounces of water did Henry drink each day?
    (C) Henry drank 12 ounces of water each day for 96 days. How many total ounces of water did Henry drink?
    (D) Henry drank 9 ounces of water on Tuesday and 12 ounces of water on Wednesday. How many total ounces of water did Henry drink?

8. Mrs. Hanson is buying tickets for her family to go see a play. She knows how many tickets she will need to purchase, and how much each ticket costs. How would she figure out how much total money, t, she will spend on the play tickets?

    (A) $t =$ the cost of each ticket $+$ the number of tickets she needs to purchase
    (B) $t =$ the cost of each ticket $\div$ the number of tickets she needs to purchase
    (C) $t =$ the cost of each ticket $\times$ the number of tickets she needs to purchase
    (D) $t =$ the cost of each ticket $-$ the number of tickets she needs to purchase

9. Lucille is organizing buses for a school trip. She knows how many students are going on the trip, and she knows how many students can fit in one bus. How would she figure out how many buses, b, she needs to fit all of the students?

    (A) $b =$ the number of students that can fit on one bus $-$ the number of students that are going on the trip
    (B) $b =$ the number of students that can fit on one bus $\div$ the number of students that are going on the trip
    (C) $b =$ the number of students going on the trip $-$ the number of students that can fit in one bus
    (D) $b =$ the number of students going on the trip $\div$ the number of students that can fit in one bus

10. Which story best fits the expression $(60 + 40) \times 4$?

   (A) Lauren baked 60 cupcakes on Monday and 40 cupcakes on Tuesday. She made gift boxes with 4 cupcakes in each box. How many gift boxes did Lauren make?
   (B) Lauren baked 60 cupcakes each day for 4 days. The next day, she baked 40 cupcakes. How many total cupcakes did Lauren bake?
   (C) Lauren and her three friends each baked 60 cupcakes on Monday and 40 cupcakes on Tuesday. How many total cupcakes did they bake?
   (D) Lauren's friend baked 60 cupcakes. Lauren baked 40 cupcakes each day for 4 days. How many total cupcakes did they bake?

Story Word Problems Practice Set 2

1. Which story best fits the expression $17 + 9$?

   (A) Nancy ran a race in 17 minutes. Paul ran the race 9 minutes faster than Nancy. How long did it take Paul to run the race?
   (B) Nancy ran a race in 17 minutes. Paul ran the race in 9 minutes. How many more minutes did it take Nancy to run the race?
   (C) Nancy ran a race in 17 minutes. Paul ran the race 9 minutes slower than Nancy. How long did it take Paul to run the race?
   (D) Nancy ran a race in 17 minutes. Paul ran the race 9 times as fast as Nancy. How long did it take Paul to run the race?

2. Which story best fits the equation $61 - 43 = 18$?

   (A) Fred has $61 and he wants to go shopping. He needs to have $18 left over after his shopping trip. How much money can Fred spend?
   (B) Fred spent $61 shopping on Monday and $18 shopping on Tuesday. How much total money did Fred spend shopping?
   (C) Fred spent $61 shopping on Friday on 43 equally priced items. How much did each item cost?
   (D) Fred spent $43 shopping on Wednesday and $18 shopping on Thursday. How much more money did Fred spend on Wednesday than on Thursday?

3. Samantha is 15 years old. This is 5 times as old as Jenny. Which equation can be used to figure out Jenny's age, a?

   (A) $15 + 5 = a$
   (B) $15 \times 5 = a$
   (C) $15 - 5 = a$
   (D) $15 \div 5 = a$

4. Serena recently lost weight. She knows how many pounds she lost and she knows how many pounds she currently weights. How could she figure out her starting weight, w?

   (A) w = how many pounds she lost + how many pounds she weighs
   (B) w = how many pounds she lost × how many pounds she weighs
   (C) w = how many pounds she lost ÷ how many pounds she weighs
   (D) w = how many pounds she lost − how many pounds she weighs

5. Which story best fits the expression 5×20?

   (A) A tennis coach buys 20 packs of tennis balls. Each pack comes with 5 tennis balls. How many total tennis balls did the coach buy?
   (B) A tennis coach buys 20 packs of tennis balls. He returns 5 packs. How many packs of tennis balls does he have left?
   (C) A tennis coach buys 20 packs of tennis balls. He gives each player on his team 5 packs of tennis balls. How many players are on his team?
   (D) A tennis coach buys 20 packs of tennis balls. His friend gives him 5 more packs. How many total packs of tennis balls does he have?

6. Zane is painting the walls in his house. He knows how many square feet of wall he will need to paint and how many square feet each can of paint covers. How would he figure out how many cans of paint, p, he needs to buy?

   (A) p = the number square feet of wall he needs to paint + the number of square feet each can of paint covers
   (B) p = the number square feet of wall he needs to paint ÷ the number of square feet each can of paint covers
   (C) p = the number square feet of wall he needs to paint − the number of square feet each can of paint covers
   (D) p = the number square feet of wall he needs to paint × the number of square feet each can of paint covers

7. Which story best fits the equation $45 \div 9 = 5$?

   (A) Mr. Linden has 45 students in his gym class. 9 students from Mr. Linden's class switch into another gym class. How many students are left in Mr. Linden's gym class?
   (B) Mr. Linden has 45 students in his gym class. He wants to make 5 teams. How many students should he put on each team?
   (C) Mr. Linden has 45 students in his gym class. 5 more students join Mr. Linden's class. How many total students are in Mr. Linden's gym class?
   (D) Mr. Linden has 45 students in his gym class. Each student receives 9 points for participating in a game. How many total points do the students receive?

8. Carl purchases 8 gallons of milk. If each gallon costs $2, which equation can be used to find the total cost, c, of the milk?

(A) $2 + 8 = c$
(B) $8 \div 2 = c$
(C) $2 \times 8 = c$
(D) $8 - 2 = c$

9. Which story best fits the expression $12 \times 6 - 4$?

(A) Greta bakes 6 batches of muffins. She throws away 4 batches of muffins. If each batch has 12 muffins, how many muffins does she have left?
(B) Greta bakes 12 muffins on Monday and 6 times as many muffins on Tuesday. If she eats 4 muffins, how many muffins does she have left?
(C) Greta bakes 6 muffins and eats 4 of them. The next day, she bakes 12 more muffins. How many muffins does Greta have left?
(D) Greta bakes 6 batches of muffins. Each batch has 12 muffins. If she eats 4 muffins, how many does she have left?

10. Will wants to fill his gas tank. He knows how many gallons his gas tank can hold and he knows the price of each gallon of gas. How can Will figure out how much money, m, it will cost him to fill his gas tank?

(A) m = the number of gallons his tank can hold – the price of each gallon of gas
(B) m = the number of gallons his tank can hold ÷ the price of each gallon of gas
(C) m = the number of gallons his tank can hold + the price of each gallon of gas
(D) m = the number of gallons his tank can hold × the price of each gallon of gas

Patterns Practice Set 1

1. Use the figure below to answer the question.

    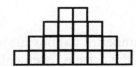

    If the pattern continues, and three more rows are added, how many squares will be in the seventh row?

    (A) 10
    (B) 12
    (C) 13
    (D) 14

2. Find the missing number in the following sequence: 1, 3, 9, 27, ___, 243, 729

    (A) 45
    (B) 81
    (C) 87
    (D) 91

3. At age 13, Trevor could run 3 miles. At age 14, he could run 5 miles. At age 15, he could run 7 miles. At age 18, he could run 13 miles. According to the pattern, how many more miles could Trevor run at age 17 than at age 12?

    (A) 6
    (B) 9
    (C) 10
    (D) 11

4. Find the next number in the following sequence: 4, –1, –6, –11 …

    (A) –17
    (B) –16
    (C) –15
    (D) –14

5. Use the figure below to answer the question.

    If the pattern continues, what will be the 23rd shape in the pattern?

    (A) ☺

    (B) ✴

    (C) ⚡

    (D) ✚

6. The price of a certain stock doubles every month. At month 1, the stock costs a dollars. How much will it cost at month 4?

    (A) $4a$ dollars
    (B) 4 dollars
    (C) $8a$ dollars
    (D) 8 dollars

7. Use the figures below to answer the question.

    If the pattern continues, how many squares will be in the sixth figure?

    (A) 25
    (B) 30
    (C) 36
    (D) 49

8. The table shows the cost of a carnival.

Number of People	Total Cost
1	$12
2	$22
3	$30
4	$36

Based on the pattern, what is the total cost for 5 people?

(A) $40
(B) $42
(C) $44
(D) $45

9. Find the next number in the following sequence: 19, 21, 16, 18, 13 …

(A) 8
(B) 11
(C) 14
(D) 15

10. The table shows the number of pushups George could do at different ages.

Age	Number of Pushups
10	5
12	6
14	8
16	?
18	15
20	20

Based on the pattern, how many pushups could George do at age 16?

(A) 9
(B) 10
(C) 11
(D) 12

Patterns Practice Set 2

1. Use the figures to answer the question.

If the pattern continues, how many circles will be in the eighth figure?

(A) 9
(B) 13
(C) 14
(D) 15

2. Find the missing number in the sequence: −10, −1, 8, ___, 26, 35

(A) 17
(B) 19
(C) 21
(D) 44

3. Use the figure to answer the question.

If the pattern continues, what will be the 36th shape in the pattern?

(A) ▽
(B) ◇
(C) ☆
(D) ○

4. Use the figures to answer the question.

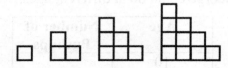

If the pattern continues, how many squares will be in the sixth figure?

(A) 15
(B) 20
(C) 21
(D) 28

5. The price of a stock triples every year. At year 1, the stock costs x dollars. How much will the stock cost at year 3?

(A) 9 dollars
(B) $9x$ dollars
(C) 27 dollars
(D) $27x$ dollars

6. The table shows Demi's salary over 5 years.

Years Working	Salary
Start	$50,000
1 Year	$60,000
2 Years	?
3 Years	$74,000
4 Years	$78,000
5 Years	$80,000

Based on the pattern, what will Demi's salary be after 2 years?

(A) $62,000
(B) $64,000
(C) $68,000
(D) $70,000

7. Find the next number in the following sequence: 8, 16, 32, 64, 128…

(A) 192
(B) 246
(C) 254
(D) 256

8. Shane is trying to save money to go on vacation. Week 1, he saves $10. Week 2, he saves $20. The following week he saves $40. If Shane keeps saving at this rate, how much money will he save week 6?

(A) $160
(B) $310
(C) $320
(D) $640

9. The table below shows the annual precipitation in two towns.

Year	Town A	Town B
2001	20 in	64 in
2002	19 in	32 in
2003	17 in	16 in
2004	14 in	8 in
2005	10 in	4 in

Based on the patterns in the table, how much rainfall is expected in 2006 in Town B?

(A) 0 in
(B) 2 in
(C) 5 in
(D) 6 in

10. Find the next number in the following sequence: 8, 10, 13, 15, 18, 20 …

(A) 22
(B) 23
(C) 24
(D) 25

Properties Practice Set 1

1. Which of the following illustrates the commutative property of addition?

   (A) $y + z = z + y$
   (B) $yz = zy$
   (C) $(x + y) + z = x + (y + z)$
   (D) $(xy)z = x(yz)$

2. Which of the following properties is illustrated by: $a \times 1 = a$?

   (A) commutative property
   (B) identity property of multiplication
   (C) associative property
   (D) identity property of addition

3. Which of the following illustrates the associative property?

   (A) $(8 - 5) + 3 = 8 - (5 + 3)$
   (B) $(8 \times 5) \times 3 = 8 \times (5 \times 3)$
   (C) $(8 - 5) - 3 = 8 - (5 - 3)$
   (D) $(8 \div 5) \times 3 = 8 \div (5 \times 3)$

4. Which of the following represents the identity property for addition?

   (A) $30 + 1 = 31$
   (B) $30 + 5 = 5 + 30$
   (C) $30 + 10 = 3(10 + 1)$
   (D) $30 + 0 = 30$

5. Which of the following properties is illustrated by: $5 \times (4 \times 7) = (5 \times 4) \times 7$?

   (A) distributive property
   (B) identity property of multiplication
   (C) commutative property
   (D) associative property

6. Which of the following represents the identity property for multiplication?

   (A) $15 \times 0 = 0$
   (B) $15 \times 3 = 3 \times 15$
   (C) $15 \times 1 = 15$
   (D) $15 \times 3 = 10(3) + 5(3)$

7. Which of the following properties is illustrated by: $56 + 0 = 56$?

   (A) associative property
   (B) commutative property
   (C) identity property of addition
   (D) none of the above

8. Which of the following illustrates the distributive property?

   (A) $3(4 \times 5) = (3 \times 4) + (3 \times 5)$
   (B) $3(4 - 5) = (3 \times 4) - (3 \times 5)$
   (C) $3(4 + 5) = (3 + 4) \times (3 + 5)$
   (D) $3(4 + 5) = (3 + 4) + (3 + 5)$

9. Which of the following properties is illustrated by: $a(b + c) = ab + ac$?

   (A) distributive property
   (B) commutative property
   (C) associative property
   (D) none of the above

10. Which of the following properties is illustrated by: $4x + 3x = 3x + 4x$?

   (A) commutative property
   (B) associative property
   (C) distributive property
   (D) identity property of addition

Properties Practice Set 2

1. Which of the following properties is illustrated by: $8+4=4+8$?

   (A) associative property
   (B) distributive property
   (C) identity property of addition
   (D) commutative property

2. Which of the following properties is illustrated by: $6\times1=6$?

   (A) identity property of multiplication
   (B) associative property
   (C) commutative property
   (D) none of the above

3. Which of the following illustrates the commutative property of addition?

   (A) $6(2+7)=(6\times2)+(6\times7)$
   (B) $6+(5+1)=(6+5)+1$
   (C) $8+3+4=3+8+4$
   (D) $6\times12=12\times6$

4. Which of the following properties is illustrated by: $b+0=b$?

   (A) identity property of multiplication
   (B) commutative property
   (C) associative property
   (D) identity property of addition

5. Which of the following illustrates the associative property?

   (A) $(10-7)+12=(10-12)+7$
   (B) $(10\times7)+12=10\times(7+12)$
   (C) $(10+7)+12=10+(7+12)$
   (D) $(10+7)\times12=10+(7\times12)$

6. Which of the following properties is illustrated by: $5(10-2)=5(10)-5(2)$?

   (A) commutative property
   (B) associative property
   (C) distributive property
   (D) identity property of multiplication

7. Which of the following illustrates the distributive property?

   (A) $4(x+y)=(4+x)\times(4+y)$
   (B) $4(xy)=4x+4y$
   (C) $4(x+y)=(4+x)+(4+y)$
   (D) $4(x+y)=4x+4y$

8. Which of the following illustrates the identity property for multiplication?

   (A) $d\times1=d$
   (B) $d\times0=0$
   (C) $d\times c=dc$
   (D) $d\times c\times e=d\times e\times c$

9. Which of the following properties is illustrated by: $m+(n+k)=(m+n)+k$?

   (A) distributive property
   (B) associative property
   (C) identity property of multiplication
   (D) commutative property

10. Which of the following illustrates the identity property for addition?

   (A) $56+1=57$
   (B) $56+0=56$
   (C) $56=50+6$
   (D) $56+1=1+56$

Vocabulary Practice Set 1

1. Which of the following is NOT an integer?

   (A) 9
   (B) −18
   (C) 0
   (D) 3.25

2. Which of the following describes the set of numbers below?

   {1, 3, 5, 7, 9, 11}

   (A) odd numbers
   (B) prime numbers
   (C) composite numbers
   (D) even numbers

3. Which of the following is irrational?

   (A) $\sqrt{6}$
   (B) $3.\overline{4}$
   (C) −10
   (D) 2/5

4. Which of the following describes the set of number below?

   {7, 14, 21, 28, 35, 42}

   (A) multiples of 7
   (B) factors of 7
   (C) odd numbers
   (D) irrational numbers

5. Which of the following describes the number 9.5?

   (A) irrational
   (B) integer
   (C) rational
   (D) odd

6. Which of the following fractions have the same denominators?

   (A) 2/3 and 2/5
   (B) 5/7 and 3/7
   (C) $3\frac{2}{5}, 3\frac{1}{4}$
   (D) None of the above

7. Which of the following sets consists of only prime numbers?

   (A) {0, 1, 7, 13}
   (B) {1, 2, 3, 5, 7}
   (C) {2, 3, 11, 13, 17}
   (D) {3, 5, 9}

8. Which of the following does NOT describe the number −8?

   (A) composite
   (B) even
   (C) integer
   (D) irrational

9. Which of the following describes the set of numbers below?

   {1, 2, 3, 4, 6, 12}

   (A) even numbers
   (B) factors of 12
   (C) multiples of 12
   (D) composite numbers

10. Which of the following sets of numbers consists of consecutive numbers?

    (A) {3, 5, 7, 9}
    (B) {1, 2, 4, 7}
    (C) {7, 8, 9, 10}
    (D) {-8, -6, 6, 8}

Vocabulary Practice Set 2

1. Which of the following pairs of fractions have the same numerators?

   (A) $\frac{4}{11}, \frac{3}{11}$

   (B) $\frac{7}{3}, \frac{7}{12}$

   (C) $4\frac{1}{2}, 4\frac{1}{3}$

   (D) None of the above

2. Which of the following is an integer?

   (A) 8.5
   (B) 1/2
   (C) -4
   (D) -9.2

3. Which of the following is irrational?

   (A) π
   (B) 5
   (C) 3.75
   (D) $1.\overline{23}$

4. Which of the following describes the number $2\frac{1}{3}$?

   (A) integer
   (B) rational
   (C) irrational
   (D) even

5. Which describes the set of numbers?

   $\{4, 8, 10, 16\}$

   (A) odd numbers
   (B) multiples of 4
   (C) consecutive numbers
   (D) even numbers

6. Which of the following describes the set of numbers below?

   $\{1, 2, 4, 5, 10, 20\}$

   (A) factors of 20
   (B) even numbers
   (C) multiples of 20
   (D) composite numbers

7. Which of the following sets of numbers consists of consecutive odd numbers?

   (A) $\{1, 2, 3, 4\}$
   (B) $\{3, 5, 7, 9\}$
   (C) $\{3, 7, 11, 15\}$
   (D) $\{2, 4, 6, 8\}$

8. Which of the following describes the set of number below?

   $\{5, 10, 15, 20, 25, 30\}$

   (A) multiples of 5
   (B) factors of 5
   (C) odd numbers
   (D) irrational numbers

9. Which of the following does NOT describe the number 11?

   (A) odd
   (B) whole number
   (C) integer
   (D) composite

10. Which of the following sets consists of only composite numbers?

    (A) $\{2, 4, 6, 8\}$
    (B) $\{0, 1, 4, 10\}$
    (C) $\{4, 6, 9, 15\}$
    (D) $\{3, 6, 9, 12\}$

Fractions Practice Set 1

1. What is the value of $\dfrac{2}{3} + \dfrac{5}{6}$?

   (A) $\dfrac{2}{3}$

   (B) $\dfrac{7}{6}$

   (C) $\dfrac{11}{6}$

   (D) $\dfrac{3}{2}$

2. What is the value of $\dfrac{7}{9} - \dfrac{3}{7}$?

   (A) $\dfrac{22}{63}$

   (B) $\dfrac{76}{63}$

   (C) $\dfrac{23}{63}$

   (D) $\dfrac{4}{9}$

3. What is the value of $1\dfrac{1}{2} + 2\dfrac{3}{4} + \dfrac{5}{8}$?

   (A) $3\dfrac{7}{8}$

   (B) $4\dfrac{1}{8}$

   (C) $4\dfrac{7}{8}$

   (D) $4\dfrac{3}{8}$

4. What is the value of $1\dfrac{3}{4} \div 1\dfrac{1}{12}$?

   (A) $\dfrac{21}{13}$

   (B) $\dfrac{91}{48}$

   (C) $\dfrac{13}{21}$

   (D) $\dfrac{21}{11}$

5. What is the value of $3\dfrac{1}{3} - 1\dfrac{7}{12} - \dfrac{5}{6}$?

   (A) $2\dfrac{7}{12}$

   (B) $\dfrac{3}{4}$

   (C) $\dfrac{11}{12}$

   (D) $\dfrac{1}{12}$

6. What is the value of $1\dfrac{2}{5} \times 2\dfrac{6}{7}$?

   (A) $\dfrac{49}{100}$

   (B) 4

   (C) 5

   (D) $\dfrac{1}{4}$

7. What is the value of $\dfrac{4}{9} \times \dfrac{5}{7} \times \dfrac{18}{25}$?

(A) $\dfrac{72}{325}$

(B) $1\dfrac{1}{35}$

(C) $\dfrac{9}{35}$

(D) $\dfrac{8}{35}$

8. What is the value of $\dfrac{1}{3} + \dfrac{3}{4} \times \dfrac{8}{9}$?

(A) $\dfrac{26}{27}$

(B) 1

(C) $1\dfrac{2}{3}$

(D) $\dfrac{2}{3}$

9. What is the value of $1\dfrac{1}{2} - \dfrac{1}{2} \div 4$?

(A) $-\dfrac{1}{2}$

(B) $\dfrac{1}{4}$

(C) $1\dfrac{3}{8}$

(D) $1\dfrac{5}{8}$

10. What is the value of $\dfrac{15}{2} + \dfrac{9}{5} - \dfrac{13}{10}$?

(A) 7

(B) 9

(C) 8

(D) 6

Fractions Practice Set 2

1. What is the value of $\dfrac{5}{8}+\dfrac{3}{4}$?

   (A) 1

   (B) $\dfrac{2}{3}$

   (C) $1\dfrac{3}{8}$

   (D) $1\dfrac{1}{4}$

2. What is the value of $\dfrac{4}{5}-\dfrac{1}{6}$?

   (A) $\dfrac{19}{30}$

   (B) $\dfrac{1}{10}$

   (C) $\dfrac{7}{10}$

   (D) $\dfrac{19}{36}$

3. What is the value of $3\dfrac{1}{3}+\dfrac{5}{6}+1\dfrac{1}{9}$?

   (A) $\dfrac{85}{18}$

   (B) $\dfrac{95}{18}$

   (C) $\dfrac{25}{18}$

   (D) $\dfrac{125}{18}$

4. What is the value of $2\dfrac{1}{5}\div 1\dfrac{3}{10}$?

   (A) $1\dfrac{9}{13}$

   (B) $1\dfrac{11}{13}$

   (C) $2\dfrac{43}{50}$

   (D) $\dfrac{13}{22}$

5. What is the value of $4\dfrac{1}{2}-1\dfrac{2}{3}-\dfrac{4}{6}$?

   (A) $2\dfrac{1}{3}$

   (B) $3\dfrac{1}{2}$

   (C) $2\dfrac{1}{6}$

   (D) $1\dfrac{5}{6}$

6. What is the value of $2\dfrac{5}{8}\times 1\dfrac{1}{3}$?

   (A) 7/4

   (B) 3

   (C) 4

   (D) 7/2

7. What is the value of $\dfrac{9}{2} - \dfrac{11}{5} + \dfrac{17}{10}$?

(A) 4
(B) 3/5
(C) 5
(D) 3

8. What is the value of $\dfrac{8}{11} \times \dfrac{3}{5} \times \dfrac{11}{24}$?

(A) 2/5
(B) 1/20
(C) 3/20
(D) 1/5

9. What is the value of $\dfrac{3}{7} + \dfrac{4}{7} \times \dfrac{5}{8}$?

(A) $\dfrac{5}{7}$
(B) $\dfrac{11}{14}$
(C) $\dfrac{17}{28}$
(D) $\dfrac{9}{14}$

10. What is the value of $3\dfrac{2}{3} - \dfrac{2}{3} \div 3$?

(A) 1
(B) $1\dfrac{2}{3}$
(C) $3\dfrac{4}{9}$
(D) $3\dfrac{1}{3}$

Comparing Fractions Practice Set 1

1. Which fraction is the largest?

   (A) $\frac{1}{2}$

   (B) $\frac{3}{4}$

   (C) $\frac{2}{5}$

   (D) $\frac{7}{8}$

2. Which fraction below is the smallest?

   (A) $\frac{2}{9}$

   (B) $\frac{1}{4}$

   (C) $\frac{3}{5}$

   (D) $\frac{3}{8}$

3. Which of the following fractions is between $\frac{1}{2}$ and $\frac{3}{4}$?

   (A) $\frac{2}{5}$

   (B) $\frac{3}{6}$

   (C) $\frac{3}{5}$

   (D) $\frac{7}{9}$

4. Which fraction is the largest?

   (A) $\frac{15}{7}$

   (B) $\frac{7}{3}$

   (C) $\frac{19}{9}$

   (D) $\frac{11}{5}$

5. Which of the following fractions is between $\frac{1}{4}$ and $\frac{3}{8}$?

   (A) $\frac{1}{5}$

   (B) $\frac{1}{3}$

   (C) $\frac{4}{9}$

   (D) $\frac{3}{7}$

6. Which fraction below is the smallest?

   (A) $\frac{8}{9}$

   (B) $\frac{5}{6}$

   (C) $\frac{2}{3}$

   (D) $\frac{7}{8}$

7. Which fraction is between $\frac{1}{3}$ and $\frac{3}{7}$?

(A) 2/5
(B) 1/2
(C) 2/8
(D) 3/9

8. Which fraction is the smallest?

(A) $1\frac{2}{3}$

(B) $\frac{11}{6}$

(C) $1\frac{3}{4}$

(D) $\frac{3}{2}$

9. Which fraction below is greatest?

(A) 3/7
(B) 6/11
(C) 1/3
(D) 3/5

10. Which fraction is between $\frac{2}{5}$ and $\frac{3}{5}$?

(A) $\frac{5}{7}$

(B) $\frac{3}{10}$

(C) $\frac{4}{9}$

(D) $\frac{1}{3}$

Comparing Fractions Practice Set 2

1. Which fraction is the largest?

(A) 3/4
(B) 5/6
(C) 4/5
(D) 6/7

2. Which fraction is the smallest?

(A) $\frac{7}{9}$

(B) $\frac{2}{5}$

(C) $\frac{3}{4}$

(D) $\frac{1}{2}$

3. Which fraction below is greatest?

(A) 7/11
(B) 3/7
(C) 5/9
(D) 6/10

4. Which fraction is between $\frac{4}{9}$ and $\frac{4}{7}$?

(A) $\frac{5}{8}$

(B) $\frac{2}{5}$

(C) $\frac{2}{3}$

(D) $\frac{1}{2}$

5. Which fraction is the smallest?

   (A) $\dfrac{5}{12}$

   (B) $\dfrac{3}{10}$

   (C) $\dfrac{6}{11}$

   (D) $\dfrac{2}{5}$

6. Which fraction is the largest?

   (A) $2\dfrac{4}{7}$

   (B) $2\dfrac{6}{11}$

   (C) $2\dfrac{1}{6}$

   (D) $2\dfrac{4}{9}$

7. Which fraction is between $\dfrac{3}{8}$ and $\dfrac{1}{2}$?

   (A) $\dfrac{4}{8}$

   (B) $\dfrac{3}{4}$

   (C) $\dfrac{3}{7}$

   (D) $\dfrac{6}{11}$

8. Which fraction is between $\dfrac{2}{7}$ and $\dfrac{4}{9}$?

   (A) $\dfrac{1}{4}$

   (B) $\dfrac{1}{2}$

   (C) $\dfrac{1}{3}$

   (D) $\dfrac{3}{5}$

9. Which fraction below is the smallest?

   (A) $\dfrac{5}{9}$

   (B) $\dfrac{5}{10}$

   (C) $\dfrac{6}{11}$

   (D) $\dfrac{6}{13}$

10. Which of the following fractions is between $3\dfrac{3}{5}$ and $3\dfrac{4}{5}$?

   (A) $\dfrac{37}{10}$

   (B) $\dfrac{38}{10}$

   (C) $\dfrac{7}{2}$

   (D) $\dfrac{23}{6}$

Fractions of Numbers Practice Set 1

1. What is $\frac{1}{5}$ of 60?

    (A) 10
    (B) 12
    (C) 13
    (D) 14

2. What is $\frac{1}{3}$ of 39?

    (A) 12
    (B) 13
    (C) 15
    (D) 18

3. What is $\frac{1}{12}$ of 24?

    (A) 2
    (B) 4
    (C) 6
    (D) 12

4. What is $\frac{1}{7}$ of 42?

    (A) 6
    (B) 7
    (C) 8
    (D) 9

5. What is $\frac{1}{2}$ of 98?

    (A) 39
    (B) 46
    (C) 48
    (D) 49

6. What is $\frac{2}{5}$ of 25?

    (A) 5
    (B) 10
    (C) 12.5
    (D) 15

7. What is $\frac{3}{4}$ of 44?

    (A) 11
    (B) 22
    (C) 33
    (D) 36

8. What is $\frac{4}{7}$ of 280?

    (A) 49
    (B) 80
    (C) 120
    (D) 160

9. What is $\frac{5}{6}$ of 54?

    (A) 35
    (B) 40
    (C) 45
    (D) 60

10. What is $\frac{9}{10}$ of 300?

    (A) 210
    (B) 240
    (C) 270
    (D) 280

Fractions of Numbers Practice Set 2

1. What is $\frac{1}{4}$ of 52?

   (A) 12
   (B) 13
   (C) 14
   (D) 16

2. What is $\frac{1}{9}$ of 81?

   (A) 9
   (B) 11
   (C) 13
   (D) 18

3. What is $\frac{1}{6}$ of 12?

   (A) 2
   (B) 3
   (C) 4
   (D) 6

4. What is $\frac{1}{8}$ of 24?

   (A) 2
   (B) 3
   (C) 4
   (D) 6

5. What is $\frac{1}{11}$ of 88?

   (A) 7
   (B) 8
   (C) 9
   (D) 11

6. What is $\frac{2}{3}$ of 36?

   (A) 24
   (B) 26
   (C) 32
   (D) 54

7. What is $\frac{4}{5}$ of 45?

   (A) 24
   (B) 32
   (C) 34
   (D) 36

8. What is $\frac{5}{9}$ of 18?

   (A) 8
   (B) 10
   (C) 12
   (D) 15

9. What is $\frac{7}{12}$ of 60?

   (A) 28
   (B) 30
   (C) 35
   (D) 42

10. What is $\frac{5}{8}$ of 32?

    (A) 15
    (B) 20
    (C) 24
    (D) 25

Fraction Word Problems Practice Set 1

1. On Tuesday, Liam worked for $3\frac{1}{2}$ hours.

   On Wednesday, he worked for $2\frac{4}{5}$ hours.

   How much longer did Liam work on Tuesday than Wednesday?

   (A) $\frac{1}{7}$ hours

   (B) $\frac{7}{10}$ hours

   (C) $\frac{4}{5}$ hours

   (D) $6\frac{3}{10}$ hours

2. A school has 360 students. If 80 students are in the band, band member make up what fraction of the school?

   (A) 2/9
   (B) 1/4
   (C) 3/4
   (D) 7/9

3. You have $360 in your piggy bank. If you spend $\frac{2}{9}$ of your money on a pair of new shoes, how much money do you have left?

   (A) $80
   (B) $100
   (C) $260
   (D) $280

4. Danielle and Whitney shared a pizza. Danielle ate 2/5 of the pizza and Whitney ate 3/7 of the pizza. What fraction of the pizza did Whitney and Danielle eat all together?

   (A) 1/35
   (B) 5/12
   (C) 29/35
   (D) 31/35

5. Claude and Veronica are writing a paper together for English class. Claude wrote 3/8 of the paper and Veronica wrote 4/9 of the paper. What fraction of the paper do they have left to write?

   (A) 5/72
   (B) 13/72
   (C) 23/72
   (D) 59/72

6. At an animal shelter there are 45 dogs. If $\frac{3}{5}$ of the dogs have spots, how many dogs have spots?

   (A) 9
   (B) 18
   (C) 27
   (D) 30

7. Sam has 60 inches of ribbon and he wants to cut it into pieces that are 2/3 inches long. How many pieces of ribbon can he cut?

   (A) 40
   (B) 45
   (C) 90
   (D) 120

8. Nick, Taylor, and Corinne own a flower shop together. On Monday, Nick made $180. On Tuesday Taylor worked for 5 hours and made $18 per hour. On Wednesday Corinne made twice as much as Nick made on Monday. If they each get to keep a third of the total money they made, how much money does each person get?

(A) $150
(B) $210
(C) $310
(D) $630

9. Fred bought a bag of candy with 125 pieces. If he ate 50 pieces of candy, what fraction of the bag of candy does Fred have left?

(A) 2/5
(B) 1/2
(C) 3/5
(D) 2/3

10. Mrs. Reynolds has $\frac{7}{8}$ of a cake that she wants to split between her five children. What fraction of the cake does each child get?

(A) $\frac{7}{40}$

(B) $\frac{7}{35}$

(C) $\frac{8}{35}$

(D) $\frac{1}{5}$

Fraction Word Problems Practice Set 2

1. Maud and Josephine are mowing their lawn together. Maud mowed 1/6 of the lawn and Josephine mowed 5/8 of the lawn. What fraction of their lawn do they have left to mow?

(A) 5/24
(B) 3/7
(C) 4/7
(D) 19/24

2. Mr. Miller drank $6\frac{3}{4}$ cups of water on Monday and $7\frac{1}{2}$ cups of water on Tuesday. How many total cups of water did he drink over the two days?

(A) $13\frac{1}{4}$

(B) $14\frac{1}{4}$

(C) $14\frac{3}{4}$

(D) $15\frac{1}{4}$

3. Mrs. Vile and Mr. Vile share a bank account with $1800 in it. Mrs. Vile spent $200 on groceries, and Mr. Vile spent $400 on house repairs. What fraction of their money did they spend?

   (A) 1/30
   (B) 1/6
   (C) 1/4
   (D) 1/3

4. You go to school for 9 hours a day. You spend 2/3 of your school day in academic classes. How many hours do you spend in academic classes?

   (A) 3 hours
   (B) 4.5 hours
   (C) 6 hours
   (D) 7.5 hours

5. Kim has 40 cm of string and she wants to cut it into pieces that are 4/5 cm long. How many pieces of string can she cut?

   (A) 32
   (B) 36
   (C) 48
   (D) 50

6. Devin ran $7\frac{1}{5}$ miles today. Yesterday he ran $1\frac{3}{10}$ fewer miles than he ran today. How many total miles did he run?

   (A) $5\frac{9}{10}$ miles

   (B) $8\frac{1}{2}$ miles

   (C) $13\frac{1}{10}$ miles

   (D) $15\frac{7}{10}$ miles

7. Vanessa spent her Saturday watching a movie marathon on television. She watched two 90-minute movies, and there were three ten-minute breaks in between the movies. Vanessa slept through 1/5 of the movie marathon. How many minutes was she awake?

   (A) 21
   (B) 42
   (C) 80
   (D) 168

8. A pizza is split into 16 slices. You and your friend eat $\frac{3}{4}$ of the pizza. How many slice of pizza are left?

   (A) 4
   (B) 6
   (C) 8
   (D) 12

9. Sofia ate 6 slices of pizza. This was $\frac{3}{7}$ of the entire pizza. How many slices were there in the whole pizza?

   (A) 7
   (B) 14
   (C) 21
   (D) 42

10. In a survey, students voted on their favorite color. 24 students said blue, 20 students said red, 12 students said yellow, and 16 students said green. What fraction of students chose green or blue as their favorite color?

    (A) 1/3
    (B) 4/9
    (C) 5/9
    (D) 5/8

Decimals Practice Set 1

1. What is the value of 487.07 + 76.049?

   (A) 563.119
   (B) 564.019
   (C) 654.109
   (D) 1247.46

2. What is the value of 0.8×7?

   (A) 0.48
   (B) 0.56
   (C) 5.4
   (D) 5.6

3. What is the value of 184.5 − 16.98?

   (A) 111.53
   (B) 167.52
   (C) 167.68
   (D) 172.48

4. What is the value of 0.3×0.6?

   (A) 0.018
   (B) 0.12
   (C) 0.18
   (D) 1.8

5. What is the value of $0.59 \div 0.04$?

   (A) 0.0678
   (B) 1.475
   (C) 14.68
   (D) 14.75

6. What is the value of the expression 20.5 + 31.21 + 4.72?

   (A) 55.33
   (B) 56.43
   (C) 58.43
   (D) 66.43

7. What is the value of the expression 90 − 13.62 − 4.91?

   (A) 71.47
   (B) 71.57
   (C) 76.38
   (D) 81.29

8. What is the value of the expression 81.245 − 15 + 3.1?

   (A) 63.145
   (B) 69.345
   (C) 69.354
   (D) 93.145

9. What is the value of $73.8 \div 0.9$?

   (A) 7.2
   (B) 8.2
   (C) 72
   (D) 82

10. What is the value of 16.12×123?

    (A) 198.276
    (B) 1972.76
    (C) 1982.76
    (D) 2982.76

Decimals Practice Set 2

1. What is the value of 0.4×7?

   (A) 0.28
   (B) 0.32
   (C) 2.4
   (D) 2.8

2. What is the value of $28.8 \div 12$?

   (A) 0.24
   (B) 0.42
   (C) 2.4
   (D) 2.8

3. What is the value of $300 - 73.32$?

   (A) 206.58
   (B) 226.68
   (C) 227.78
   (D) 233.32

4. What is the value of $56.04 + 9.97$?

   (A) 65
   (B) 65.01
   (C) 66
   (D) 66.01

5. What is the value of $0.79 \div 0.05$?

   (A) 0.158
   (B) 1.58
   (C) 15.4
   (D) 15.8

6. What is the value of 0.9×0.5?

   (A) 0.045
   (B) 0.4
   (C) 0.45
   (D) 4.5

7. What is the value of the expression $82.3 - 70 - 6.18$?

   (A) 6.12
   (B) 6.28
   (C) 16.12
   (D) 18.48

8. What is the value of $1.725 \div 0.3$?

   (A) 0.174
   (B) 0.575
   (C) 5.75
   (D) 57.5

9. What is the value of 0.57×91.2?

   (A) 42.864
   (B) 51.984
   (C) 52.784
   (D) 519.84

10. What is the value of the expression $9.1 + 43.23 - 25.97$?

    (A) 26.36
    (B) 26.46
    (C) 33.64
    (D) 36.26

Decimal Word Problems Practice Set 1

1. Vivian is making friendship bracelets. Each bracelet uses 5.2 inches of string. If she has 124.8 inches of string, how many bracelets can she make?

   (A) 14
   (B) 18
   (C) 24
   (D) 26

2. Nikhil goes to the store and buys six apples and four oranges. Each apple costs $1.15, and each orange costs $0.82. How much money did Nikhil spend?

   (A) $1.97
   (B) $9.52
   (C) $10.18
   (D) $10.78

3. Nina weighs 145.72 pounds, which is 13.94 pounds more than Johnson. How much does Johnson weigh?

   (A) 131.78 pounds
   (B) 132.22 pounds
   (C) 158.66 pounds
   (D) 159.66 pounds

4. Which of the following is closest in value to 3?

   (A) 2.98
   (B) 2.89
   (C) 2.9
   (D) 3.01

5. Mackenzie ran 6.8 miles yesterday and 2.6 miles today. Her goal is to run a total of 14.5 miles this week. How many more miles does she need to run?

   (A) 5.1 miles
   (B) 5.35 miles
   (C) 6.1 miles
   (D) 23.9 miles

6. Xavier makes $9.25 an hour at his job. Last week he worked 25 hours and this week he worked 15 hours. How much money did he make in these two weeks?

   (A) $277.50
   (B) $368.50
   (C) $370
   (D) $462.50

7. If 0.09 is equal to $\dfrac{a}{100}$, then a is equal to which of the following?

   (A) 0.9
   (B) 9
   (C) 90
   (D) 900

8. Cristina went to the store and bought 6 apples for $1.35 each. If she gave the cashier a $10, how much money did she get back?

   (A) $1.90
   (B) $2.10
   (C) $2.90
   (D) $8.10

9. The product of a number and 1.5 is 18. What is 2.9 less than the number?

(A) 8.1
(B) 9.1
(C) 10.9
(D) 24.1

10. Emma has $24 and Weston has $18. They want to put their money together and buy gift bags for their friends and family. If each gift bag costs $1.40, how many gift bags can they buy?

(A) 3
(B) 30
(C) 38
(D) 60

Decimal Word Problems Practice Set 2

1. Emily bought four packs of pencils that cost $6.07 each and seven packs of pens that cost $4.98 each. How much total money did she spend on pencils and pens?

(A) $11.05
(B) $59.14
(C) $59.18
(D) $62.41

2. Which of the following is closest in value to 1?

(A) 1.009
(B) 0.99
(C) 1.1
(D) 1.01

3. Rachel has $72.40. She splits it equally between her four children. Each child spends $12 on lunch and gives the remaining money back to Rachel. How much money does Rachel have?

(A) $18.10
(B) $20.40
(C) $24.40
(D) $48

4. If 0.4 is equal to $\dfrac{x}{100}$, then x is equal to which of the following?

(A) 0.4
(B) 4
(C) 40
(D) 400

5. Priyanka ran a race in 39.54 seconds, which is 4.78 seconds faster than Steven. What is the sum of Priyanka's and Steven's times?

(A) 34.76 seconds
(B) 44.32 seconds
(C) 74.3 seconds
(D) 83.86 seconds

6. David has $65 and Ronnie has $25. They put their money together to buy action figures. If each action figure costs $1.50, how many action figures can they buy?

(A) 60
(B) 67
(C) 90
(D) 135

7. Grant lost 0.7 pounds per week for eight weeks. He now weighs 152.8 pounds. How much did he weigh eight weeks ago?

   (A) 147.2 pounds
   (B) 147.4 pounds
   (C) 158.2 pounds
   (D) 158.4 pounds

8. Bianca drinks 7.6 cups of water every day. How many cups of water will Bianca drink in five weeks?

   (A) 38 cups
   (B) 53.2 cups
   (C) 190 cups
   (D) 266 cups

9. Sierra and Bryant went on a road trip. On Friday they drove for 4.2 hours, on Saturday they drove for 3.6 hours, and on Sunday they drove for 5.5 hours. How many total hours did they drive?

   (A) 12.3 hours
   (B) 13.3 hours
   (C) 13.4 hours
   (D) 14.3 hours

10. The sum of 15.4 and a number is 40. What is the number divided by 0.2?

   (A) 12.3
   (B) 27.7
   (C) 123
   (D) 277

Converting Decimals, Fractions, and Percents Practice Set 1

1. What is 0.5 as a percent?

   (A) 0.005%
   (B) 0.5%
   (C) 5%
   (D) 50%

2. What is 1.6 as a fraction?

   (A) $\dfrac{4}{25}$

   (B) $\dfrac{7}{6}$

   (C) $\dfrac{8}{5}$

   (D) $\dfrac{9}{5}$

3. What is 0.045 as a percent?

   (A) 0.0045%
   (B) 0.45%
   (C) 4.5%
   (D) 45%

4. What is 2.62 as a percent?

   (A) 0.0262%
   (B) 2.62%
   (C) 26.2%
   (D) 262%

5. What is 0.08 as a fraction?

   (A) 1/20
   (B) 3/50
   (C) 2/25
   (D) 4/5

6. What is $3\dfrac{3}{4}$ as a percent?

   (A) 325%
   (B) 334%
   (C) 350%
   (D) 375%

7. What is $\dfrac{17}{20}$ as a decimal?

   (A) 0.17
   (B) 0.68
   (C) 0.8
   (D) 0.85

8. What is 45% as a decimal?

   (A) 0.045
   (B) 0.45
   (C) 4.5
   (D) 450

9. What is 25% as a fraction?

   (A) $\dfrac{1}{25}$

   (B) $\dfrac{1}{5}$

   (C) $\dfrac{1}{4}$

   (D) $2\dfrac{1}{2}$

10. What is $\dfrac{3}{8}$ as a percent?

    (A) 37.5%
    (B) 38%
    (C) 62.5%
    (D) 24%

Converting Decimals, Fractions, and Percents Practice Set 2

1. What is 0.32% as a decimal?

   (A) 3.2
   (B) 0.0032
   (C) 0.032
   (D) 0.32

2. What is 0.06 as a fraction?

   (A) 3/50
   (B) 2/25
   (C) 6/50
   (D) 6/10

3. What is $\dfrac{7}{25}$ as a decimal?

   (A) 0.28
   (B) 0.32
   (C) 0.35
   (D) 0.725

4. What is 0.072 as a percent?

   (A) 0.0072%
   (B) 0.72%
   (C) 7.2%
   (D) 72%

5. What is 80% as a fraction?

   (A) $\dfrac{3}{5}$

   (B) $\dfrac{4}{5}$

   (C) $\dfrac{5}{6}$

   (D) $\dfrac{8}{9}$

6. What is $1\dfrac{3}{10}$ as a decimal?

   (A) 1.003
   (B) 1.03
   (C) 1.13
   (D) 1.3

7. What is 405% as a fraction?

   (A) $4\dfrac{1}{200}$

   (B) $4\dfrac{1}{20}$

   (C) $4\dfrac{1}{2}$

   (D) $40\dfrac{1}{2}$

8. What is 86% as a decimal?

   (A) 0.086
   (B) 0.86
   (C) 8.6
   (D) 860

9. What is $\dfrac{2}{3}$ as a percent?

   (A) 23%
   (B) 60%
   (C) 66%
   (D) 66.$\overline{6}$%

10. What is 75% as a fraction?

   (A) 1/2
   (B) 3/5
   (C) 3/4
   (D) 4/3

Percents Practice Set 1

1. What is 50% of 130?

   (A) 55
   (B) 60
   (C) 65
   (D) 75

2. What is 10% of 460?

   (A) 0.46
   (B) 4.6
   (C) 23
   (D) 46

3. What is 20% of 150?

   (A) 30
   (B) 35
   (C) 45
   (D) 75

4. What is 15% of 40?

   (A) 2
   (B) 5
   (C) 6
   (D) 8

5. 9 is what percent of 45?

   (A) 5%
   (B) 20%
   (C) 25%
   (D) 40%

6. What percent of 30 is 60?

   (A) 50%
   (B) 100%
   (C) 150%
   (D) 200%

7. 36 is what percent of 3,600?

   (A) 1%
   (B) 2%
   (C) 5%
   (D) 10%

8. 7 is 25% of what number?

   (A) 28
   (B) 35
   (C) 280
   (D) 350

9. 60 is 75% of what number?

   (A) 45
   (B) 65
   (C) 75
   (D) 80

10. 30 is 150% of what number?

   (A) 20
   (B) 25
   (C) 40
   (D) 45

Percents Practice Set 2

1. What is 75% of 48?

   (A) 12
   (B) 36
   (C) 24
   (D) 32

2. What is 80% of 50?

   (A) 30
   (B) 35
   (C) 40
   (D) 45

3. What is 5% of 700?

   (A) 3.5
   (B) 15
   (C) 35
   (D) 350

4. What is 200% of 16?

   (A) 32
   (B) 36
   (C) 42
   (D) 48

5. 24 is what percent of 30?

   (A) 45%
   (B) 60%
   (C) 80%
   (D) 125%

6. What percent of 10 is 40?

   (A) 20%
   (B) 25%
   (C) 300%
   (D) 400%

7. 63 is what percent of 630?

   (A) 1%
   (B) 2%
   (C) 10%
   (D) 63%

8. 40 is 20% of what number?

   (A) 80
   (B) 200
   (C) 400
   (D) 800

9. 90 is 150% of what number?

   (A) 60
   (B) 75
   (C) 135
   (D) 180

10. 12 is 25% of what number?

   (A) 3
   (B) 4
   (C) 36
   (D) 48

Estimating Practice Set 1

1. Which of the following is the best way to estimate the product 418×68?

   (A) 500×60
   (B) 400×60
   (C) 500×70
   (D) 400×70

2. Which of the following is the best way to estimate the quotient $19.57 \div 4.86$?

   (A) $20 \div 5$
   (B) $20 \div 4$
   (C) $19 \div 4$
   (D) $19 \div 5$

3. Lewis, the principal of a middle school, ordered 223 boxes of pencils for the school year. If each box comes with 82 pencils, which of the following expressions gives the best estimate of the total number of pencils Lewis ordered?

   (A) 200×80
   (B) 200×90
   (C) 300×80
   (D) 300×90

4. What is a reasonable estimation for the value of $\dfrac{38 \times 624}{18}$?

   (A) between 500 and 1,000
   (B) between 1,000 and 1,500
   (C) between 1,500 and 2,000
   (D) between 2,000 and 2,500

5. Lucy went to the mall and bought the following items: a shirt for \$34.49, three pairs of socks that each cost \$2.99, and a pair of shoes that cost \$67.49. What is the estimated total cost of Lucy's items?

   (A) in between \$100 and \$105
   (B) in between \$105 and \$110
   (C) in between \$110 and \$115
   (D) in between \$115 and \$120

6. Mount Everest is 29,029 feet tall. Which of the following mountains has a height closest to $\dfrac{1}{3}$ that of Mount Everest?

   (A) Mount Olympus, which has a height of 7,992 feet
   (B) Mount Norikura, which has a height of 9,928 feet
   (C) Mount Walter, which has a height of 13,123 feet
   (D) Mount Meru, which has a height of 14,980 feet

7. Both jars below would each hold 2 cups of liquid if they were filled to the top. The jars are not filled to the top.

   If the liquids in the two jars are combined, approximately how much total liquid will there be?

   (A) 1 cup
   (B) 1.5 cups
   (C) 2 cups
   (D) 3 cups

8. What is a reasonable estimation for the value of $\dfrac{77 \times 62}{41}$?

   (A) between 50 and 75
   (B) between 75 and 100
   (C) between 100 and 125
   (D) between 125 and 150

9. Each bar below represents one whole candy bar.

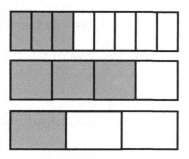

   If the Gina eats the shaded amount of each candy bar, approximately how many total candy bars will she have eaten?

   (A) 1
   (B) $1\dfrac{1}{2}$
   (C) 2
   (D) $2\dfrac{1}{2}$

10. Tim is making trail mix. The ingredients below were evenly mixed and equally divided into 8 bags.

    INGREDIENTS

    9 cups of granola
    7 cups of raisins
    5 cups of peanuts
    4 cups of chocolate chips
    2 cups of almonds

    Approximately how many cups of the mixture were placed in each bag?

    (A) 3
    (B) $3\dfrac{1}{2}$
    (C) 4
    (D) $4\dfrac{1}{2}$

Estimating Practice Set 2

1. Which of the following is the best way to estimate the product 73.87×295.74?

   (A) 80×300
   (B) 100×300
   (C) 70×250
   (D) 70×300

2. Which of the following is the best way to estimate the quotient $577 \div 27$?

   (A) $600 \div 30$
   (B) $600 \div 20$
   (C) $500 \div 30$
   (D) $500 \div 20$

3. Garret ran 17 miles each week for 52 weeks. Which of the following expressions gives the best estimate of the total number of miles Garret ran?

   (A) 10×50
   (B) 10×60
   (C) 20×50
   (D) 20×60

4. Devin bought six items costing $6.99, $3.49, $11.49, $5.49, 12.99, and 0.50. What is the estimated total cost of Devin's items?

   (A) in between $30 and $35
   (B) in between $35 and $40
   (C) in between $40 and $45
   (D) in between $45 and $50

5. What is a reasonable estimation for the value of $\dfrac{61 \times 645}{29}$?

   (A) between 800, and 1,100
   (B) between 1,100 and 1,400
   (C) between 1,400 and 1,700
   (D) between 2,000 and 2,300

6. Lake Superior has an area of 82,100 km^2. Which of the following lakes has an area closest to $\dfrac{1}{4}$ that of Lake Superior?

   (A) Lake Vostok, which has an area of 12,500 km^2
   (B) Lake Balkhash, which has an area of 16,400 km^2
   (C) Lake Ontario, which has an area of 18,960 km^2
   (D) Lake Winnipeg, which has an area of 24,514 km^2

7. Both jars below would each hold 4 cups of liquid if they were filled to the top. The jars are not filled to the top.

   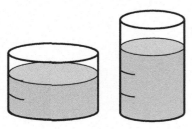

   If the liquids in the two jars are combined, approximately how much total liquid will there be?

   (A) 1.5 cups
   (B) 4 cups
   (C) 4.5 cups
   (D) 5.5 cups

8. Patricia is mixing paint together. She mixes the following amounts of each color paint:

10 pints of red paint
5 pints of blue paint
3 pints of pink paint
1 pint of white paint
1 pint of purple pain

If she splits the paint equally into 6 cans, approximately how many pints of the mixture are in each can?

(A) 3

(B) $3\frac{1}{4}$

(C) $3\frac{3}{4}$

(D) 4

9. What is a reasonable estimation for the value of $\dfrac{121 \times 28}{64}$?

(A) between 25 and 30
(B) between 30 and 45
(C) between 45 and 65
(D) between 65 and 75

10. Each bar below represents one whole candy bar.

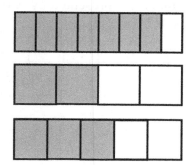

If the Ken eats the shaded amount of each candy bar, approximately how many total candy bars will he have eaten?

(A) $1\frac{1}{2}$

(B) 2

(C) $2\frac{1}{2}$

(D) 3

Number Lines Practice Set 1

1. What number is represented by A on the number line?

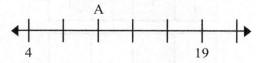

   (A) 6
   (B) 8
   (C) 10
   (D) 13

2. What number is represented by X on the number line?

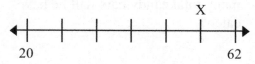

   (A) 48
   (B) 50
   (C) 54
   (D) 55

3. What number is represented by B on the number line?

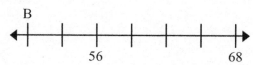

   (A) 50
   (B) 52
   (C) 53
   (D) 54

4. What numbers are represented by A, B, and C on the number line?

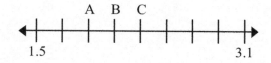

   (A) 1.7, 1.8, 1.9
   (B) 1.9, 2.1, 2.3
   (C) 2.0, 2.2, 2.4
   (D) 2.1, 2.4, 2.7

5. What numbers are represented by X, Y, and Z on the number line?

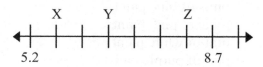

   (A) 5.6, 6.4, 7.6
   (B) 5.6, 6.4, 8.3
   (C) 5.7, 6.7, 7.7
   (D) 5.7, 6.7, 8.2

6. What numbers are represented by J, K, and L on the number line?

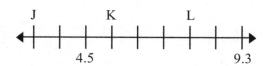

   (A) 2.8, 5.2, 7.9
   (B) 2.9, 5.3, 7.7
   (C) 3.1, 5.2, 7.9
   (D) 3.7, 5.3, 7.7

7. What is the sum of M and N on the number line?

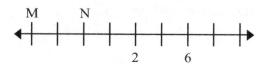

   (A) −8
   (B) −4
   (C) 4
   (D) 8

8. W is the average of V and another number. What is the other number?

(A) 3
(B) 6
(C) 12
(D) 15

9. S is the average of R and another number. What is the other number?

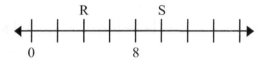

(A) 6
(B) 7
(C) 14
(D) 16

10. What number is represented by G on the number line?

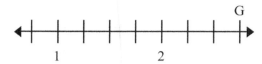

(A) $2\frac{1}{2}$

(B) $2\frac{2}{3}$

(C) $2\frac{3}{4}$

(D) 3

Number Lines Practice Set 2

1. What number is represented by Y on the number line?

(A) 17
(B) 20
(C) 23
(D) 26

2. What number is represented by F on the number line?

(A) $3\frac{1}{4}$

(B) $3\frac{1}{3}$

(C) $3\frac{3}{8}$

(D) $3\frac{1}{2}$

3. What number is represented by B on the number line?

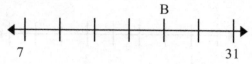

(A) 19
(B) 23
(C) 24
(D) 27

4. What numbers are represented by X, Y, and Z on the number line?

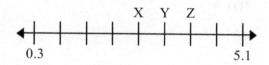

(A) 2.1, 2.7, 3.3
(B) 2.7, 3.3, 3.9
(C) 2.7, 3.4, 4.1
(D) 3.1, 3.8, 4.5

5. What numbers are represented by C, D, and E on the number line?

(A) 4.6, 4.7, 5.8
(B) 4.6, 4.8, 5.6
(C) 4.7, 4.9, 5.5
(D) 4.7, 4.9, 5.7

6. What numbers are represented by A, B, and C on the number line?

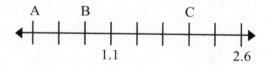

(A) 0.2, 0.8, 2.0
(B) 0.2, 0.8, 2.3
(C) 0.5, 0.9, 1.7
(D) 0.8, 1.0, 2.4

7. What is the sum of P and Q on the number line?

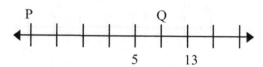

(A) −3
(B) −2
(C) 2
(D) 3

8. What number is represented by X on the number line?

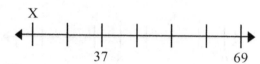

(A) 21
(B) 23
(C) 25
(D) 29

9. N is the average of M and another number. What is the other number?

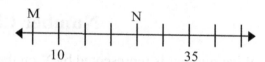

(A) 22.5
(B) 30
(C) 40
(D) 45

10. U is the average of T and another number. What is the other number?

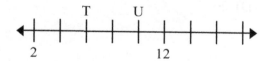

(A) 4
(B) 8
(C) 14
(D) 16

Proportions Practice Set 1

1. Brandon drives his car at a speed of 25 miles per hour. How long will it take Brandon to drive 175 miles?

   (A) 5 hours
   (B) 6 hours
   (C) 7 hours
   (D) 8 hours

2. Mia can read 5 pages every 4 minutes. How long will it take Mia to read 100 pages?

   (A) 80 minutes
   (B) 84 minutes
   (C) 100 minutes
   (D) 125 minutes

3. Morgan can do 50 jumping jacks in 30 seconds. How many jumping jacks can Morgan do in 2 minutes?

   (A) 200 jumping jacks
   (B) 225 jumping jacks
   (C) 250 jumping jacks
   (D) 300 jumping jacks

4. Last weekend, it snowed at a rate of 1.2 inches every 4 hours. At the same rate, how many hours would it take to accumulate 4.2 inches of snow?

   (A) 7 hours
   (B) 8 hours
   (C) 12 hours
   (D) 14 hours

5. If 6 apples cost $9, what is the cost of 8 apples?

   (A) $11
   (B) $12
   (C) $14
   (D) $16

6. Partha and Panu run at the same pace. If Partha runs 4 miles in 22 minutes, how long would it take Panu to run 6 miles?

   (A) 24 minutes
   (B) 33 minutes
   (C) 42 minutes
   (D) 66 minutes

7. If 5 vans can fit 65 people, how many vans are needed to fit 156 people?

   (A) 12 vans
   (B) 13 vans
   (C) 14 vans
   (D) 15 vans

8. At a carnival, you can buy 4 prizes with $3. How much money would you need to buy 10 prizes?

   (A) $6.75
   (B) $7.25
   (C) $7.50
   (D) $13.30

9. A building casts at 15-foot shadow. At the same time, a 5-foot tall child casts a 3-foot shadow. How tall is the building?

   (A) 9 ft
   (B) 20 ft
   (C) 25 ft
   (D) 35 ft

10. If 2.4 inches on map represents 36 miles in real life, how many inches on the map would represent 54 miles in real life?

   (A) 2.2 inches
   (B) 3.6 inches
   (C) 3.8 inches
   (D) 4.8 inches

Proportions Practice Set 2

1. Susan can swim 4 miles in 60 minutes. How many miles can Susan swim in 3 hours?

   (A) 12 miles
   (B) 15 miles
   (C) 18 miles
   (D) 45 miles

2. Gina makes 8 bracelets in 18 minutes. How many bracelets can Gina make in 90 minutes?

   (A) 32 bracelets
   (B) 35 bracelets
   (C) 40 bracelets
   (D) 45 bracelets

3. Daniel can type 120 words in 2 minutes. How long would it take Daniel to type 480 words?

   (A) 4 minutes
   (B) 6 minutes
   (C) 7 minutes
   (D) 8 minutes

4. If 8 buses can fit 160 students, how many buses are needed to fit 60 students?

   (A) 2 buses
   (B) 3 buses
   (C) 4 buses
   (D) 6 buses

5. Yesterday, it rained at a rate of 3.3 inches every 6 hours. At this rate, how many inches would it rain in 10 hours?

   (A) 5.5 inches
   (B) 6 inches
   (C) 7.3 inches
   (D) 11 inches

6. If 16 t-shirts cost $100, what is the cost of 12 t-shirts?

   (A) $65
   (B) $70
   (C) $73
   (D) $75

7. If eight wooden beams can support 50 pounds, how many wooden beams would it take to support 175 pounds?

   (A) 20
   (B) 24
   (C) 28
   (D) 32

8. A recipe calls for 4 tablespoons of sugar for every 12 tablespoons of water. If you use 48 tablespoons of water, how many tablespoons of sugar should you use?

   (A) 12
   (B) 16
   (C) 132
   (D) 144

9. An 18-ft flagpole casts a 24-ft shadow. At the same time of day, how long of a shadow does a 6-ft tall person cast?

   (A) 4 ft
   (B) 4.5 ft
   (C) 6 ft
   (D) 8 ft

10. If 4.2 cm on map represents 30 miles in real life, how many cm on the map would represent 20 miles in real life?

   (A) 2.1 cm
   (B) 2.8 cm
   (C) 3.1 cm
   (D) 6.3 cm

Ratios Practice Set 1

1. There are 16 peaches and 12 pears in a basket. In simplest terms, what is the ratio of peaches to pears?

   (A) 4:3
   (B) 3:4
   (C) 4:7
   (D) 1:2

2. Which of the following ratios is equivalent to 12:9?

   (A) 24:16
   (B) 9:12
   (C) 9:6
   (D) 4:3

3. A bag of marbles contains 15 red marbles, 5 blue marbles, and 10 green marbles. What is the ratio of red to green marbles?

   (A) 1:2
   (B) 3:2
   (C) 3:1
   (D) 2:3

4. The ratio of blue markers to green markers in Lauren's desk is 2:3. If there are 6 blue markers, how many green markers are there?

   (A) 4
   (B) 6
   (C) 9
   (D) 15

5. The ratio of soccer balls to basketballs at a sporting goods store is 4:7. If there are 28 soccer balls, how many basketballs are there?

   (A) 28
   (B) 31
   (C) 42
   (D) 49

6. A basket is filled with green and yellow apples. The ratio of green to yellow apples is 8:3. If there are 88 apples in the basket, how many of the apples are green?

   (A) 24
   (B) 56
   (C) 64
   (D) 80

7. The ratio of boys to girls in a class is 5:4. If there are 20 boys in the class how many total students are in the class?

   (A) 16
   (B) 25
   (C) 36
   (D) 45

8. The ratio of adults to children at a school play is 3:5. If there are 30 children at the play, how many total people are at the play?

   (A) 18
   (B) 48
   (C) 50
   (D) 80

9. There are 8 black blocks and an unknown number of white blocks in a bucket. The ratio of black blocks to total blocks is 4:7. How many white blocks are in the bucket?

(A) 3
(B) 6
(C) 7
(D) 14

10. The ratio of shirts to pants in Jean's closet is 5:2. Which of the following could be the combination of clothes in Jean's closet?

(A) 15 shirts and 6 pants
(B) 10 shirts and 6 pants
(C) 6 shirts and 20 pants
(D) 8 shirts and 40 pants

Ratios Practice Set 2

1. Annalisa has 15 pairs of sandals and 18 pairs of sneakers in her closet. In simplest terms, what is the ratio of pairs of sneakers to pairs of sandals?

(A) 6:5
(B) 5:6
(C) 3:2
(D) 6:11

2. The radius of circle A is 6 yards and the radius of circle B is 9 feet. What is the ratio of the radius of circle A to the radius of circle B?

(A) 2:3
(B) 2:9
(C) 3:2
(D) 2:1

3. A bag of candy contains 12 chocolates, 24 gummies, and 4 hard candies. What is the ratio of gummies to chocolates?

(A) 2:1
(B) 6:1
(C) 1:2
(D) 1:3

4. The ratio of Angela's age to Patricia's age is 6:7. If Patricia is 42 years old, how old is Angela?

(A) 32 years
(B) 36 years
(C) 41 years
(D) 49 years

5. Rachel drank 4 gallons of water last week and 6 gallons of water this week What is the ratio of the amount of water that Rachel drank this week to the total water Rachel drank over the two weeks?

(A) 2:3
(B) 3:2
(C) 3:5
(D) 2:5

6. A bucket is filled with purple and orange marbles. The ratio of purple to orange marbles is 11:4. There 60 marbles in the bucket. How many marbles are purple?

(A) 16
(B) 40
(C) 44
(D) 55

7. The ratio of boys to girls in a class is 3:7. If there are 21 girls in the class, how many total students are in the class?

    (A) 9
    (B) 30
    (C) 49
    (D) 70

8. The ratio of fiction books to non-fiction books in a bookstore is 5:2. If there are 120 non-fiction books, how many fiction books are there?

    (A) 48
    (B) 300
    (C) 360
    (D) 420

9. The ratio of cupcakes to muffins at a bake sale is 7:3. Which of the following could be the combination of cupcakes and muffins at the bake sale?

    (A) 54 cupcakes and 24 muffins
    (B) 30 cupcakes and 70 muffins
    (C) 42 cupcakes and 24 muffins
    (D) 28 cupcakes and 12 muffins

10. There are 6 pink socks and an unknown number of green socks in a drawer. If the ratio of pink socks to total socks is 2:9, how many green socks are in the drawer?

    (A) 7
    (B) 14
    (C) 21
    (D) 27

Probability Practice Set 1

1. There are 3 blue, 7 red, and 5 yellow hats in a closet. If you randomly choose a hat, what is the probability it is blue?

   (A) 1/5
   (B) 1/4
   (C) 3/4
   (D) 4/5

2. A spinner is broken up into 12 sections. 4 sections are black, 6 sections are white, and 2 sections are red. What is the probability of spinning the spinner and NOT landing on a red section?

   (A) 1/6
   (B) 2/3
   (C) 4/5
   (D) 5/6

3. There are 5 milk chocolates, 9 dark chocolates, and 6 white chocolates in a box of chocolates. If you choose a chocolate at random, what is the chance you choose a dark chocolate or a milk chocolate?

   (A) 3/10
   (B) 3/5
   (C) 7/10
   (D) 3/4

4. A bucket is filled with 4 red, 2 blue, 6 purple, and 8 green balls. If a ball is randomly selected from the bucket, which color has a 2 out of 5 chance of being chosen?

   (A) red
   (B) blue
   (C) purple
   (D) green

5. A dartboard is broken up into 18 equal sized sections. If you throw a dart and it hits the board, the probability that you hit a blue section is 2/9. How many sections are blue?

   (A) 2
   (B) 4
   (C) 6
   (D) 9

6. Carlton randomly selects five cards from a stack of cards labeled C through N. If none of the cards repeat, what is the probability that the first card picked is labeled with the letter G?

   (A) 1/12
   (B) 1/11
   (C) 5/12
   (D) 12/26

7. A number between 1 and 20 inclusive is chosen at random. What is the probability that the number is no more than 5?

   (A) 1/5
   (B) 1/4
   (C) 3/4
   (D) 4/5

8. In a class of 30 students, the probability of choosing a student who plays soccer is 3 out of 5. How many students in the class do NOT play soccer?

   (A) 10
   (B) 12
   (C) 15
   (D) 18

9. Lauren has a box filled with different flavored juice boxes: orange, grape, apple, and pineapple. The probability of choosing a grape juice box is 3 out of 8. Which of the following is a possible combination of juice boxes?

(A) 3 grape juice boxes and 8 other
(B) 6 grape juice boxes and 12 other
(C) 8 grape juice boxes and 11 other
(D) 9 grape juice boxes and 15 other

10. The probability of NOT choosing a white marble from a bag of marbles is 5/7. Which of the following could be a possible combination of marbles in the bag?

(A) 5 white marbles and 7 other marbles
(B) 6 white marbles and 21 other marbles
(C) 4 white marbles and 10 other marbles
(D) 15 white marbles and 6 other marbles

Probability Practice Set 2

1. There are 9 gray blocks, 4 brown blocks, and 8 white blocks in a bucket. If you randomly choose a block, what is the probability that it is gray?

(A) 4/21
(B) 3/7
(C) 4/7
(D) 3/4

2. A sheet is filled with 24 equal sized stickers. 12 stickers are silver, 4 stickers are gold, and 8 stickers are pink. If you randomly choose a sticker from the sheet, what is the probability that it is NOT silver or gold?

(A) 1/6
(B) 1/3
(C) 1/2
(D) 2/3

3. A box of waffles is filled with 3 blueberry, 4 plain, and 3 cinnamon waffles. If you pick a waffle at random, what is the probability you pick a blueberry or a cinnamon waffle?

(A) 2/5
(B) 3/5
(C) 2/3
(D) 7/10

4. You flip a six-sided number cube, numbered 1 through 6, four times. What is the probability that the first roll lands on an even number?

(A) 1/6
(B) 1/3
(C) 1/2
(D) 3/5

5. A dartboard is broken up into 15 sections. 5 sections are green, 6 sections are white, 1 section is black, and 3 sections are blue. If you throw a dart and it hits the board, which color has a 1 out of 5 chance of being hit?

   (A) green
   (B) white
   (C) black
   (D) blue

6. A basket is filled with 20 different colored pencils. The probability of choosing a brown pencil from the basket is 2/5. How many brown pencils are in the basket?

   (A) 6
   (B) 8
   (C) 12
   (D) 16

7. A spinner is broken up into 12 equal sized sections. The probability of spinning the spinner and NOT landing on an orange section is 5 out of 6. How many sections are orange?

   (A) 2
   (B) 4
   (C) 5
   (D) 10

8. The probability of choosing a strawberry flavored candy from a bag is 1/4. If there are 12 strawberry flavored candies in the bag, how many other candies are in the bag?

   (A) 24
   (B) 32
   (C) 36
   (D) 48

9. Vanessa has a box of colored markers: orange, red, blue, yellow, and green. The probability of choosing a yellow marker is 2 out of 9. Which of the following is a possible combination of markers?

   (A) 2 yellow markers and 9 other
   (B) 4 yellow markers and 12 other
   (C) 6 yellow markers and 24 other
   (D) 8 yellow markers and 28 other

10. The probability of choosing a pink marble from a bag of marbles is 4/11. Which of the following could NOT be a possible combination of marbles in the bag?

   (A) 4 pink marbles and 7 other marbles
   (B) 8 pink marbles and 22 other marbles
   (C) 16 pink marbles and 28 other marbles
   (D) 20 pink marbles and 35 other marbles

Unit Conversions Practice Set 1

1. How many quarts are in two and a half gallons? (1 gallon = 4 quarts)

    (A) 5 quarts
    (B) 8 quarts
    (C) 10 quarts
    (D) 20 quarts

2. How many grams are in 2.4 kilograms?

    (A) 24 grams
    (B) 240 grams
    (C) 2,400 grams
    (D) 24,000 grams

3. 4,000 milliliters is equal to how many kiloliters?

    (A) 0.004 kiloliters
    (B) 0.04 kiloliters
    (C) 40,000 kiloliters
    (D) 4,000,000 kiloliters

4. 144 inches is equal to how many yards? (1 yard = 3 feet and 1 feet = 12 inches)

    (A) 4 yards
    (B) 6 yards
    (C) 8 yards
    (D) 12 yards

5. How many minutes are in 2 days?

    (A) 1,440 minutes
    (B) 2,880 minutes
    (C) 5,760 minutes
    (D) 172,800 minutes

6. How many feet are in 18 yards? (1 yard = 3 feet)

    (A) 6 feet
    (B) 36 feet
    (C) 54 feet
    (D) 216 feet

7. 120 seconds is equal to how many hours?

    (A) $\dfrac{1}{60}$ hours
    (B) $\dfrac{1}{30}$ hours
    (C) 0.2 hours
    (D) 2 hours

8. 24 cups is equal to how many pints? (1 pint = 2 cups)

    (A) 6 pints
    (B) 8 pints
    (C) 12 pints
    (D) 48 pints

9. Which of the following is equal to 6 quarts? (1 gallon = 4 quarts, 1 quart = 2 pints, 1 pint = 2 cups, 1 cup = 8 fluid ounces)

    (A) 2 gallons
    (B) 12 fluid ounces
    (C) 18 pints
    (D) 24 cups

10. Which of the following is equal to 200 centimeters?

    (A) 0.02 kilometers
    (B) 2 meters
    (C) 20 meters
    (D) 20,000 millimeters

Unit Conversions Practice Set 2

1. 530 milliliters is equal to how many liters?

   (A) 0.53 liters
   (B) 5.3 liters
   (C) 53 liters
   (D) 530,000 liters

2. How many inches are in 24 feet? (1 ft = 12 inches)

   (A) 2 inches
   (B) 96 inches
   (C) 144 inches
   (D) 288 inches

3. How many pints are in one and a half gallons? (1 gallon = 4 quarts, 1 quart = 2 pints)

   (A) 8 pints
   (B) 12 pints
   (C) 16 pints
   (D) 20 pints

4. How many seconds are in half of a day?

   (A) 360 seconds
   (B) 720 seconds
   (C) 43,200 seconds
   (D) 86,400 seconds

5. How many milligrams are in 0.06 kilograms?

   (A) 60 milligrams
   (B) 6,000 milligrams
   (C) 60,000 milligrams
   (D) 600,000 milligrams

6. 9 yards is equal to how many inches? (1 yard = 3 feet, 1 feet = 12 inches)

   (A) 27 inches
   (B) 81 inches
   (C) 108 inches
   (D) 324 inches

7. 4 cups is equal to how many fluid ounces? (1 cup = 8 fluid ounces)

   (A) 8 fluid ounces
   (B) 16 fluid ounces
   (C) 28 fluid ounces
   (D) 32 fluid ounces

8. 195 minutes is equal to how many hours?

   (A) 1.95 hours
   (B) 2.25 hours
   (C) 3.15 hours
   (D) 3.25 hours

9. Which of the following is equal to 70 centimeters?

   (A) 0.007 kilometers
   (B) 0.07 meters
   (C) 0.7 meters
   (D) 7,000 millimeters

10. Which of the following is equal to 16 pints? (1 gallon = 4 quarts, 1 quart = 2 pints, 1 pint = 2 cups, 1 cup = 8 fluid ounces)

    (A) 2 gallons
    (B) 4 quarts
    (C) 32 fluid ounces
    (D) 36 cups

Appropriate Units Practice Set 1

1. Which is the most reasonable unit to use when measuring the volume of water in a lake?

   (A) square feet
   (B) kiloliters
   (C) kilograms
   (D) miles

2. Which is the most reasonable unit to use when measuring the length of a pencil?

   (A) feet
   (B) milliliters
   (C) centimeters
   (D) square inches

3. Which is the most reasonable unit to use when measuring the weight of a truck?

   (A) tons
   (B) milligrams
   (C) cubic centimeters
   (D) kilometers

4. Which is the most reasonable unit to use when measuring the height of a tree?

   (A) miles
   (B) grams
   (C) feet
   (D) square yards

5. Which is the most reasonable unit to use when measuring the height of a person?

   (A) kilometers
   (B) inches
   (C) milligrams
   (D) liters

6. Which is the most reasonable unit to use when measuring the length of football field?

   (A) liters
   (B) grams
   (C) yards
   (D) square feet

7. Which is the most reasonable unit to use when measuring the volume of liquid in a water bottle?

   (A) pounds
   (B) cups
   (C) kilograms
   (D) square feet

8. Which is the most reasonable unit to use when measuring the area of a rug?

   (A) cubic feet
   (B) kilograms
   (C) yards
   (D) square feet

9. Which is the most reasonable unit to use when measuring the distance between two cities?

   (A) inches
   (B) liters
   (C) grams
   (D) kilometers

10. Which is the most reasonable unit to use when measuring the weight of a toothbrush?

   (A) grams
   (B) tons
   (C) centimeters
   (D) milliliters

Appropriate Units Practice Set 2

1. Which is the most reasonable unit to use when measuring the width of a piece of paper?

   (A) miles
   (B) milliliters
   (C) inches
   (D) square centimeters

2. Which is the most reasonable unit to use when measuring the time it takes to drive between two cities?

   (A) seconds
   (B) square feet
   (C) miles
   (D) hours

3. Which is the most reasonable unit to use when measuring the depth of an ocean?

   (A) kilometers
   (B) kilograms
   (C) cubic feet
   (D) square yards

4. Which is the most reasonable unit to use when measuring the volume of water in a pool?

   (A) cubic feet
   (B) square feet
   (C) kilograms
   (D) kilometers

5. Which is the most reasonable unit to use when measuring the weight of a dog?

   (A) meters
   (B) kilograms
   (C) liters
   (D) square centimeters

6. Which is the most reasonable unit to use when measuring the volume of milk in a carton?

   (A) tons
   (B) gallons
   (C) feet
   (D) square centimeters

7. Which is the most reasonable unit to use when measuring the area of a soccer field?

   (A) kiloliters
   (B) miles
   (C) feet
   (D) square yards

8. Which is the most reasonable unit to use when measuring the weight of couch?

   (A) grams
   (B) pounds
   (C) square centimeters
   (D) liters

9. Which is the most reasonable unit to use when measuring the height of a high-rise building?

   (A) liters
   (B) meters
   (C) millimeters
   (D) kilograms

10. Which is the most reasonable unit to use when measuring the circumference of a lake?

    (A) kilometers
    (B) liters
    (C) kilograms
    (D) milliliters

Solving Equations Practice Set 1

1. What is the value of x in the equation $x - 8 = 10$?

   (A) −18
   (B) −2
   (C) 2
   (D) 18

2. Use the equations below to answer the question.

   $9 + m = 28$

   $n - 7 = 16$

   What is the value of $n - m$?

   (A) 4
   (B) 5
   (C) 14
   (D) 28

3. If $2(\square + 5) = 36$, then what does $\square$ equal?

   (A) 12
   (B) 13
   (C) 18
   (D) 23

4. Use the equations below to answer the question.

   $a \div 3 = 9$

   $b + 3 = 11$

   What is the sum of a and b?

   (A) 11
   (B) 29
   (C) 35
   (D) 41

5. What is the value of y in the equation

   $\dfrac{y}{3} - 7 = 13$?

   (A) 2
   (B) 18
   (C) 45
   (D) 60

6. Use the equations below to answer the question.

   $-5x = 20$

   $12 - y = 9$

   What is the product of x and y?

   (A) −15
   (B) −12
   (C) 12
   (D) 15

7. What is the value of x in the equation $6 - 2x = 4$?

   (A) −1
   (B) 1
   (C) 2
   (D) 5

8. If $\dfrac{20}{\Delta} + 8 = 12$, then what does Δ equal?

   (A) 1
   (B) 4
   (C) 5
   (D) 10

9. What is the value of b in the equation $12 + b = 18 - b$?

(A) 3
(B) 4
(C) 6
(D) 10

10. Use the equations below to answer the question.

$$24 \div x = 8$$
$$x + y = 14$$

What is the value of y?

(A) 3
(B) 6
(C) 10
(D) 11

Solving Equations Practice Set 2

1. What is the value of x in the equation $x + 7 = 16$?

(A) 9
(B) 11
(C) 22
(D) 23

2. If $4(\bigcirc - 8) = 20$, then what does $\bigcirc$ equal?

(A) 5
(B) 7
(C) 13
(D) 24

3. Use the equations below to answer the question.

$$a + 11 = 17$$
$$23 - b = 10$$

What is the value of $a + b$?

(A) 19
(B) 21
(C) 29
(D) 41

4. What is the value of a in the equation $5a + 10 = 25$?

(A) 2
(B) 3
(C) 5
(D) 7

5. Use the equations below to answer the question.

$$\frac{x}{3} = -8$$
$$6y = -12$$

What is the product of x and y?

(A) -48
(B) -12
(C) 12
(D) 48

6. If $\dfrac{@}{2} - 12 = 8$, then what does $@$ equal?

(A) 10
(B) 16
(C) 28
(D) 40

7. What is the value of k in the equation $2k - 6 = k + 2$?

(A) 2
(B) 4
(C) 6
(D) 8

8. What is the value of b in the equation $\dfrac{12}{b} + 5 = 7$?

(A) 2
(B) 6
(C) 12
(D) 24

9. Use the equations below to answer the question.

$$4n = 28$$
$$16 - m = 7$$

What is the value of $m - n$?

(A) 1
(B) 2
(C) 4
(D) 16

10. Use the equations below to answer the question.

$$x - 5 = 7$$
$$xy = 72$$

What is the value of y?

(A) 6
(B) 7
(C) 12
(D) 36

Creating Equations and Expressions Practice Set 1

1. Vishak has x dollars. After Vishak gave $6 to Hasti, he had y dollars remaining. Which of the following equations can be used to find out how much money Vishak started with?

   (A) $x = y - 6$
   (B) $x = 6y$
   (C) $x = y + 6$
   (D) $x + y = 6$

2. The total cost of buying eight boxes of paper is $76. If c represents the cost of one box of paper, which equation can be used to find the price of one box of paper?

   (A) $76 \div c = 8$
   (B) $76 \times 8 = c$
   (C) $c \div 8 = 76$
   (D) $76 - c = 8$

3. The total price of three apples and one banana is $3.50. If the cost of each apple is twice the cost of each banana, which equation can be used to find the cost of each banana, b?

   (A) $b + 3 = 3.50$
   (B) $7b = 3.50$
   (C) $4b = 3.50$
   (D) $5b = 3.50$

4. Which of the following represents "eight less than six times a number"?

   (A) $6x - 8$
   (B) $8x - 6$
   (C) $8 - 6x$
   (D) $6 - 8x$

5. Which expression can be read as three times the sum of a number and 8 is equal to 5 less than half of the number?

   (A) $3(n + 8) = 5 - \dfrac{1}{2}n$
   (B) $3(n + 8) = \dfrac{1}{2}n - 5$
   (C) $3n + 8 = \dfrac{1}{2}n - 5$
   (D) $3n + 8 = 5 - \dfrac{1}{2}n$

6. Which of the following represents "four more than twice a number is 16"?

   (A) $2(n + 4) = 16$
   (B) $4n + 2 = 16$
   (C) $2n - 4 = 16$
   (D) $2n + 4 = 16$

7. If the volume of a rectangular prism is 60 m^3, which equation can be used to determine the height of the rectangular prism? ($V = lwh$, where V = volume, l = length, w = width, and h = height)

   (A) $h = 60lw$
   (B) $h = \dfrac{60l}{w}$
   (C) $h = \dfrac{lw}{60}$
   (D) $h = \dfrac{60}{lw}$

8. Ryan went to the store and bought a pair of shoes for $50 and six pairs of socks. If he spent a total of $68, which equation can be used to find the cost of each pair of socks, s?

(A) $50 + s = 68$
(B) $6(50) + s = 68$
(C) $50 + 6s = 68$
(D) $50 - 6s = 68$

9. Brenda and Gerald were having a contest to see who could eat the most marshmallows. Brenda ate x marshmallows and Gerald ate y marshmallows. If Brenda won the contest, which expression can be used to find how many more marshmallows Brenda ate than Gerald?

(A) $x + y$
(B) $x - y$
(C) $y - x$
(D) $x \div y$

10. The area of a triangle is 40 square inches. Which equation can be used to determine the height of the triangle?

($A = \dfrac{1}{2}bh$, where A = area, b = base, and h = height.)

(A) $h = \dfrac{2(40)}{b}$

(B) $h = \dfrac{40b}{2}$

(C) $h = 2(40) \times b$
(D) $h = 2(40) - b$

Creating Equations and Expressions Practice Set 2

1. Roger and Cory play on the same basketball team. During the last game, Roger and Cory scored a total of 34 points. If Roger scored 6 more points than Cory, which equation can be used to determine how many points Cory scored. (c represents how many points Cory scored.)

   (A) $c+6=34$
   (B) $c-6=34$
   (C) $2c+6=34$
   (D) $2c-6=34$

2. Sonja has x dollars on Monday. On Tuesday, Sonja makes \$25 babysitting, and now she has y dollars. Which of the following equations can be used to find out how much money Sonja has after babysitting?

   (A) $x=y+25$
   (B) $x=25-y$
   (C) $x-y=25$
   (D) $y-x=25$

3. Alice is older than Brett. If Alice is a years old and Brett is b years old, which expression can help answer the question, "Alice is how many times as old as Brett?"

   (A) ab
   (B) $a+b$
   (C) $a \div b$
   (D) $b \div a$

4. Which of the following represents "five more than half of a number is three less than twice the number?"

   (A) $\dfrac{1}{2}n+5=2n-3$

   (B) $\dfrac{1}{2}n+5=3-2n$

   (C) $\dfrac{1}{2}(n+5)=2n-3$

   (D) $\dfrac{1}{2}(n+5)=3-2n$

5. Which of the following represents "ten less than one fourth of a number"?

   (A) $\dfrac{x-10}{4}$

   (B) $\dfrac{1}{4}x-10$

   (C) $10-\dfrac{1}{4}x$

   (D) $\dfrac{10-x}{4}$

6. Which of the following represents "four times the sum of a number and one is twenty-four"?

   (A) $4n+1=24$
   (B) $4(n+1)=24$
   (C) $4(n-1)=24$
   (D) $4n-1=24$

7. Ryan has 12 action figures and b boxes of toy cars. If each box of toy cars has 10 toy cars in it, and Ryan has a total of 42 action figures and toy cars, which equation can be used to find how many boxes of toy cars Ryan has?

(A) $10(12)+b=42$

(B) $12+10b=42$

(C) $12+\dfrac{b}{10}=42$

(D) $12+\dfrac{10}{b}=42$

8. Junior purchased a notebook for $12 and b boxes of pencils. If each box of pencils costs $3, which expressions represents the total amount of money that Junior spent?

(A) $12+b$

(B) $12(3)+3b$

(C) $12+3b$

(D) $12b+3$

9. If the area of a rectangle is 24 m², which equation can be used to determine the base of the rectangle? ($A=bh$ where $A=$ area, $b=$ base, and $h=$ height.)

(A) $b=\dfrac{24}{h}$

(B) $b=24h$

(C) $b=24-h$

(D) $b=\dfrac{h}{24}$

10. The volume of a pyramid is 75 in³. Which equation can be used to determine the width of the pyramid? ($V=\dfrac{1}{3}lwh$, where $V=$ volume, $l=$ length, $w=$ width, and $h=$ height)

(A) $w=3(75)\times lh$

(B) $w=\dfrac{(75)}{3lh}$

(C) $w=3(75)-lh$

(D) $w=\dfrac{3(75)}{lh}$

Function Tables Practice Set 1

1. Use the table below to answer the question.

Input	Output
4	1
6	3
8	5
10	7

What output will be created with an input of 17?

(A) 14
(B) 15
(C) 18
(D) 20

2. Use the table to determine the rule.

Input a	Output b
4	9
5	11
8	17
10	21

What is the rule for the table?

(A) $a = b - 5$
(B) $b = 2a + 1$
(C) $b = 3a - 4$
(D) $a = b - 6$

3. Use the table to determine the rule.

Input x	Output y
1	1
2	0
7	−5
10	−8

What is the rule for the table?

(A) $x = y$
(B) $y = x - 12$
(C) $y = -x + 2$
(D) $y = -x - 2$

4. Use the table below to answer the question.

Input	Output
12	35
15	44
18	a
21	62
24	71

What is the value of a?

(A) 53
(B) 54
(C) 58
(D) 80

5. Use the table below to answer the question.

Input	Output
7	16
5	12
3	8
1	4

Which input value creates an output value of 24?

(A) 8
(B) 11
(C) 12
(D) 13

6. Use the table below to answer the question.

Input	Output
1	2
2	5
3	8
4	11
x	20

What is the value of x?

(A) 5
(B) 7
(C) 8
(D) 10

7. Use the table to determine the rule.

Input ◆	Output ☐
1	6
2	9
4	15
8	27

What is the rule for the table?

(A) $5◆ + 1 = ☐$
(B) $2(◆ + 1) = ☐$
(C) $◆ + 3 = ☐$
(D) $3(◆ + 1) = ☐$

8. Use the table to determine the rule.

Input ◆	Output ☐
9	−2
5	0
3	1
−1	3

What is the rule for the table?

(A) $◆ = 5 − 2☐$
(B) $◆ = ☐ + 11$
(C) $◆ = 5 + 2☐$
(D) $◆ = 2☐ + 1$

9. Use the table below to answer the question.

Input □	Output Δ
1	x
2	2
y	8
7	17

The rule for the table is $\Delta = 3\square - 4$. What does $x + y$ equal?

(A) 3
(B) 4
(C) 5
(D) 6

10. Use the table below to answer the question.

Input	Output
x	10
20	12
25	14
30	16
45	y

What does $x + y$ equal?

(A) 33
(B) 35
(C) 37
(D) 39

Function Tables Practice Set 2

1. Use the table below to answer the question.

Input a	Output b
0	5
x	3
−4	y
−5	0

The rule for the table above is $a = b - 5$. What does $x - y$ equal?

(A) −3
(B) −2
(C) −1
(D) 3

2. Use the table to determine the rule.

Input ◆	Output □
3	4
4	6
7	12
12	22

What is the rule for the table?

(A) $3\blacklozenge - 5 = \square$
(B) $\blacklozenge + 1 = \square$
(C) $\blacklozenge + 5 = \square$
(D) $2\blacklozenge - 2 = \square$

3. Use the table to determine the rule.

Input ◆	Output ☐
–2	1
0	2
4	4
6	5

What is the rule for the table?

(A) $\blacklozenge = 2 \times (\square - 2)$
(B) $\blacklozenge = \square - 3$
(C) $\blacklozenge = -2 \times \square$
(D) $\blacklozenge = 2 \times (\square + 2)$

4. Use the table below to answer the question.

Input	Output
3	19
5	31
7	43
9	55
x	73

What is the value of x?

(A) 10
(B) 11
(C) 12
(D) 14

5. Use the table below to answer the question.

Input	Output
19	13
21	15
23	17
25	19

What output will be created with an input of 47?

(A) 21
(B) 39
(C) 41
(D) 54

6. Use the table to determine the rule.

Input w	Output z
10	17
12	21
15	27
20	37

What is the rule for the table?

(A) $z = w + 7$
(B) $z = 3w - 13$
(C) $z = w + 9$
(D) $z = 2w - 3$

7. Use the table to determine the rule.

Input x	Output y
4	−3
8	−1
14	2
20	5

What is the rule for the table?

(A) $y = x - 7$

(B) $y = \dfrac{1}{2}x - 5$

(C) $y = -x + 1$

(D) $y = x \div 4$

8. Use the table below to answer the question.

Input	Output
□	4
18	9
20	10
44	△
52	26

What does □ + △ equal?

(A) 24
(B) 30
(C) 38
(D) 90

9. Use the table below to answer the question.

Input	Output
10	4
12	5
18	8
24	b
28	13

What is the value of b?

(A) 9
(B) 10
(C) 11
(D) 12

10. Use the table below to answer the question.

Input	Output
4	9
8	17
12	25
14	29

Which input value creates an output value of 61?

(A) 18
(B) 20
(C) 28
(D) 30

Mixed Word Problems Practice Set 1

1. During a basketball game, Wilson scored 18 points. Ryan scored 7 more points than Wilson. How many points did they score all together?

   (A) 25
   (B) 29
   (C) 32
   (D) 43

2. Leo went to the school carnival last weekend and played a total of 28 games. If he lost 6 fewer games than he won, how many games did his lose?

   (A) 8 games
   (B) 11 games
   (C) 17 games
   (D) 21 games

3. Benji is baking cookies for his school's bake sale. He split his cookies into 5 boxes, and each box had 25 cookies. If he sold each cookie for $2, how much money did Benji make?

   (A) $10
   (B) $50
   (C) $200
   (D) $250

4. Caroline wrote down an even number greater than 12 and less than 18. When Rich tried to guess the number, Caroline told him that it is greater than 14 and less than 20. What is Caroline's number?

   (A) 14
   (B) 15
   (C) 16
   (D) 18

5. Hansel has 56 pieces of candy and Gretel has 40 pieces of candy. How many pieces of candy will Hansel need to give Gretel if each are to have the same number?

   (A) 8
   (B) 9
   (C) 12
   (D) 16

6. Vinny wrote down a whole number greater than 30 and less than 40. When Rea tried to guess the number, Vinny told her that it was a multiple of four and six. What is Vinny's number?

   (A) 24
   (B) 32
   (C) 36
   (D) 38

7. Harold currently has $ −40 in his bank account. Each week he deposits $20 into his account. How much money will he have saved after 14 weeks?

   (A) $240
   (B) $260
   (C) $280
   (D) $320

8. Eight people split the cost of an office space equally each month. Right now they each pay $75. If three people decide they don't need the office space anymore, and the remaining people split the cost equally, how much will each person pay?

   (A) $15
   (B) $100
   (C) $120
   (D) $200

9. Anthony is 8 inches taller than Lucas, but 3 inches shorter than Danielle. Danielle is twice as tall as Yasmin. If Yasmin is 36 inches tall, what is the combined height of Anthony and Lucas?

(A) 22 inches
(B) 130 inches
(C) 136 inches
(D) 146 inches

10. The total combined ages of Ronnie, Sam, and Jenny is 42. If Ronnie is twice as old as Sam and Jenny is half as old as Sam, what is Sam's age?

(A) 6 years
(B) 12 years
(C) 16 years
(D) 24 years

Mixed Word Problems Practice Set 2

1. A middle school is made up of sixth grade, seventh grade, and eighth grade students. There are a total of 254 students at the school. If there are 97 sixth graders and 84 seventh graders, how many eighth graders are at the school?

(A) 64
(B) 73
(C) 75
(D) 181

2. Owen wrote down an odd number greater than 20 and less than 30. Liam guessed the number 29, which was wrong. Owen then told Liam that the number is greater than 25 and less than 32. What is Owen's number?

(A) 25
(B) 27
(C) 29
(D) 31

3. Carla plants carrots in her garden. Last week, she planted 24 carrots. This week, she planted 3 equal rows of 6 carrots. If she wants to split all of her carrots equally into 6 boxes, how many carrots will be in each box?

(A) 4
(B) 6
(C) 7
(D) 8

4. Greg is trying to pay off his college loans. He owes $4200 on one of his loans and $1200 on his other loan. If he pays a total of $300 every month, how many months will it take for his to pay off both of his loans?

(A) 14 months
(B) 17 months
(C) 18 months
(D) 19 months

5. Maria has $4 fewer than twice the amount of money that her brother has. If her brother has $48, how much do Maria and her brother have all together?

    (A) $88
    (B) $92
    (C) $136
    (D) $140

6. Christina wrote down a whole number greater than 20 and less than 29. When Rebecca tried to guess the number, Christina told her that it was a prime number. What is Christina's number?

    (A) 23
    (B) 25
    (C) 27
    (D) 29

7. There are 25 people waiting in line for a ride at an amusement park. If each car can hold no more than 7 people, and no two cars can have the same number of people, what is the least number of cars that can fit all 25 people?

    (A) 3
    (B) 4
    (C) 5
    (D) 6

8. In a basketball game, the winning team scored 8 more points than the losing team. Both teams scored 94 points all together. How many points did the losing team score?

    (A) 39 points
    (B) 43 points
    (C) 51 points
    (D) 55 points

9. The total combined weight of a cylinder, a cube, and a prism is 30 grams. If the cylinder weighs 5 more grams than the cube, and the prism's weight is half of the cubes, what is the weight of the prism?

    (A) 5 grams
    (B) 8 grams
    (C) 10 grams
    (D) 15 grams

10. Tom's age is one third of Lara's age. Lara is 14 years younger than Brynn. If Tom is 18 years old, how old is Brynn?

    (A) 20 years
    (B) 40 years
    (C) 62 years
    (D) 68 years

Mean, Median, Mode, and Range Practice Set 1

1. Find the mean of 10, 340, 15, 223, 55, and 77.

   (A) 120
   (B) 130
   (C) 150
   (D) 720

2. Find the median of the following set of numbers: 45, 48, 45, 52, 60, 120, 45, 90

   (A) 45
   (B) 48
   (C) 50
   (D) 52

3. Find the mode of 23, 47, 7, 19, 26, 47, and 80, 47, 19.

   (A) 19
   (B) 23
   (C) 26
   (D) 47

4. Find the range of 18, 96, 7, 13, 55, 88, and 35.

   (A) 81
   (B) 83
   (C) 89
   (D) 96

5. Brian and his twin brother are 15 years old. Their mother is 45 years old, their father is 50 years old, and their younger sister is 5 years old. What is the mean age of Brian and his family members?

   (A) 23 years
   (B) 26 years
   (C) 28.75 years
   (D) 32.5 years

6. Which of the following statements is true given the data set: 20, 20, 20, 30, 40, 50, 60?

   (A) The median is the same as the mode.
   (B) The median is higher than the range.
   (C) The range is lower than the mode.
   (D) The mean is higher than the mode.

7. Which of the following statements is false given the data set: 45, 50, 3, 40, 45, 45?

   (A) The mean is lower than the median.
   (B) The mode is equal to the median.
   (C) The range is lower than the median.
   (D) The mode is higher than the mean.

8. The range of ages of a group of people is 23 years. If the oldest member of the group is 41 years old, how old is the youngest member?

   (A) 8 years
   (B) 18 years
   (C) 28 years
   (D) 64 years

9. What is the average of $3\frac{1}{2}$, $1\frac{1}{4}$, $2\frac{3}{4}$, and 5?

   (A) $3\frac{1}{8}$

   (B) $3\frac{1}{4}$

   (C) $4\frac{1}{4}$

   (D) $12\frac{1}{2}$

10. Five kittens weigh 1.4 pounds, $3\frac{5}{8}$ pounds, $2\frac{2}{3}$ pounds, $5\frac{1}{3}$ pounds, and 7.6 pounds respectively. What is the average weight of all five kittens?

(A) $3\frac{7}{8}$ pounds

(B) $4\frac{1}{8}$ pounds

(C) $4\frac{1}{4}$ pounds

(D) $4\frac{3}{4}$ pounds

Mean, Median, Mode, and Range Practice Set 2

1. Find the mode of the following set of numbers: 13, 86, 14, 86, 23, 23, 86, 19, 7, 12, 1

   (A) 19
   (B) 23
   (C) 85
   (D) 86

2. Find the median of the following set of numbers: 4, 18, 23, 17, 6, 29, 4

   (A) 4
   (B) 15
   (C) 17
   (D) 18

3. Which of the following statements is true given the data set: 15, 18, 15, 15, 16, 17?

   (A) The mean is higher than the mode.
   (B) The mean is lower than the range.
   (C) The median is equal to the mode.
   (D) The median is equal to the mean.

4. Find the mean of the data set: 80, 53, 22, 57, 100, 30, 8

   (A) 50
   (B) 53
   (C) 57
   (D) 70

5. What is the range of 22, 87, 60, 31 31, 19, 40, and 50?

   (A) 19
   (B) 65
   (C) 68
   (D) 87

6. Which of the following statements is false given the data set: 10, 25, 20, 20, 25, 30, 20, 30?

   (A) The mean is higher than the mode.
   (B) The median is higher than the range.
   (C) The mode is equal to the range.
   (D) The median is equal to the mode.

7. Robert has two twin daughters, one son, and a wife. Robert is 50 years old, his twin daughters are 12 years old, his wife is 45 years old, and his son is 6 years old. What is the average of their ages?

(A) 20 years
(B) 25 years
(C) 28.25 years
(D) 31.25 years

8. What is the average of $6\frac{1}{8}$, $3\frac{1}{4}$, $\frac{3}{2}$, $2\frac{1}{2}$ and $2\frac{5}{8}$?

(A) $2\frac{4}{5}$

(B) $3\frac{1}{5}$

(C) $3\frac{1}{4}$

(D) $3\frac{1}{2}$

9. In a group of seven consecutive odd numbers, the median is 13. What is the smallest number in the group?

(A) 7
(B) 9
(C) 10
(D) 19

10. On Monday it rained $\frac{9}{10}$ inches, it rained $\frac{3}{5}$ inches on Tuesday and Wednesday, and it rained $1\frac{1}{10}$ inches on Thursday, Friday, and Saturday. What is the average rainfall over the six days?

(A) $\frac{4}{5}$ inches

(B) $\frac{9}{10}$ inches

(C) $1\frac{1}{10}$ inches

(D) $1\frac{4}{5}$ inches

Charts, Graphs, and Tables Practice Set 1

1. The table below shows the items that Sean bought at the farmers market.

Item	Price for One	Total Spent on Items
Orange	$0.50	$5.50
Apple	$1.25	
Avocado	$1.50	$6.00
Onion	$0.75	$3.75

If Sean spent a total of $21.50, how many apples did he buy?

(A) 4
(B) 5
(C) 6
(D) 6.5

2. The chart below shows the number of tickets a group of four kids won at the carnival.

Hank	⬭⬭⬭
Danny	⬭⬭⬭⬭⬭⬭
Gina	⬭⬭⬭⬭
Greta	⬭⬭

⬭ = 25 tickets

How many more tickets did Danny win than Greta?

(A) 4
(B) 75
(C) 50
(D) 100

3. The graph below shows the heart rates of three people over the course of a 30-minute workout.

	Julie	Kenny	Lauren
Start	70 BPM	75 BPM	83 BPM
10 min	90 BPM	100 BPM	93 BPM
20 min	120 BPM	120 BPM	103 BPM
30 min	160 BPM	135 BPM	113 BPM

At 30 minutes, how much higher was Julie's heart rate than Lauren's?

(A) 15 BPM
(B) 17 BPM
(C) 37 BPM
(D) 47 BPM

4. The bar graph below shows the favorite colors of a group of children. What is the difference between the number of girls who chose yellow and the number of boys who chose red?

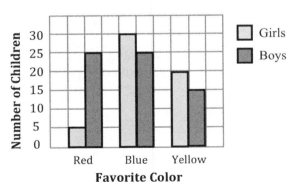

(A) 1
(B) 5
(C) 15
(D) 20

5. A survey of 80 students' favorite colors is displayed in the circle graph.

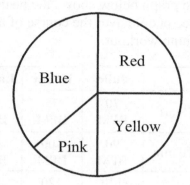

About what fraction of students chose blue as their favorite color?

(A) $\frac{1}{4}$

(B) $\frac{3}{8}$

(C) $\frac{1}{2}$

(D) $\frac{2}{3}$

6. The table below shows the price of red and blue paint at two different paint stores. Based on the table below, what is the price of 3 gallons of red paint from Paint With Me?

	Red Paint (per gallon)	Blue Paint (per gallon)
Paint With Me	$2.75	$3.50
Paint and More	$4.25	$3.25

(A) $8.25
(B) $8.75
(C) $10.50
(D) $12.75

7. Use the Venn diagram to answer the question.

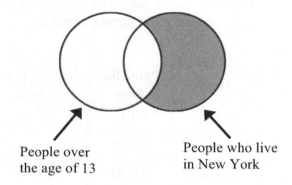

People over the age of 13   People who live in New York

Which person could be found in the shaded part of the Venn diagram?

(A) Julie who is 12 years old and lives in California
(B) Manny who is 54 years old and lives in New Jersey
(C) Luis who is 13 years old and lives in New York
(D) Brenda who is 18 years old and lives in New York

8. The graph shows the revenue of a business.

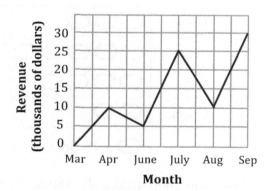

Between which 2 months was there the least change in revenue?

(A) April and June
(B) March and April
(C) July and August
(D) August and September

9. Use the Venn diagram below to answer the question.

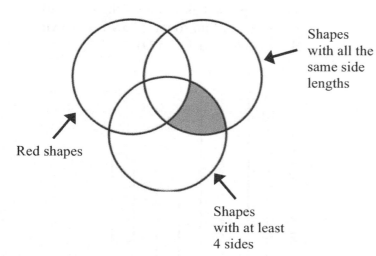

Shapes with all the same side lengths

Red shapes

Shapes with at least 4 sides

Which shape could be found in the shaded part of the Venn diagram?

(A) A yellow equilateral triangle
(B) A red square
(C) A green rectangle
(D) A blue regular pentagon

10. Five students recorded the number of minutes spent completing a homework assignment and recorded their data in the graph shown.

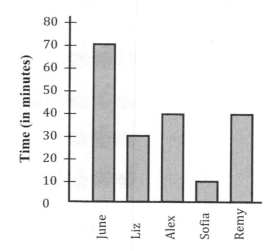

Which of the following is false based on the graph?

(A) Alex spent the same amount of time as Liz and Sofia combined
(B) The mean is between 35 and 40.
(C) The median is lower than the mode
(D) The range is higher than the number of minutes Remy took to complete the assignment.

Charts, Graphs, and Tables Practice Set 2

1. Katia, Lucille, David, and Reggie went apple picking. The chart below shows how many apples they each picked.

Katia	🍎🍎🍎
Lucille	🍎🍎🍎🍎🍎
Reggie	🍎🍎🍎
David	🍎🍎🍎🍎

🍎 = 10 apples

How many total apples did David and Lucille pick?

(A) 9
(B) 60
(C) 80
(D) 90

2. The table below shows the number of men and women who do their own laundry. What fraction of women don't do their own laundry?

	Men	Women	Total
Do Own Laundry	8	18	26
Don't Do Own Laundry	12	12	24
Total	20	30	50

(A) 6/25
(B) 9/25
(C) 2/5
(D) 3/5

3. The bar graph below shows the snowfall, in inches, of four towns (Town A, Town B, Town C, and Town D)

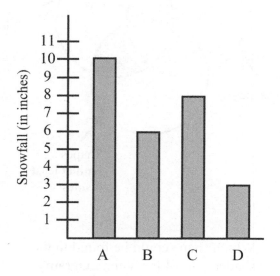

Which statement is true based on the graph?

(A) The difference between the snowfall in Town A and Town C equals the snowfall in Town D.
(B) The sum of the snowfall in Town A and Town D equals the sum of the snowfall in Town B and Town C.
(C) The difference between the snowfall in Town C and Town B is greater than the snowfall in Town D.
(D) The sum of the snowfall in Town B and Town D is less than the snowfall in Town A.

4. The table shows the items Bethany bought at the mall.

Item	Price for One	Total Items Purchased
Shirt	$10	4
Socks	$2	8
Hat	$8	1
Shorts	$12	?

If Bethany spent a total of $112, how many pairs of shorts did she buy?

(A) 3
(B) 4
(C) 6
(D) 48

5. A survey of 100 students' favorite pets is displayed in the circle graph.

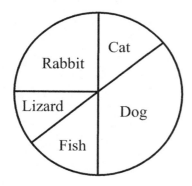

About what fraction of students chose rabbits as their favorite pets?

(A) $\dfrac{1}{8}$

(B) $\dfrac{1}{5}$

(C) $\dfrac{1}{4}$

(D) $\dfrac{1}{2}$

6. The table below shows the temperature of three buckets of water.

	Bucket 1	Bucket 2	Bucket 3
Start	42° F	30° F	60° F
20 min	54° F	36° F	63° F
40 min	66° F	41° F	67° F
60 min	78° F	45° F	72° F

What was the difference between the temperatures of Bucket 1 and Bucket 3 after 20 minutes?

(A) 9° F
(B) 11° F
(C) 18° F
(D) 27° F

7. The graph shows the revenue of a business.

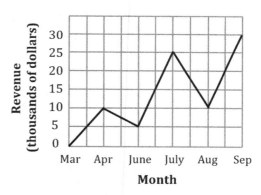

What was the difference in revenue between September and June?

(A) $5,000
(B) $20,000
(C) $25,000
(D) $30,000

8. Use the Venn diagram to answer the question.

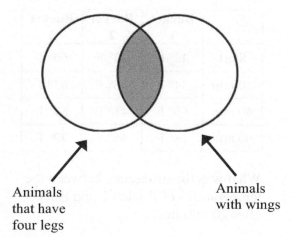

Animals that have four legs

Animals with wings

Which animals could be found in the shaded part of the Venn diagram?

(A) Fish
(B) Chickens
(C) Cats
(D) None of the above

9. The graph below shows the favorite pet of a group of 3rd and 4th graders.

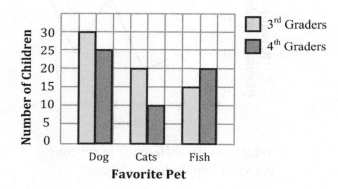

What is the difference between the number of 4th graders who like dogs and 3rd graders who like fish?

(A) 10
(B) 15
(C) 20
(D) 25

10. Use the Venn diagram below to answer the question.

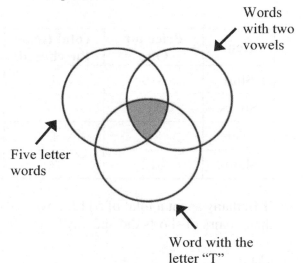

Words with two vowels

Five letter words

Word with the letter "T"

Which word could be found in the shaded part of the Venn diagram?

(A) "Plant"
(B) "Later"
(C) "Teas"
(D) "Plead"

Naming Shapes Practice Set 1

1. What is the name of a triangle with exactly two equal sides?

   (A) isosceles
   (B) scalene
   (C) obtuse
   (D) acute

2. What is the name of a rectangle with all equal sides?

   (A) square
   (B) parallelogram
   (C) pentagon
   (D) trapezoid

3. What is the name of the shape below?

   (A) pentagon
   (B) hexagon
   (C) octagon
   (D) heptagon

4. How many sides does an octagon have?

   (A) 5
   (B) 6
   (C) 7
   (D) 8

5. Which of the following is a parallelogram?

   (A) trapezoid
   (B) rhombus
   (C) pentagon
   (D) circle

6. What type of triangle is shown below?

   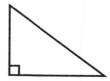

   (A) acute
   (B) equiangular
   (C) obtuse
   (D) right

7. Which statement is false?

   (A) a square is a rectangle
   (B) a rectangle is a parallelogram
   (C) a parallelogram is a quadrilateral
   (D) a rhombus is a square

8. What is the name of the shape below?

   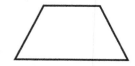

   (A) parallelogram
   (B) rhombus
   (C) trapezoid
   (D) rectangle

9. Which shape is NOT a quadrilateral?

   (A) trapezoid
   (B) kite
   (C) rectangle
   (D) pentagon

10. Which of the following shapes has the least number of sides?

    (A) parallelogram
    (B) pentagon
    (C) octagon
    (D) heptagon

Naming Shapes Practice Set 2

1. What is the name of a triangle with three equal sides?

   (A) equilateral
   (B) isosceles
   (C) congruent
   (D) scalene

2. What type of triangle is shown below?

   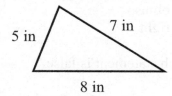

   (A) isosceles
   (B) scalene
   (C) equiangular
   (D) equilateral

3. Which shape is NOT a parallelogram?

   (A) rhombus
   (B) square
   (C) trapezoid
   (D) rectangle

4. Which shape is a quadrilateral?

   (A) rhombus
   (B) pentagon
   (C) triangle
   (D) circle

5. What is the name of the shape below?

   (A) quadrilateral
   (B) hexagon
   (C) octagon
   (D) pentagon

6. How many sides does a heptagon have?

   (A) 5
   (B) 6
   (C) 7
   (D) 8

7. Which statement is true?

   (A) a rectangle is a quadrilateral
   (B) a trapezoid is a parallelogram
   (C) a pentagon has more sides than a hexagon
   (D) an octagon has six sides

8. What is the name of the shape below?

   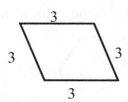

   (A) square
   (B) trapezoid
   (C) rectangle
   (D) rhombus

9. Which shape has the most number of sides?

   (A) triangle
   (B) hexagon
   (C) rhombus
   (D) pentagon

10. A square is all of the following EXCEPT

    (A) a rectangle
    (B) a quadrilateral
    (C) a parallelogram
    (D) a pentagon

Basic Area and Perimeter Practice Set 1

1. What is the area of a square with a side length of 5 inches?

   (A) 10 in^2
   (B) 20 in^2
   (C) 25 in^2
   (D) 50 in^2

2. What is the perimeter of the rectangle below?

   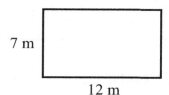

   (A) 19 m
   (B) 38 m
   (C) 48 m
   (D) 84 m

3. A triangle has a height of 6 ft and a base of 8 ft. What is the area of the triangle?

   (A) 14 ft^2
   (B) 24 ft^2
   (C) 28 ft^2
   (D) 48 ft^2

4. What is the perimeter of the triangle below?

   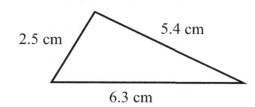

   (A) 14.2 cm
   (B) 14.4 cm
   (C) 28.4 cm
   (D) 28.8 cm

5. What is the side length of a square with a perimeter of 36 inches?

   (A) 6 inches
   (B) 9 inches
   (C) 12 inches
   (D) 18 inches

6. What is the area of a rectangle with a width of 3 inches and a length of 9 inches?

   (A) 12 in^2
   (B) 21 in^2
   (C) 24 in^2
   (D) 27 in^2

7. What is the area of the isosceles trapezoid below?

   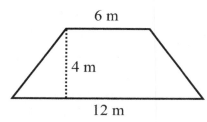

   (A) 24 m^2
   (B) 32 m^2
   (C) 36 m^2
   (D) 48 m^2

8. What is the perimeter of a regular octagon with a side length of 7 cm?

   (A) 35 cm
   (B) 42 cm
   (C) 49 cm
   (D) 56 cm

9. What is the perimeter of the shape below?

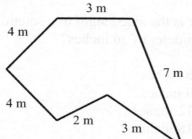

(A) 16 m
(B) 19 m
(C) 20 m
(D) 23 m

10. What is the perimeter of the shape below?

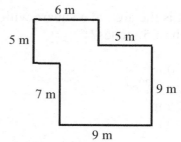

(A) 41 m
(B) 42 m
(C) 45 m
(D) 46 m

Basic Area and Perimeter Practice Set 2

1. What is the side length of a square that has an area of 64 cm^2?

   (A) 8 cm
   (B) 9 cm
   (C) 16 cm
   (D) 32 cm

2. What is the area of the rectangle below?

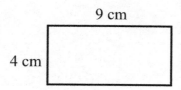

   (A) 13 cm^2
   (B) 26 cm^2
   (C) 32 cm^2
   (D) 36 cm^2

3. What is the perimeter of a square with a side length of 7 ft?

   (A) 14 ft
   (B) 28 ft
   (C) 49 ft
   (D) 98 ft

4. What is the perimeter of the shape below?

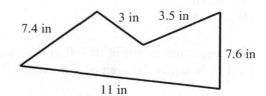

   (A) 29.5 in
   (B) 32.5 in
   (C) 33.5 in
   (D) 36 in

5. The perimeter of a regular hexagon is 48 cm. What is the side length of the hexagon?

   (A) 6 cm
   (B) 8 cm
   (C) 12 cm
   (D) 24 cm

6. What is the perimeter of the triangle below?

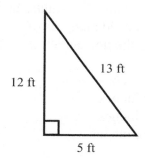

(A) 30 ft
(B) 40 ft
(C) 60 ft
(D) 65 ft

7. What is the perimeter of the figure below?

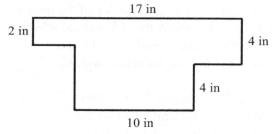

(A) 37 in
(B) 43 in
(C) 49 in
(D) 50 in

8. What is the area of a triangle with a base of 12 m and a height of 11 m?

(A) 23 m^2
(B) 43 m^2
(C) 66 m^2
(D) 132 m^2

9. What is the area of the trapezoid below?

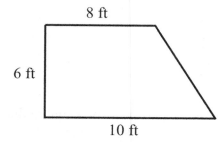

(A) 48 ft^2
(B) 54 ft^2
(C) 56 ft^2
(D) 60 ft^2

10. What is the perimeter of a rectangle with a width of 20 in and a length of 24 in?

(A) 44 in
(B) 84 in
(C) 88 in
(D) 480 in

Area and Perimeter Word Problems Practice Set 1

1. The rectangle below has a perimeter of 24 cm. What is the area of the rectangle?

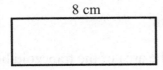

   8 cm

   (A) 22 cm^2
   (B) 32 cm^2
   (C) 36 cm^2
   (D) 128 cm^2

2. What is the perimeter of a square that has an area of 36 square inches?

   (A) 12 in
   (B) 18 in
   (C) 24 in
   (D) 81 in

3. The triangle below has an area of 24 square cm. What is the perimeter of the triangle?

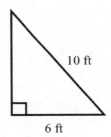

   10 ft

   6 ft

   (A) 8 ft
   (B) 20 ft
   (C) 24 ft
   (D) 48 ft

4. The perimeter of a square is 12a. What is the length of one side?

   (A) 3
   (B) 6
   (C) 3a
   (D) 6a

5. The area of a square is 16 square inches. If you double the side lengths of the square, what is the new area?

   (A) 32 square inches
   (B) 64 square inches
   (C) 48 square inches
   (D) 256 square inches

6. A square and a rectangle have the same perimeter. If the square has a side length of 8 ft, which of the following could be the dimensions of the rectangle?

   (A) 16 ft and 4 ft
   (B) 6 ft and 2 ft
   (C) 12 ft and 3 ft
   (D) 11 ft and 5 ft

7. A triangle has a perimeter of 40 inches. If one side measures 15 inches, which of the following could NOT be the dimensions of the other two sides?

   (A) 10 inches and 15 inches
   (B) 12 inches and 13 inches
   (C) 8 inches and 17 inches
   (D) 9 inches and 14 inches

8. A square is shown below.

   $x + 4$

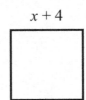

   What is the perimeter of the square, in terms of x?

   (A) 4x + 4
   (B) x + 16
   (C) 2x + 8
   (D) 4x + 16

9. The area of a rectangle is $18x$ meters. If one side measures 9 meters, what is the length of the other side of the rectangle?

(A) $2x$ meters
(B) $9x$ meters
(C) 2 meters
(D) 9 meters

10. A can of paint covers 10 square yards. How many cans of paint are needed to cover a wall that measures 18 ft by 15 ft?

(A) 3
(B) 6
(C) 9
(D) 27

Area and Perimeter Word Problems Practice Set 2

1. The area of a triangle is 20 square yards. If the base of the triangle is 10 yards, what is the height of the triangle?

(A) 1 yard
(B) 2 yards
(C) 4 yards
(D) 10 yards

2. A rectangle has a perimeter of 56 inches. Which of the following could be the dimensions of the rectangle?

(A) 16 inches and 12 inches
(B) 7 inches and 8 inches
(C) 26 inches and 30 inches
(D) 15 inches and 11 inches

3. The rectangle below has an area of 108 cm^2. What is the perimeter of the rectangle?

9 cm

x cm

(A) 12 cm
(B) 21 cm
(C) 42 cm
(D) 44 cm

4. The area of a triangle is twice the area of a square. If the area of the triangle is 72 square ft, what is the perimeter of the square?

(A) 6 ft
(B) 24 ft
(C) 28 ft
(D) 36 ft

5. A rectangle has a width of $4b$ and a length of 6. What is the area of the rectangle?

(A) 20
(B) 24
(C) $20b$
(D) $24b$

6. What is the area of a square that has a perimeter of 64 inches?

(A) 32 in^2
(B) 64 in^2
(C) 216 in^2
(D) 256 in^2

7. A rug store sells rugs for $3.25 per square foot. How much would a rug cost that measures 12 ft by 8 ft?

(A) $96
(B) $130
(C) $302
(D) $312

8. Which of the following could be the perimeter of an isosceles triangle if one side measures 6 cm and another side measures 8 cm?

(A) 14 cm
(B) 22 cm
(C) 24 cm
(D) 28 cm

9. What is the perimeter of a square with a side length of $5x$?

(A) $20x$
(B) $25x$
(C) 20
(D) 25

10. A triangle is shown below.

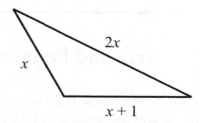

In terms of x, what is the perimeter of the triangle?

(A) $5x$
(B) $4x + 1$
(C) $4x + 2$
(D) $3x + 1$

Shaded Area Practice Set 1

1. The figure below shows a triangle inside of a rectangle.

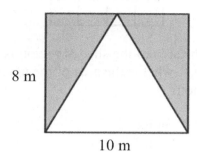

8 m

10 m

What is the area of the shaded region?

(A) 18 m^2
(B) 20 m^2
(C) 40 m^2
(D) 80 m^2

2. Each square in the grid shown has an area of 2 units^2.

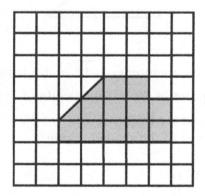

What is the area of the shaded region?

(A) 12 units^2
(B) 14 units^2
(C) 22 units^2
(D) 24 units^2

3. A rectangular garden is 9 meters long and 7 meters wide. There is a walkway around the garden, as shown by the shaded region in the figure below.

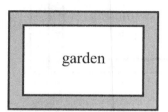

garden

If the walkway is 1 meter wide, what is the area of the walkway?

(A) 17 m^2
(B) 36 m^2
(C) 63 m^2
(D) 99 m^2

4. The figure below shows a large square with two smaller squares cut out.

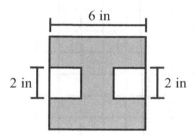

6 in

2 in   2 in

What is the area of the shaded region?

(A) 8 in^2
(B) 16 in^2
(C) 28 in^2
(D) 32 in^2

5. The path around a rectangular swimming pool is 18 ft long and 16 ft wide, as shown by the shaded region below.

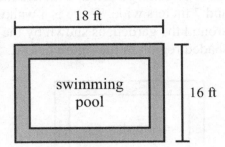

18 ft

swimming pool

16 ft

If the path is 2 ft wide, what is the area of the path?

(A) 64 ft^2
(B) 120 ft^2
(C) 140 ft^2
(D) 168 ft^2

6. Each square in the grid shown has a perimeter of 12 units.

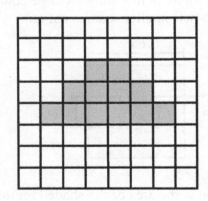

What is the area of the shaded region?

(A) 12 units^2
(B) 36 units^2
(C) 108 units^2
(D) 144 units^2

7. The figure below is made up of equal sized squares.

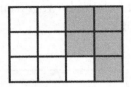

If the area of the shaded region is 15 units^2, what is the area of the non-shaded region?

(A) 21 units^2
(B) 24 units^2
(C) 27 units^2
(D) 36 units^2

8. The figure below shows a right triangle with a rectangle cut out.

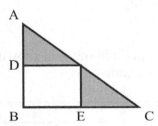

A

D

B   E   C

D is the midpoint of $\overline{AB}$ and E is the midpoint of $\overline{BC}$. If the length of $\overline{AB}$ is 6 ft and the length of $\overline{BC}$ is 8 ft, what is the area of the shaded region?

(A) 12 ft^2
(B) 18 ft^2
(C) 24 ft^2
(D) 48 ft^2

9. The total area of the large triangle below is 27 units^2.

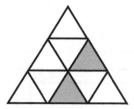

What is the area of the shaded region?

(A) 2 units^2
(B) 3 units^2
(C) 6 units^2
(D) 9 units^2

10. The figure below is made up of two overlapping squares.

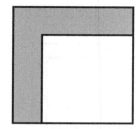

The perimeter of the outer square is 36 inches and the perimeter of the inner square is 24 inches. What is the area of the shaded region?

(A) 12 inches^2
(B) 24 inches^2
(C) 32 inches^2
(D) 45 inches^2

Shaded Area Practice Set 2

1. The figure below shows a triangle inside of a rectangle.

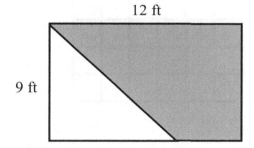

If the base of the triangle measures 8 ft, what is the area of the shaded region?

(A) 36 ft^2
(B) 60 ft^2
(C) 62 ft^2
(D) 72 ft^2

2. Each square in the grid shown has an area of 1.5 units^2.

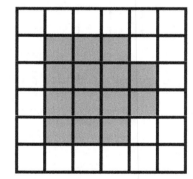

What is the area of the shaded region?

(A) 14 units^2
(B) 21 units^2
(C) 22 units^2
(D) 28 units^2

3. A rectangular garden is 12 yards long and 10 yards wide. There is a walkway around the garden, as shown by the shaded region in the figure below.

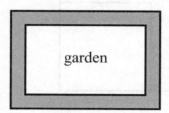

garden

If the walkway is 2 yards wide, what is the area of the walkway?

(A) 40 yd^2
(B) 48 yd^2
(C) 72 yd^2
(D) 104 yd^2

4. The figure below shows a large square with four smaller, equal sized squares cut out.

12 in

4 in

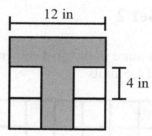

What is the area of the shaded region?

(A) 80 in^2
(B) 96 in^2
(C) 112 in^2
(D) 128 in^2

5. The path around a rectangular swimming pool is 15 meters long and 11 meters wide, as shown by the shaded region below.

15 m

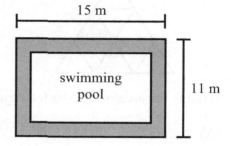

swimming pool

11 m

If the path is 1 meter wide, what is the area of the path?

(A) 25 m^2
(B) 48 m^2
(C) 117 m^2
(D) 140 m^2

6. Each square in the grid shown has a perimeter of 20 units.

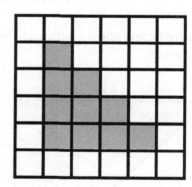

What is the area of the shaded region?

(A) 50 units^2
(B) 200 units^2
(C) 225 units^2
(D) 250 units^2

7. The figure below is made up of equal sized squares.

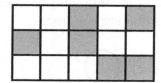

   If the area of the entire figure is 90 units^2, what is the area of the shaded region?

   (A) 12 units^2
   (B) 30 units^2
   (C) 36 units^2
   (D) 42 units^2

8. In the rectangle below, E is a midpoint of $\overline{AB}$, F is a midpoint of $\overline{BC}$, G is a midpoint of $\overline{DC}$, and H is a midpoint of $\overline{DA}$.

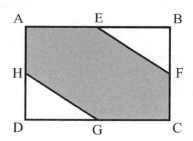

   If the length of $\overline{AB}$ is 10 ft and the length of $\overline{BC}$ is 8 ft, what is the area of the shaded region?

   (A) 20 ft^2
   (B) 40 ft^2
   (C) 60 ft^2
   (D) 64 ft^2

9. The non-shaded area in the figure below is 20 units^2.

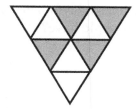

   What is the area of the shaded region?

   (A) 12 units^2
   (B) 16 units^2
   (C) 20 units^2
   (D) 25 units^2

10. Use the figure below to answer the question.

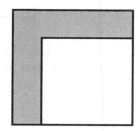

   The side length of the smaller square is 5 ft, and the area of the shaded region is 11 ft^2. What is the side length of the larger square?

   (A) 4 ft
   (B) 6 ft
   (C) 8 ft
   (D) 36 ft

Properties of Shapes and Figures Practice Set 1

1. How many lines of symmetry does an equilateral triangle have?

    (A) 1
    (B) 3
    (C) 6
    (D) 9

2. Which shape below has exactly one pair of parallel lines?

    (A) 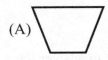   (B)

    (C) 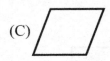   (D)

3. In which pair of capital letters do both letters have an equal number of lines of symmetry?

    (A) E and O
    (B) W and G
    (C) L and A
    (D) T and Y

4. Which of the following shapes has exactly four lines of symmetry?

    (A) 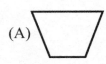   (B)

    (C)    (D)

5. Which of the following pairs shows figures that are congruent?

    (A)

    (B)

    (C)

    (D)

6. Use the figures to answer the question.

    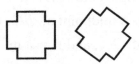

    The two shapes shown can be described as

    (A) congruent
    (B) similar
    (C) symmetric
    (D) none of the above

7. Use the figures to answer the question.

    The two shapes shown can be described as

    (A) perpendicular
    (B) congruent
    (C) similar
    (D) parallel

8. Which shape below has perpendicular lines?

(A)    (B)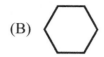

(C) 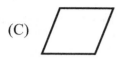   (D)

9. Use the figure to answer the question.

How many edges does the cube have?

(A) 6
(B) 8
(C) 12
(D) 16

10. Use the figure to answer the question.

How many faces does the triangular pyramid have?

(A) 3
(B) 4
(C) 6
(D) 8

Properties of Shapes and Figures Practice Set 2

1. How many lines of symmetry does a square have?

(A) 2
(B) 4
(C) 6
(D) 8

2. Which shape below has no lines of symmetry?

(A) 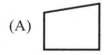   (B)

(C)    (D)

3. In which pair of capital letters do both letters have an equal number of lines of symmetry?

(A) P and M
(B) D and X
(C) B and L
(D) H and I

4. Which shape below has no perpendicular lines?

(A) 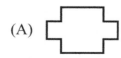   (B)

(C) 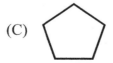   (D)

5. Which of the following pairs shows figures that are similar?

(A)

(B)

(C)

(D)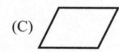

6. Which shape below has more than one pair of parallel lines?

(A)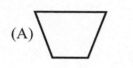

(B)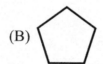

(C)

(D)

7. Use the figures below to answer the question

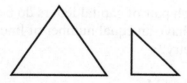

The two shapes can be described as

(A) similar
(B) congruent
(C) parallel
(D) none of the above

8. Use the figure to answer the question.

How many vertices does the cube have?

(A) 4
(B) 6
(C) 8
(D) 12

9. Use the figures to answer the question.

The two shapes shown can be described as

(A) similar
(B) congruent
(C) perpendicular
(D) none of the above

10. Use the figure to answer the question.

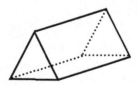

How many faces does the triangular prism have?

(A) 2
(B) 5
(C) 6
(D) 9

Coordinate Geometry Practice Set 1

1. What are the coordinates of point A below?

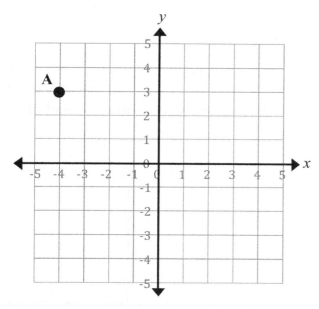

   (A) (3, –4)
   (B) (–3, 4)
   (C) (–4, –3)
   (D) (–4, 3)

2. Point W has coordinates (7, –5). If the point is translated 4 units left and 3 units up, what are the new coordinates of the point?

   (A) (3, –8)
   (B) (11, –2)
   (C) (3, –2)
   (D) (10, –9)

3. Point A has coordinates of (5, 1). If point A is reflected over the y-axis, what are the new coordinates of point A?

   (A) (–5, 1)
   (B) (1, 5)
   (C) (5, –1)
   (D) (–5, –1)

4. The points with coordinates (–3, 1) (–1, 4), (5, 1), (5, 4) are used to form a quadrilateral. If all four points are connected to form the quadrilateral, which term best describes the quadrilateral formed?

   (A) trapezoid
   (B) kite
   (C) rectangle
   (D) parallelogram

5. Use the coordinate grid to answer the question.

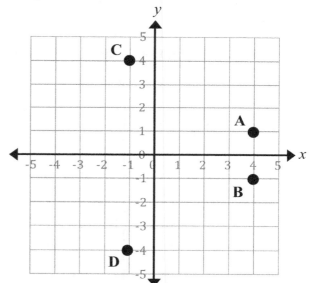

   Which point has coordinates (4, –1)?

   (A) Point A
   (B) Point B
   (C) Point C
   (D) Point D

6. The points with coordinates (–2, 0), (–2, 3), and (4, 0) are used to form a triangle. If all three points are connected to form the triangle, which term best describes the triangle formed?

   (A) obtuse
   (B) acute
   (C) equilateral
   (D) right

7. What is the area of a triangle with vertices (5, 2), (1, 2), and (2, 4)?

   (A) 4 units^2
   (B) 6 units^2
   (C) 8 units^2
   (D) 9 units^2

8. Eden is walking from point A to point B.

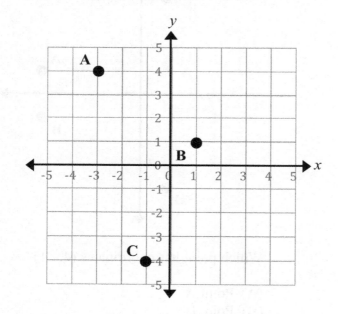

   If she can only move left, right, up, and down, what is the shortest distance she can travel to get from point A to B?

   (A) 5 grid units
   (B) 7 grid units
   (C) 10 grid units
   (D) 12 grid units

9. Point K is translated 2 units down and 3 units right. The new coordinates of point K are (–6, 1). What were the starting coordinates of point K?

   (A) (–3, –1)
   (B) (–4, –4)
   (C) (–9, 3)
   (D) (–9, –1)

10. The grid below shows three vertices of a rectangle.

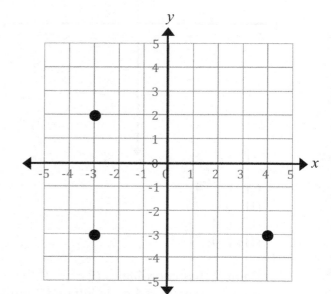

   Which of the following could be the fourth coordinate of the rectangle?

   (A) (2, 4)
   (B) (5, 2)
   (C) (4, 3)
   (D) (4, 2)

Coordinate Geometry Practice Set 2

1. What are the coordinates of point C below?

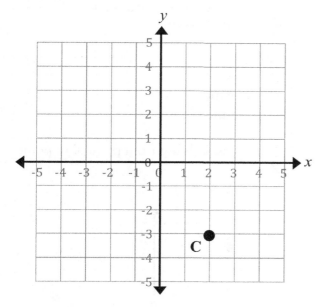

   (A) (−3, 2)
   (B) (2, 3)
   (C) (2, −3)
   (D) (−3, −2)

2. Point E has coordinates (5, 8). If point E is translated 3 units down and 2 units right, what are the new coordinates of point E?

   (A) (7, 5)
   (B) (2, 10)
   (C) (3, 5)
   (D) (7, 11)

3. Point B has coordinates of (5, −7). If point B is reflected over the x-axis, what are the new coordinates of point B?

   (A) (5, 7)
   (B) (−7, 5)
   (C) (−5, −7)
   (D) (−5, 7)

4. Use the coordinate grid to answer the question.

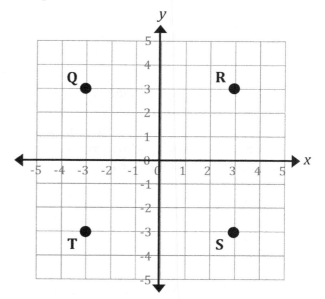

   Which point has coordinates (3, −3)?

   (A) Point Q
   (B) Point R
   (C) Point S
   (D) Point T

5. Point B lies in between points A and C. Point A has coordinates (−3, 4). If point B is 5 units to the right of A, and is 3 units left of point C, what are the coordinates of point C?

   (A) (2, 4)
   (B) (5, 4)
   (C) (−11, 4)
   (D) (−3, 12)

6. What is the perimeter of a rectangle with vertices (6, 1), (6, 3), (–1, 3), and (–1, 1)?

(A) 9 units
(B) 14 units
(C) 18 units
(D) 22 units

7. The points with coordinates (–1, 2), (–1, 4), and (5, 0) are used to form a triangle. If all three points are connected to form the triangle, which term best describes the triangle formed?

(A) acute
(B) right
(C) equilateral
(D) obtuse

8. The grid below shows three vertices of a trapezoid.

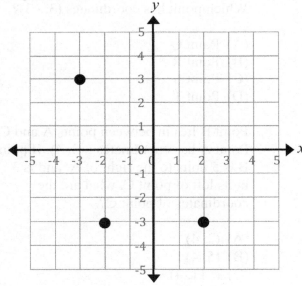

Which of the following could be the fourth coordinate of the trapezoid?

(A) (2, 2)
(B) (4, 3)
(C) (3, 4)
(D) (5, 0)

9. The points with coordinates (3, –2) (–3, –2), (–1, 2), (5, 2) are used to form a quadrilateral. If all four points are connected to form the quadrilateral, which term best describes the quadrilateral formed?

(A) square
(B) kite
(C) rectangle
(D) parallelogram

10. Katrina is walking from point X to point Z.

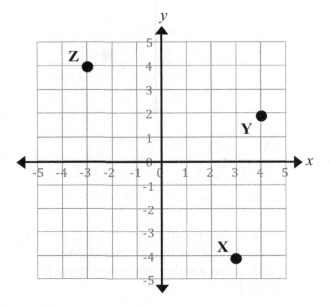

If she can only move left, right, up, and down, what is the shortest distance she can travel to get from point X to Z?

(A) 7 grid units
(B) 10 grid units
(C) 14 grid units
(D) 16 grid units

Volume, Surface Area, and 3D Shapes Practice Set 1

1. What is the volume of a cube that has a side length of 3 in?

   (A) 9 in³
   (B) 27 in³
   (C) 54 in³
   (D) 81 in³

2. What is the surface area of a cube that has a volume of 8 cubic feet?

   (A) 2 square feet
   (B) 12 square feet
   (C) 24 square feet
   (D) 64 square feet

3. What is the surface area of a rectangular prism that measures 4 inches by 7 inches by 1 inch?

   (A) 28 in²
   (B) 39 in²
   (C) 68 in²
   (D) 78 in²

4. The net below will form which shape?

   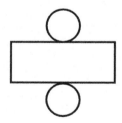

   (A) cylinder
   (B) cone
   (C) cube
   (D) sphere

5. What is the volume of the rectangular prism shown below?

   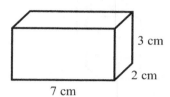

   (A) 12 cm³
   (B) 35 cm³
   (C) 42 cm³
   (D) 82 cm³

6. What shape is shown below?

   (A) pyramid
   (B) cylinder
   (C) cone
   (D) prism

7. The volume of the small, shaded cube is 4 cubic feet.

   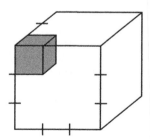

   What is the volume of the larger cube?

   (A) 27 cubic ft
   (B) 36 cubic ft
   (C) 108 cubic ft
   (D) 216 cubic ft

8. The rectangular prism below is made up of small cubes. If each small cube below has a volume of 1.5 cubic cm, what is the volume of the rectangular prism?

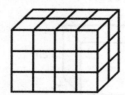

(A) 24 cubic cm
(B) 32 cubic cm
(C) 36 cubic cm
(D) 16 cubic cm

9. The volume of the larger cube shown below is 54 in^3.

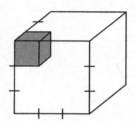

What is the volume of the small, shaded cube?

(A) 1 in^3
(B) 2 in^3
(C) 3 in^3
(D) 9 in^3

10. The figure below represents a rectangular piece of cardboard with dimensions 15 in by 8 in.

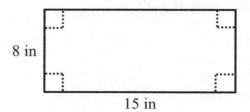

8 in

15 in

If 2 in by 2 in squares are cut out of each corner of the cardboard, as shown by the dotted lines, and the remaining piece of cardboard is folded into a box without a top, what is the volume of the box?

(A) 88 in^3
(B) 120 in^3
(C) 156 in^3
(D) 240 in^3

Volume, Surface Area, and 3D Shapes Practice Set 2

1. What is the surface area of a cube that has a side length of 4 in?

    (A) 24 in²
    (B) 64 in²
    (C) 96 in²
    (D) 144 in²

2. What is the volume of a cube that has a surface area of 54 cm²?

    (A) 9 cm³
    (B) 27 cm³
    (C) 81 cm³
    (D) 6,561 cm³

3. What is the volume of a rectangular prism that has a width of 5 km, a height of 3 km, and a length of 6 km?

    (A) 48 km³
    (B) 75 km³
    (C) 90 km³
    (D) 180 km³

4. What shape is shown below?

    (A) cylinder
    (B) cone
    (C) oval
    (D) sphere

5. What is the surface area of the rectangular prism shown below?

    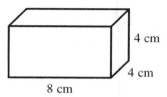

    (A) 64 cm²
    (B) 80 cm²
    (C) 128 cm²
    (D) 160 cm²

6. The net will form which type of shape?

    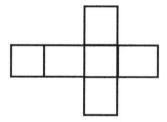

    (A) rectangular prism
    (B) pyramid
    (C) rectangle
    (D) triangular prism

7. The volume of the small, shaded cube is 2.5 cubic feet.

    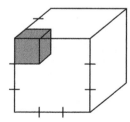

    What is the volume of the larger cube?

    (A) 54 cubic ft
    (B) 67.5 cubic ft
    (C) 77.5 cubic ft
    (D) 135 cubic ft

8. The volume of the cube below is 27 in³.

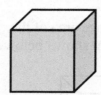

What is the shaded area?

(A) 9 in²
(B) 12 in²
(C) 18 in²
(D) 162 in²

9. A small cube has a base area that measures 4 square cm. A larger cube has a side length of 4 cm. How many small cubes could fit inside the larger cube?

(A) 2
(B) 4
(C) 8
(D) 16

10. The surface area of the larger cube shown below is 54 in³.

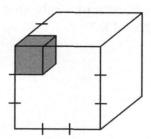

What is the surface area of the small, shaded cube?

(A) 2 in³
(B) 6 in³
(C) 9 in³
(D) 12 in³

Spatial Reasoning Practice Set 1

1. Use the figure to answer the question.

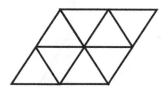

How many triangles are in the figure?

(A) 8
(B) 9
(C) 10
(D) 12

2. With one, straight-line cut, what shape or shapes can be made from a rectangle?

(A) triangle only
(B) rectangle only
(C) rectangle or triangle
(D) rectangle, or triangle, or trapezoid

3. The figure below is made up of four squares.

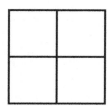

If the perimeter of each square is 20 cm, what is the perimeter of the entire figure?

(A) 32 cm
(B) 40 cm
(C) 60 cm
(D) 80 cm

4. Use the diagram to answer the question.

Which figure would complete the diagram to make a square?

(A)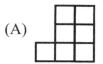

(B)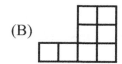

(C)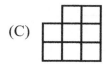

(D)

5. The length of *XY* is *a* and the length of *XZ* is *b*. what is the length of *YZ*?

(A) $b - a$
(B) $a - b$
(C) $a + b$
(D) ab

6. Use the figure to answer the question.

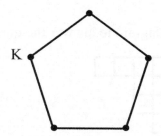

If lines are drawn from vertex K to each of the other vertices, how many triangular regions are formed?

(A) 2
(B) 3
(C) 4
(D) 5

7. Use the figure to answer the question.

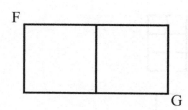

How many paths can be draw from point G to point F if you can only move up and left?

(A) 2
(B) 3
(C) 4
(D) 6

8. The figure below may be folded along one or more of the dotted lines.

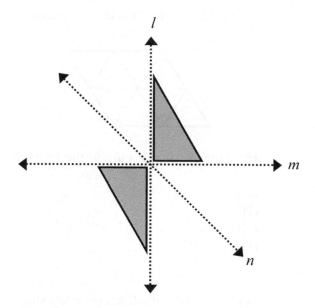

Which line or pair of lines, when folded, will allow the triangles to exactly match the original figure?

(A) line *n* only
(B) line *m* only
(C) both line *l* and line *m*
(D) both line *l* and line *n*

9. Use the diagram to answer the question.

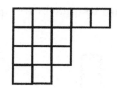

Which figure would complete the diagram to make a square?

(A)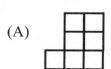

(B)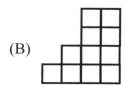

(C)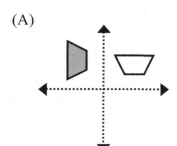

(D)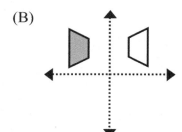

10. In which figure is the white trapezoid a translation of the shaded trapezoid?

(A)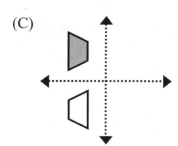

(B)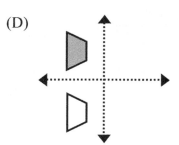

(C)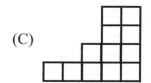

(D)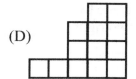

Spatial Reasoning Practice Set 2

1. Use the figure to answer the question.

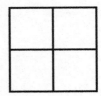

How many rectangles are in the figure?

(A) 4
(B) 6
(C) 7
(D) 9

2. What shape or shapes can be made by the overlapping region when two right triangles overlap?

(A) triangle only
(B) square only
(C) triangle or square
(D) square, or triangle, or trapezoid

3. The figure below is made up of five squares.

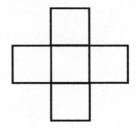

If the perimeter of each square is 4 in, what is the perimeter of the entire figure?

(A) 9 in
(B) 12 in
(C) 16 in
(D) 20 in

4. Use the diagram to answer the question.

Which figure would complete the diagram to make a square?

(A)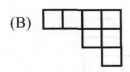

(B)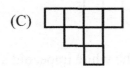

(C)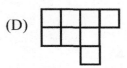

(D)

5. The length of *AB* is *x*, and the length of *BC* is *y*. If *CD* is the same length as *AB*, what is the length of *AD*?

(A) $2x + y$
(B) $x + y$
(C) $x + 2y$
(D) $2x - y$

6. Use the figure to answer the question.

How many lines can be drawn between all non-consecutive vertices?

(A) 6
(B) 8
(C) 9
(D) 11

7. Use the figure to answer the question.

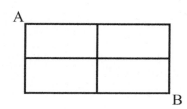

How many paths can be drawn from point A to point B if you can only move right and down?

(A) 2
(B) 3
(C) 4
(D) 6

8. The figure below may be folded along any of the three dotted lines.

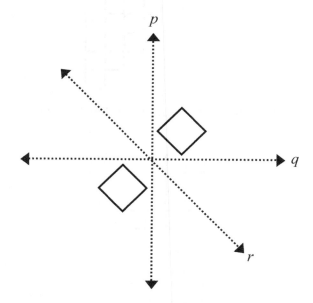

If only one fold is allowed, folding over which line, or lines, will allow the diamonds to exactly match the original figure?

(A) line *r* only
(B) only line *r* or line *p*
(C) only line *r* or line *q*
(D) line *r*, line *p*, or line *q*

9. Use the diagram to answer the question.

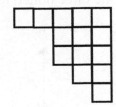

Which figure would complete the diagram to make a square?

(A)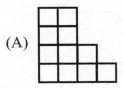

(B)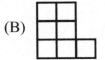

(C)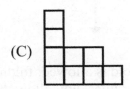

(D)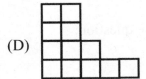

10. In which figure is the white trapezoid a reflection of the shaded trapezoid?

(A)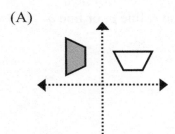

(B)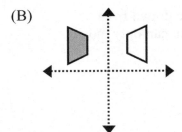

(C)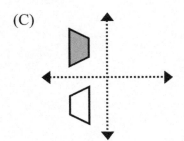

(D)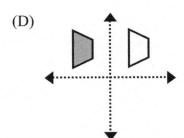

Math Multiple Choice Chapter Answer Key

Fundamentals Practice Set 1

1. C
2. D
3. A
4. B
5. B
6. D
7. C
8. B
9. A
10. B

Fundamentals Practice Set 2

1. C
2. C
3. A
4. B
5. D
6. C
7. D
8. A
9. C
10. B

Writing Numbers as Words Practice Set 1

1. A
2. B
3. D
4. B
5. C
6. C
7. D
8. B
9. A
10. C

Writing Numbers as Words Practice Set 2

1. B
2. B
3. A
4. C
5. D

6. C
7. B
8. A
9. D
10. C

Place Value Practice Set 1

1. D
2. D
3. B
4. C
5. C
6. D
7. C
8. C
9. B
10. A

Place Value Practice Set 2

1. A
2. C
3. A
4. C
5. B
6. A
7. C
8. D
9. B
10. D

Divisibility and Remainders Practice Set 1

1. B
2. D
3. D
4. D
5. C
6. A
7. B
8. C
9. D
10. D

Divisibility and Remainders Practice Set 2

1. A
2. D
3. D
4. B
5. D
6. D
7. C
8. A
9. A
10. C

Multiples and Factors Practice Set 1

1. C
2. C
3. D
4. C
5. A
6. D
7. C
8. C
9. B
10. A

Multiples and Factors Practice Set 2

1. A
2. B
3. B
4. C
5. A
6. C
7. B
8. D
9. D
10. C

Prime Factorization Practice Set 1

1. A
2. B
3. B
4. C

5. D
6. A
7. D
8. A
9. B
10. A

Prime Factorization Practice Set 2

1. D
2. D
3. A
4. B
5. C
6. B
7. A
8. D
9. A
10. D

Order of Operations Practice Set 1

1. B
2. D
3. C
4. B
5. A
6. B
7. A
8. C
9. A
10. D

Order of Operations Practice Set 2

1. A
2. D
3. B
4. A
5. C
6. C
7. B
8. C
9. B
10. D

**Story Word
Problems Practice
Set 1**

1. A
2. D
3. C
4. B
5. A
6. A
7. B
8. C
9. D
10. C

**Story Word
Problems Practice
Set 2**

1. C
2. A
3. D
4. A
5. A
6. B
7. B
8. C
9. D
10. D

**Patterns Practice
Set 1**

1. D
2. B
3. C
4. B
5. A
6. C
7. C
8. A
9. D
10. C

**Patterns Practice
Set 2**

1. D
2. A
3. D
4. C
5. B
6. C

7. D
8. C
9. B
10. B

**Properties Practice
Set 1**

1. A
2. B
3. B
4. D
5. D
6. C
7. C
8. B
9. A
10. A

**Properties Practice
Set 2**

1. D
2. A
3. C
4. D
5. C
6. C
7. D
8. A
9. B
10. B

**Vocabulary Practice
Set 1**

1. D
2. A
3. A
4. A
5. C
6. B
7. C
8. D
9. B
10. C

**Vocabulary Practice
Set 2**

1. B
2. C
3. A

4. B
5. D
6. A
7. B
8. A
9. D
10. C

**Fractions Practice
Set 1**

1. D
2. A
3. C
4. A
5. C
6. B
7. D
8. B
9. C
10. C

**Fractions Practice
Set 2**

1. C
2. A
3. B
4. A
5. C
6. D
7. A
8. D
9. B
10. C

**Comparing Fractions
Practice Set 1**

1. D
2. A
3. C
4. B
5. B
6. C
7. A
8. D
9. D
10. C

**Comparing Fractions
Practice Set 2**

1. D
2. B
3. A
4. D
5. B
6. A
7. C
8. C
9. D
10. A

**Fractions of
Numbers Practice Set
1**

1. B
2. B
3. A
4. A
5. D
6. B
7. C
8. D
9. C
10. C

**Fractions of
Numbers Practice Set
2**

1. B
2. A
3. A
4. B
5. B
6. A
7. D
8. B
9. C
10. B

**Fraction Word
Problems Practice
Set 1**

1. B
2. A
3. D
4. C
5. B
6. C
7. C
8. B

9. C
10. A

Fraction Word Problems Practice Set 2

1. A
2. B
3. D
4. C
5. D
6. C
7. D
8. A
9. B
10. C

Decimals Practice Set 1

1. A
2. D
3. B
4. C
5. D
6. B
7. A
8. B
9. D
10. C

Decimals Practice Set 2

1. D
2. C
3. B
4. D
5. D
6. C
7. A
8. C
9. B
10. A

Decimal Word Problems Practice Set 1

1. C
2. C
3. A

4. D
5. A
6. C
7. B
8. A
9. B
10. B

Decimal Word Problems Practice Set 2

1. B
2. A
3. C
4. C
5. D
6. A
7. D
8. D
9. B
10. C

Converting Decimals, Fractions, and Percents Practice Set 1

1. D
2. C
3. C
4. D
5. C
6. D
7. D
8. B
9. C
10. A

Converting Decimals, Fractions, and Percents Practice Set 2

1. B
2. A
3. A
4. C
5. B
6. D
7. B
8. B
9. D

10. C

Percents Practice Set 1

1. C
2. D
3. A
4. C
5. B
6. D
7. A
8. A
9. D
10. A

Percents Practice Set 2

1. B
2. C
3. C
4. A
5. C
6. D
7. C
8. B
9. A
10. D

Estimating Practice Set 1

1. D
2. A
3. A
4. B
5. C
6. B
7. C
8. C
9. B
10. B

Estimating Practice Set 2

1. D
2. A
3. C
4. C
5. B
6. C

7. D
8. B
9. C
10. B

Number Lines Practice Set 1

1. C
2. D
3. A
4. B
5. D
6. B
7. A
8. C
9. D
10. C

Number Lines Practice Set 2

1. C
2. A
3. B
4. B
5. D
6. A
7. B
8. A
9. D
10. C

Proportions Practice Set 1

1. C
2. A
3. A
4. D
5. B
6. B
7. A
8. C
9. C
10. B

Proportions Practice Set 2

1. A
2. C
3. D

4. B
5. A
6. D
7. C
8. B
9. D
10. B

Ratios Practice Set 1

1. A
2. D
3. B
4. C
5. D
6. C
7. C
8. B
9. B
10. A

Ratios Practice Set 2

1. A
2. D
3. A
4. B
5. C
6. C
7. B
8. B
9. D
10. C
11.

Probability Practice Set 1

1. A
2. D
3. C
4. D
5. B
6. A
7. B
8. B
9. D
10. C

Probability Practice Set 2

1. B
2. B

3. B
4. C
5. D
6. B
7. A
8. C
9. D
10. B

Unit Conversions Practice Set 1

1. C
2. C
3. A
4. A
5. B
6. C
7. B
8. C
9. D
10. B

Unit Conversions Practice Set 2

1. A
2. D
3. B
4. C
5. C
6. D
7. D
8. D
9. C
10. A

Appropriate Units Practice Set 1

1. B
2. C
3. A
4. C
5. B
6. C
7. B
8. D
9. D
10. A

Appropriate Units Practice Set 2

1. C
2. D
3. A
4. A
5. B
6. B
7. D
8. B
9. B
10. A

Solving Equations Practice Set 1

1. D
2. A
3. B
4. C
5. D
6. B
7. B
8. C
9. A
10. D

Solving Equations Practice Set 2

1. A
2. C
3. A
4. B
5. D
6. D
7. D
8. B
9. B
10. A

Creating Equations and Expressions Practice Set 1

1. C
2. A
3. B
4. A
5. B
6. D
7. D
8. C
9. B

10. A

Creating Equations and Expressions Practice Set 2

1. C
2. D
3. C
4. A
5. B
6. B
7. C
8. C
9. A
10. D

Function Tables Practice Set 1

1. A
2. B
3. C
4. A
5. B
6. B
7. D
8. A
9. A
10. C

Function Tables Practice Set 2

1. A
2. D
3. A
4. C
5. C
6. D
7. B
8. B
9. C
10. D

Mixed Word Problems Practice Set 1

1. D
2. B
3. D
4. C

5. A
6. C
7. A
8. C
9. B
10. B

Mixed Word Problems Practice Set 2

1. B
2. B
3. C
4. C
5. D
6. A
7. C
8. B
9. A
10. D

Mean, Median, Mode, and Range Practice Set 1

1. A
2. C
3. D
4. C
5. B
6. D
7. C
8. B
9. A
10. B

Mean, Median, Mode, and Range Practice Set 2

1. D
2. C
3. A
4. A
5. C
6. D
7. B
8. B
9. A
10. B

Charts, Graphs, and Tables Practice Set 1

1. B
2. D
3. D
4. B
5. B
6. A
7. C
8. A
9. D
10. C

Charts, Graphs, and Tables Practice Set 2

1. D
2. C
3. D
4. B
5. C
6. A
7. C
8. D
9. A
10. B

Naming Shapes Practice Set 1

1. A
2. A
3. B
4. D
5. B
6. D
7. D
8. C
9. D
10. A

Naming Shapes Practice Set 2

1. A
2. B
3. C
4. A
5. D
6. C
7. A
8. D

9. B
10. D

Basic Area and Perimeter Practice Set 1

1. C
2. B
3. B
4. A
5. B
6. D
7. C
8. D
9. D
10. D

Basic Area and Perimeter Practice Set 2

1. A
2. D
3. B
4. B
5. B
6. A
7. D
8. C
9. B
10. C

Area and Perimeter Word Problems Practice Set 1

1. B
2. C
3. C
4. C
5. B
6. D
7. D
8. D
9. A
10. A

Area and Perimeter Word Problems Practice Set 2

1. C

2. A
3. C
4. B
5. D
6. D
7. D
8. B
9. A
10. B

Shaded Area Practice Set 1

1. C
2. D
3. B
4. C
5. B
6. C
7. A
8. A
9. C
10. D

Shaded Area Practice Set 2

1. D
2. B
3. D
4. A
5. B
6. D
7. C
8. C
9. B
10. B

Properties of Shapes and Figures Practice Set 1

1. B
2. A
3. D
4. B
5. D
6. A
7. C
8. D
9. C
10. B

**Properties of Shapes
and Figures Practice
Set 2**

1. B
2. A
3. D
4. C
5. A
6. C
7. D
8. C
9. B
10. B

**Coordinate
Geometry Practice
Set 1**

1. D
2. C
3. A
4. A
5. B
6. D
7. A

8. B
9. C
10. D

**Coordinate
Geometry Practice
Set 2**

1. C
2. A
3. A
4. C
5. B
6. C
7. D
8. B
9. D
10. C

**Volume, Surface
Area, and 3D Shapes
Practice Set 1**

1. B
2. C
3. D

4. A
5. C
6. A
7. C
8. C
9. B
10. A

**Volume, Surface
Area, and 3D Shapes
Practice Set 2**

1. C
2. B
3. C
4. A
5. D
6. A
7. B
8. C
9. C
10. B

**Spatial Reasoning
Practice Set 1**

1. C
2. D
3. B
4. A
5. A
6. B
7. B
8. C
9. C
10. D

**Spatial Reasoning
Practice Set 2**

1. D
2. D
3. B
4. C
5. A
6. C
7. D
8. A
9. A
10. B

Reading

THIS PAGE IS INTENTIONALLY LEFT BLANK

How to Use the Reading Chapter

Chapter Overview

This chapter of the book covers the Reading Comprehension section. The purpose of this chapter is to present students with test-like passages and questions so they can become familiar with the style and difficulty of questions that show up on the ISEE Lower Level.

Using the Practice Passages

The chapter contains 40 fiction and non-fiction practice passages, each with 5 multiple-choice questions. You can work through the passages one at a time, or you can complete 5 passages at a time to mimic the actual ISEE Lower Level exam. If you are struggling with the Reading Comprehension section of the test, we suggest working through all 40 passages. The best way to improve your Reading Comprehension score is to practice!

Tips for Working Through this Chapter

1. **Time yourself**. Time yourself as you're working through the passages. If you are comfortable finishing the Reading Comprehension section of the ISEE Lower Level in the given time, give yourself 5 minutes for each practice passage and set of questions. If you have trouble finishing the Reading Comprehension section of the ISEE Lower Level in the given time, start by giving yourself 6 to 8 minutes for each passage and set of questions, depending on your reading speed. As you work through the 40 practice passages, gradually decrease your time and work your way down to 5 minutes per passage and set of questions. This will allow you to slowly work on speeding up so you'll eventually be able to complete each passage and set of questions in 5 minutes.

2. **Understand your mistakes.** For the Reading Comprehension section, it's important to understand your mistakes in order to really improve your scores. If you answer a question incorrectly, go back to the passage and try to re-answer the question. Focus on understanding why your initial answer was incorrect and why the correct answer is correct. Make a mental note of any mistakes you made, and think of ways you can improve when answering similar questions in the future.

3. **Break up your practice.** Remember to break up your practice into small chunks. Don't try and cram all of the practice sets into a short amount of time. If you try to complete all of the reading practice passages right before your official ISEE Lower Level exam, you won't give yourself time to improve and learn from your mistakes.

Reading Passage 1

1   I knew that Risa and I would be friends
2 from the moment she showed up on my
3 doorstep. I remember that night like it was
4 yesterday. While eating dinner with my
5 parents, I heard a scratching sound near our
6 door. "That's odd," I thought out loud.
7 Walking slowly towards the front hallway, I
8 peered through the small, tinted window. I
9 saw nothing. Undeterred, I opened the door
10 and almost tripped over my future
11 companion: a small brown dog.
12   "You have to find the dog's owners,"
13 my parents would say every night at dinner.
14 They brought up a very good point; I would
15 miss Risa if she had ran away from my
16 home, too. By that time, she had been
17 staying with us for two weeks, and I had
18 practically adopted her. I convinced my
19 mom to help me buy necessary supplies: a
20 bowl, food, toys, and a collar. She
21 begrudgingly agreed to help if I promised to
22 make signs to hang up around the
23 neighborhood. That was the last thing I
24 wanted to do.
25   All in all, my father and I hung fifty

26 posters up around the neighborhood. I knew
27 that finding Risa's – or whatever her real
28 name is – real owners was the right thing to
29 do, but I just didn't want to lose her. We
30 had put our home phone number down on
31 the posters, and every time I heard the
32 electronic trill, my gut wrenched.
33   It happened on a Sunday. The phone
34 rang and I heard my father discussing
35 something in hushed tones. He confirmed
36 an address, hung up the phone, and slowly
37 started walking up the steps. He knocked on
38 my door and told me it was time.
39   As we drove through the city I noticed
40 something odd: we weren't near any
41 houses. My dad pulled up to a dull, brown
42 building and parked the car. "We're here!"
43 he said cheerily. I squinted to see the sign
44 out front of the building; it said 'Humane
45 Society'. I couldn't understand what we
46 were doing. My dad explained that Risa's
47 'owner' was the Humane Society and that
48 she had run away. I quickly asked if that
49 meant she could be ours. "All that's left is
50 the paperwork," he said through a smile.

1. The passage is primarily concerned with

   (A) promoting the Humane Society.
   (B) informing the reader how to
       properly care for a lost dog.
   (C) telling a story about a lost dog.
   (D) warning dog owners about theft.

2. As used in line 21, the word
   "begrudgingly" most nearly means

   (A) happily.
   (B) angrily.
   (C) reluctantly.
   (D) willingly.

3. The passage supplies information to
   answer which question?

   (A) What dog breed is Risa?
   (B) Where did the narrator originally
       find Risa?
   (C) In which state does the narrator's
       family live?
   (D) What is the narrator's name?

4. Based on the passage we can infer that

   (A) Risa will find a new home at the
       Humane Society.
   (B) the narrator's mother dislikes dogs.
   (C) Risa is a mutt.
   (D) the narrator is going to keep Risa.

5. In lines 27 – 28, the author uses the
   phrase "or whatever her real name is" to
   demonstrate that

   (A) the narrator doesn't actually care
       about Risa.
   (B) the narrator's mother wants to keep
       the dog.
   (C) the narrator's father wants to put
       Risa's real name on the poster.
   (D) the narrator doesn't actually know
       Risa's real name.

Reading Passage 2

1   It is a miracle that Wilma Rudolph
2 survived infancy. She was born
3 prematurely in 1940 in Tennessee,
4 weighing only 4.5 pounds. Her childhood
5 was plagued with diseases including
6 pneumonia, scarlet fever, and infantile
7 paralysis. Pushing past these hardships,
8 Rudolph would go on to become the first
9 American woman to win three gold medals
10 in a single Olympic Games as well as one
11 of the most celebrated African American
12 athletes of her time.
13   Rudolph started her career at Burt High
14 School where she began to run track as a
15 way to keep busy during the offseason for
16 basketball. She was spotted at a high
17 school race by Ed Temple, a college track
18 coach, who immediately saw her potential.
19 Rudolph began training with the Tennessee
20 State track program and was an instant
21 star.
22   That summer, Rudolph attended the
23 1956 Olympic Trials in Seattle,
24 Washington. Primarily a sprinter, she
25 competed in the 100 meter, 200 meter, and
26 400 meter races. She took second place in
27 the 200 meters and qualified for the 1956

28 Olympic Games in Melbourne, Australia
29 by over a second.
30   When Rudolph attended the Games,
31 she was the youngest member of the
32 United States delegation at only 16 years
33 old. Unfortunately, she was defeated in the
34 preliminary heat of the 200-meter race, but
35 her time wasn't up yet. She ran the third
36 leg of the 4x100 meter relay, earning a
37 bronze medal and breaking a world record.
38 Rudolph returned to the Olympic Games in
39 1960; this time she vowed to win gold. She
40 competed in three events in Rome: 100
41 meter, 200 meter, and the 4x100 meter
42 relay. Setting world records in every event
43 along the way, she would go on to win
44 gold in all three events, cementing her
45 place in Olympic history.
46   Rudolph retired from competitive sport
47 relatively soon after the Rome Olympics.
48 She would go on to be a teacher, mother,
49 and civil rights activist. Due to her success,
50 Rudolph served as a prominent role model
51 for young African American athletes and
52 helped to elevate women's track and field.
53 She leaves behind a legacy of
54 perseverance, dedication, and athletic
55 excellence.

1. The primary purpose of the passage is to

    (A) discuss the history of sprinting at the 1956 and 1960 Olympic Games.
    (B) inform the reader about the life of an incredible athlete.
    (C) talk about why Wilma Rudolph is the greatest American athlete ever.
    (D) compare and contrast different African American athletes.

2. In line 32 the word "delegation" most nearly means

    (A) officials.
    (B) audience.
    (C) team.
    (D) high jumpers.

3. At age 16, Rudolph

    (A) broke an Olympic world record.
    (B) came in second place at the Olympics.
    (C) won three Olympic gold medals.
    (D) was the youngest person to compete in the Olympics.

4. What can be assumed from the passage?

    (A) Ed Temple never had faith in Wilma Rudolph.
    (B) Rudolph liked the 1956 Games more than the 1960 Games.
    (C) The 200-meter sprint in Rome was a very close race.
    (D) Rudolph was originally going to be a basketball player.

5. What word best describes Wilma Rudolph's attitude toward the 1960 Olympics?

    (A) Spiteful
    (B) Nervous
    (C) Confident
    (D) Amused

Reading Passage 3

Animals made their debut appearance in space long before humans. Shortly after World War II, scientists began to ponder the viability of living organisms in space. In 1947, they got their answer. Using technology developed during the war, scientists launched a rocket from New Mexico past the upper atmosphere. Fruit flies were amongst the living organisms aboard, and several hours after launch they were recovered, alive.

Several years later, Russia became the next nation to send an animal into space. On July 22nd, 1951, the dogs Tsygan and Dezik were launched into the abyss. Unlike previous missions by the United States involving monkeys, both dogs were successfully recovered alive.

Launching an animal into space is quite different from launching an animal in orbit (meaning the spacecraft is circling the earth like a satellite). NASA defines the boundary of 'space' as 50 miles above the earth's surface; various international bodies use the Kármán Line to define space as 100 kilometers above earth's surface. Both the previous US and Russian missions launched animals roughly 70 miles upwards, but these ships quickly fell back to earth. In 1957, Russia launched their spacecraft, Sputnik 2, into orbit with the dog Laika aboard.

Finally, in 1961, Yuri Alekseyevich Gagarin became the first human being in space. The 27-year-old launched from Russia in 1961 and circled the earth in 89 minutes. His flight, pioneered by countless insects, mice, rats, dogs, and monkeys, marked the beginning of a new era for humankind. Eight years later, in 1969, Neil Armstrong would become the first human to walk on the surface of the moon.

These animals paved the way for human space exploration by providing invaluable data about how space and spaceflight affects living organisms. While it is relatively rare for animals to be sent to space now, human beings are able to live and work in space, on the International Space Station, in part due to sacrifices by these animals.

1. The primary purpose of this passage is to

   (A) discuss the first space walk.
   (B) educate the reader about Russian space exploration.
   (C) examine the history of animals in space.
   (D) tell the story of the first dog in space.

2. What is meant by the phrase 'debut appearance' as used in line 1?

   (A) In 1947, animals were launched into space on television.
   (B) This was the first time animals had been in space.
   (C) Humans accompanied animals into space for the first time in 1947.
   (D) The first Russian dog was launched into space in 1947.

3. The author mentions all of the following EXCEPT

   (A) Russia was the second nation to send animals into space.
   (B) some of the animals launched into space did not survive.
   (C) Russian astronauts first walked on the surface of the moon in 1969.
   (D) Yuri Alekseyevich Gagarin was the first human in space.

4. Based on the passage we can infer that

   (A) animals have been extremely useful in the development of human space exploration.
   (B) it is certain that animals will never be sent to space again.
   (C) Russian astronauts are superior to American astronauts..
   (D) the first animal was actually launched into space in 1939.

5. In the last paragraph, the author mentions the International Space Station primarily to

   (A) demonstrate the progress humans have made in space thanks to animals.
   (B) show that humans can unite around a common goal: space exploration.
   (C) provide contrast to Neil Armstrong walking on the moon.
   (D) reinforce the idea that humans can't live out in the open in space.

Reading Passage 4

1 Evidence suggests that smallpox
2 existed on planet earth for over 4,000
3 years. It is a viral disease that causes
4 bumps and lumps on the skin similar to
5 chickenpox. One of the major differences
6 between the two is the outcome: about
7 0.002% of patients die from chickenpox,
8 while almost 30% of smallpox patients will
9 eventually die.
10 Thankfully, the start of a cure for
11 smallpox began as early as 1796. Edward
12 Jenner, a British scientist, observed that
13 individuals infected with a similar, but
14 non-lethal type of pox, cowpox, seemed to
15 be immune to smallpox. In other words,
16 people who were sick with cowpox first
17 were not able to contract smallpox. He
18 began purposefully infecting patients with
19 cowpox, and his hypothesis was correct:
20 almost none of these individuals became
21 sick from smallpox.
22 Over the course of the next 100 years
23 this practice, now known as vaccination,
24 became quite common throughout the
25 world. By 1900, the percent of total deaths
26 in London due to smallpox fell to less than
27 0.01%, compared to about 9% in 1800. A
28 similar decline in cases occurred
29 throughout most of the developed world
30 from 1900 to 1950.
31 By 1955, over 95% of smallpox cases
32 were found in South America and Africa.
33 The disease had been eliminated in
34 Western countries like the US, Canada,
35 and almost all of Europe. Scientists
36 worked tirelessly to vaccinate individuals
37 in countries where the disease still
38 remained. By 1975 there were fewer than
39 20,000 reported cases, and by 1978, there
40 were 0 individuals infected with the virus.
41 Smallpox remains the only disease that
42 humans have eradicated from planet earth.
43 It is estimated that over 500 million people
44 died from the virus while it still existed.
45 The elimination of smallpox is one
46 example of what humans can accomplish
47 when they come together and embrace
48 science.

1. What is the main idea of the passage?

    (A) Vaccination eventually helped
        eliminate smallpox.
    (B) Smallpox was eliminated in 1978.
    (C) Cowpox was a vital part of curing
        smallpox.
    (D) Everyone should get vaccinated.

2. As used in line 42, the word "eradicated"
    most nearly means

    (A) cured.
    (B) eliminated.
    (C) isolated.
    (D) maneuvered.

3. Why did Edward Jenner infect people
    with cowpox?

    (A) To prove that cowpox and smallpox
        were the same diseases.
    (B) To test if cowpox was lethal.
    (C) To test a vaccine for cowpox.
    (D) To test his hypothesis.

4. Based on the passage we can infer that

    (A) Edward Jenner died from smallpox.
    (B) in 2007 there were no cases of
        smallpox in the United States.
    (C) smallpox evolved 20,000 years ago.
    (D) smallpox is likely to come back
        very soon.

5. In this passage, the author's tone could
    be be described as

    (A) excited.
    (B) worrisome.
    (C) informative.
    (D) persuasive.

Reading Passage 5

In 2019, a flight from New York to Paris took about seven hours. This duration has been the same for almost forty years. These flights take place on giant aircrafts that are hundreds of feet long and can carry hundreds of passengers. When Charles Lindberg became the first person to cross the Atlantic Ocean, he did it in a 30-foot plane that weighed less than most modern cars, and he did it solo.

The beginning of Lindberg's journey across the pond came in 1903 - when the Wright Brothers became the first humans to successfully fly a basic aircraft. Lindberg was born only a year earlier and spent his childhood fascinated by the quickly-changing world of aviation. He attended several years of college where he studied engineering, which no doubt was vital to his transatlantic success.

In 1922, Lindberg dropped out of college and began flight school in Nebraska. He spent his summers working as a flying stuntman, walking on wings and parachuting from aircraft. He spent the better part of the next five years honing his flight skills and traveling as an aviation stuntman.

The announcement of the Orteig Prize would alter the course of Lindberg's life forever. Around 1920, Raymond Orteig, a New York hotelier, offered $25,000 to anyone who could successfully cross the Atlantic Ocean by plane. Over the course of the next six years, dozens of teams would try. Many of them died, and they often went missing, likely lost in the Atlantic Ocean.

Beginning in 1926, Lindberg began gathering financing for a plane he would help design: *The Spirit of St. Louis.* For several weeks in the spring of 1927, Lindberg test-flew his plane around the United States. He eventually made his way to Long Island, New York.

Lindberg began his flight in the early morning of May 20, 1927. He flew *The Spirit of St. Louis* for 33½ hours straight across the Atlantic Ocean, fighting poor weather and failing instruments. On schedule, Lindberg landed on an airstrip in Paris to an estimated crowd of 150,000 people. His journey was praised around the world, and marked a turning point in aviation that shaped how people fly around the world today.

1. This passage is primarily concerned with

   (A) commercial flights between the United States and Europe.
   (B) exploring the advancements in aviation technology.
   (C) an analysis of the aviation career of Charles Lindberg.
   (D) the first solo flight across the Atlantic Ocean.

2. The weather Lindberg encountered on his Atlantic flight could likely be described as

   (A) stormy and rainy.
   (B) sunny and warm.
   (C) unpredictable but good.
   (D) partly cloudy but mostly clear.

3. As used in line 53, the word "praised" most nearly means

   (A) ignored.
   (B) recognized.
   (C) discovered.
   (D) celebrated.

4. Why did the Orteig Prize alter the course of Lindberg's life?

   (A) Lindberg desperately needed the $25,000 prize.
   (B) The prize inspired Lindberg to attempt his famous journey.
   (C) Many of Lindberg's pilot friends died competing for the prize.
   (D) The prize inspired him to become interested in aviation.

5. Based on the last line of the first paragraph, one can infer that

   (A) Lindberg had originally wanted to fly from New York to London.
   (B) Lindberg was struggling to find a flight partner.
   (C) a solo flight of such great length was unheard of at the time.
   (D) the goal of Lindberg's flight was to reduce flight time across the Atlantic.

Reading Passage 6

1   Surrealism is a style of painting
2 originating in the early 20th century. It
3 focuses on presenting odd, sometimes off
4 putting objects in settings which they
5 normally would not be found. A well-
6 known example of this style can be seen in
7 the 1931 painting *The Persistence of*
8 *Memory*. This oil on canvas painting
9 depicts watches and clocks melting as if
10 being heated by the sun. The painting's
11 artist, Salvador Dalí, is one of the most
12 celebrated surrealist artists ever.
13   Dalí was born in 1904 in Catalonia,
14 Spain. He showed a passion for art early in
15 life and was enrolled in drawing school by
16 1916. He continued his art education at the
17 Real Academia de Bellas Artes de San
18 Fernando in Madrid, Spain through 1926.
19 There, he honed his painting skills through
20 one of his first works, *Basket of Bread*. It
21 was during this time that he met another
22 famous artist, Pablo Picasso, who would
23 help shape Dalí's art.
24   For the next 20 years, Dalí would go
25 on to paint some of his most famous
26 works: *The First Days of Spring,*
27 *Metamorphosis of Narcissus, and The*
28 *Face of War*, among many others. It was
29 around this time that he was introduced to
30 the American public; he was an instant
31 phenomenon. His surrealist art was
32 something that Americans had never
33 experienced before, and during the war-
34 torn period in the early 1940's, Dalí
35 relocated to the United States.
36   After World War II, Dalí and his wife,
37 Gala, moved back to Spain. For the next 25
38 years, Dalí would produce paintings,
39 sculptures, recordings, and drawings on an
40 irregular basis. During this period, his art
41 and style were heavily influenced by his
42 new-found love of math and science.
43   Dalí died in his home of heart failure in
44 1989; he was 84 years old. Interestingly,
45 the location of his death was only ¼ mile
46 from his place of birth, baptism, and
47 funeral. During his career, Dalí produced
48 over 1,500 paintings, many of which today
49 serve as the finest examples of surrealism
50 ever produced.

1. The primary purpose of the passage is to

   (A) discuss the history of surrealism.
   (B) explain the importance of a piece of artwork.
   (C) show how World War II affected Salvador Dalí.
   (D) describe the life and work of Salvador Dalí.

2. Which of the following is the earliest of Dalí's works?

   (A) *The Persistence of Memory*
   (B) *Basket of Bread*
   (C) *The First Days of Spring*
   (D) *The Face of War*

3. Based on the definition of surrealism, which of the following is an example of surrealism?

   (A) A painting of boats sailing through the clouds.
   (B) A painting of a bowl of fruit on a kitchen table.
   (C) A realistic self-portrait.
   (D) A photograph of a sunset.

4. As used in line 9, the word "depicts" most nearly means

   (A) shows.
   (B) admires.
   (C) erases.
   (D) explains.

5. We can infer that Pablo Picasso

   (A) taught Dalí everything he knows about surrealism.
   (B) was a better artist than Dalí.
   (C) played a role is Dali's success as an artist.
   (D) collaborated with Dalí on some of his paintings.

Reading Passage 7

1   Every year roughly 1.5 million
2   wildebeest migrate in East Africa. Every 2-
3   3 months, giant herds move further
4   clockwise in their migration pattern. These
5   400-pound animals are chasing the
6   seasonal rains that nourish the grasslands
7   wildebeest depend on for food. The
8   African mammals aren't alone, either.
9   Every year thousands of different species
10 undertake migrations of various sizes and
11 types.
12   Animals migrate for many different
13 reasons. One of the most common is
14 climate. The monarch butterfly is one such
15 species. These beautiful, delicate insects
16 are unable to survive the harsh
17 temperatures of the American winter, so
18 they are forced to migrate south to Mexico.
19 The butterflies make the 3,000 mile
20 journey over the course of four separate
21 generations; no single butterfly will cover
22 the distance to Mexico and back.
23   Other animals migrate because their
24 mating grounds are in a different location
25 than where they live. American Salmon are
26 a good example of this. These fish spend
27 the vast majority of their lives in the
28 Pacific Ocean off the coast of Alaska and

29 Russia. When they mature, the salmon
30 return to the freshwater rivers and lakes
31 they were born in to breed.
32   Some animals migrate due to better
33 hunting opportunities, like the Osprey.
34 These birds primarily take roost in Canada
35 and the Midwest of the United States:
36 Ohio, Pennsylvania, and New York,
37 among others. Starting in the fall, these
38 birds will begin to fly south, but they don't
39 stop in Florida. They continue flying
40 across the Gulf of Mexico, stopping on
41 islands like Cuba, Jamaica, and Haiti.
42 Once they arrive in their final destination,
43 typically South America, Osprey will
44 spend the winter hunting along the fruitful
45 coast.
46   While every migratory animal migrates
47 according to different schedules, lengths,
48 patterns, and reasons, one thing is the
49 same: migration is a necessary part of our
50 ecosystem. Without this process, billions
51 of insects, birds, mammals, and reptiles
52 wouldn't be able to complete their life
53 cycles. As today's scientists learn more
54 about migration, they learn more about
55 how to protect these amazing animals with
56 which we share planet earth.

1. The main purpose of the passage is to

   (A) explain how Wildebeest migrate the entire year in East Africa.
   (B) compare and contrast the migration of American Salmon and butterflies.
   (C) describe various features and habits of different animals .
   (D) describe the different reasons animals migrate.

2. All of the following were mentioned as a reason for migration EXCEPT

   (A) competition.
   (B) mating.
   (C) food availability.
   (D) climate.

3. Based on the passage, what is the normal number of generations that is required for Monarch butterflies to migrate?

   (A) One
   (B) Two
   (C) Three
   (D) Four

4. As used in line 16, the word "harsh" most nearly means

   (A) dry.
   (B) hot.
   (C) cold.
   (D) wet.

5. The passage supplies information to answer which of the following questions?

   (A) How many miles do Osprey migrate each year?
   (B) How many wildebeest migrate each year?
   (C) What South American countries do Osprey migrate to?
   (D) How much does an American Salmon weigh?

Reading Passage 8

Mother's Day was still a few months away, but this year I needed much more time for my gift. I had presented my mom with the classics before: flowers, gift cards, and certificates to clean the house. But this time I wanted to give her something original that she would love. I decided on a coffee table.

Every morning while I was getting ready for school, my mom would sit on the couch in our living room and drink her coffee. She would read the paper and plan her day; I think it was one of her favorite times. We've had the same table since I was four or five years old, and it was nothing special. It bore the marks of raising three children, covered in water marks, scratches, and burns from hot dishes.

My dad helped me buy the lumber. I picked out a dark red cherry for the top and a light pine for the legs. According to my father, we needed a few other things at the hardware store, as well. Once all the supplies were in our basement, it was time to start cutting. Each piece needed to be measured and cut - both to the right length and at the right angle

After many hours of working, we finally had all the pieces laid out. Each of the four legs matched, and the top of the table was in a few different sections. I held each of the top pieces as my dad slowly applied glue to them. After lining them up perfectly, we clamped them all together.

After waiting a whole day, it was finally time to place the top onto the legs. Together my dad and I carefully rested the cherry slab upon the legs. We spent the next few hours painstakingly screwing and nailing the entire structure together, taking care to hide the screws and nails out of sight.

Suddenly, it was Mother's Day. My father and I woke up early and placed the new coffee table in our living room. It looked perfect. We heard my mom begin to walk down the stairs, eventually rounding the corner where she could see us. She stopped, smiling. "I'll go make some coffee." That was all she needed to say.

1. The primary purpose of the passage is to

   (A) provide an accurate guide to building a coffee table.
   (B) make the reader think about their Mother's Day gift ideas.
   (C) show the importance of creating thoughtful gifts.
   (D) detail the process of creating a meaningful gift.

2. In line 39, the word "slab" most nearly means

   (A) section of leg.
   (B) piece of wood.
   (C) paint.
   (D) picture frame.

3. Based on the last line, one can infer that the narrator's mother feels what emotion from seeing her gift?

   (A) Joy
   (B) Interest
   (C) Frustration
   (D) Sadness

4. According to the passage, which of the following happened last?

   (A) The narrator and their father cut the leg pieces for the table.
   (B) The narrator thought of the idea to make their mom a coffee table.
   (C) The narrator bought wood.
   (D) The narrator's mom was drinking coffee at the coffee table.

5. In line 40, the word "painstakingly" most nearly means

   (A) slowly.
   (B) carefully.
   (C) quickly.
   (D) easily.

Reading Passage 9

On October 31st, 2000, the space shuttle *Soyuz TM-31* launched into space from Kazakhstan. Aboard the ship were three astronauts: two Russians and an American. Two days later, after 33 orbits of planet Earth, the crew docked their ship aboard the International Space Station (ISS). This was the start of the longest continuous human presence in outer space.

Construction of the ISS began in 1998. Both American and Russian teams manufactured and launched various pieces into space, one at a time. Once these sections of the station reached space, they were manually assembled by astronauts during short missions. Over 160 pieces had to be installed, ranging from the size of a dishwasher to the size of a large house. Since its initial construction, Canada, Japan, and Europe have been added to the list of cooperating nations.

The ISS serves many purposes. Scientists are able to conduct unique experiments in the zero-gravity environment in fields such as biology, chemistry, physics, and medicine. The station also serves as a staging area for possible future missions to the Moon, Mars, and various asteroids. Astronauts are also considered as major educational figures; they often will film educational videos for schools or conduct experiments on the behalf of students.

Life on the space station can be very different from life on earth. One of the most obvious distinctions is the absence of gravity. This affects everyday tasks such as eating, bathing, and using the bathroom. Partially for this reason, almost all of the food that astronauts consume is dehydrated and pre-cooked. Each individual has their own supply of food and is able to warm meals in various kitchens aboard the ISS. The crew looks forward to resupply missions from earth as they usually contain fresh fruits and vegetables.

All in all, the ISS has cost roughly $150 billion; it is sometimes referred to as the single most expensive item ever created. Since its inception, that money has helped fund valuable discoveries about the human body, dark matter, and growing crystals for medicine. The ISS has funding to continue to operate from both the US and Russia through 2024. Past that point, there have been international talks about developing a new, modern space station.

1. The main purpose of the passage is

   (A) to prove that US and Russia are the biggest space powers.
   (B) to provide information about the ISS.
   (C) to explain the difficulties of living in space.
   (D) to detail the construction of the ISS.

2. Relative to life on Earth, the passage implies that tasks on the ISS are relatively

   (A) easier.
   (B) more boring.
   (C) harder to complete.
   (D) more fun.

3. According to the passage

   (A) the ISS will likely be operational until at least 2024.
   (B) Canada and Japan were the first countries to think of the ISS.
   (C) the first human entered space in 2000.
   (D) the first mission to the ISS was launched from the United States.

4. As used in line 36, the word "distinctions" most nearly means

   (A) benefits.
   (B) issues.
   (C) problems.
   (D) differences.

5. The author's tone could best be described as

   (A) informational and optimistic.
   (B) excited but scared.
   (C) apprehensive but thoughtful.
   (D) boring and uninterested.

Reading Passage 10

Rosa didn't think she had ever gotten up at 4 AM before. Her older brother, Jaime, had always gotten to go fishing with their father, but Rosa wasn't previously allowed to go. Now that she had officially turned 10, it was her turn.

For her first trip, Rosa wanted to go alone with her father. Even though the lunch she had promised to make them was simple, it still took her much longer than expected. Rosa eagerly ran upstairs to wake her father up, "It's time to fish!"

Driving down the road, it seemed like they were the only people awake in the world. They parked at the dock and Rosa helped her father unhook the boat. They had taken many trips on the lake as a family in the past, so Rosa was well versed in this process. Her father grabbed their rods, reels, and tackle box. They were off.

By this point, the sun was just starting to rise. The early morning light illuminated the steam evaporating from the surface of the water. Her father handed Rosa a rod and helped her cast it into the water. "Nice throw!" he exclaimed, proud.

For the next few hours they talked about where to find the biggest fish, how to choose the right bait, and everything in-between. Every time Rosa stood up her father reminded her to always use one hand to stabilize herself. "If you don't have three points of contact with the boat, you're bound to fall in sometime."

After a few hours of fishing, it was finally time for lunch. Rosa proudly unpacked sandwiches and bags of chips she had packed for them. Halfway through his sandwich, Rosa's father stood up to grab a bottle of water. He reached down into the cooler and sifted through the ice. As he stood up, he used both hands to twist the cap off. "Dad, you always told me that-" *Splash!* Her father plunged into the cold water. "I always told you to keep three points of contact with the boat."

1. The main purpose of the passage is to

   (A) instruct the reader on how to prepare for a fishing trip.
   (B) show the love between a father and daughter.
   (C) describe a memorable first experience.
   (D) discuss the pros and cons of fishing.

2. In line 22, the word "illuminated" most nearly means

   (A) increased.
   (B) concealed.
   (C) highlighted.
   (D) ignited.

3. It can be inferred that Rosa wasn't allowed to go fishing in the past because

   (A) she didn't want to go.
   (B) her dad was worried she was scared.
   (C) her older brother didn't want her to go.
   (D) she wasn't old enough.

4. According to the passage,

   (A) Rosa and her brother do not get along well.
   (B) Rosa made lunch for her and her father.
   (C) Jaime was too sick to attend this fishing trip.
   (D) no one else was out fishing on the lake that day.

5. The incident that occurs in the last paragraph could be best characterized as

   (A) dangerous and scary.
   (B) funny and ironic.
   (C) interesting and thought-provoking.
   (D) awkward and obtuse.

Reading Passage 11

The Boundary Waters Canoe Area (BWCA) is a vast, wooded national forest located in Northern Minnesota. As a whole, the area is three times larger than the state of Rhode Island. Due to the nearly 5,000 lakes in this area, it is also the most popular canoeing destination in the world. Canoeists will travel dozens if not hundreds of miles into the backcountry, carrying everything they need to survive in their canoes. Up until 1986, a canoeist also was able to get a homemade bottle of ice cold root beer from the only building left in the BWCA: the Root Beer Lady's cabin.

Dorothy Molter became the owner of a resort in the BWCA, the *Isle of Pines,* in 1948. The resort had been operating in a typical way for the time, but that quickly changed due to a new set of laws officially designating the area as national forest. Originally, people could reach her location by seaplane or motorboat, but new rules outlawed motorized travel in the region. A year later, in 1949, the United States Forest Service began its attempts to purchase her resort and cabin.

Around this time, Molter began to change her business model. Instead of renting cabins, she began to create root beer. Her cabin had no electricity, and tanks of propane were carried into her cabin as her only source of power. During the winters, she would hire a team of workers to cut blocks of ice to keep her rootbeer cold; this ice would last from March to August most years.

On busy days, Molter would see over 100 people who specifically canoed out to her cabin to buy root beer. In busy seasons, she could see as many as 7,000 guests. In 1964 the US Wilderness Act deemed the sale of her root beer illegal, so she began giving it away in exchange for a "donation" from people.

In 1975, Molter was appointed as a Forest Service "volunteer in service", which allowed for a legal loophole for her property in the BWCA. She sold root beer from her cabin until her death in 1986. Her cabin was deconstructed and moved to Ely, MN, where it now serves as a museum.

1. The primary purpose of the passage is to

    (A) provide a brief history of Dorothy
        Molter's root beer business.
    (B) discuss the root beer sales tactics of
        Dorothy Molter.
    (C) discuss why the BWCA is a popular
        canoeing spot.
    (D) discuss the reasons that people
        choose to canoe.

2. The BWCA is the most popular
    canoeing destination because

    (A) the area is three times larger than
        the state of Rhode Island.
    (B) people could buy homeade root
        beer.
    (C) it was in a wooded, secluded area.
    (D) it had thousands of places to canoe.

3. As used in line 2, the word "vast" most
    nearly means

    (A) crowded.
    (B) empty.
    (C) large.
    (D) wooded.

4. What did Molter do once the sale of root
    beer was declared illegal?

    (A) she didn't change her sales strategy
        at all.
    (B) she stopped making root beer for
        people.
    (C) she began donating her root beer to
        people for free.
    (D) she received donations from people
        in exchange for her root beer.

5. From the last paragraph, one can infer
    that

    (A) Molter's house was torn down and
        destroyed.
    (B) Molter's cabin is no longer in the
        BWCA.
    (C) Molter was hired by the forest
        service due to her knowledge of the
        area.
    (D) Molter's root beer is still sold in
        stores today.

Reading Passage 12

On October 7th, 2001, the United States invaded Afghanistan in-part as retaliation for the terrorist attacks occuring on September 11th, 2001. In 2020, the war entered its 18th year, making it the longest conflict in United States' history. While that may seem long, its length is significantly shorter than the 355 Years' War between Sicily and the United Kingdom from 1651 to 1986. Both of these conflicts top the list of longest armed conflicts, but one war stands out as holding the record for the shortest war ever fought in history: the Anglo-Zanzibar War.

During the late 19th and early 20th centuries, Britain claimed ownership over a kingdom in Eastern Africa known as the Zanzibar Sultanate. The British allowed the Zanzibaris to more or less rule over themselves under the condition that any change to their leader, the Sultan, would first be approved by the British.

On August 25th, 1896, Sultan Hamad bin Thuwaini died and was quickly replaced by Sultan Khalid bin Barghash. The British did not approve of this change, and immediately ordered the Sultan to step down on August 26th.

Since the Zanzibaris didn't listen to the order, the British had gathered several boats and about 1,000 soldiers outside the Sultan's palace. At 9:02 AM, the British began to fire at the palace, setting it on fire. They also sunk all three of the defending Zanzibar Sultanate ships.

The Sultan escaped during the fight, but the palace was taken by the British. The attack ended at 9:46 AM that same day. In total, the Sultan's forces suffered over 500 deaths and injuries, while only a single British soldier was injured. To this day, the Anglo-Zanzibar War remains the shortest conflict in history, lasting somewhere between 38 and 45 minutes.

1. The primary purpose of the passage is to

   (A) convince the reader that war should be avoided at all costs.
   (B) compare the lengths of various wars.
   (C) talk about the War in Afghanistan.
   (D) describe the events of the world's shortest war.

2. As used in line 3, the word "retaliation" most nearly means

   (A) apology.
   (B) revenge.
   (C) violence.
   (D) warning.

3. Based on the passage, one can infer that during the Anglo-Zanzibar war

   (A) the British army cheated during the attack.
   (B) the Zanzibaris didn't have an army.
   (C) the British eventually killed the Sultan.
   (D) the British forces were more powerful than the Zanzibaris.

4. What caused the Anglo-Zanzibar war to start?

   (A) The British wanted to take land from the Zanzibaris.
   (B) The Zanzibaris were tired of being ruled by the British.
   (C) The Zanzibaris didn't get permission from the British about their new leader.
   (D) The British elected a new leader.

5. In the last line of the passage, why is the duration of the war given as a range?

   (A) It is impossible to accurately time a war.
   (B) Historians always use a range when talking about the length of wars.
   (C) The exact timing of the war is unknown.
   (D) The British and Zanzibaris each claim a different length of the war.

Reading Passage 13

1   James had just crossed the 75-mile
2 mark, and his legs were entering new
3 territory. As a last resort, he had decided to
4 enter the Chattanooga Century - a 100-mile
5 bike race through the forest and foothills of
6 Tennessee. It's not as if he wasn't a cyclist,
7 but James had only ever ridden ¾ of a
8 competitive century before this race.
9   Two weeks prior he came close -
10 excruciatingly close - to qualifying for
11 Nationals the next month, for the chance to
12 compete in the 75-mile race with some of
13 the best cyclists in the country. To be
14 eligible, a racer needed to finish top 5 in
15 any of the qualifying races throughout the
16 season. In the Atlanta 50-Mile, the race
17 two weeks ago, he was leading the pack
18 with a mile left. Victory seemed inevitable,
19 but his flat tire changed that. Being so
20 close to the finish, there was never going
21 to be enough time to change and continue
22 fast enough. James finished in 31st place.
23   While Atlanta was his best chance to
24 qualify, it wasn't his last. James
25 immediately registered for the Tennessee
26 race and began training for the longest
27 competitive ride of his life.

28   Now, at mile 95, James knew that the
29 cyclists more experienced with this length
30 of race would start to creep up behind him.
31 He had been holding on to a lonely fourth
32 place for almost 40 miles, sandwiched
33 between a group of three riders both ahead
34 of and behind him. "At mile 99, I'll give it
35 everything I've got," James thought to
36 himself. By now the clump of seven riders
37 had condensed to within a few of each
38 other.
39   Half-mile left, he stands in his saddle,
40 pedaling so hard, it felt as if his bike would
41 snap. One hundred meters left and instinct
42 is the only thing keeping James moving
43 forward. Out of the corner of his eye he
44 sees the timing gate whiz above his head.
45 The race is over.
46   He looks up and sees nobody ahead of
47 him, confusingly. As James turns around
48 he realizes what has happened. The rest of
49 the riders were only a few feet behind, but
50 they were behind him. Panting, James says
51 out loud, "at least Nationals is only 75
52 miles!"

1. The passage tells the story of

   (A) a failure followed by a triumph.
   (B) the difficulties of being a professional cyclist.
   (C) the pain caused by not achieving your dreams.
   (D) one of the world's greatest cyclists.

2. Based on the opening paragraph, one can assume that a ¾ century is how many miles?

   (A) 25
   (B) 50
   (C) 75
   (D) 100

3. As used in line 10, the word "excruciatingly" most nearly means

   (A) extremely.
   (B) dangerously.
   (C) not very.
   (D) impulsively.

4. Why did James enter the Chattanooga Century race?

   (A) It was the only way that riders could qualify for Nationals.
   (B) It was his final chance to qualify for Nationals.
   (C) He wanted to prove to himself that he could complete a 100-mile race.
   (D) It was a good way to train for Nationals.

5. James lost his race in Atlanta because

   (A) he didn't train enough.
   (B) he had never ridden 100 miles before.
   (C) he was competing against the best cyclists in the country.
   (D) he had an issue with his bike.

Reading Passage 14

Tulip Fever remains one of the most fascinating eras of Dutch history. Tulips were first introduced to the Netherlands in 1593 from the Ottoman Empire. The brightly colored tulips were unlike any flower the region had seen, and because they could withstand the harsh winters, mania ensued.

The world's wealthiest and the poorest descended upon local Dutch taverns to buy and sell the prized flowers. Because tulips only bloomed for one week in April and May, most sales were simply for the dormant bulbs in the ground or future ownership of the flower at the end of the season. Therefore, in one day, a flower could easily exchange ten hands, inflating prices by as much as 300% to 500%.

Everyone assumed the tulip's value would always increase, but, in February of 1637, the bubonic plague brought trading to a halt. With no buyers, speculators holding on to contracts faced the harsh reality of having to pay exorbitant prices for tulips. Those already in possession of tulips saw the value of their investment plummet. The courts offered little respite, as the trades were considered gambling and thus unenforceable under Dutch law. Tulip Fever had officially come to a chilly stop.

To this day, many use the phrase "Tulip Fever" or "Tulip Mania" to describe unpredictable markets like the dot-com bubble in the 1990's, the subprime mortgage crisis that led to the Great Recession in 2008, and the current bitcoin exchanges happening today. It remains an accurate lesson of ethics in the world of business and finance.

1. The main point of the passage is to

   (A) compare and contrast "Tulip Fever" and "Tulip Mania".
   (B) provide a brief Dutch history.
   (C) describe a specific economic event in the Netherlands.
   (D) explain the popularity and importance of tulips.

2. Tulips were so popular because

   (A) they were brightly colored.
   (B) they were cheap, so both poor and rich people could buy them.
   (C) they only bloomed for one week each year.
   (D) they could survive the winter.

3. As used in line 14, the word "dormant" most nearly means

   (A) dead.
   (B) flourishing.
   (C) inactive.
   (D) expensive.

4. Since tulips only bloomed for one week a year,

   (A) many people bought future ownership of tulips.
   (B) people only purchased tulips in April or May.
   (C) tulips were not traded very often.
   (D) people purchased tulip seeds to plant themselves.

5. Tulip trading stopped because of

   (A) inflation.
   (B) the bubonic plague.
   (C) law enforcement.
   (D) decrease in value of tulips.

Reading Passage 15

1   What do you get when you cross a
2 beaver, an otter, and a duck? You get one
3 of nature's most intriguing animals: the
4 platypus. When the first platypus was
5 examined, scientists actually thought it was
6 a hoax. "It naturally excites the idea of
7 some deceptive preparation by artificial
8 means," English zoologist George Shaw
9 wrote in 1799. The platypus' body is
10 covered with brown and black fur like an
11 otter's. Its feet are webbed, similar to that
12 of a duck, and it also possesses a bill with
13 sensitive receptors that can detect the
14 slightest changes in water movement. The
15 animal also features a beaver-sized tail,
16 which serves as a rudder for swimming.
17 Because of these odd features, Shaw
18 believed that someone took the bill of a
19 duck, the body of an otter, and the tail of a
20 beaver and put them together to form this
21 odd creature.

22   After close and careful examination,
23 Shaw confirmed that the animal was
24 indeed real, and he named it the
25 "platypus". Soon, other unique features of
26 the platypus were discovered. Coming out
27 of the webbed feet were retractable claws
28 that were used to burrow and dig for food;
29 their large flat tail wasn't just for show – it
30 actually stores fat that helps prevent the
31 animal from starving.
32   While all of the features discussed
33 above are indeed interesting, what makes
34 platypuses the most fascinating creatures is
35 their ability to lay eggs. While mammals
36 are known to give birth to live young,
37 platypuses actually preserved the reptile-
38 like capability to lay eggs. In fact, they are
39 one of only two known mammalian species
40 (the other being echidnas) that lay eggs.

1. The main point of the passage is to

   (A) describe similarities between beavers, otters, and ducks.
   (B) explain a scientific prank that went wrong.
   (C) prove that the platypus is the world's only mammal that lays eggs.
   (D) describe the strange discovery of a unique animal.

2. As used in line 6, the word "hoax" most nearly means

   (A) a mistake.
   (B) an artificial creation.
   (C) a prank.
   (D) an imposter.

3. A platypus's tail

   (A) stores fat incase of food shortage.
   (B) is similar to that of an otter.
   (C) doesn't have a useful function.
   (D) is used for digging for food.

4. Platypuses and echidnas are similar because they both

   (A) are half mammal half reptile.
   (B) are mammals that lay eggs.
   (C) were thought to be hoaxes.
   (D) give birth to live young.

5. The author implies that Shaw

   (A) was gullible and easily tricked.
   (B) was a persistent scientist.
   (C) was the first person to ever see a Platypus.
   (D) discovered many animals in his life.

Reading Passage 16

China is one of the world's oldest cultures. It's written history dates back as far as 4,000 years ago, and archaeological evidence supports origins as early as 8,000 years ago. It is also considered the only surviving ancient civilization, outlasting the likes of the Roman, Babylonian, and Egyptian empires.

Over that time, the Chinese culture has naturally made substantial contributions to the modern world. Ancient China is credited for the Four Great Inventions: gunpowder, paper, the printing press, and a compass. The Chinese additionally invented many universal items that we use today, such as silk, wheelbarrows, kites, umbrellas, and even noodles. More so, in an effort to boost its economy, China became the world's manufacturer, fabricating everything from plastic bottles to plush toy animals for global consumers.

However, within the last half-century, we have seen the reverse phenomenon also occurring, where Western cultures are contributing to and influencing the ancient Asian country. The Chinese population has adopted a new and remarkably ravenous appetite for technology, smart phones, apps, and fast food, which Western companies are more than eager to feed. Global fashion houses based in Paris, Spain, Italy, and New York now cater to a growing segment of the Chinese population hungry for brand name fashion, jewelry, and handbags. Even Hollywood films, once completely shut out from the country, are now making valuable contributions to Chinese pop culture.

As technology and consumer tastes continue to evolve, this trend will only continue, and the door to China will remain open to accept more contributions from the 'newer' countries and cultures that exist.

1. The main purpose of this passage is to

   (A) explain the contributions made by and to China throughout the past.
   (B) compare and contrast the contributions made by China and other countries.
   (C) persuade readers that China is the most influential country.
   (D) provide a brief history of China.

2. Which of the following is *not* mentioned as one of the Four Great Inventions from Ancient China?

   (A) gunpowder
   (B) printing press
   (C) wheelbarrows.
   (D) compasses

3. What does the author mean when he says that China has become the "world's manufacturer," in lines 18 – 19?

   (A) China has more factories than any other country in the world.
   (B) China's economy is dependent on the manufacturing of goods.
   (C) China creates and exports many useful goods to countries around the world.
   (D) Without China, the world would have no items manufactured.

4. As used in line 20, the word "fabricating" most nearly means

   (A) lying.
   (B) destroying.
   (C) selling.
   (D) creating.

5. The author seems to believe that

   (A) as time goes on, China will benefit more from Western cultures.
   (B) China has made more significant contributions to the world than the Babylonian and Roman Empires.
   (C) in the future, China will always be the world's manufacturer.
   (D) soon Chinese culture will be almost identical to Western cultures.

Reading Passage 17

1   After rigorous scientific research,
2   lengthy experimentation, and detailed
3   notes, we've finally determined how to
4   create the perfect grilled cheese. What is
5   the secret? Well for starters, you have to
6   cut the sandwich into two triangular
7   pieces. If you accidentally slice your
8   grilled cheese into rectangular halves, you
9   may as well throw the whole thing away.
10   Before you even get down to the
11   decision of how to slice your sandwich,
12   you'll need to know how to prepare it.
13   First, you need to choose your bread of
14   choice. We highly recommend using
15   potato bread, but buttermilk, sourdough,
16   and pumpernickel are all good options.
17   Whatever you do, don't settle for basic
18   white bread: it's basically a death sentence
19   for your grilled cheese.
20   Once you've chosen your bread, it's
21   time to decide on the perfect combination
22   of cheeses. With so many cheeses to
23   choose from, this is the most difficult part
24   of the process. If you want the most flavor,
25   use a combination of sharp cheddar and
26   American cheese; if you want an extra
27   kick, add a slice of pepper jack. If you
28   want to experiment with other types of
29   cheese, make sure to choose cheese that
30   easily melts – that means no parmesan or
31   feta.
32   Now this next step is imperative and
33   often overlooked by even the most
34   experienced grilled cheese chefs: spread a
35   thin layer of mayonnaise on the bread
36   before you add the cheese. This will add
37   extra flavor. Once you spread the
38   mayonnaise and carefully lay the cheese,
39   you're ready to put your cooking skills to
40   the test!
41   Melt a small amount of butter in a
42   nonstick pan, and cook each side of your
43   sandwich for 3 minutes over low heat.
44   Once you're done, don't forget our biggest
45   secret: triangles over rectangles.

1. Which of the following titles is best for this passage?

   (A) Perfection in a Pan
   (B) The Death of a Sandwich
   (C) Triangles over Rectangles
   (D) Cooking like a King

2. The author implies that you cannot have a perfect grilled cheese if you

   (A) use sourdough bread.
   (B) don't use pepper jack cheese.
   (C) use too much butter.
   (D) forget to use mayonnaise.

3. As used in line 32, the word imperative means

   (A) overlooked.
   (B) relevant.
   (C) delicious.
   (D) crucial.

4. The primary purpose of this passage is to

   (A) persuade.
   (B) instruct.
   (C) entertain.
   (D) inform.

5. You should cook your grilled cheese for

   (A) only 3 minutes over low heat.
   (B) a total of 6 minutes over low heat.
   (C) 3 minutes on each side over medium heat.
   (D) a total of 6 minutes over high heat.

Reading Passage 18

Silk is a much better fabric than cotton because of its moisture-wicking abilities, anti-ageing properties, and incredible sleep support. Given silk's denser, lighter material, it is easier for the fabric to regulate the body's temperature. It promotes and preserves coolness and allows your skin to breathe in order to prevent unwanted moisture.

Silk can also slow down aging. Because silk is a natural material harvested from silkworm cocoons, it contains a naturally-occurring chemical called albumen. This wonder enzyme helps speed up skin metabolism, reinvigorating dying and tired skin cells for a more youthful glow.

What really makes silk one of the leading fabrics for bedding and nightwear is its extremely soft texture. The material is light, cool, breathable, and extremely soft. It facilitates a better sleeping experience, leaving users to a night of moisture-free slumber.

While more expensive than cotton, silk's durability makes any product a sound investment. Whether it's towels, bedding, table napkins, or everyday clothing, this wonder fabric can improve your health and quality of life with just a little more cost.

1. The best title for this selection would be

   (A) "A Comparison of Silk and Cotton."
   (B) "The Benefits of Silk."
   (C) "Silk: The Superior Fabric."
   (D) "Choosing the Right Fabric."

2. As used in line 11, the word "harvested" most nearly means

   (A) chosen.
   (B) created.
   (C) grown.
   (D) collected.

3. Why is silk one of the leading fabrics for bedding and nightwear?

   (A) It eliminates all moisture.
   (B) Its texture is breathable and soft.
   (C) It speeds up skin metabolism.
   (D) It's harvested from silkworm cocoons.

4. Which of the following is *not* mentioned as a benefit of silk?

   (A) It facilitates better sleep.
   (B) It controls body temperature.
   (C) It's soft and breathable.
   (D) It's an inexpensive material.

5. What is the purpose of the first paragraph?

   (A) To make an argument about silk.
   (B) To explain one benefit of silk in detail.
   (C) To compare and contrast silk and cotton.
   (D) To explain why cotton is superior to silk.

Reading Passage 19

Imagine suddenly discovering a strange, dark, egg-shaped stone covered in mysterious carvings. What would you think? How would you react? Who would you tell, if anyone?

This is what happened to a group of construction workers, hired by local businessman Seneca Ladd, in 1872 near Lake Winnipesaukee in New Hampshire. While digging in the clay near the shore of the lake, these workers unearthed an unusual artifact that is known today as "New England's Mystery Stone". Today, Seneca Ladd is credited with the discovery of the stone.

The artifact measures four inches in length and two and a half inches in width and is made out of quartzite, which is a smooth rock that is the result of shifting rock layers. The stone is shaped like an egg and is covered in carvings of a face, a teepee, an ear of corn, and geometric figures resembling circles. While these symbols have led some researchers to believe that the stone is a Native American artifact, others claim that it may be of Celtic or Inuit origins.

Ever since its discovery, naturalists, geologists, and archaeologists have come up with theories about the New England Mystery Stone, but many questions still remain unanswered. Who created this mysterious artifact? What are the meanings of the cryptic carvings? What purpose did this stone serve in ancient times?

Maybe one day we will discover the true story of this mysterious stone. Until then, we can continue coming up with our own theories about one of America's most curious artifacts.

1. What is the main purpose of the passage?

   (A) To explain that some mysteries are better left unsolved.
   (B) To show that scientist's theories are often false.
   (C) To prove that a discovery can be made when you least expect it.
   (D) To provide information about an unusual discovery.

2. As used in line 11, the word "unearthed" most nearly means

   (A) buried.
   (B) stole.
   (C) uncovered.
   (D) stumbled upon.

3. Who discovered the mystery stone?

   (A) A local businessman.
   (B) Archaeologists studying Lake Winnipesaukee.
   (C) A Native American tribe.
   (D) A group of construction workers.

4. As used in line 34, the word "cryptic" most nearly means

   (A) dangerous.
   (B) mysterious.
   (C) obvious.
   (D) diverse.

5. The stone was probably named the "Mystery Stone" because

   (A) no one knows the names of the construction workers who discovered the stone.
   (B) there are still many questions about the stone that are unanswered.
   (C) researchers question where the stone is located today.
   (D) New England is home to many unsolved mysteries.

Reading Passage 20

1   The Cold War, beginning shortly after
2 World War II in 1945, was a decades long
3 stalemate between the United States, and
4 the former Soviet Union. The U.S. led
5 Western Powers wanted to spread
6 democracy and eliminate communism
7 throughout the world, and the U.S.S.R. led
8 Eastern Powers wanted the exact opposite.

9   Both sides had always existed and held
10 an unfriendly relationship. However, it
11 wasn't until post World War II that both
12 adapted the technology to make and test
13 atomic bombs. The swords so to speak
14 made way for weapons that could cause
15 mass destruction, and it was a very real
16 threat.

17   At its height, the Cold War held an icy
18 grip of terror throughout the country. In
19 fear of an atomic bomb dropping at any
20 moment, schools held emergency duck-
21 and-cover drills; families built fortified
22 bunkers under their homes; armed forces
23 ran air raids over even the most remote
24 towns. Many would call the Cold War one
25 of the most fearful times in U.S. history,
26 and yet not a single civilian's life was ever
27 in danger.

28   The real battleground was overseas, in
29 countries caught in the middle between
30 pro-democratic and pro-communist
31 movements. Many parts of Eastern Europe,
32 such as East Germany, Hungary, and
33 Czechoslovakia, eagerly joined the Eastern
34 bloc in the early part of the war. The U.S.
35 helped fight for Democracy in regions
36 close to home, such as the Dominican
37 Republic, Grenada, Guatemala, and Cuba.

38   The Nuclear Test-Ban Treaty of 1963
39 brought an end to the terror everyday
40 citizens felt at home, work, and school.
41 However, the efforts became even more
42 drawn-out and bloody. The greatest
43 examples being the years long Vietnam
44 War, in which millions of people lost their
45 lives and the Korean War, where, to this
46 day, there is still a militarized line between
47 communist North Korea and democratic
48 South Korea.

49   Only with the fall of the Soviet Union
50 in 1991, did the Cold War end. However,
51 with increasing tensions between the U.S.
52 and Russia many question whether it ended
53 at all.

1. What is the main purpose of the passage?

   (A) To compare and contrast the two sides fighting in the Cold War.
   (B) To give a brief background on the Cold War.
   (C) To explain why the Cold War was the most devastating war in U.S. history.
   (D) To suggest that the Cold War really never ended.

2. The U.S. and Western Powers were fighting for

   (A) the spread of democracy.
   (B) the spread of communism.
   (C) complete control over all nuclear weapons.
   (D) the elimination of democracy.

3. As used in line 23, the word "remote" most nearly means

   (A) populated.
   (B) dangerous.
   (C) faraway.
   (D) famous.

4. The Cold War was one of the most fearful times in U.S. history because

   (A) many innocent civilians were attacked and killed.
   (B) school children were often targeted.
   (C) atomic bombs were used on a regular basis.
   (D) there was a constant fear of nuclear attack.

5. From the passage it can be inferred that the Nuclear Test-Ban Treaty

   (A) completely ended the Cold War.
   (B) caused the Vietnam War and the Korean War.
   (C) was essentially ineffective and useless.
   (D) restricted the use of nuclear weapons.

Reading Passage 21

Some of the most popular and beloved children's books were written over a five-year period from 1955 to 1960. These classics include *Horton Hears a Who!*, *The Cat in the Hat*, *How the Grinch Stole Christmas!*, and *Green Eggs and Ham*. Not only were these books were written in the same time period, but they were also written by the same author: the famous Dr. Seuss.

Born in 1904 and raised in Springfield, Massachusetts, Dr. Seuss wasn't always Dr. Seuss; his given name was Theodor Seuss "Ted" Geisel. During his time as an undergraduate at Dartmouth College, he started to write under the pen name "Dr. Seuss." After gaining praise for his initial writings and short stories, he stuck with the name during his studies at Lincoln College, Oxford, England.

While many people may know Geisel for his writings, he started his career mainly as an illustrator. For the first 15 years of his professional career, Dr. Seuss illustrated comics and cartoons for magazines and companies like *Judge*, *Vanity Fair*, and *Life*. During this part of his career, his subject matter mostly focused on light-hearted observations and advertising.

The lighthearted nature of Geisel's comics and illustrations changed at the onset of WWII in the late 1930's. Dr. Seuss began to create political cartoons for a variety of different publications. He was staunchly critical of Hitler and Mussolini as well as public figures who did not want the US to enter the war. During a short two-year period, Geisel created over 400 political illustrations which are now collected in the book *Dr. Seuss Goes to War*.

After WWII, Geisel settled into the most prolific writing period of his career. It was during the period of 1950 to 1975 that Dr. Seuss wrote his best selling books that would go on to sell over 650 million copies. Geisel died of cancer in 1991 at the age of 87. Following his death, a number of libraries, gardens, and museums were dedicated in his name to honor his contributions to education and literacy.

1. The passage is primarily concerned with

   (A) the origin of how Theodor Geisel received the name Dr. Seuss.
   (B) the literary career and life of Dr. Seuss.
   (C) the number of books that Dr. Seuss wrote.
   (D) the influence WWII had on the Dr. Seuss's writing.

2. In line 16, what is meant by the phrase "pen name?"

   (A) It is a name adopted by an author to avoid using their real name.
   (B) It is a nickname given to an author by their friends.
   (C) It references the tool that authors use to write: a pen.
   (D) It is a traditional name given to authors at Dartmouth.

3. According to the passage, Dr. Seuss worked as all of the following EXCEPT

   (A) an illustrator.
   (B) a cartoonist.
   (C) a photographer.
   (D) an author.

4. According to the passage, which of the following happened first?

   (A) WWII broke out in the late 1930's.
   (B) Geisel wrote for *Vanity Fair*.
   (C) Geisel's stories were compiled into *Dr. Seuss Goes to War*.
   (D) Dr. Seuss wrote *Horton Hears a Who*.

5. The author's tone towards Dr. Seuss could best be described as

   (A) admiring.
   (B) apathetic.
   (C) jealous.
   (D) skeptical.

Reading Passage 22

The largest stock market crash in United States history occurred in September of 1929. The crash followed the "Roaring 20's" and marked the beginning of the Great Depression. Realizing that the economy may require federal assistance, President Franklin D. Roosevelt pioneered a now-famous program: the Civilian Conservation Corps.

The Civilian Conservation Corps, typically referred to by its initials, CCC, was one of the major programs under the larger New Deal program. While the entire New Deal was intended to stimulate the economy and reform American banking institutions, the CCC was specifically aimed at young, unemployed men. The major goal of the CCC was to provide manual labor jobs to men aged 17 to 28, mostly working in the development of natural resources in rural lands.

The CCC accomplished an incredible number of projects during its 10-year lifespan. In the vein of public works, the program built over 125,000 miles of road, enough to cover the distance from LA to New York almost 50 times. Along these roads they also built bridges, almost 47,000 in total.

The CCC was also very active in the environment. Starting in 1934, the organization planted over 3 billion trees across the United States. At the same time, CCC workers put in over 8 million hours fighting forest fires in every corner of the United States. Today, many of the trails and paths that hikers used were originally built by the CCC.

In 1942, the United States entered into WWII shortly after the bombing of Pearl Harbor. With this declaration came the draft, and millions of young men were commissioned to fight. This provided work for millions of Americans and effectively ended the CCC. While the organization hasn't existed for over 75 years, its legacy will continue to live on for generations.

1. The passage is primarily concerned with

   (A) the legacy Franklin D. Roosevelt left behind.
   (B) the impact of the Great Depression.
   (C) the history of the leaders of the CCC.
   (D) the history of some of the CCC projects.

2. As used in line 7, the word "pioneered" most nearly means

   (A) ended.
   (B) developed.
   (C) fought against.
   (D) discovered.

3. According to the author, the CCC

   (A) built over 3 billion miles of road.
   (B) hasn't existed in over 100 years.
   (C) essentially ended because of WWII.
   (D) only hired men in between the ages of 17 and 28.

4. Based on the passage, one can assume that the CCC

   (A) was instrumental in the development of air travel in the US.
   (B) helped pull the United States out of the Great Depression.
   (C) quickly failed, leading to its demise after only ten years.
   (D) was developed during WWI.

5. As used in line 43, the word "commissioned" most nearly means

   (A) trying.
   (B) attempting.
   (C) commanded.
   (D) insisting.

Reading Passage 23

1

1   In 1904, Lizzie Magie self-published
2 the board game *The Landlord's Game.* As
3 an avid anti-monopolist, she created the
4 game as an approachable teaching tool to
5 discuss and understand why concentrating
6 land and money into the hands of only a
7 few wealthy individuals was not ideal. Her
8 game was met with a moderate amount of
9 success but was largely forgotten.
10   Roughly 30 years later, Charles
11 Darrow, a board game inventor, discovered
12 the game. He was introduced to *The*
13 *Landlord's Game* at a dinner party where
14 he played several times over the course of
15 the night. Over the next several months,
16 Darrow adapted and changed the game,
17 eventually selling the rights to game-
18 producing company Parker Brothers. They
19 would patent the game as *Monopoly* in
20 1935.
21   Very quickly after patenting the game,
22 Parker Brothers began distributing
23 *Monopoly* outside the US. During WWII,
24 the British Secret Intelligence Service even
25 produced their own special version to
26 distribute to prisoners of war held by the
27 Nazis. These versions contained "maps,
28 compasses, real money, and other objects
29 useful for escaping" according to
30 historians.
31   Since its inception in the early 20th
32 century, *Monopoly* has gone on to produce
33 hundreds of different versions in dozens of
34 different countries. Typically, the spaces
35 and idioms used for each game are country
36 specific. For example, the Canadian
37 version includes buildings and monuments
38 in Canadian cities like Montreal and
39 Quebec City.
40   *Monopoly* is one of the most popular
41 board games to ever be produced. Since it
42 was patented in 1935, over 275 million
43 units have been sold. Hasbro, the company
44 that now owns *Monopoly,* claims that they
45 print over $30 billion in game money
46 every year. Considering that the only
47 games that sell more copies every year are
48 chess, checkers, and backgammon, it is
49 likely that *Monopoly* will continue to be a
50 popular game for decades to come.

1. The primary purpose of the passage is to

   (A) convince the reader that monopolies are bad.
   (B) make the argument that *Monopoly* is the best board game ever.
   (C) discuss the origin and history of *Monopoly*.
   (D) discuss Lizzie Magie's role in the creation of *Monopoly*.

2. Why did Lizzie Magie create *The Landlord's Game?*

   (A) She was passionate about board games.
   (B) She was a huge supporter of big businesses and monopolies.
   (C) She was confident that it would be one of the most popular games ever created.
   (D) She wanted to use it to promote her values and beliefs.

3. As used in line 19, the word "patent" most nearly means

   (A) sell.
   (B) trademark.
   (C) buy.
   (D) create.

4. As used in line 31, the word "inception" most nearly means

   (A) collapse.
   (B) popularity.
   (C) discovery.
   (D) creation.

5. Based on the last paragraph, it can be inferred that

   (A) Parker Brothers sold *Monopoly* to Hasbro.
   (B) *Monopoly* will sell 275 million copies this year.
   (C) checkers and chess each sell twice as many copies as *Monopoly*.
   (D) *Monopoly* will eventually become the world's most popular game.

Reading Passage 24

Bananas are one of the world's favorite fruits, with over 100 million tons of bananas produced and sold annually throughout the world. However, the banana as we know it is in imminent danger.

Today's banana, known as the Cavendish species, is actually a genetic clone of its forefathers. Unlike other fruits, such as apples or oranges, the Cavendish banana is sterile and cannot reproduce on its own. As a result, while there are over 1,000 species of wild bananas, the Cavendish banana we buy at the grocery store are all the same, or a monoculture.

Being a clone does have its benefits. They are seedless and non-acidic fruit, making them a favored fruit for many. Additionally, bananas last longer on the shelf, and can be shipped farther distances at lower prices across the world. However, left to the forces of nature and evolution, the Cavendish banana stands little to no chance of survival.

Shocking it has happened before and may happen again. During the 1950's and 1960's, the Gros Michel banana, which once ruled the supermarket shelves, was completely wiped out by a fungal disease called Fusarium Wilt. The Cavendish banana was simply chosen as its replacement because of its resistance to that particular strain of disease.

However, over time new diseases have evolved, such as the Black Sigatoka and Panama disease. Now, food scientists and genetic researchers around the world are racing against the clock to generate solutions before the next potential outbreak.

1. What is the main purpose of the passage?

   (A) To describe the difference between a banana and apples.
   (B) To explain how scientists prepare for disease outbreaks.
   (C) To discuss a possible threat to bananas.
   (D) To show how strong bananas are today.

2. As used in line 5, "imminent" most nearly means

   (A) important.
   (B) severe.
   (C) insignificant.
   (D) approaching.

3. The Cavendish banana differs from apples and oranges because

   (A) it is resistant to certain fungal diseases.
   (B) it cannot reproduce on its own.
   (C) it is not sterile.
   (D) it is not a genetic clone.

4. The Cavendish banana was chosen to replace the Gros Michel banana because

   (A) it was resistant to Fusarium Wilt.
   (B) it could fight off any disease.
   (C) it had a better taste.
   (D) it has a longer shelf life.

5. We can assume that the greatest threat to the modern-day banana is

   (A) changing customer tastes.
   (B) the evolution of fungal diseases.
   (C) global labor disputes.
   (D) increasing costs of the banana.

Reading Passage 25

The idea of living completely isolated from the modern-day world may sound impossible. Surprisingly though, on an island in the Indian Ocean roughly the size of a theme park, the Sentinelese are one of the few existing cultures today that maintain no contact with the outside world.

The people of North Sentinel Island, located in the Bay of Bengal, have reportedly been there for tens of thousands of years. First contact with the island was made in the late 1800s, when the British used surrounding islands in the same archipelago as a penal colony. An explorer by the name of W.V. Portman kidnapped six of the natives, but because many of them died of disease while in captivity and the island lacked "valuable" resources, the British largely left the Sentinelese people to themselves during the height of the colonial years.

The contact, however, was enough for the local Sentinelese tribe to fear foreigners. All outsiders are seen as a threat, and the people have been known to protect themselves with whatever means possible. Over the years, stranded ships, fishing boats, and illegal hunters have succumbed to the arrows of the Sentinelese people should they get too close.

The Indian government, who successfully made brief and peaceful excursion to the islands in the 1990s, now strictly prohibits anyone from coming within five nautical miles of the island. This is not only to protect foreigners, but more so to protect the people. Due to the population's small size and lack of genetic diversity, their immune systems are comprised. Contact with even the most common illnesses, like the cold or flu, can be potentially fatal to the average citizen.

Therefore, as the world has continued to advance around the island, staying disconnected from the outside world is no longer a choice, but a biological necessity for the continued survival of the people of North Sentinel Island.

1. The author's main purpose in writing this passage is to

   (A) condemn an ancient tribe.
   (B) describe a unique cultural group.
   (C) explore the characteristics of a mysterious island.
   (D) explain the importance of foreign exploration.

2. The Indian government prohibits anyone getting too close to the North Sentinel Island mainly because

   (A) the Sentinelese people are dangerous and armed.
   (B) the Indian government is scared of the Sentinelese people.
   (C) the Sentinelese people are very susceptible to outside illnesses.
   (D) the Sentinelese people carry unknown and deadly diseases.

3. As used in line 29, the word succumbed most nearly means

   (A) surrendered.
   (B) attacked.
   (C) stolen.
   (D) triumphed.

4. Why did the British eventually decide to leave the Sentinelese people to themselves?

   (A) The British didn't find any resources that were useful to them.
   (B) The British realized it was unjust to capture innocent people.
   (C) The Sentinelese tribe killed some of the British soldiers.
   (D) The British died of diseases while on the island.

5. As used in line 40 passage, the word "compromised" most nearly means

   (A) cooperated.
   (B) settled.
   (C) weakened.
   (D) strengthened.

Reading Passage 26

Did you know the human body has more bacteria than human cells? Bacteria actually outnumber human cells by 10 to 1, and more than 10,000 different species inhabit the human body. They are found everywhere: on your skin, in your eye, up your nose and in your stomach.

While many of these microorganisms are known to cause illnesses among the sick, in healthy individuals they peacefully coexist with their host (our bodies) and, contrary to popular opinion, play a vital role in many bodily functions.

The bacteria in our gastro-intestinal tract, for example, carry the genes and produce the enzymes necessary for us to digest foods and absorb nutrients. Microbes are also known to generate vitamins and anti-inflammatories, and even allow certain minerals, such as magnesium and sulfur, to become more bioavailable.

Only under certain conditions can these advantageous bacteria become pathogenic and cause disease or death. Things like environmental stress, smoking, or acidic foods can upset the delicate equilibrium between human cells and microbes. Powerful antibiotics are also known to kill not only bad bacteria, but also decimate large populations of beneficial bacteria as well. As the latter take longer to take root, this can often leave the body exposed to be overtaken by fast growing, disease causing organisms.

Therefore, being 'healthy' is not just a matter of eating right, drinking water, getting plenty of sleep. It is also a matter of keeping the 'good' bacteria in our bodies happy.

1. Which of the following is a good title for this passage?

    (A) How to Avoid Dangerous Bacteria
    (B) Surprising Truth about Bacteria
    (C) The Wonders of the Human Body
    (D) Tips for Staying Healthy

2. Which of the following is an example of how bacteria is beneficial?

    (A) Bacteria can cause disease or death.
    (B) Bacteria can help our body absorb nutrients.
    (C) Bacteria can fight off antibiotics.
    (D) Bacteria can create new genes in our body.

3. According in line 23, the word pathogenic most nearly means

    (A) insignificant.
    (B) beneficial.
    (C) annoying.
    (D) harmful.

4. The balance between human cells and microbes can be disturbed by

    (A) a lack of non-acidic foods.
    (B) drinking too much water.
    (C) smoking and stress.
    (D) taking too many vitamins.

5. It can be inferred from the passage that some people

    (A) don't know that some bacteria is helpful.
    (B) don't have any helpful bacteria in their bodies.
    (C) weren't taught about bacteria in school.
    (D) purposely use antibiotics to kill useful bacteria.

Reading Passage 27

1   The day we had all been dreading this
2 year had finally arrived: Thanksgiving.
3 There wasn't anything wrong with the
4 holiday itself, per say, but rather with what
5 it marked. Every year we would eat our
6 Thanksgiving dinner in the afternoon, pile
7 into the car, and cut down a Christmas tree.
8 This year would be hard, though. My mom
9 had died six months earlier.
10   Her death had been sudden and
11 surprising. She worked as a night manager
12 for a hardware store, taking shipments and
13 getting things ready for the morning. She
14 was on her way home, a mile from our
15 house, when she was hit by a pickup truck.
16 We had the chance to go see her that night,
17 but she fell into a coma and only lasted for
18 a few more days.
19   I was supposed to head off to the
20 University of Washington that fall, but I
21 delayed school for a while. I knew that my
22 brother and sister, 13 and 16, would need
23 as much family as they could get during
24 this time. Now, with the holidays
25 approaching, it would be a real test of how
26 much we had recovered.

27   The day started off pretty normal. We
28 went over to our Aunt Scholzy's house and
29 ate with some of our close family. There
30 were a lot of condolences and many people
31 saying "I know this must be hard." At
32 times, it was easy to get lost in
33 conversation, to pretend that mom was just
34 in the bathroom.
35   Also like normal, we all jumped into
36 the car with our hot chocolate and began
37 the drive to "our" section of forest where
38 we always cut the tree down. Winters in
39 Washington usually don't bring snow this
40 early, but there was a dusting spread over
41 the entire forest that afternoon.
42   The youngest in the family
43 traditionally got their first pick of a tree,
44 pending my mother's approval. Arthur
45 excitedly ran over to a 7-foot tall pine and
46 began to shout, "I found it! Mom, do you
47 think that–" He stopped. We gathered
48 around Arthur and my dad was the first to
49 speak, "It's okay for us to have new
50 traditions, and I think your mother would
51 want us to trust your judgment. Your
52 pick."

1. The primary purpose of the passage is to

   (A) argue why Christmas trees are so important.
   (B) talk about the death of a mother.
   (C) discuss the traditions of a family.
   (D) describe part of the recovery process for a family.

2. Thanksgiving was a difficult time for the narrator because

   (A) Thanksgiving was a special day traditionally spent with his whole family.
   (B) his mother had passed away last Thanksgiving.
   (C) Thanksgiving was his mom's favorite holiday.
   (D) he was worried his family wouldn't be able to find a good tree without their mother.

3. Based on the last paragraph, one can infer that

   (A) the narrator doesn't approve of Arthur's choice.
   (B) the narrator's father is no longer upset by his wife's death.
   (C) the family chose Arthur's tree.
   (D) the tree Arthur wants to pick may not fit in the house.

4. As used in line 30, the word "condolences" most nearly means

   (A) helping hands.
   (B) frustrations.
   (C) sympathies.
   (D) experiences.

5. According to lines 35 through 41, the family

   (A) owned part of the tree farm.
   (B) had a tradition about where they chose their tree.
   (C) chose a tree from their mother's favorite spot.
   (D) changed their plans based on the snow.

Reading Passage 28

1   Lindsey Caroline Kildow was born in
2 St. Paul, Minnesota in 1984. Her father,
3 Alan Lee Kildow, was a talented skier who
4 won a US national junior title before a
5 career-ending knee injury. Her grandfather,
6 Don Kildow, taught her to ski before the
7 age of two. Lindsey's family, friends, and
8 coaches helped to push and develop her
9 into the world-class alpine skier that the
10 world now knows by a different household
11 name: Lindsey Vonn.
12   Kildow grew up skiing in the flatlands
13 of Minnesota near the town of Burnsville.
14 There, she learned and raced on a team that
15 operated out of Buck Hill Ski Resort. This
16 wasn't the only location she skied, though.
17 Her family would routinely undergo a 16-
18 hour car ride from Minnesota to Vail,
19 Colorado where she learned to ski bigger
20 terrain than what Minnesota had to offer.
21 These locations, in addition to spring
22 skiing in Oregon, allowed Kildow to ski
23 almost year round.
24   Kildow's professional career began at
25 the Skiing World Cup in Park City, Utah,
26 in 2000. That event was largely uneventful,

27 but helped to prepare her for Kildow's
28 Olympic debut two years later in Salt Lake
29 City, Utah. There she raced both slalom
30 and combined; her best finish was 6th
31 place in the combined event.
32   The beginning of the most successful
33 period of Kildow's career came a year later
34 in Puy Saint-Vincent, France, in 2003.
35 There, she earned a silver medal at the
36 Junior World Championship in the
37 downhill event. She would go on to
38 compete in the 2006 Olympics in San
39 Sicario, Italy, but suffered a crash that
40 required her to be evacuated by helicopter.
41 She would still return to compete, but
42 without success.
43   Kildow, who married and changed her
44 name to Vonn in 2007, spent the next two
45 years recovering and training. This paid off
46 as she won the world championships back
47 to back to back from 2008-2010. Vonn
48 would go on to compete in the 2010 and
49 2018 Winter Olympics, eventually
50 amassing two bronze and one gold medal.
51 She remains the most decorated athlete in
52 American skiing history.

1. The primary purpose of this passage is to

   (A) provide a detailed account of Vonn's Olympic career.
   (B) discuss the career and accomplishments of Lindsey Vonn.
   (C) show the importance of dedication in sports.
   (D) inform the reader about Vonn's junior ski racing career.

2. The passage states that Lindsey's father

   (A) won an Olympic medal.
   (B) taught Lindsey to ski at the age of 2.
   (C) ended his skiing career because of an injury.
   (D) was Lindsey's primary ski trainer.

3. Based on the second paragraph, lines 12 through 23, we can infer that

   (A) Minnesota had better ski slopes than Colorado.
   (B) Lindsey didn't enjoy the 16-hour car rides to Colorado.
   (C) If Lindsey hadn't skied in Colorado, she would not be famous today.
   (D) Lindsey's family was dedicated to helping her succeed.

4. As used in line 50, the word "amassing" most nearly means

   (A) earning.
   (B) founding.
   (C) fighting for.
   (D) discovering.

5. As used in line 51, the word "decorated" most nearly means

   (A) attractive.
   (B) visible.
   (C) accomplished.
   (D) forgotten.

Reading Passage 29

Steve lived in Florida. The highest point in Florida is an unassuming hill near the Alabama border. When he looked out of the plane over the Rocky Mountains, Steve almost couldn't believe what he was seeing. As far as the small window allowed him to look, all that he could see were mountains. He gulped thinking about the reason he was on this plane in the first place: skiing.

Steve's older sister, Lydia, had always been the adventurous one in their family. She liked outdoor activities like camping and biking, and she moved to Colorado for school as a freshman in college. She was considerably older than Steve, so while Steve was still in high school and deciding where he wanted to go to school, Lydia was working as a kindergarten teacher in Denver. She loved her job because it gave her time to explore her passion for skiing. She had started while in college and never stopped.

Lydia would always talk about skiing or biking when she came home to visit, but until now, no one else in the family had ever gone out west to try those things. "I promise it won't be scary, Steve." she reassured him. They went to bed early that night in anticipation of the next day.

The mountains were even bigger driving up to them. Steve kept thinking that they must be close, but the peaks just kept getting bigger. They parked in a snow-covered parking lot and Lydia grabbed her gear. "We'll have to head to the rental shop to get you some skis." It took a half hour to get boots and skis and sign all the paperwork, but soon enough they were holding skis at the base of the hill.

"Okay, so you're going to take your boot and sort of press it down onto your ski." Lydia instructed. Steve fumbled for a moment. "Try doing it with more force." *Click.* "Okay, now what do we do?" Steve said half-jokingly. Lydia looked at him through her goggles with a grin, "We go up there!" Steve followed her finger as Lydia pointed impossibly high on the mountain. She started to ski away from Steve, "But don't forget, that's only the bunny hill."

1. The main purpose of the passage is to

   (A) persuade people that that skiing is dangerous.
   (B) argue why Steve has avoided skiing until now.
   (C) explain Lydia's first time teaching a family member to ski.
   (D) describe Steve's lead-up to trying something new.

2. In line 2, the word "unassuming" most nearly means

   (A) huge.
   (B) boring.
   (C) tall.
   (D) modest.

3. Steve could be described as

   (A) annoyed and upset that his sister is pressuring him.
   (B) adventurous and excited to experience thrilling activities.
   (C) worried and hesitant to trust his sister.
   (D) cautious but willing to try new things.

4. Based on last two lines, one can infer that

   (A) the mountain is much larger than Steve anticipated.
   (B) Lydia believes Steve may get hurt on this trip.
   (C) Steve decided to not go skiing after seeing the size of the mountain.
   (D) Lydia previously lied to Steve about the size of the mountain.

5. Why did Lydia love her job?

   (A) She enjoyed working with young children.
   (B) Her job allowed her to have a good work-life balance.
   (C) She could take time off work to go skiing whenever she wanted.
   (D) Her employer paid for her ski trips.

Reading Passage 30

The climbing gym in Baltimore had been open for seven years, but Carlos had avoided going there like the plague. "Why would I climb up something just so that I can climb down, then do it again?" he would ask his friends when they invited him to come along. "Heights have never been a 'fun' thing," he would add. Little did he know, this might change quickly.

Your attendance to Lilly's Birthday Climbing Extravaganza is requested on March 13th. Carlos stopped walking while reading his invite email. Lilly was one of his best friends, and Carlos hadn't missed her birthday party in more than 10 years. *I can just go and not climb, right?*

March 13th was finally here and Carlos was standing in his bedroom getting ready. *What the heck do I wear to climb?* He sorted through his drawers, eventually picking out a pair of athletic shorts and a t-shirt. As he stepped out of his house he sent a quick message to Lilly: *leaving my house now!*

Walking up to the front doors of the gym, Carlos saw a few people he knew, "Hey guys, glad you could make it!" he said with a nervous twinge in his voice. "Carlos, today is finally going to be the day we see you climb!" They walked in together and began filling out paperwork. The employee asked them for their shoe size then fitted each of them into a climbing harness.

As Carlos walked out into the main part of the gym, his eyes were drawn upwards. Everywhere he saw people scaling walls, hanging on ropes, and notably, laughing. *Maybe this isn't so bad...*

"You ready, Carlos?" Lilly yelled over at him. He looked at her nervously, "I guess as ready as I will be?" She showed him how to tie into the rope and talked about the safety procedures. "Keep in mind, you're going to be fine."

Carlos breathed out and stepped off the ground. He climbed slowly, making sure to keep both hands on the wall when possible. He quietly laughed to himself along the way. *This isn't so bad!* Before he knew it, Carlos was on top. "Lilly, what do I do now?" he yelled. "Whoops, I forgot to tell you!" Lilly said while smirking, "JUMP!"

1. The passage is primarily concerned with

   (A) describing the anxiety of a first experience.
   (B) describing the struggles faced by children.
   (C) explaining the importance of facing your fears.
   (D) discussing the need to support your friends.

2. In line 3, what is meant by the phrase "like the plague?"

   (A) Carlos was afraid he would get sick if he went there.
   (B) The gym had a reputation for being dirty.
   (C) Carlos avoided going there at all costs.
   (D) Carlos was not allowed to go to the gym.

3. Based on the last paragraph, we can assume

   (A) Lilly was a bad friend to Carlos.
   (B) Lilly purposely forgot to tell Carlos how to get down.
   (C) Carlos will likely buy a gym membership.
   (D) Carlos will never climb again.

4. Carlos felt obligated to attend Lilly's birthday party because

   (A) he knew he needed to face his fear of heights.
   (B) he didn't want to get made fun of.
   (C) Lilly was one of his best friends.
   (D) he knew that he didn't have to climb if he went.

5. Why had Carlos never climbed before?

   (A) he was afraid of getting hurt.
   (B) he thought climbing up and down the wall was repetitive.
   (C) his friends had never invited him.
   (D) he was scared of heights.

Reading Passage 31

Many animal rights activists argue that zoos are prisons for animals rather than shelters. Even in the best living conditions, captivity cannot replicate the natural habitats of wild animals. Many animals are not provided with adequate living space and are often prevented from participating in activities that are important to them: running, flying, climbing, and foraging. These conditions lead to feelings of isolation, boredom, and loneliness.

Animals in captivity are often not allowed to bond with other members of their kind, so they are deprived of their natural social structure. Instead, animals are forced to be in close proximity with species they may not be familiar with, such as humans. Research has shown that when animals imprint on humans, this prevents them from experiencing their own identities as animals.

Advocates of zoos argue that people benefit from zoos because zoos serve as an educational and economic resource for communities. Supporters claim that zoos play a critical role in educating children, provide jobs, and create tourism opportunities.

Unfortunately, these advantages don't outweigh the disadvantages. Holding animals in captivity is unethical, even if it provides benefits to humans.

1. The main purpose of this passage is to

   (A) provide facts about a certain zoo.
   (B) argue that zoos are unethical.
   (C) compare the advantages and disadvantages of zoos.
   (D) insist that all zoos be shut down immediately.

2. All of the following are mentioned as benefits of zoos EXCEPT

   (A) providing educational resources.
   (B) creating jobs.
   (C) helping the tourism industry.
   (D) healing injured animals.

3. One negative aspect of zoos is

   (A) animals are forced to live in small spaces.
   (B) animals are surrounded by their own species.
   (C) animals learn how to communicate with other species.
   (D) animals are antagonized by humans.

4. The passage suggests that animals in zoos experience

   (A) premature death due to neglect.
   (B) living conditions similar to their natural habitat.
   (C) mental effects due to their living conditions.
   (D) life-threatening contact with humans.

5. What does the author most likely mean by "animals imprint on humans," in line 19?

   (A) Animals learn behaviors from humans.
   (B) Animals leave a mark on humans.
   (C) Animals learn behaviors from their parents.
   (D) Humans intentionally train animals to act like them.

Reading Passage 32

Despite its small size, the praying mantis is perfectly designed for hunting prey. The name "praying mantis" comes from the structure and shape of the insect's body: the front legs are bent at an angle that suggests a position of prayer.

These predators are crafty and aggressive hunters. They have many physical features that aid them in hunting, such as a head that can turn 180 degrees, two large compound eyes with three simple eyes in between, and a greenish brown color that allows them to easily camouflage themselves with plants. While these features are extremely helpful for catching prey, the praying mantis' legs are their most useful feature. Praying mantis' use their front legs to snare their prey, with reflexes so fast that they are difficult to see with the naked eye. Each leg also has spikes used to pin the prey in place.

These creatures are so skilled at hunting that they can catch things over twice their size. A 2017 study found that praying mantises around the world have been able to catch and eat small birds. More impressively, a praying mantis was recently seen catching a fish. And while the sheer difference in size between predator and prey is shocking, what is more surprising is the timing of incident: the praying mantis has evolved to hunt in daylight, but this legendary catch was made in the middle of the night.

1. The main purpose of the passage is to

   (A) prove that the praying mantis is the strongest insect.
   (B) explain what makes the praying mantis a great hunter.
   (C) compare the praying mantis to other insects.
   (D) describe what the praying mantis looks like.

2. What is the reason behind the name "praying mantis".

   (A) The insect is a religious symbol.
   (B) The name describes the body of the insect.
   (C) The insect is known for hunting prey.
   (D) The name refers to the history of the insect.

3. As used in line 18, the word "snare" most nearly means

   (A) find.
   (B) kill.
   (C) scare.
   (D) trap.

4. The author would most likely agree with which of the following statements?

   (A) Don't underestimate praying mantises because of their size.
   (B) The praying mantis is the most dangerous predator.
   (C) Praying mantises are stronger than most fish and birds.
   (D) Praying mantises are the most aggressive insects.

5. We can assume that the praying mantis' ability to turn its head 180 degrees is most useful for

   (A) confusing other creatures.
   (B) looking out for potential threats.
   (C) scanning its surroundings for prey.
   (D) finding shelter during bad weather.

Reading Passage 33

As a child, you were probably tricked by this question at least once: "Is a tomato a fruit or a vegetable?" And while many would laugh if you made the mistake of calling a tomato a vegetable, the answer is actually trickier than most people know. Botanically, the tomato is a fruit. Legally, the tomato is a vegetable.

Before we get into where this discrepancy comes from, let's take a look at why tomatoes are botanically considered fruits. The botanical definition of a fruit is "the seed-bearing structure in flowering plants formed from the ovary." In simpler terms, fruits grow from the flower of a plant and contain seeds. Since tomatoes form from small yellow flowers on vines and naturally contain seeds, they are scientifically considered plants.

So who decided that tomatoes should legally be considered vegetables? The U.S. Supreme Court. During a 1893 court case in which the Supreme Court had to rule on whether tomatoes should be taxed as a fruit or a vegetable, the Supreme Court devised its own rules for distinguishing between fruits and vegetables: vegetables are generally served with the main part of a meal and fruits are generally served with dessert. Today, many people use this definition when classifying tomatoes.

So what should you say when someone asks the question, "Is a tomato a fruit or a vegetable?" That is up to you, but at least now you can explain to them the history behind all of the confusion surrounding this vegetable like fruit.

1. What is the main purpose of this passage?

   (A) To compare and contrast fruits and vegetables.
   (B) To present fruits that people consider vegetables.
   (C) To discuss the confusion around the classification of tomatoes.
   (D) To condemn a controversial court decision.

2. We can infer from the passage that

   (A) some people don't know that the tomato is legally a vegetable.
   (B) everyone has heard of the Supreme Court ruling on tomatoes.
   (C) some people think the Supreme Court shouldn't have the authority to define tomatoes.
   (D) no one respects the botanical definition of tomatoes.

3. As used in line 25, the word "devised" most nearly means

   (A) created.
   (B) ignored.
   (C) suggested.
   (D) banned.

4. Why was the Supreme Court asked to rule on the classification of tomatoes?

   (A) The public was confused by the botanical definition.
   (B) They needed to decide how tomatoes should be taxed.
   (C) They didn't know about the scientific definition.
   (D) People weren't sure if they should eat tomatoes with dinner or dessert.

5. The botanical definition of fruits

   (A) is easily understood by most people.
   (B) doesn't have much influence on how many people classify tomatoes.
   (C) is similar to the legal definition of fruits.
   (D) doesn't apply to tomatoes anymore.

Reading Passage 34

I was initially woken up by my alarm clock yelling at me to get up and a few seconds later by my mother shouting, "Devin! Devin! It's time to get up! We are leaving in ten minutes, and I can't be late to work again. If you're not down here by 7:45, I'm leaving without you."

It was April 15th. That meant only 42 days left of school. 336 more hours of teachers droning on and on about things that no one cared, making jokes that no one laughed at, and assigning homework on topics that no one would ever use in the real world.

I dragged myself out of bed, grabbed a pair of jeans, and put on the same Nirvana sweatshirt I wear every day – not that anyone at school would even notice. "42 days left," I said to myself, "then I'll be free from this place forever."

The car ride to school was the same as always: my mom complained about her boss, badgered me about my grades, and I just sat in the back seat nodding my head, not actually listening or responding. As we pulled up to the school, I dragged myself out of the car, pulled my hood over my head, and walked into school.

The hallways were crawling with overachievers, arrogant jocks, and peppy cheerleaders, and I slowly made my way to my first period class: physics. I hated physics, along with all other classes except band. As I slid into my seat in the back of the class, I noticed a new kid sitting next to me. He turned to me and said, "Cool sweatshirt. That's my favorite band."

"Thanks," I replied. Taken aback that someone was actually talking to me. "I'm Devin, what's your name?"

"I'm Sean. I just moved here from Seattle. Nice to see there is at least one person in this school who has good taste in music."

I smiled and thought to myself, "42 days left. Maybe it won't be as bad as I thought."

1. What is the main idea of the passage?

   (A) Even when times are tough, things can get better.
   (B) High school is a challenging time for many teenagers.
   (C) Good friends often have many things in common.
   (D) Some teenagers complain about everything.

2. We can assume Devin doesn't like school because

   (A) he feels invisible.
   (B) he can't stand jocks and cheerleaders.
   (C) he hates his physic's teacher.
   (D) he doesn't like waking up early.

3. Devin and Sean initially bond over

   (A) the fact that they have the same sweatshirt.
   (B) their mutual hatred of physics.
   (C) their mutual taste in music.
   (D) the fact that Sean is from Seattle.

4. The repetition of the phrase "42 days left" was used to

   (A) remind the reader how many school days Devin had left.
   (B) emphasize Devin's desire to be done with high school.
   (C) show Devin's excitement for going to college after graduation.
   (D) reiterate that Devin was going to miss high school.

5. From the beginning to the end of the story, Devin's feelings towards school shifted from

   (A) terrified to manageable.
   (B) indifferent to content.
   (C) depressed to excited.
   (D) miserable to bearable.

Reading Passage 35

The Pyramid of Giza is the last remaining wonder of the ancient world. Originally standing at 481 feet tall, the pyramid is the largest of all the Egyptian pyramids; up until 1889 it was the tallest structure made by human hands. Due to erosion and the removal of the top piece, the current height of the pyramid is only about 455 feet tall. The base of the pyramid is a square with each side measuring around 755 feet long. To give you an idea of how large the pyramid is, a football field has length of about 350 feet.

Along with its enormous dimensions, the pyramid is also incredibly massive: it was constructed out of more than 2 million stone blocks that each weigh over 2000 pounds, and the entire pyramid covers an area of over 13 acres.

Today, no one is certain how a pyramid so large could have been built. How were the Egyptians able to lift such heavy stones let alone transport them to the top of the pyramid? Some theories suggest that the Egyptians used ramps to move the stones. Others believe that wooden sleds could have helped with the building process and water could have been used to reduce friction.

While we may never come to a consensus about what methods were used to create such an amazing structure, there is one thing we should all be able to agree on: a lot of thought and effort went into building the Pyramid of Giza.

1. The main purpose of the passage is to

   (A) compare and contrast a variety of pyramids.
   (B) describe the wonders of the ancient world.
   (C) provide information about the Pyramid of Giza.
   (D) explain how the Egyptians built the Pyramid of Giza.

2. We can infer that erosion

   (A) causes stone to wear away.
   (B) eventually destroyed the Pyramid of Giza.
   (C) is the removal of the top piece of a structure.
   (D) is a chemical used to shrink things.

3. As used in line 31, the word "consensus" most nearly means

   (A) fact.
   (B) opinion.
   (C) agreement.
   (D) decision.

4. Which of the following is NOT mentioned as a theory for how the Egyptians constructed the Pyramid of Giza?

   (A) Ramps were used to transport stones.
   (B) Water was used to help the stones slide better.
   (C) Wooden sleds were used during the process.
   (D) Ladders were built to place the higher stones.

5. The author implies that in 1889

   (A) the tallest human-built structure known to date was built.
   (B) a taller pyramid was constructed by the Egyptians.
   (C) a 460 foot tall structure was created by human hands.
   (D) a man-made structure over 481 feet tall was constructed.

Reading Passage 36

At 11:40 PM on April 14th, 1912, the *RMS Titanic* hit an iceberg in the North Atlantic Ocean off the coast of North America. The ship had departed four days prior from Ireland and was heading for New York City. The 900-foot long ship took on water for the next two hours until lifting into the air, breaking into two pieces, and sinking to the ocean floor, 2.4 miles below the ocean's surface. There the wreck would lie until its discovery 73 years later in 1985.

Almost immediately after news of the *Titanic's* sinking spread around the world, interested parties began discussing the best ways to salvage the sunken ship. Several wealthy families of passengers hired a diving company to raise the *Titanic*. The idea of divers finding the ship was quickly abandoned after they couldn't even reach a small fraction of the depth of the wreck.

Over the next forty years, many entertaining and ultimately fruitless ideas were put forward to raise the ship. Charles Smith, an architect from Denver, Colorado, proposed attaching magnets to the main body of the ship and pulling it upwards towards the surface. Another idea suggested attaching balloons to the ship and raising it to the surface. This idea was scrapped after engineers realized that the balloons would be crushed by water pressure before they made it down to the *Titanic*.

The ideas to raise the ship out of the water ignored the bigger, more difficult problem: finding the ship. The first real attempt to simply locate the ship came in 1977. Robert Ballard, an oceanographer, formed a company with the purpose of finding the ship. After several years and many failed attempts, his company folded and the project was abandoned.

Several years later, in 1985, the US Navy hired Ballard to work on several military projects, many still classified, concerned with finding sunken submarines. Ballard agreed in exchange for using the military's advanced technology to look for the *Titanic* as well. The machine mainly used a remote-controlled submarine with a camera attached to it. At 12:48 AM on September 1st, 1985, the first piece of debris from the ship was seen. Later that day the main ship was found, making headlines around the world.

1. The main purpose of the passage is to

   (A) describe the events that led to the sinking of the *Titanic* in 1912.
   (B) discuss the efforts to raise and find the *Titanic*.
   (C) argue the ideas people suggested to recover the *Titanic* were absurd.
   (D) inform the reader as to the general history of the *Titanic*.

2. Based on the passage it can be inferred that it was difficult to initially find the *Titanic* due to a lack of

   (A) money to spend on finding the ship.
   (B) knowledge about when the ship sank.
   (C) proper technology to locate the ship.
   (D) experienced divers to look for the ship.

3. As used in line 16, the word "salvage" most nearly means

   (A) discover.
   (B) explore.
   (C) recover.
   (D) destroy.

4. According to the passage which of the following happened first?

   (A) Ballard formed a company to find the *Titanic*.
   (B) Newspapers began to report that the *Titanic* had been found.
   (C) Debris from the *Titanic* was first located.
   (D) The US Navy hired Ballard to work on several projects for them.

5. The U.S. Navy intially hired Robert Ballard to

   (A) locate the *Titanic*.
   (B) repair old submarines.
   (C) test their submarine technology.
   (D) recover sunken submarines.

Reading Passage 37

1　In some cultures, particularly some
2　Western cultures, it can be unacceptable to
3　be late. In American and Canadian culture,
4　arriving 15 minutes late to a business
5　meeting reflects very poorly on the one
6　who is late. In Spanish culture, the exact
7　opposite can be true. A meeting at 1 PM
8　might not start until 2 PM, and being late
9　isn't considered to be as poor form as in
10　the United States. Regardless of how any
11　individual culture views time, the ability to
12　do so is made possible by one invention:
13　the clock.
14　　The ability to tell the time dates back
15　thousands of years to the first "clock."
16　Over 3,000 years ago, the Egyptians
17　realized that the position of the sun could
18　tell the time. At noon, the sun would be
19　directly overhead. After that point, the
20　shadow cast by a stick in the ground would
21　fall at different angles, showing different
22　"times." This method still works perfectly
23　well today, unless it's cloudy.
24　　Fast forward to the 1600's and clocks
25　had started to incorporate pendulums -
26　large swinging arms. These are often found
27　in clocks that Americans may call

28　"grandfather clocks." These were very
29　accurate, but also very heavy, hard to
30　transport, and very expensive.
31　　By the late 1600's and early 1700's,
32　the first portable wrist and pocket watches
33　started to appear in Europe. These used
34　springs to keep their time accurately. Over
35　the course of the 17th century, watches
36　went from losing several hours a day to
37　less than 15 minutes.
38　　Over the next two centuries, watches
39　and clocks became so precise that they did
40　not need to be fixed, or 'wound', except
41　every few weeks or months. By the mid
42　19th century, electrical clocks had begun
43　to gain popularity. These time keeping
44　devices used small batteries to ensure their
45　accuracy.
46　　Now, in the 21st century, the most
47　accurate of clocks use atomic radiation to
48　keep their time. These clocks are so
49　accurate they only lose one second every
50　30 million years. While these clocks likely
51　represent the future of timekeeping, only
52　time will tell what new inventions will
53　affect how the average person reads a
54　clock.

1. The passage is primarily concerned with

   (A) discussing the history of grandfather clocks.
   (B) comparing the ways that different cultures view time.
   (C) the history of timekeeping pieces.
   (D) providing an account of how to construct timekeeping pieces.

2. It can be inferred from the second paragraph that the first "clock"

   (A) wasn't able to tell time at night.
   (B) was more effective at telling time than moden clocks.
   (C) was an accidental discovery made by Egyptians.
   (D) was more accurate during the summer.

3. As used in line 25, the word "incorporate" most nearly means

   (A) create.
   (B) find.
   (C) benefit from.
   (D) utilize.

4. According to the passage, all of the following were disadvantages of grandfather clocks EXCEPT

   (A) they weighed a lot.
   (B) they were difficult to move.
   (C) they weren't very accurate.
   (D) they cost a lot of money.

5. The tone of this passage could be best described as

   (A) persuasive.
   (B) enthusiastic.
   (C) cautionary.
   (D) objective.

Reading Passage 38

I could tell the roads were bad because Edward had stopped talking with me 15 minutes ago. All that we could hear was the dull talk radio and the wind blowing on the car. I could only see 15 or 20 feet ahead of the vehicle, and I assumed that Edward wasn't faring any better. There weren't many other cars on the road, which made sense. The forecast had called for blizzard conditions, but I had an interview to make tomorrow. "Hey Kurt, do you see that light up ahead?" I looked forward, "Ugh I can barely make anything out; it's probably far away." We found out within a few seconds it wasn't far away.

It only took a few seconds for us to crash. The light we saw was a car on the side of the road. Edward realized this too late to safely move around the car, so he swerved to the side, suddenly.

We ended up about 20 feet off the road. Thankfully, we didn't flip or roll or end up on our side. Neither of us said much of anything for a few minutes, we just sat and thought as the storm raged on around us. "Edward... does your phone have service?" He looked, "No."

"Okay, can try to walk to the nearest town, maybe?" I asked. Edward had a good reason as to why I wasn't thinking straight. "Kurt, think about it. We can't even see the road from here and it's only 20 feet. If we leave and try to walk on the road, one of us isn't going to make it." It was true: we couldn't make out what direction the road was from our car, let alone know which direction to walk.

"Let's wait for a car to pass by and we can get help from them." Edward offered. I thought about that for a moment. "I don't think they'll ever be able to see us and stop in time." He nodded. We made eye contact as we both realized what was going to happen. "Ever slept in the passenger seat of a car, Kurt?" I laughed and looked at the small interior of the car. "I guess there's a first time for everything."

1. The passage is primarily concerned with

   (A) teaching a lesson about the dangers of driving in a blizzard.
   (B) telling the story of a disagreement between two friends.
   (C) telling the story of two friends in an unfortunate situation.
   (D) teaching a lesson about the importance of staying positive.

2. As used in line 4, the word "dull" most nearly means

   (A) boring.
   (B) political.
   (C) frustrating.
   (D) quiet.

3. Based on the last paragraph, one can assume that Kurt and Edward

   (A) are starting to get annoyed with each other.
   (B) ended up flagging down a passing car.
   (C) walked to the nearest town to get help.
   (D) were forced to sleep in the car during the storm.

4. Which of the following is stated in the passage?

   (A) Edward is not an experienced winter driver.
   (B) Kurt wanted to make his interview the next day.
   (C) The pair crashed into another car.
   (D) Edward lives in Idaho, where it snows a lot.

5. Throughout the passage, Kurt and Edward can be described as

   (A) terrified and regretful of their decision to drive.
   (B) angry and frustrated with each other.
   (C) concerned about dying in the storm.
   (D) nervous but relatively calm.

Reading Passage 39

"For the benefit and enjoyment of the people" is the inscription displayed on the arch at the entrance to Yellowstone National Park. Located in Wyoming, Montana, and Idaho, Yellowstone National Park was the first national park, established on March 1st, 1872. Its inception began a worldwide trend of setting aside valuable and beautiful lands for public use.

Over the next 40 years, many other parks were established. 18 years after the first national park, Yosemite National Park in California was founded in 1890. A slew of parks followed: Mount Rainier (1899), Crater Lake (1902), Wind Cave (1903), Mesa Verde (1906), and Glacier (1910). These early parks are now some of the most popular outdoor tourist destinations in the US.

Beginning in 1916, the national parks were grouped together into their own part of government: the National Park System. For the first 60 years after the establishment of Yellowstone National Park, the only 'parks' in the National Park System were those already designated as National Parks. Monuments, conservation areas, cultural sites, and areas of scientific importance were not included in this system and were managed by a random assortment of agencies. This changed in 1933 when President Roosevelt signed the *Organization of Executive Agencies.* This declared that all 56 existing non-National Park areas would now be managed by the National Park System.

The most recent additions to the National Park System are Indiana Dunes and White Sands National Parks, both added in 2019. Those additions bring the total number of Parks to 62, and the total number of areas in the National Park System stands at 419. The National Parks themselves protect over 52 million acres, bigger than over 100 countries. The system has been referred to as "America's best idea" because it strives to protect wild and natural places for the public to enjoy, forever.

1. The primary purpose of the passage is to

    (A) provide an overview of the history of the National Park System.
    (B) convince the reader that the National Parks should be saved.
    (C) discuss the establishment of the National Park System.
    (D) discuss the different areas where National Parks are located.

2. As used in line 8, the word "inception" most nearly means

    (A) creation.
    (B) recovery.
    (C) popularity.
    (D) significance.

3. As used in line 14, the phrase "a slew" most nearly means

    (A) one or two.
    (B) thousands.
    (C) a large number.
    (D) a specific collection.

4. The purpose of the *Organizations of Executive Agencies* was to

    (A) require the National Park System to only manage areas that were not designated as National Parks.
    (B) create a new branch of government to manage areas that were not National Parks.
    (C) officially designate 56 more areas as National Parks.
    (D) expand the types of areas that would be managed by the National Park System.

5. From the last paragraph, one can infer that the purpose of the National Park System is to

    (A) encourage tourists to visit National Parks.
    (B) preserve and protect National Parks.
    (C) prevent humans from harming wildlife at National Parks.
    (D) rebuild and renovate National Parks.

Reading Passage 40

1   Kiara had decided she wanted to be an
2 author in 7th grade. One of her poems, *A*
3 *Breezy Kansas Night,* had been selected to
4 be part of a book featuring middle-school
5 poets. She was asked to read her work in
6 front of an all-school assembly, and she
7 loved being able to show off her talents.
8 Now, as a 31-year-old woman, she had the
9 chance to publish something for real.
10   Kiara had studied literature in college.
11 She found it comical that other students
12 complained about "having" to read every
13 night. *All I have to do is read books and*
14 *then write about it?* She would think to
15 herself. During her time at Kansas State,
16 Kiara was able to publish some of her short
17 stories and poems in the school newspaper,
18 but she had never made any money.
19   After college, Kiara began to work for
20 a publishing company. There, she was able
21 to be close to writers, authors, editors, and
22 everyone else involved with books and
23 their publication. She loved being able to
24 talk with her coworkers about their jobs
25 over lunch, but she had been stuck as a
26 copyeditor for nearly a decade.

27   Her job may have given Kiara access
28 to people she wanted to learn about, but
29 the work itself wasn't her favorite. She was
30 tasked with making sure the grammar in
31 client's work was correct. She loved
32 reading their text, but all she could do was
33 fix the placement of commas and correct
34 the occasional incorrectly-used semicolon.
35   Now, she had finally written a series of
36 poems she felt would be worth publication.
37 Using her connections, she had submitted
38 her work to a local publisher, and today
39 was the final day by which she would hear
40 what the publishing team thought.
41   Her poems were a collective about
42 writing. They were about her journey
43 through what felt like every other part of
44 publishing besides the creation part. The
45 waiting game to find out her fate felt like it
46 was all part of the process, part of the
47 journey to realizing a 20-year dream. Her
48 phone pinged with a new email, she took a
49 deep breath and opened it.
50 *"Congratulations, Kiara!"*

1. What is the main purpose of this passage?

   (A) It explores an author's journey to publishing a book.
   (B) It details the necessary steps to publish a book of poems.
   (C) It argues why publishing is a difficult industry to work in.
   (D) It tells the story of a child who won a poetry competition in middle school.

2. In line 12, the word "having" is in quotation marks because

   (A) Kiara was frustrated that her classmates complained.
   (B) the assignments don't actually have to be completed.
   (C) Kiara didn't enjoy her reading assignments.
   (D) Kiara enjoys reading and doesn't feel like it's a chore.

3. In line 47, the word "realizing" most nearly means

   (A) understanding.
   (B) achieving.
   (C) losing.
   (D) finding.

4. How did Kiara feel about her job as a copyeditor?

   (A) She hated it and felt she was superior to her coworkers.
   (B) She enjoyed parts of the work but wanted a more fulfilling job.
   (C) She loved her coworkers and felt that she had found her dream job.
   (D) She was bored by the work and tolerated her coworkers.

5. From the last paragraph, it can be inferred that Kiara

   (A) earned an interview for her dream job.
   (B) is not hopeful of her chances.
   (C) will not continue working with the publisher.
   (D) is going to have her book published.

Reading Chapter Answer Key

Reading Passage 1

1. C
2. C
3. B
4. D
5. D

Reading Passage 2

1. B
2. C
3. A
4. D
5. C

Reading Passage 3

1. C
2. B
3. C
4. A
5. A

Reading Passage 4

1. A
2. B
3. D
4. B
5. C

Reading Passage 5

1. D
2. A
3. D
4. B
5. C

Reading Passage 6

1. D
2. B
3. A
4. A
5. C

Reading Passage 7

1. D
2. A
3. D
4. C
5. B

Reading Passage 8

1. D
2. B
3. A
4. A
5. B

Reading Passage 9

1. B
2. C
3. A
4. D
5. A

Reading Passage 10

1. C
2. C
3. D
4. B
5. B

Reading Passage 11

1. A
2. D
3. C
4. D
5. B

Reading Passage 12

1. D
2. B
3. D
4. C
5. C

Reading Passage 13

1. A
2. C
3. A
4. B
5. D

Reading Passage 14

1. C
2. D
3. C
4. A
5. B

Reading Passage 15

1. D
2. C
3. A
4. B
5. B

Reading Passage 16

1. A
2. C
3. C
4. D
5. A

Reading Passage 17

1. A
2. D
3. D
4. B
5. B

Reading Passage 18

1. B
2. D
3. B
4. D
5. A

Reading Passage 19

1. D
2. C
3. D
4. B
5. B

Reading Passage 20

1. B
2. A
3. C
4. D
5. D

Reading Passage 21

1. B
2. A
3. C
4. B
5. A

Reading Passage 22

1. D
2. B
3. C
4. B
5. C

Reading Passage 23

1. C
2. D
3. B
4. D
5. A

Reading Passage 24

1. C
2. D
3. B
4. A
5. B

Reading Passage 25

1. B
2. C
3. A
4. A
5. C

Reading Passage 26

1. B
2. B
3. D
4. C
5. A

Reading Passage 27

1. D
2. A
3. C
4. C
5. B

Reading Passage 28

1. B
2. C
3. D
4. A
5. C

Reading Passage 29

1. D
2. D
3. D
4. A
5. B

Reading Passage 30

1. A
2. C
3. B
4. C
5. D

Reading Passage 31

1. B
2. D
3. A
4. C
5. A

Reading Passage 32

1. B
2. B
3. D
4. A
5. C

Reading Passage 33

1. C
2. A
3. A
4. B
5. B

Reading Passage 34

1. A
2. A
3. C
4. B
5. D

Reading Passage 35

1. C
2. A
3. C
4. D
5. D

Reading Passage 36

1. B
2. C
3. C
4. A
5. D

Reading Passage 37

1. C
2. A
3. D
4. C
5. D

Reading Passage 38

1. C
2. A
3. D
4. B
5. D

Reading Passage 39

1. A
2. A
3. C
4. D
5. B

Reading Passage 40

1. A
2. D
3. B
4. B
5. D

Essay

The Essay

Essay Overview

The ISEE essay is the last section of the ISEE Lower Level. Students are given 30 minutes to respond to a prompt. The essay is not scored, but a copy of the writing sample is sent to the schools to which the ISEE score report is sent.

The essay has two purposes: it shows schools how well you can write and it also gives the admissions officers another opportunity to learn about you. Keep this in mind when writing your essay. Make sure to focus your essay on yourself. For example, if the essay asks you to talk about someone you look up to, talk about the person you choose, but make sure to also talk about yourself. How does this person inspire you? How has this person impacted your life?

Essay Tips

- **Read the Directions:** On the official ISEE, you're asked to write in a blue or black pen. You're also asked to rewrite the essay prompt at the top of the first page of your essay. Make sure to carefully read the directions before starting your essay.
- **Manage your Time:** Make sure you manage your time effectively. Give yourself time to organize your essay, time to write your essay, and time to revise and edit your essay.
- **Structure your Essay:** While there are no rules for how to structure your essay, it is recommended to have an introduction, a body, and a conclusion. We recommend the body of your essay be 1-3 paragraphs long.
- **Write Neatly:** You are not graded on how neatly you write your essay, but make sure to write neatly enough so someone can read your writing.

How to Use the Practice Essay Prompts

On the next page, you'll find 10 practice essay prompts. For each prompt, set a timer for 30 minutes. Make sure to go somewhere quiet to write your essay. Write your essay on a sheet of lined paper (you can use the front and back of the sheet, but no more).

Once you've finished, have an adult read over your essay and give you feedback.

Essay Prompts

1. What is your favorite subject in school? What do you enjoy about this subject?

2. What is your favorite after school activity and why?

3. What are the most important qualities in a friend?

4. What is the best gift you've every received? Why was this gift so special to you?

5. Who is a character that you like from a book you've read or a movie you've watched? What do you like about this character?

6. If you could take a vacation anywhere, where would you go and why?

7. Write about a person that you look up to. Why do you look up to this person?

8. If you had an entire day to do anything that you wanted, what would you do?

9. If you could change one thing about your school, what would it be and why?

10. If you could build a robot, what type of robot would you build? What types of things would your robot do?

Practice Tests

THIS PAGE IS INTENTIONALLY LEFT BLANK

Elevate Prep

PRACTICE TEST

ISEE

LOWER LEVEL TEST 1

Test Instructions

The format of this practice test is the same format as the actual ISEE. The number of questions and the number of minutes allowed for each section are both listed on the instruction page of each section, under the title of the section. The chart below also shows the number of questions and the number of minutes allowed for each section.

Section	Number of Questions	Number of Minutes
Verbal Reasoning	34 Questions	20 Minutes
Quantitative Reasoning	38 Questions	35 Minutes
Reading Comprehension	25 Questions	25 Minutes
Mathematics Achievement	30 Questions	30 Minutes
Essay	-----	30 Minutes

Use the answer sheet provided on the next two pages to record your answers. We suggest tearing the answer sheet out of the book. **You can also download and print a free answer sheet on our website: www.elevateprep.com/isee-lower-level**

When you've finished taking the test, grade your test using the answer key at the end of the test. On the pages following the answer key, you will see information on how to score your test, including how to find your raw score, percentile, and stanine for each section.

*The Independent School Entrance Examination and ISEE are trademarks owned by Educational Records Bureau which is not affiliated with and does not endorse this practice test.

Elevate Prep

ISEE Lower Level

Answer Sheet

SECTION 1: VERBAL REASONING		
1 Ⓐ Ⓑ Ⓒ Ⓓ	15 Ⓐ Ⓑ Ⓒ Ⓓ	29 Ⓐ Ⓑ Ⓒ Ⓓ
2 Ⓐ Ⓑ Ⓒ Ⓓ	16 Ⓐ Ⓑ Ⓒ Ⓓ	30 Ⓐ Ⓑ Ⓒ Ⓓ
3 Ⓐ Ⓑ Ⓒ Ⓓ	17 Ⓐ Ⓑ Ⓒ Ⓓ	31 Ⓐ Ⓑ Ⓒ Ⓓ
4 Ⓐ Ⓑ Ⓒ Ⓓ	18 Ⓐ Ⓑ Ⓒ Ⓓ	32 Ⓐ Ⓑ Ⓒ Ⓓ
5 Ⓐ Ⓑ Ⓒ Ⓓ	19 Ⓐ Ⓑ Ⓒ Ⓓ	33 Ⓐ Ⓑ Ⓒ Ⓓ
6 Ⓐ Ⓑ Ⓒ Ⓓ	20 Ⓐ Ⓑ Ⓒ Ⓓ	34 Ⓐ Ⓑ Ⓒ Ⓓ
7 Ⓐ Ⓑ Ⓒ Ⓓ	21 Ⓐ Ⓑ Ⓒ Ⓓ	
8 Ⓐ Ⓑ Ⓒ Ⓓ	22 Ⓐ Ⓑ Ⓒ Ⓓ	
9 Ⓐ Ⓑ Ⓒ Ⓓ	23 Ⓐ Ⓑ Ⓒ Ⓓ	
10 Ⓐ Ⓑ Ⓒ Ⓓ	24 Ⓐ Ⓑ Ⓒ Ⓓ	
11 Ⓐ Ⓑ Ⓒ Ⓓ	25 Ⓐ Ⓑ Ⓒ Ⓓ	
12 Ⓐ Ⓑ Ⓒ Ⓓ	26 Ⓐ Ⓑ Ⓒ Ⓓ	
13 Ⓐ Ⓑ Ⓒ Ⓓ	27 Ⓐ Ⓑ Ⓒ Ⓓ	
14 Ⓐ Ⓑ Ⓒ Ⓓ	28 Ⓐ Ⓑ Ⓒ Ⓓ	

SECTION 2: QUANTITATIVE REASONING		
1 Ⓐ Ⓑ Ⓒ Ⓓ	15 Ⓐ Ⓑ Ⓒ Ⓓ	29 Ⓐ Ⓑ Ⓒ Ⓓ
2 Ⓐ Ⓑ Ⓒ Ⓓ	16 Ⓐ Ⓑ Ⓒ Ⓓ	30 Ⓐ Ⓑ Ⓒ Ⓓ
3 Ⓐ Ⓑ Ⓒ Ⓓ	17 Ⓐ Ⓑ Ⓒ Ⓓ	31 Ⓐ Ⓑ Ⓒ Ⓓ
4 Ⓐ Ⓑ Ⓒ Ⓓ	18 Ⓐ Ⓑ Ⓒ Ⓓ	32 Ⓐ Ⓑ Ⓒ Ⓓ
5 Ⓐ Ⓑ Ⓒ Ⓓ	19 Ⓐ Ⓑ Ⓒ Ⓓ	33 Ⓐ Ⓑ Ⓒ Ⓓ
6 Ⓐ Ⓑ Ⓒ Ⓓ	20 Ⓐ Ⓑ Ⓒ Ⓓ	34 Ⓐ Ⓑ Ⓒ Ⓓ
7 Ⓐ Ⓑ Ⓒ Ⓓ	21 Ⓐ Ⓑ Ⓒ Ⓓ	35 Ⓐ Ⓑ Ⓒ Ⓓ
8 Ⓐ Ⓑ Ⓒ Ⓓ	22 Ⓐ Ⓑ Ⓒ Ⓓ	36 Ⓐ Ⓑ Ⓒ Ⓓ
9 Ⓐ Ⓑ Ⓒ Ⓓ	23 Ⓐ Ⓑ Ⓒ Ⓓ	37 Ⓐ Ⓑ Ⓒ Ⓓ
10 Ⓐ Ⓑ Ⓒ Ⓓ	24 Ⓐ Ⓑ Ⓒ Ⓓ	38 Ⓐ Ⓑ Ⓒ Ⓓ
11 Ⓐ Ⓑ Ⓒ Ⓓ	25 Ⓐ Ⓑ Ⓒ Ⓓ	
12 Ⓐ Ⓑ Ⓒ Ⓓ	26 Ⓐ Ⓑ Ⓒ Ⓓ	
13 Ⓐ Ⓑ Ⓒ Ⓓ	27 Ⓐ Ⓑ Ⓒ Ⓓ	
14 Ⓐ Ⓑ Ⓒ Ⓓ	28 Ⓐ Ⓑ Ⓒ Ⓓ	

SECTION 3: READING COMPREHENSION

1 (A)(B)(C)(D)   15 (A)(B)(C)(D)
2 (A)(B)(C)(D)   16 (A)(B)(C)(D)
3 (A)(B)(C)(D)   17 (A)(B)(C)(D)
4 (A)(B)(C)(D)   18 (A)(B)(C)(D)
5 (A)(B)(C)(D)   19 (A)(B)(C)(D)
6 (A)(B)(C)(D)   20 (A)(B)(C)(D)
7 (A)(B)(C)(D)   21 (A)(B)(C)(D)
8 (A)(B)(C)(D)   22 (A)(B)(C)(D)
9 (A)(B)(C)(D)   23 (A)(B)(C)(D)
10 (A)(B)(C)(D)   24 (A)(B)(C)(D)
11 (A)(B)(C)(D)   25 (A)(B)(C)(D)
12 (A)(B)(C)(D)
13 (A)(B)(C)(D)
14 (A)(B)(C)(D)

SECTION 4: MATHEMATICS ACHIEVEMENT

1 (A)(B)(C)(D)   18 (A)(B)(C)(D)
2 (A)(B)(C)(D)   19 (A)(B)(C)(D)
3 (A)(B)(C)(D)   20 (A)(B)(C)(D)
4 (A)(B)(C)(D)   21 (A)(B)(C)(D)
5 (A)(B)(C)(D)   22 (A)(B)(C)(D)
6 (A)(B)(C)(D)   23 (A)(B)(C)(D)
7 (A)(B)(C)(D)   24 (A)(B)(C)(D)
8 (A)(B)(C)(D)   25 (A)(B)(C)(D)
9 (A)(B)(C)(D)   26 (A)(B)(C)(D)
10 (A)(B)(C)(D)   27 (A)(B)(C)(D)
11 (A)(B)(C)(D)   28 (A)(B)(C)(D)
12 (A)(B)(C)(D)   29 (A)(B)(C)(D)
13 (A)(B)(C)(D)   30 (A)(B)(C)(D)
14 (A)(B)(C)(D)
15 (A)(B)(C)(D)
16 (A)(B)(C)(D)
17 (A)(B)(C)(D)

ISEE

Verbal Reasoning

LOWER LEVEL

Practice Test

Section 1
Verbal Reasoning

34 Questions   **Time: 20 Minutes**

This section is split into two parts that contain two different question types. Once you've finished Part One, move on to Part Two. You may write anywhere in your test booklet. For each answer you select, fill in the corresponding answer choice on your bubble sheet.

Part One – Synonyms

Each question in Part One includes a word in capital letters followed by four answer choices. Choose the word that has the closest meaning as the capitalized word.

SAMPLE QUESTION: Sample Answer

    ABANDON:

       (A) claim
       (B) desert
       (C) abuse
       (D) neglect

Part Two – Sentence Completion

Each question in Part Two includes a sentence with one blank. The blank indicates that a word or phrase is missing. Each sentence is followed by four answer choices. Choose the answer choice with the word or phrase that best completes the sentence.

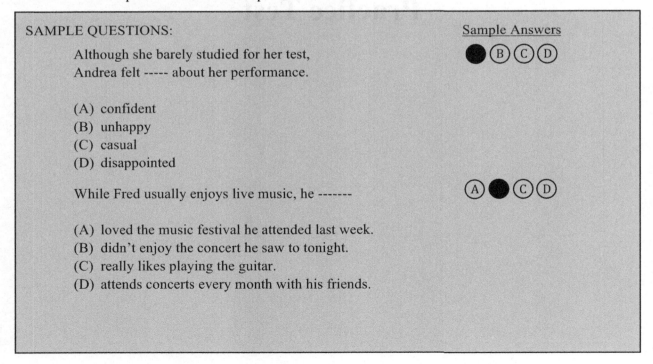

SAMPLE QUESTIONS: Sample Answers

    Although she barely studied for her test,
    Andrea felt ----- about her performance.

       (A) confident
       (B) unhappy
       (C) casual
       (D) disappointed

    While Fred usually enjoys live music, he -------

       (A) loved the music festival he attended last week.
       (B) didn't enjoy the concert he saw to tonight.
       (C) really likes playing the guitar.
       (D) attends concerts every month with his friends.

Part 1 – Synonyms

Directions: Select the word that is closest in meaning to the word in capital letters.

1. SPONTANEOUS

   (A) energetic
   (B) rehearsed
   (C) impromptu
   (D) unusual

2. INCAPABLE

   (A) unintelligent
   (B) sufficient
   (C) beginner
   (D) inadequate

3. DIVERSE

   (A) interesting
   (B) uniform
   (C) varied
   (D) odd

4. INTIMIDATE

   (A) threaten
   (B) anger
   (C) disagree
   (D) scream

5. ENCOURAGE

   (A) escalate
   (B) motivate
   (C) listen
   (D) agree

6. IMITATE

   (A) annoy
   (B) copy
   (C) admire
   (D) invent

7. MORAL

   (A) honest
   (B) corrupt
   (C) political
   (D) valuable

8. DAUNTING

   (A) haunted
   (B) intimidating
   (C) impossible
   (D) alarming

9. WIDESPREAD

   (A) local
   (B) enormous
   (C) contagious
   (D) common

10. RESENTFUL

    (A) apologetic
    (B) sensitive
    (C) brutal
    (D) bitter

11. OPPOSE

    (A) resist
    (B) promote
    (C) destroy
    (D) assume

12. DETRIMENTAL

    (A) disrespectful
    (B) beneficial
    (C) harmful
    (D) uncomfortable

Go on to the next page →

13. OMIT

    (A) mislead
    (B) exclude
    (C) permit
    (D) remember

14. INSISTENT

    (A) bothersome
    (B) lenient
    (C) demanding
    (D) fierce

15. ASSURED

    (A) protected
    (B) probable
    (C) uncertain
    (D) confident

16. FUSE

    (A) merge
    (B) repair
    (C) explode
    (D) ignite

17. SCARCE

    (A) frightened
    (B) generous
    (C) rare
    (D) unfortunate

Go on to the next page →

Part 2 – Sentence Completion

Directions: Select the word or phrase that best completes the sentence.

18. Cara did not understand why she had to take etiquette classes, finding the practices to be ------- and irrelevant in modern times.

    (A) classy
    (B) annoying
    (C) humorous
    (D) outdated

19. Emily Dickenson had a(n) ------- style of writing and challenged the existing definition of poetry by experimenting with different techniques.

    (A) unconventional
    (B) standard
    (C) simple
    (D) attractive

20. Susie thought the hair dye would wash out easily, but it was ------- and did not come out when she took a shower.

    (A) temporary
    (B) permanent
    (C) vibrant
    (D) menacing

21. Without written ------- from his parents, Frank would not be allowed to participate in the class field trip.

    (A) permission
    (B) explanation
    (C) stipulation
    (D) information

22. Brett had always been very good at math, but he was struggling in calculus and found it to be much more ------- than algebra and geometry.

    (A) straightforward
    (B) boring
    (C) challenging
    (D) impractical

23. Since Mr. Ferris required all students to wear black dress pants to the chorus concert, it was not ------- attire for Billy to wear blue jeans.

    (A) appropriate
    (B) unusual
    (C) stylish
    (D) obedient

24. Judging from the ------- expression on Sam's face as he stood in front of the class, it was obvious that he wasn't comfortable presenting in front of people.

    (A) confident
    (B) aggressive
    (C) unusual
    (D) nervous

25. After being interrogated for hours, the suspect was released when the lab results proved his DNA was not ------- to the sample found at the crime scene.

    (A) different
    (B) identical
    (C) related
    (D) suspicious

Go on to the next page →

26. World War II was one of the most ------- wars in human history, killing around 70 million people.

(A) lengthy
(B) intense
(C) deadly
(D) expensive

27. In many cultures, it is important to remove your shoes before entering sacred places like temples and churches, not only for sanitary reasons, but also as a sign of -------.

(A) interest
(B) mockery
(C) respect
(D) cleanliness

28. When Harry sprained his ankle, the doctor suggested taking salt baths to ------- the pain.

(A) increase
(B) demolish
(C) pinpoint
(D) soothe

29. Even though Mariah had been to the store many times, she still -------.

(A) had no idea which aisle the pickles were in.
(B) was frustrated that her car had a flat tire.
(C) decided to go with her friend, Jake.
(D) knew exactly where to find the canned fruit.

30. Most people believe that all great musicians can read music, but Elvis Presley was extremely successful -------.

(A) and became famous for writing catchy rock songs.
(B) despite not being able to read or write sheet music.
(C) because he learned how to read sheet music at a young age.
(D) even though he learned how to play music as a teenager.

31. Since the children looked exhausted, their -------.

(A) coach ended practice early.
(B) teacher assigned more homework.
(C) parents let them stay up late.
(D) friends continued to make jokes.

32. Roger was normally unmotivated and lazy when it came to his schoolwork, so his teacher was pleasantly surprised when he -------.

(A) turned in a half-completed assignment.
(B) spent his free time playing soccer.
(C) didn't have any questions about the homework.
(D) completed his science fair project early.

33. Without running water and electricity, people were -------.

(A) forced to pay higher electricity bills.
(B) unable to complete many of their daily tasks.
(C) encouraged to sleep on the floor.
(D) able to spend more time with their families.

Go on to the next page →

34. Contrary to Malcolm X, who was willing to use physical force to fight for equality, Martin Luther King Jr. -------.

    (A) would do whatever was necessary to get what he wanted.
    (B) is one of the greatest civil rights activists of all times.
    (C) believed in non-violent practices, such as peaceful protests.
    (D) stood up for the rights of African Americans.

STOP. Do not go on to the next section until you are told to do so.

STOP

ISEE

Quantitative Reasoning

LOWER LEVEL

Practice Test

Section 2
Quantitative Reasoning

38 Questions   **Time: 35 Minutes**

Each question is followed by four answer choices. Read each question and decide which answer choice is correct.

Find the question number on your answer sheet and mark the space having the same letter as the answer choice that you chose. You may show your work in your test booklet.

EXAMPLE 1:   Sample Answer

   What is the value of the expression $10 - 7 + 2$?   Ⓐ Ⓑ ● Ⓓ

   (A) 1
   (B) 3
   (C) 5
   (D) 6

   The correct answer is 5, so circle C is darkened.

EXAMPLE 2:   Sample Answer

   Which could be the dimensions of a triangle with   Ⓐ ● Ⓒ Ⓓ
   an area of 12 in^2?

   (A) 1 in × 6 in
   (B) 3 in × 8 in
   (C) 6 in × 2 in
   (D) 10 in × 2 in

   The correct answer is 3 in × 8 in, so circle B is darkened.

---

1. Tom wrote down an odd number greater than 20 and less than 30. When Sue tried to guess the number, Tom told her that it is greater than 27 and less than 32. What is Tom's number?

   (A) 27
   (B) 28
   (C) 29
   (D) 31

2. The side length of a regular hexagon is $3s$. What is the perimeter of the hexagon?

   (A) 15
   (B) 18
   (C) $15s$
   (D) $18s$

3. The ratio of pop songs to rock songs on Cary's playlist is 7:3. If she has 21 rock songs on her playlist, how many pop songs are on her playlist?

   (A) 9
   (B) 25
   (C) 49
   (D) 63

4. Talia is twice as old as Wilson. Wilson is three times as old as Wendy. The sum of all of their ages is 50 years. How old is Talia?

   (A) 5 years
   (B) 15 years
   (C) 20 years
   (D) 30 years

5. The perimeter of the rectangle below is 24 cm.

   8 cm

   What is the area of the rectangle?

   (A) 22 cm^2
   (B) 28 cm^2
   (C) 32 cm^2
   (D) 128 cm^2

6. Which fraction is in between $\frac{1}{2}$ and $\frac{6}{7}$?

   (A) $\frac{4}{9}$

   (B) $\frac{4}{8}$

   (C) $\frac{3}{5}$

   (D) $\frac{7}{8}$

7. Tyler and Hannah are driving at the same speed. If Tyler drives 80 miles in 90 minutes, how long would it take Hannah to drive 120 miles?

   (A) 130 minutes
   (B) 135 minutes
   (C) 145 minutes
   (D) 180 minutes

Go on to the next page →

8. The combined area of all of the surfaces of the small, shaded cube is 12 square feet.

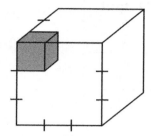

What is the total combined area of the surfaces of the larger cube?

(A) 18 square ft
(B) 36 square ft
(C) 54 square ft
(D) 108 square ft

9. Use the equations below to answer the question.

$$6x = -30$$
$$4 + y = 10$$

What is the product of x and y?

(A) −30
(B) −1
(C) 11
(D) 30

10. If a can be divided by 4 and 6 without leaving a remainder, then a can also be divided by which number without leaving a remainder?

(A) 10
(B) 12
(C) 18
(D) 24

11. Use the Venn diagram to answer the question.

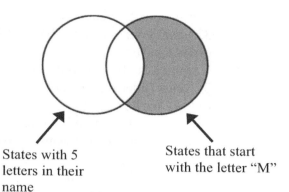

States with 5 letters in their name

States that start with the letter "M"

Which state could be found in the shaded part of the Venn diagram?

(A) Maine
(B) Texas
(C) Oregon
(D) Montana

12. Megan had a pitcher of juice that had 24 pints in it. If she wants to place 3/4 pints of juice into smaller cups, what is the maximum number of cups she can fill?

(A) 18
(B) 24
(C) 32
(D) 48

13. What number is represented by B on the number line?

(A) 3.7
(B) 3.9
(C) 4.2
(D) 4.3

Go on to the next page →

14. Which story best fits the expression
50 – 32?

(A) Veronica is 50 years old, which is
32 years younger than Charlie. How
old is Charlie?
(B) Veronica is 50 years old, which is
32 years older than Charlie. How
old is Charlie?
(C) Charlie is 50 years old, which is 32
years younger than Veronica. How
old is Veronica?
(D) Charlie is 32 years old, which is 50
years younger than Veronica. How
old is Veronica?

15. The data below represents Xavier's test
scores in science class, with one score
missing.

79, 88, 80, 75, ___, 85, 80

If the range of Xavier's scores is 14,
which of the following could be the
missing score?

(A) 73
(B) 74
(C) 76
(D) 90

16. Use the figure to answer the question.

If the pattern continues, how many
circles will be in the sixth figure?

(A) 15
(B) 18
(C) 20
(D) 21

17. Use the table to determine the rule.

Input a	Output b
2	5
3	8
6	17
11	32

What is the rule for the table?

(A) $a = b - 3$
(B) $b = 3a - 1$
(C) $b = 2a + 1$
(D) $a = \dfrac{1}{2}b - 1$

18. What is the value of x in the equation
$2x - 4 = 10$?

(A) 3
(B) 6
(C) 7
(D) 12

19. Which equation can be read as "4 less
than twice a number is equal to the sum
of the number and 11"?

(A) $2x - 4 = x + 11$
(B) $2x - 4 = x - 11$
(C) $4 - 2x = x + 11$
(D) $4 - 2x = x - 11$

20. What is the value of the expression
$\dfrac{90 \times 100}{50(85 - 25)}$?

(A) 3
(B) 30
(C) 300
(D) 3,000

Go on to the next page →

21. Olga is growing three plants in her backyard. The table below shows the heights of each plant over the period of 5 days.

	Plant 1	Plant 2	Plant 3
Start	5 cm	10 cm	1 cm
Day 1	6 cm	12 cm	2 cm
Day 2	8 cm	14 cm	4 cm
Day 3	11 cm	16 cm	8 cm
Day 4	15 cm	18 cm	16 cm
Day 5	20 cm	20 cm	32 cm

According to the pattern from the data, what is the predicted height of Plant 3 on day 7?

(A) 32 cm
(B) 64 cm
(C) 96 cm
(D) 128 cm

---

22. Each bar represents 1 chocolate bar.

If Miles eats the shaded amount of each chocolate bar, approximately how many total chocolate bars will he have eaten?

(A) 1
(B) $1\frac{1}{2}$
(C) 2
(D) $2\frac{1}{4}$

23. A deck of cards contains 6 red cards, 4 blue cards, 8 green cards, 1 yellow card, and 5 white cards. If a card is randomly selected from the deck, which color has a 1 out of 4 chance of being selected?

(A) blue
(B) green
(C) yellow
(D) red

24. The points with coordinates (3, 1) (5, 2), (3, 6), (1, 2) are used to form a quadrilateral. If all four points are connected to form the quadrilateral, which term best describes the quadrilateral formed?

(A) kite
(B) trapezoid
(C) rectangle
(D) diamond

Go on to the next page →

25. The figure shown may be reflected over any of the three dotted lines.

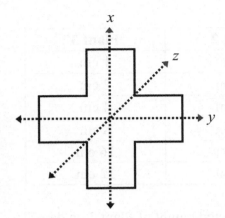

The figure will exactly match the original figure when it is reflected over which of the lines?

(A) line x only
(B) line y only
(C) line x or line y only
(D) line x, line y, or line z

26. The figure below is a large cube made up of smaller cubes.

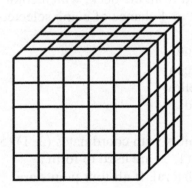

How many small cubes are used to make the larger cube?

(A) 75
(B) 125
(C) 150
(D) 175

27. What is a reasonable estimation for the value of $\dfrac{58 \times 453}{29}$?

(A) between 600 and 800
(B) between 800 and 1200
(C) between 1200 and 1600
(D) between 1600 and 1800

28. Which of the following illustrates the identity property for multiplication?

(A) $x \cdot y = y \cdot x$
(B) $x \cdot 0 = 0$
(C) $x + 0 = x$
(D) $x \cdot 1 = x$

29. The regular hexagon below is divided into equal sized triangles.

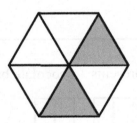

If the area of the entire hexagon is 42 cm^2, what is the area of the shaded region?

(A) 14 cm^2
(B) 16 cm^2
(C) 21 cm^2
(D) 28 cm^2

30. The average age of Paul and Meyli is 32. If Paul is 40 years old, how old is Meyli?

(A) 24
(B) 26
(C) 28
(D) 36

Go on to the next page →

2

31. The figure shows a rectangle with four equal sized squares cut out.

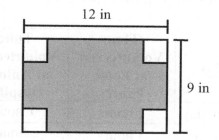

12 in

9 in

If the side length of each square is 2 in, what is the area of the shaded region?

(A) 64 in²
(B) 76 in²
(C) 92 in²
(D) 100 in²

32. A survey of 120 people's favorite month is shown in the circle graph below.

Approximately how many people chose June as their favorite month?

(A) 10
(B) 15
(C) 30
(D) 60

33. The bar graph below shows the results of a survey where students were asked their favorite subject.

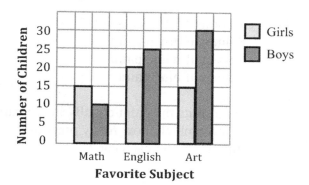

Favorite Subject

Which of the following statements is true based on the graph?

(A) The same number of girls and boys chose math or English.
(B) The total number of boys surveyed was 20 more than the total number of girls surveyed.
(C) The difference between the number of boys who chose art and the number of girls who chose art is 3.
(D) The sum of the number of boys who chose English and the number of girls who chose art is 50.

34. A bag is filled with red, blue, yellow, and green marbles. The probability of choosing a red marble out of the bag is 7 out of 10. Which combination of marbles is possible?

(A) 7 red marbles and 10 other marbles
(B) 14 red marbles and 20 other marbles
(C) 16 red marbles and 6 other marbles
(D) 21 red marbles and 9 other marbles

Go on to the next page →

35. Jim is mixing paint together. He mixes the following amounts of each color paint:

16 pints of yellow paint
8 pints of green paint
5 pints of white paint
3 pints of blue paint

If he splits the paint equally into 5 cans, approximately how many pints of the mixture are in each can?

(A) $5\frac{1}{2}$

(B) 6

(C) $6\frac{1}{2}$

(D) 7

36. Use the figure to answer the question.

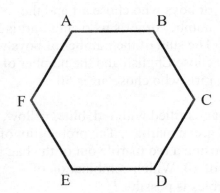

How many triangular regions will be formed in the figure by only drawing line segments from vertex A to all of the other vertices and line segments from vertex D to all of the other vertices?

(A) 4
(B) 6
(C) 8
(D) 10

37. The table shows how long Michael has volunteered at the food pantry and animal hospital over four days.

Day	Time Volunteered at Food Pantry	Time Volunteered at Animal Hospital
Thursday	2 hours	1 hour
Friday	3 hours	2 hours
Saturday	4 hours	3 hours
Sunday	?	?

On Sunday, Michael spent three times as long volunteering at the food pantry than he did at the animal hospital. If Michael volunteered for a total of 15 hours at the food pantry over the four days, how long did he volunteer at the animal hospital on Sunday?

(A) 1 hour
(B) 2 hours
(C) 6 hours
(D) 18 hours

38. Use the triangle to answer the question.

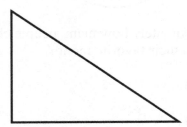

If one straight line cut is made to the triangle, which of the following shape or shapes could be made?

(A) a triangle only
(B) a triangle or a rectangle
(C) a triangle or a trapezoid
(D) a triangle, rectangle, or trapezoid

STOP. Do not go on to the next section until you are told to do so.

STOP

THIS PAGE IS INTENTIONALLY LEFT BLANK

ISEE

Reading Comprehension

LOWER LEVEL

Practice Test

Section 3
Reading Comprehension

25 Questions   **Time: 25 Minutes**

This section includes five reading passages followed by five questions about that passage. Answer each question based on what is <u>stated</u> or <u>implied</u> in the passage. You may write anywhere in your test booklet. For each answer you select, fill in the corresponding answer choice on your bubble sheet.

Questions 1 – 5

1   Many legends exist to explain the
2 origins of American baseball. Some say it
3 was invented by graduates of West Point
4 Academy who needed something to do in
5 their free time. Others falsely imply that it
6 started as a modified form of golf. The
7 simple truth is that the "founder" of
8 baseball isn't one single person, but rather
9 a collection of rules and ideas that have
10 morphed over time.
11   Most historians believe that baseball
12 can trace its roots back to two different
13 British games: rounders and cricket. By the
14 time of the American Revolution, each of
15 these games was widely played throughout
16 the United States. Over the next 75 years,
17 the rules would gradually change to
18 resemble a game that is similar to modern
19 day baseball.
20   One of the first recorded instances of
21 these rules being written down was in 1845
22 by the New York Knickerbocker Baseball
23 Club. One of its members, Alexander Joy
24 Cartwright, was instrumental in suggesting

25 several rule changes that persist to this day,
26 namely the diamond shape of the field and
27 the three-strike rule.
28   The first professional leagues that
29 formed in the United States are the same
30 leagues that exist today: the National and
31 American Leagues. During their first years
32 of competition, each had eight teams, most
33 of them concentrated on the East Coast.
34 The first World Series was played in 1903
35 and was won by the Boston Americans, a
36 now-non-existent team.
37   Baseball has been growing since the
38 early 20th century, and it remains the most
39 popular sport in America by ticket sales.
40 The start of the 21st century saw the
41 highest number of fans ever. A staggering
42 80 million people attended professional
43 baseball games in 2007. Although ticket
44 sales have been declining since that time,
45 there is little doubt that baseball will
46 remain America's favorite pastime for the
47 foreseeable future.

Go on to the next page →

1. The passage is primarily concerned with

   (A) praising the creator of baseball.
   (B) showing the importance of the American League.
   (C) giving a brief history of baseball.
   (D) explaining why baseball is so popular in America.

2. In line 10, the word "morphed" most nearly means

   (A) transformed.
   (B) improved.
   (C) disappeared.
   (D) continued.

3. Which of the following can be answered by the passage?

   (A) What year were the first major league teams formed?
   (B) Who invented cricket?
   (C) Who was the first World Series champion?
   (D) What was the name of the first major league team?

4. Based on the first paragraph, one can assume that

   (A) the person who invented baseball never told anyone.
   (B) the origins of baseball are complex and involve many people.
   (C) golf is an early form of baseball.
   (D) American baseball came before British baseball.

5. In line 7, the word "founder" is in quotation marks to emphasize

   (A) that the author thinks baseball is a silly game.
   (B) that no one really knows who started the game of baseball.
   (C) the ridiculous nature of the origins of baseball.
   (D) how long ago baseball was first played.

Go on to the next page →

Questions 6 – 10

1   For six years, I had walked the same
2 winding trail through Bear Creek Park. I
3 loved the path because it paralleled a
4 stream for most of its length. The quiet
5 babble was everything that I needed after a
6 long day managing the bike shop. A few
7 months ago, I noticed a rather odd-shaped
8 lump in the middle of the path. I slowly
9 walked forward to find that it was
10 breathing! I carefully bent down and
11 realized what I was looking at: a red tailed
12 hawk.
13   Thankfully, I had my phone with me
14 that particular day. Often, I'll leave it in
15 the car so I'm not distracted by calls and
16 work emails. I quickly pulled it out before
17 realizing I didn't even know who to call.
18 *This isn't a police matter... right?* I opted
19 to look up the number for the local
20 Humane Society. After a few minutes, a
21 veterinarian informed me that there was a
22 local raptor center in town and that I
23 should give them a call.
24   Within an hour, volunteers from the
25 raptor center had hiked from the parking

26 lot to where I was standing next to the
27 injured bird. The volunteer turned to me,
28 "Did you see what happened, ma'am?" I
29 shook my head no. "I just happened to find
30 him on the path." As the crew examined
31 the hawk, it was making low murmuring
32 noises: it seemed like it was in pain.
33   I drove back to the raptor center with
34 the volunteers, but they informed me that
35 there wasn't much, if anything, that I could
36 do. They said I could call back in a few
37 days to check on the bird, and if everything
38 went well, I would be able to see it in a
39 few weeks.
40   I had called a few times to no avail.
41 They always told me that he was
42 recovering, but they weren't quite sure yet.
43 After a few weeks, I stopped calling. They
44 had told me there was a good chance they
45 would have to euthanize the bird. Injured
46 birds don't last long in the wild. So, when I
47 received a call from the raptor center, you
48 can imagine my surprise. "If you have time
49 this afternoon, we'll be releasing your
50 hawk in Bear Creek!"

Go on to the next page →

6. The passage is primarily concerned with

   (A) the process by which someone can save a hawk's life.
   (B) a hiker who finds an injured hawk.
   (C) the steps to rehabilitate a hawk.
   (D) the work done by a local raptor center.

7. The passage implies that red tailed hawks are

   (A) small birds.
   (B) birds of northern flight.
   (C) raptors.
   (D) almost extinct.

8. As used in line 40, the phrase "to no avail" most nearly means

   (A) consistently.
   (B) in a short span of time.
   (C) while waiting for a response.
   (D) without success.

9. The main character's tone as she waited to find out news about the bird could best be described as

   (A) indifferent.
   (B) terrified.
   (C) optimistic.
   (D) concerned.

10. In the final paragraph, the narrator was surprised because

    (A) she wasn't expecting the injured hawk to be released.
    (B) she wasn't able to get an answer from the raptor center.
    (C) no one was answering her phone calls.
    (D) the hawk was going to be euthanized.

Go on to the next page →

Questions 11 – 15

1 The day before Valentine's Day,
2 February 14th, 2020, residents in Bristol,
3 United Kingdom awoke to find a stunning
4 mural on the side of a local building. It
5 depicted a young girl firing a slingshot of
6 red flowers and leaves. The flowers and
7 leaves were real: someone had actually
8 glued red roses to the side of the building.
9 As a crowd gathered to look at the mural,
10 people began to wonder who had created
11 this fabulous piece of art. Later that day,
12 posted on his website, it became clear:
13 Banksy.
14 Little is known about the true identity
15 of Banksy. He is an anonymous, England-
16 based street artist. This means that his
17 work appears overnight, and there is no
18 one to witness the act of his drawing or
19 painting. Banksy's messages often center
20 around topics such as anti-war, anti-
21 violence, and anti-capitalism.
22 While not much is known about his
23 identity, the world knows much about
24 Banksy's artistic history. He began
25 creating street art, primarily graffiti, in the
26 early 1990's. He was very active in Bristol,
27 UK, and it was during this time that his
28 artistic style began to use stenciling. He
29 credits this change to the fact that
30 stenciling is much faster than free-hand
31 drawing, which is vital when illegally
32 drawing art throughout the city.
33 In 2004, Banksy revealed his most
34 famous series: *Girl With a Balloon*. As the
35 name implies, the murals that sprung up
36 around England featured a young girl that
37 seems to have just let go of a bright red
38 balloon. These works have continued to
39 appear in response to various world events
40 like the Syrian refugee crisis and various
41 UK elections.
42 It is unknown whether the real identity
43 of Banksy will ever be revealed. Many
44 people claim to know who he is. Some say
45 his name is Robin Gunningham, born in
46 1973. Others believe he is Robert Del
47 Naja, born 1955. Regardless of his true
48 identity, it is likely that Banksy will
49 continue to stun the UK and the world with
50 his thought-provoking art.

Go on to the next page →

11. The primary purpose of the passage is to

 (A) propose one theory about the true
     identity of Banksy.
 (B) discuss the work of a unique street
     artist.
 (C) describe Banksy's famous series,
     Girl With a Balloon.
 (D) enlighten the reader about the rich
     history of street art in the UK.

12. As used in line 5, the word "depicted"
    most nearly means

 (A) erased.
 (B) mocked.
 (C) showed.
 (D) fabricated.

13. Based on the passage, we can assume
    that the purpose of Banksy's street art is
    to

 (A) confuse and annoy people.
 (B) entertain people and make them
     smile.
 (C) make people think about important
     world issues.
 (D) increase his fame as an artist.

14. Why did Banksy use stencils for his
    street art?

 (A) Stenciling helped him efficiently
     create his murals without getting
     caught.
 (B) Stenciling added to the
     mysteriousness of his art.
 (C) It was legal to use stencils when
     creating street art.
 (D) Stenciling was more precise than
     freehand drawing.

15. What is the function of the last
    paragraph?

 (A) It informs the reader about the only
     two individuals who could possibly
     be Banksy.
 (B) It reveals Banksy's true identity.
 (C) It shows that the author also doesn't
     know who Banksy is.
 (D) It demonstrates that people have
     different opinions about Banksy's
     identity.

Go on to the next page →

Questions 16 – 20

1   The elections for student council were
2 always tough. Students recruited their
3 friends to draw campaign posters, speak
4 with fellow classmates, and offer much-
5 needed help on missed homework
6 assignments. The whole process took about
7 a month, and it was the only thing that
8 anyone cared about. All this made it even
9 worse when Jules lost.
10   She had first come up with the idea of
11 running during her sophomore year. The
12 homecoming dance was fast approaching,
13 and it seemed as if no one on the student
14 council had even heard of it, let alone
15 planned anything. When the dance arrived,
16 Jules was right. There were no decorations,
17 no theme, and no food!
18   Now, as a junior, Jules felt that she
19 could change all that. During the first week
20 of school, her and her team of friends
21 covered the entire school in posters. *Only*
22 *fools don't vote for Jules.* Every lunch she
23 would visit new tables with students whom
24 she didn't know well, and once a week
25 Jules visited a different student group:
26 boy's basketball, theatre, speech club.
27   Election day was September 29th. "I
28 must have spoken with every single

29 student in this school," Jules thought. She
30 cast her ballot during lunch like everyone
31 else; she felt proud to check her name.
32 There were only 221 students in her junior
33 class, so the voting committee said they
34 would be able to announce the results by
35 the end of the day.
36   "Good afternoon Douglas High. We
37 are pleased to announce the results of this
38 year's student council election," the
39 loudspeaker boomed. Jules nervously
40 squirmed in her seat. Many of her
41 classmates turned their gazes, waiting to
42 see how she would react. The loudspeaker
43 continued, "And for your junior class, we
44 are pleased to welcome Mark Watters and
45 Stella Manning!"
46   Jules shrunk in her chair. She had
47 worked so hard for this: all the posters and
48 all the conversations were for nothing.
49 Stella happened to be in her class and came
50 over to offer her sympathies. "I'm sorry
51 Jules. You would have been great on the
52 council." Jules just nodded as Stella
53 continued, "We have a spot for a non-
54 council member on the spring dance
55 planning committee if you're interested?"

Go on to the next page →

16. The primary purpose of the passage is to

   (A) explain the unfairness of school elections.
   (B) discuss the benefits of student government.
   (C) tell the story of a girl losing an election.
   (D) describe the process of getting ready for student council elections.

17. According to the passage

   (A) Jules was pretty sure that she would lose the election.
   (B) Jules was inspired to run because of the school dance.
   (C) Jules made different promises to each group of students she talked to.
   (D) Jules first decided to run during her freshman year.

18. As used in line 41, the phrase "turned their gazes" most nearly means

   (A) looked.
   (B) joked.
   (C) laughed.
   (D) silenced.

19. Based on the last paragraph, one can infer that

   (A) Stella is offering Jules a spot on the committee because she pities her.
   (B) Jules rejected Stella's offer to join the spring dance planning committee.
   (C) Jules placed third in the election granting her a spot on the dance committee.
   (D) Jules will still get a chance to help with a school dance.

20. The passage supplies information to answer which of the following questions?

   (A) How many students were elected to the junior student council?
   (B) How many students ran for junior student council?
   (C) How old is Jules?
   (D) Where is Douglas High?

Go on to the next page →

RC

Questions 21 – 25

1   On March 4th, 1841, President William
2 Henry Harrison delivered his inaugural
3 address to an eager crowd on a cold, wet
4 day in Washington, D.C. Wanting to
5 appear strong, he declined to wear a coat
6 and spoke for nearly two hours. 22 days
7 later on March 26, then-President Harrison
8 started to develop cold-like symptoms. The
9 doctors of the day incorrectly thought the
10 cold and wet weather had caused his
11 illness. They treated him with a variety of
12 techniques including bloodletting (a
13 practice whereby doctors intentionally
14 cause bleeding to "free" the disease from a
15 patient) and giving him a mixture of
16 petroleum and snakeroot. Modern doctors
17 believe that he likely had typhoid fever and
18 that his doctor's treatments possibly
19 exacerbated Harrison's condition. He died
20 nine days later, making his 31 days in
21 office the shortest amount of time served
22 by any US president.
23   Prior to Harrison's untimely death, he
24 served in both the United States military
25 and government for over 50 years. His
26 military career began in 1791 when

27 Harrison was persuaded to join the Army.
28 He quickly rose through the ranks and
29 retired as a Captain in 1798, although this
30 would not be the end of his military career.
31   Harrison used his reputation and
32 popularity to win a seat as the Northwest
33 Territory's first congressional delegate in
34 1798. Shortly after, he was appointed as
35 the Governor of the Indiana Territory by
36 President John Adams. He resigned the
37 governorship in 1812 to rejoin the military
38 in the War of 1812.
39   After the war, Harrison quickly
40 returned to public life. He was elected in
41 1816 as a US representative from Ohio,
42 eventually serving as a senator in 1817.
43 After the 1817 election, he served on-and-
44 off in government as a senator, presidential
45 elector, and ambassador to Colombia.
46   It was this combination of military and
47 government experience that helped
48 Harrison become president. While William
49 Harrison may have had a short time in the
50 Oval Office, his grandson, Benjamin
51 Harrison, held the office for a full term,
52 1,461 days.

Go on to the next page →

21. The primary purpose of the passage is to

    (A) argue that President Harrison would have done a good job had he served longer.
    (B) discuss what caused the death of President Harrison.
    (C) make the case that President Harrison died of pneumonia.
    (D) inform the reader about the life and career of President Harrison.

22. Which can be inferred from the first paragraph?

    (A) Doctors back then didn't have much education.
    (B) President Harrison wouldn't have gotten sick if he had worn a coat.
    (C) The cold and wet weather didn't cause Harrison's illness.
    (D) President Harrison did not know that the weather was going to be cold and wet the day of his speech.

23. As used in line 19, the word "exacerbated" most nearly means

    (A) improved.
    (B) sparked.
    (C) confused.
    (D) made worse.

24. According to the passage, all of the following are true about Harrison EXCEPT

    (A) he served as president for less time than any other US president.
    (B) his son also served as president.
    (C) his military experience helped him become president.
    (D) he was a governor before he was president.

25. Which of the following best describes the organization of the passage?

    (A) The passage is organized by time.
    (B) The passage is organized around Harrison's military achievements.
    (C) The passage is organized around the battles that Harrison fought in.
    (D) The passage is organized around Harrison's political contributions.

ISEE

Mathematics Achievement

LOWER LEVEL

Practice Test

Section 4
Mathematics Achievement

30 Questions   **Time: 30 Minutes**

Each question is followed by four answer choices. Read each question and decide which answer choice is correct.

Find the question number on your answer sheet and mark the space having the same letter as the answer choice that you chose. You may show your work in your test booklet.

SAMPLE QUESTION:

    Which number is divisible by 5?

    (A) 89
    (B) 154
    (C) 203
    (D) 275

    The correct answer is 275, so circle D is darkened.

<u>Sample Answer</u>

---

1. What is the name of a polygon with eight sides?

   (A) pentagon
   (B) hexagon
   (C) decagon
   (D) octagon

2. Use the number line to answer the question.

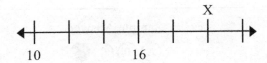

   What number is represented by X on the number line?

   (A) 18
   (B) 20
   (C) 21
   (D) 22

3. Use the triangle to answer the question.

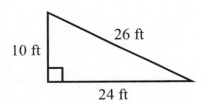

   What is the area of the triangle?

   (A) 120 ft^2
   (B) 130 ft^2
   (C) 240 ft^2
   (D) 260 ft^2

4. Michelle is 18 years old. Sophie is 7 years younger than Michelle. What is their combined age?

   (A) 11 years
   (B) 25 years
   (C) 29 years
   (D) 43 years

5. What is the value of the expression $5,003 - 476$?

   (A) 4,427
   (B) 4,477
   (C) 4,527
   (D) 4,637

6. Use the diagram to answer the question.

   If one shape is picked at random, what is the probability that it will be a ⬤ ?

   (A) 1 out of 6
   (B) 1 out of 4
   (C) 1 out of 3
   (D) 1 out of 2

7. If $50 - (\square + 3) = 40$, then what does $\square$ equal?

   (A) 7
   (B) 8
   (C) 10
   (D) 13

Go on to the next page →

8. Use the coordinate grid to answer the question.

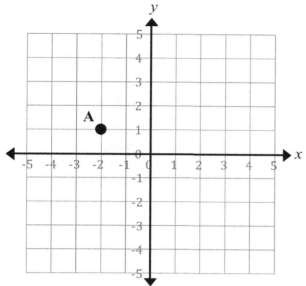

If point A is translated 3 units right and 4 units down, what are the new coordinates?

(A) (1, −3)
(B) (−1, 5)
(C) (−5, 5)
(D) (−3, 1)

9. Which expression is equal to 15?

(A) $3+(2\times 5-10)$
(B) $(3+2)\times 5-10$
(C) $3+2\times 5-10$
(D) $3+2\times(5-10)$

10. Which decimal is equivalent to $\dfrac{3}{5}$?

(A) 0.35
(B) 0.53
(C) 0.6
(D) 0.8

11. Use the set of numbers shown to answer the question.

{2, 11, 17, 23, 29}

Which describes this set of numbers?

(A) odd numbers
(B) composite numbers
(C) irrational numbers
(D) prime numbers

12. What is the value of the expression 57×46?

(A) 567
(B) 570
(C) 2,622
(D) 2,682

13. Veronica went to the store and bought juice for $2.49, chips for $0.75, gum for $1.49, and a candy bar for $1.25. If she gave the cashier $10, approximately how much money did she get back?

(A) $2
(B) $4
(C) $6
(D) $7

14. A basket of fruit has 16 apples, 8 oranges, and 12 pears. What is the ratio of apples to pears?

(A) 1:2
(B) 3:4
(C) 4:3
(D) 2:1

15. What is the value of $9-2.82$?

(A) 6.18
(B) 6.28
(C) 7.18
(D) 7.28

Go on to the next page →

16. The chart below shows the number of sunny days in a town over a four-month period.

May	☀ ☀
June	☀ ☀ ☀ ☀ ☀
July	☀ ☀ ☀ ☀
August	☀ ☀ ☀

☀ = 5 days

How many total sunny days were there is June and August?

(A) 8
(B) 35
(C) 40
(D) 45

17. The population of Austin, Texas is about 964,254. The population of Austin is about one-fourth of the population of which of the following cities?

(A) Madison, Wisconsin which has a population of 233,209
(B) Houston, Texas which has a population of 2,325,502
(C) Kuwait City, Kuwait which has a population of 3,114,553
(D) Los Angeles, California which has a population of 3,793,621

18. Which is the most reasonable unit to use when measuring the length of a toothbrush?

(A) kilometers
(B) inches
(C) milliliters
(D) ounces

19. The table below shows the test scores of an English class.

87	83	87	90	80	96
75	75	90	98	87	85
71	67	87	70	93	85

What is the range of the data?

(A) 26
(B) 29
(C) 31
(D) 98

20. Which number is in the hundredths place in the number 547.638?

(A) 3
(B) 4
(C) 5
(D) 8

21. Which fraction is the smallest?

(A) $\frac{4}{9}$

(B) $\frac{7}{12}$

(C) $\frac{3}{5}$

(D) $\frac{3}{7}$

22. Carly ran 3.8 miles on Monday, 2.6 miles on Tuesday, and 1.75 miles on Wednesday. How many total miles did she run over the three days?

(A) 7.15 miles
(B) 7.25 miles
(C) 8.05 miles
(D) 8.15 miles

Go on to the next page →

23. How many inches are in 3 yards?
(1 yd = 3 ft and 1 ft = 12 inches)

(A) 12 inches
(B) 36 inches
(C) 72 inches
(D) 108 inches

24. Which of the following represents "three less than four times a number"?

(A) $3x - 4$
(B) $4x - 3$
(C) $3 - 4x$
(D) $4 - 3x$

25. Use the number sequence to answer the question.

3, 6, 11, 18, 27, ____

What is the next number in the sequence?

(A) 30
(B) 36
(C) 38
(D) 48

26. The length of a rectangle is $4\frac{1}{6}$ meters and the width is $2\frac{2}{3}$ meters. How many meters longer is the length of the rectangle than the width?

(A) $1\frac{1}{2}$

(B) $1\frac{5}{6}$

(C) $2\frac{1}{2}$

(D) $2\frac{5}{6}$

27. Which of the following pairs of shapes are similar?

(A)

(B)

(C)

(D)

28. The number machine performs the same operation on each input number to create an output number.

Input	Output
19	10
13	7
9	5
5	3
3	2

What input gives an output of 12?

(A) 21
(B) 23
(C) 25
(D) 27

29. The perimeter of a square is 12 units. What is the area of the square?

(A) 3 units^2
(B) 6 units^2
(C) 9 units^2
(D) 16 units^2

Go on to the next page →

30. The graph below shows how Anthony's weight varies with his age.

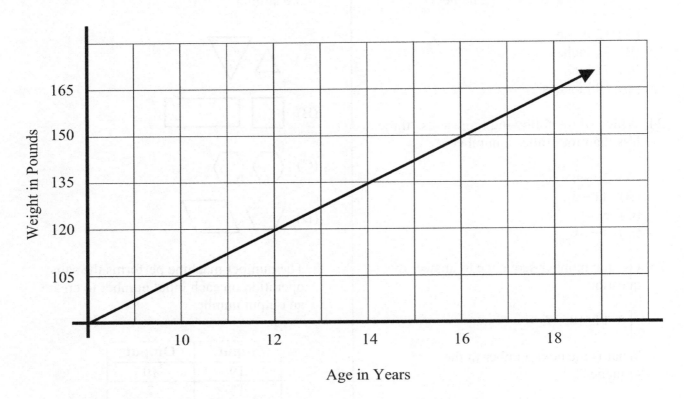

Age in Years

If the line continues, what is Anthony's predicted weight at age 24?

(A) 195 pounds
(B) 210 pounds
(C) 220 pounds
(D) 225 pounds

*STOP. Do not go on to
the next section until
you are told to do so.*

STOP

ISEE

Essay

LOWER LEVEL

Practice Test

Essay Topic Sheet

You will have 30 minutes to plan and write an essay on the topic given on the other side of this page.

The essay is designed to give you the chance to show how well you can write. Be sure to express your thoughts clearly. The quality of your writing is much more important than how much you write, but it is important to write enough for a reader to understand what you mean. You will probably want to write more than a short paragraph.

You are only allowed to write in the appropriate section of the answer sheet. Please write or print neatly; you may write your essay in print or cursive.

You may take notes and plan your essay on the backside of the page. You must copy the essay topic into the box provided on your essay sheet. Please remember to write the final draft of your essay on the two lined sheets provided and to write it in blue or black pen. These are the only sheets that will be sent to the schools.

Directions continue on the next page.

REMINDER: Please write this essay topic in the box provided on your essay sheet.

Essay Topic

You have the opportunity to volunteer anywhere. Where would you choose to volunteer and why?

- Only write on this essay question
- Only the next two pages will be sent to schools
- Only write in blue or black pen

Notes

_____

_____

_____

_____

_____

_____

_____

_____

_____

_____

_____

STUDENT NAME _____ GRADE APPLYING FOR _____

Use a blue or black ballpoint pen to write the final draft of your essay on this sheet.

You must write your essay topic in this space.

_____

_____

_____

Use specific details and examples in your response.

_____

_____

_____

_____

_____

_____

_____

_____

_____

_____

_____

_____

_____

_____

_____

_____

_____

_____

_____

_____

_____

_____

_____

_____

_____

_____

_____

ISEE LL Practice Test 1 Answer Key

Verbal Reasoning	Quantitative Reasoning	Reading Comprehension	Mathematics Achievement
1. C	1. C	1. C	1. D
2. D	2. D	2. A	2. B
3. C	3. C	3. C	3. A
4. A	4. D	4. B	4. C
5. B	5. C	5. B	5. C
6. B	6. A	6. B	6. B
7. A	7. B	7. C	7. A
8. B	8. D	8. D	8. A
9. D	9. A	9. D	9. B
10. D	10. B	10. A	10. C
11. A	11. D	11. B	11. D
12. C	12. C	12. C	12. C
13. B	13. B	13. C	13. B
14. C	14. B	14. A	14. C
15. D	15. B	15. D	15. A
16. A	16. D	16. C	16. C
17. C	17. B	17. B	17. D
18. D	18. C	18. A	18. B
19. A	19. A	19. D	19. C
20. B	20. A	20. A	20. A
21. A	21. D	21. D	21. D
22. C	22. B	22. C	22. D
23. A	23. D	23. D	23. D
24. D	24. A	24. B	24. B
25. B	25. D	25. A	25. C
26. C	26. B		26. A
27. C	27. B		27. A
28. D	28. D		28. B
29. A	29. A		29. C
30. B	30. A		30. B
31. A	31. C		
32. D	32. C		
33. B	33. A		
34. C	34. D		
	35. C		
	36. C		
	37. B		
	38. C		

Scoring Your Test

On the ISEE you receive one point for every question you answer correctly, and you receive no points for questions you answer incorrectly. The ISEE also includes 3 to 5 experimental questions on each section that do not count towards your score; you will not be told which questions are not scored. This means that it is not possible to determine your exact scores for each section of this practice test, but you can estimate your scores using the tables and charts below.

Calculating Raw Score

To calculate your raw score, add up all of the questions you answered correctly in each section, and then subtract 3 to 5 points for each section to account for the experimental questions. Use the table below to calculate your raw score.

CALCULATING RAW SCORE			
Section	Number of Correct Answers		Raw Score
Verbal Reasoning		$-4=$	
Quantitative Reasoning		$-3=$	
Reading Comprehension		$-5=$	
Mathematics Achievement		$-5=$	

Calculating Scaled Scores and Percentiles

Now that you've found your raw score, you can convert it into approximate scaled scores and percentiles using the tables below. Since these scores are estimates, they may differ slightly from your scaled scores and percentiles when you take your official ISEE exam, depending on the specific scaling for that version of the exam.

Verbal Reasoning Conversion Tables

Raw Score	Scaled Score Range	
30	874	904
29	870	900
28	866	896
27	862	892
26	859	889
25	855	885
24	851	881
23	847	877
22	843	873
21	840	870
20	836	866
19	832	862
18	828	858
17	824	854
16	820	850
15	817	847
14	813	843
13	809	839
12	805	835
11	801	831
10	798	828
9	794	824
8	790	820
7	786	816
6	782	812
5	779	809
4	775	805
3	771	801
2	767	797
1	763	793
0	760	790

Percentiles from Scaled Scores			
Grade Applying To	75th	50th	25th
5	858	841	827
6	867	855	840

Quantitative Reasoning Conversion Tables

Raw Score	Scaled Score Range	
35	877	907
34	874	904
33	870	900
32	867	897
31	864	894
30	861	891
29	858	888
28	854	884
27	851	881
26	848	878
25	845	875
24	841	871
23	838	868
22	835	865
21	832	862
20	829	859
19	826	856
18	822	852
17	819	849
16	816	846
15	813	843
14	810	840
13	806	836
12	803	833
11	800	830
10	797	827
9	793	823
8	790	820
7	787	817
6	784	814
5	780	810
4	777	807
3	774	804
2	771	801
1	768	798
0	764	794

Percentiles from Scaled Scores			
Grade Applying To	75th	50th	25th
5	861	845	829
6	874	858	843

Reading Comprehension Conversion Tables

Raw Score	Scaled Score Range	
20	883	913
19	877	907
18	871	901
17	865	895
16	859	889
15	853	883
14	847	877
13	841	871
12	835	865
11	829	859
10	823	853
9	816	846
8	810	840
7	804	834
6	798	828
5	792	822
4	786	816
3	780	810
2	774	804
1	768	798
0	762	792

Percentiles from Scaled Scores			
Grade Applying To	75th	50th	25th
5	855	832	815
6	868	849	827

Mathematics Achievement Conversion Tables

Raw Score	Scaled Score Range	
25	874	904
24	870	900
23	866	896
22	862	892
21	859	889
20	855	885
19	851	881
18	847	877
17	844	874
16	840	870
15	836	866
14	833	863
13	829	859
12	825	855
11	822	852
10	818	848
9	814	844
8	811	841
7	807	837
6	803	833
5	800	830
4	796	826
3	792	822
2	788	818
1	785	815
0	781	811

Percentiles from Scaled Scores			
Grade Applying To	75th	50th	25th
5	865	850	834
6	876	864	849

Calculating Stanines

Now that you've calculated your scaled scores and percentiles, you can use the table below to calculate your stanine for each section. A stanine is a number from 1-9 obtained by dividing the range percentile scores into 9 segments, as shown in the table below.

Percentile Range	Stanine Score
1-3	1
4-10	2
11-22	3
23-39	4
40-59	5
60-76	6
77-88	7
89-95	8
96-99	9

Although it is not possible to calculate an exact stanine score from this practice test, since the percentiles are ranges rather than exact scores, you can still estimate your stanine using the percentile ranges. For example, if you scored in between the 50th and 75th percentile your stanine score would be in between 5 and 6.

Elevate Prep

PRACTICE TEST

ISEE

LOWER LEVEL TEST 2

Test Instructions

The format of this practice test is the same format as the actual ISEE. The number of questions and the number of minutes allowed for each section are both listed on the instruction page of each section, under the title of the section. The chart below also shows the number of questions and the number of minutes allowed for each section.

Section	Number of Questions	Number of Minutes
Verbal Reasoning	34 Questions	20 Minutes
Quantitative Reasoning	38 Questions	35 Minutes
Reading Comprehension	25 Questions	25 Minutes
Mathematics Achievement	30 Questions	30 Minutes
Essay	-----	30 Minutes

Use the answer sheet provided on the next two pages to record your answers. We suggest tearing the answer sheet out of the book. **You can also download and print a free answer sheet on our website: www.elevateprep.com/isee-lower-level**

When you've finished taking the test, grade your test using the answer key at the end of the test. On the pages following the answer key, you will see information on how to score your test, including how to find your raw score, percentile, and stanine for each section.

The Independent School Entrance Examination and ISEE are trademarks owned by Educational Records Bureau which is not affiliated with and does not endorse this practice test.

Elevate Prep

ISEE Lower Level

Answer Sheet

SECTION 1: VERBAL REASONING		
1 Ⓐ Ⓑ Ⓒ Ⓓ	15 Ⓐ Ⓑ Ⓒ Ⓓ	29 Ⓐ Ⓑ Ⓒ Ⓓ
2 Ⓐ Ⓑ Ⓒ Ⓓ	16 Ⓐ Ⓑ Ⓒ Ⓓ	30 Ⓐ Ⓑ Ⓒ Ⓓ
3 Ⓐ Ⓑ Ⓒ Ⓓ	17 Ⓐ Ⓑ Ⓒ Ⓓ	31 Ⓐ Ⓑ Ⓒ Ⓓ
4 Ⓐ Ⓑ Ⓒ Ⓓ	18 Ⓐ Ⓑ Ⓒ Ⓓ	32 Ⓐ Ⓑ Ⓒ Ⓓ
5 Ⓐ Ⓑ Ⓒ Ⓓ	19 Ⓐ Ⓑ Ⓒ Ⓓ	33 Ⓐ Ⓑ Ⓒ Ⓓ
6 Ⓐ Ⓑ Ⓒ Ⓓ	20 Ⓐ Ⓑ Ⓒ Ⓓ	34 Ⓐ Ⓑ Ⓒ Ⓓ
7 Ⓐ Ⓑ Ⓒ Ⓓ	21 Ⓐ Ⓑ Ⓒ Ⓓ	
8 Ⓐ Ⓑ Ⓒ Ⓓ	22 Ⓐ Ⓑ Ⓒ Ⓓ	
9 Ⓐ Ⓑ Ⓒ Ⓓ	23 Ⓐ Ⓑ Ⓒ Ⓓ	
10 Ⓐ Ⓑ Ⓒ Ⓓ	24 Ⓐ Ⓑ Ⓒ Ⓓ	
11 Ⓐ Ⓑ Ⓒ Ⓓ	25 Ⓐ Ⓑ Ⓒ Ⓓ	
12 Ⓐ Ⓑ Ⓒ Ⓓ	26 Ⓐ Ⓑ Ⓒ Ⓓ	
13 Ⓐ Ⓑ Ⓒ Ⓓ	27 Ⓐ Ⓑ Ⓒ Ⓓ	
14 Ⓐ Ⓑ Ⓒ Ⓓ	28 Ⓐ Ⓑ Ⓒ Ⓓ	

SECTION 2: QUANTITATIVE REASONING		
1 Ⓐ Ⓑ Ⓒ Ⓓ	15 Ⓐ Ⓑ Ⓒ Ⓓ	29 Ⓐ Ⓑ Ⓒ Ⓓ
2 Ⓐ Ⓑ Ⓒ Ⓓ	16 Ⓐ Ⓑ Ⓒ Ⓓ	30 Ⓐ Ⓑ Ⓒ Ⓓ
3 Ⓐ Ⓑ Ⓒ Ⓓ	17 Ⓐ Ⓑ Ⓒ Ⓓ	31 Ⓐ Ⓑ Ⓒ Ⓓ
4 Ⓐ Ⓑ Ⓒ Ⓓ	18 Ⓐ Ⓑ Ⓒ Ⓓ	32 Ⓐ Ⓑ Ⓒ Ⓓ
5 Ⓐ Ⓑ Ⓒ Ⓓ	19 Ⓐ Ⓑ Ⓒ Ⓓ	33 Ⓐ Ⓑ Ⓒ Ⓓ
6 Ⓐ Ⓑ Ⓒ Ⓓ	20 Ⓐ Ⓑ Ⓒ Ⓓ	34 Ⓐ Ⓑ Ⓒ Ⓓ
7 Ⓐ Ⓑ Ⓒ Ⓓ	21 Ⓐ Ⓑ Ⓒ Ⓓ	35 Ⓐ Ⓑ Ⓒ Ⓓ
8 Ⓐ Ⓑ Ⓒ Ⓓ	22 Ⓐ Ⓑ Ⓒ Ⓓ	36 Ⓐ Ⓑ Ⓒ Ⓓ
9 Ⓐ Ⓑ Ⓒ Ⓓ	23 Ⓐ Ⓑ Ⓒ Ⓓ	37 Ⓐ Ⓑ Ⓒ Ⓓ
10 Ⓐ Ⓑ Ⓒ Ⓓ	24 Ⓐ Ⓑ Ⓒ Ⓓ	38 Ⓐ Ⓑ Ⓒ Ⓓ
11 Ⓐ Ⓑ Ⓒ Ⓓ	25 Ⓐ Ⓑ Ⓒ Ⓓ	
12 Ⓐ Ⓑ Ⓒ Ⓓ	26 Ⓐ Ⓑ Ⓒ Ⓓ	
13 Ⓐ Ⓑ Ⓒ Ⓓ	27 Ⓐ Ⓑ Ⓒ Ⓓ	
14 Ⓐ Ⓑ Ⓒ Ⓓ	28 Ⓐ Ⓑ Ⓒ Ⓓ	

SECTION 3: READING COMPREHENSION

1 (A)(B)(C)(D)   15 (A)(B)(C)(D)
2 (A)(B)(C)(D)   16 (A)(B)(C)(D)
3 (A)(B)(C)(D)   17 (A)(B)(C)(D)
4 (A)(B)(C)(D)   18 (A)(B)(C)(D)
5 (A)(B)(C)(D)   19 (A)(B)(C)(D)
6 (A)(B)(C)(D)   20 (A)(B)(C)(D)
7 (A)(B)(C)(D)   21 (A)(B)(C)(D)
8 (A)(B)(C)(D)   22 (A)(B)(C)(D)
9 (A)(B)(C)(D)   23 (A)(B)(C)(D)
10 (A)(B)(C)(D) 24 (A)(B)(C)(D)
11 (A)(B)(C)(D) 25 (A)(B)(C)(D)
12 (A)(B)(C)(D)
13 (A)(B)(C)(D)
14 (A)(B)(C)(D)

SECTION 4: MATHEMATICS ACHIEVEMENT

1 (A)(B)(C)(D)   18 (A)(B)(C)(D)
2 (A)(B)(C)(D)   19 (A)(B)(C)(D)
3 (A)(B)(C)(D)   20 (A)(B)(C)(D)
4 (A)(B)(C)(D)   21 (A)(B)(C)(D)
5 (A)(B)(C)(D)   22 (A)(B)(C)(D)
6 (A)(B)(C)(D)   23 (A)(B)(C)(D)
7 (A)(B)(C)(D)   24 (A)(B)(C)(D)
8 (A)(B)(C)(D)   25 (A)(B)(C)(D)
9 (A)(B)(C)(D)   26 (A)(B)(C)(D)
10 (A)(B)(C)(D) 27 (A)(B)(C)(D)
11 (A)(B)(C)(D) 28 (A)(B)(C)(D)
12 (A)(B)(C)(D) 29 (A)(B)(C)(D)
13 (A)(B)(C)(D) 30 (A)(B)(C)(D)
14 (A)(B)(C)(D)
15 (A)(B)(C)(D)
16 (A)(B)(C)(D)
17 (A)(B)(C)(D)

ISEE

Verbal Reasoning

LOWER LEVEL

Practice Test

Section 1
Verbal Reasoning

34 Questions   **Time: 20 Minutes**

This section is split into two parts that contain two different question types. Once you've finished Part One, move on to Part Two. You may write anywhere in your test booklet. For each answer you select, fill in the corresponding answer choice on your bubble sheet.

Part One – Synonyms

Each question in Part One includes a word in capital letters followed by four answer choices. Choose the word that has the closest meaning as the capitalized word.

SAMPLE QUESTION:	Sample Answer
ABANDON:	Ⓐ ● Ⓒ Ⓓ
(A) claim	
(B) desert	
(C) abuse	
(D) neglect	

Part Two – Sentence Completion

Each question in Part Two includes a sentence with one blank. The blank indicates that a word or phrase is missing. Each sentence is followed by four answer choices. Choose the answer choice with the word or phrase that best completes the sentence.

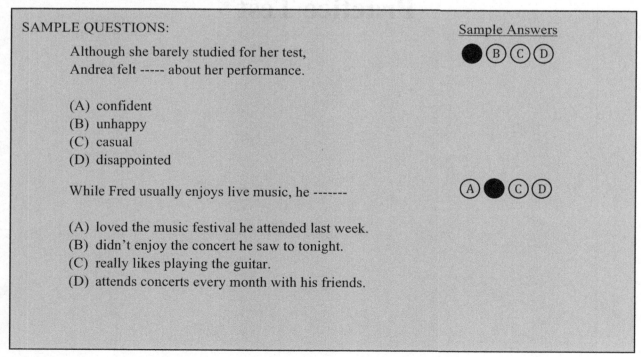

SAMPLE QUESTIONS: Sample Answers

Although she barely studied for her test,   ● Ⓑ Ⓒ Ⓓ
Andrea felt ----- about her performance.

(A) confident
(B) unhappy
(C) casual
(D) disappointed

While Fred usually enjoys live music, he -------   Ⓐ ● Ⓒ Ⓓ

(A) loved the music festival he attended last week.
(B) didn't enjoy the concert he saw to tonight.
(C) really likes playing the guitar.
(D) attends concerts every month with his friends.

Part 1 – Synonyms

Directions: Select the word that is closest in meaning to the word in capital letters.

1. IRRELEVANT

   (A) incorrect
   (B) applicable
   (C) ignorant
   (D) unrelated

2. ASTONISHING

   (A) exciting
   (B) surprising
   (C) frightening
   (D) predictable

3. CAUTIOUS

   (A) scared
   (B) anxious
   (C) careful
   (D) reckless

4. COLLABORATE

   (A) cooperate
   (B) copy
   (C) ponder
   (D) celebrate

5. ALLY

   (A) opponent
   (B) coach
   (C) friend
   (D) trainee

6. GRATITUDE

   (A) luck
   (B) positivity
   (C) regret
   (D) appreciation

7. RESTORE

   (A) purchase
   (B) decorate
   (C) repair
   (D) simplify

8. ATTENTIVE

   (A) observant
   (B) worried
   (C) patient
   (D) hardworking

9. EMULATE

   (A) praise
   (B) imitate
   (C) defend
   (D) innovate

10. INVENTIVE

    (A) boring
    (B) conventional
    (C) creative
    (D) professional

11. ENDURE

    (A) obtain
    (B) tolerate
    (C) triumph
    (D) quit

12. TIMID

    (A) nerdy
    (B) talkative
    (C) unsafe
    (D) shy

Go on to the next page →

13. PROVOKE

(A) support
(B) annoy
(C) scold
(D) pursue

14. TRANQUIL

(A) peaceful
(B) restless
(C) sleepy
(D) friendly

15. MEAGER

(A) limited
(B) sufficient
(C) enthusiastic
(D) unhappy

16. CONTRACT

(A) suggestion
(B) statement
(C) agreement
(D) marriage

17. STINGY

(A) burning
(B) harmful
(C) rich
(D) greedy

Go on to the next page →

Part 2 – Sentence Completion

Directions: Select the word or phrase that best completes the sentence.

18. Although Cassandra was not excited about getting braces, she took comfort in knowing that they were ------- and would be off by the time she graduated.

    (A) fashionable
    (B) mandatory
    (C) painless
    (D) temporary

19. The benefit to having a laptop computer over a desktop is that it is ------- and can be taken with you anywhere.

    (A) stylish
    (B) portable
    (C) efficient
    (D) expensive

20. Although Nadia's symptoms were ------- with the flu, the doctor determined that her nausea, fever, and headache were actually caused by extreme anxiety.

    (A) unusual
    (B) dangerous
    (C) curable
    (D) consistent

21. Jake, who had an extreme ------- of the dark, was unable to fall asleep unless all of the lights in his room were turned on.

    (A) phobia
    (B) doubt
    (C) disrespect
    (D) anticipation

22. Chris ------- his Uncle Tom so much that people often mistook Chris for Tom's son.

    (A) loved
    (B) admired
    (C) resembled
    (D) mimicked

23. Marty enjoyed his school's ------- demographic because it allowed him to meet people with different backgrounds, cultures, and life experiences.

    (A) dense
    (B) uniform
    (C) diverse
    (D) friendly

24. Though his suggested solution to the company's dilemma was -------, it was far too expensive and would take too long to implement.

    (A) practical
    (B) unrealistic
    (C) costly
    (D) perfect

25. When Tom woke up with a minor headache, he ------- his symptoms to his parents so that he wouldn't have to go to school.

    (A) understated
    (B) cured
    (C) increased
    (D) exaggerated

Go on to the next page →

26. Though the weather forecasted ------- rain for the entire week, the sky remained sunny through Friday.

(A) continuous
(B) minimal
(C) terrifying
(D) unexpected

27. The teacher grew more and more ------- as the student continued to tap his pen against the desk, despite being asked numerous times to stop.

(A) amused
(B) worried
(C) irritated
(D) violent

28. Although once widespread, the population of wild tigers has been drastically ------- by poachers who profit from hunting tigers and selling their pelts.

(A) increased
(B) threatened
(C) interrupted
(D) manipulated

29. Although the price of a plane ticket had gone up by $300 because Anna waited so long, she still decided to -----------.

(A) drive home instead of fly.
(B) ask her brother if he was planning on flying home.
(C) change her travel plans to a later date.
(D) purchase a ticket to visit her family.

30. Since Chris is extremely dedicated to his Christian religion, he -------

(A) has many friends who are Jewish.
(B) often forgets to pray before bed.
(C) goes to church at least twice a week.
(D) invited his friends to church.

31. Vincent Van Gogh and Pablo Picasso were both incredibly talented artists, but while Picasso earned millions of dollars throughout his lifetime, Van Gogh -------

(A) was known for his impressionist paintings.
(B) lived most of his life in poverty.
(C) sold his paintings for thousands of dollars.
(D) died almost 100 years before Picasso.

32. Most players on Zoe's soccer team started playing at a young age, but Zoe

(A) started playing basketball at age 15.
(B) was more talented than most of her teammates.
(C) plays both offense and goalie.
(D) just started playing soccer this year.

33. Because Alison had forgotten to close her bedroom window, ----------.

(A) her desk got wet during the storm.
(B) her mom left the door open.
(C) her cat was hiding in the closet.
(D) her brother couldn't sleep that night.

34. Thinking her physics exam would be easy, Tonya -------.

(A) didn't spend any time studying.
(B) cheated during the test.
(C) accidentally slept through the exam.
(D) asked her friends to form a study group.

STOP. Do not go on to the next section until you are told to do so.

STOP

ISEE

Quantitative Reasoning

LOWER LEVEL

Practice Test

Section 2
Quantitative Reasoning

38 Questions   **Time: 35 Minutes**

Each question is followed by four answer choices. Read each question and decide which answer choice is correct.

Find the question number on your answer sheet and mark the space having the same letter as the answer choice that you chose. You may show your work in your test booklet.

EXAMPLE 1:   Sample Answer

What is the value of the expression $10 - 7 + 2$?   (A) (B) ● (D)

(A) 1
(B) 3
(C) 5
(D) 6

The correct answer is 5, so circle C is darkened.

EXAMPLE 2:   Sample Answer

Which could be the dimensions of a triangle with   (A) ● (C) (D)
an area of 12 in²?

(A) 1 in × 6 in
(B) 3 in × 8 in
(C) 6 in × 2 in
(D) 10 in × 2 in

The correct answer is 3 in × 8 in, so circle B is darkened.

1. The rectangle below is divided into equal sized triangles.

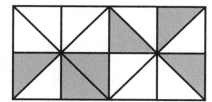

    What fraction of the figure is shaded?

    (A) $\dfrac{3}{8}$

    (B) $\dfrac{7}{16}$

    (C) $\dfrac{1}{2}$

    (D) $\dfrac{5}{8}$

2. Ruth is making gift bags filled with jellybeans. She knows how many total jellybeans she has and she knows how many jellybeans she wants to put into each gift bag. How would she figure out how many total gift bags, b, that she can make?

    (A) b = the total number of jellybeans ÷ the number of jellybeans in each gift bag
    (B) b = the total number of jellybeans × the number of jellybeans in each gift bag
    (C) b = the total number of jellybeans + the number of jellybeans in each gift bag
    (D) b = the total number of jellybeans − the number of jellybeans in each gift bag

3. An isosceles triangle has two sides measuring 6 cm and 10 cm. Which of the following could be the perimeter of the triangle?

    (A) 22 cm
    (B) 24 cm
    (C) 28 cm
    (D) 32 cm

4. Use the equations below to answer the question.

    $$a \div 4 = 8$$
    $$5 + b = 12$$

    What is the sum of a and b?

    (A) 9
    (B) 39
    (C) 43
    (D) 49

5. The total combined cost of a mug, a plate, and a bowl is $24. If the mug costs the same as three plates and the bowl costs the same as two plates, how much does the bowl cost?

    (A) $4
    (B) $6
    (C) $8
    (D) $12

6. Nina is packing up the items in her apartment into equal sized boxes. If 4 boxes can hold 50 pounds worth of items, how many pounds worth of items can 10 boxes hold?

    (A) 100 pounds
    (B) 125 pounds
    (C) 130 pounds
    (D) 150 pounds

Go on to the next page →

7. Use the figure below to answer the question.

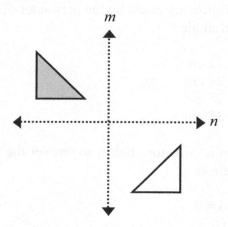

Which set of transformations done to the shaded triangle will result with it exactly on top of the white triangle?

(A) reflection across line *m* followed by a reflection across line *n*
(B) translation right followed by a translation down
(C) translation up followed by a reflection across line *m*
(D) reflection across line *m* followed by a translation down

8. The scale on a map shows that 6 cm represents 48 km. How many cm represents 12 km?

(A) 1 cm
(B) 1.5 cm
(C) 2 cm
(D) 3 cm

9. What is the value of the expression $\dfrac{80(95+25)}{4}$?

(A) 1,200
(B) 2,400
(C) 4,800
(D) 9,600

10. Which is the largest fraction?

(A) $\dfrac{2}{3}$

(B) $\dfrac{6}{7}$

(C) $\dfrac{4}{5}$

(D) $\dfrac{7}{8}$

11. When 183 is divided by a number, the remainder is 3. Which of the following could be the number?

(A) 3
(B) 7
(C) 8
(D) 9

12. Use the Venn diagram below to answer the question.

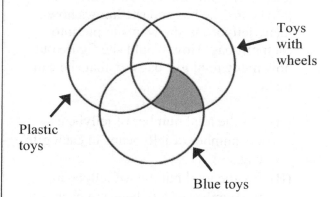

Which shape could be found in the shaded part of the Venn diagram?

(A) A plastic toy car
(B) A green toy motorcycle
(C) A blue wooden toy truck
(D) A blue action figure

Go on to the next page →

13. The table below shows the items that Yael bought at the grocery store.

Item	Price for One	Total Spent on Items
Banana	$0.25	$2.25
Peach	$1.25	$2.50
Plum	$0.75	
Grapefruit	$1.50	$6.00

If Yael spent a total of $13, how many plums did she buy?

(A) 2
(B) 3
(C) 4
(D) 5

14. At the paint store, Lillian bought 8 cans of paint that cost $3 each and a paintbrush. Her total before tax was $37. Which equation could be used to find the cost of the paintbrush (p)?

(A) $3(8) + p = \$37$
(B) $3(p) + 8 = \$37$
(C) $3(8) + 3p = \$37$
(D) $3 + p = \$37$

15. The points with coordinates (0, 3) (5, 1), and (0, 0) are used to form a triangle. If all three points are connected to form the triangle, what type of triangle is formed?

(A) acute
(B) right
(C) obtuse
(D) equilateral

16. A rectangular garden is 12 meters long and 10 meters wide. There is a walkway around the garden, as shown by the shaded region in the figure below.

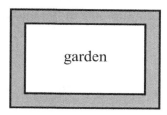

If the walkway is 1 meter wide, what is the area of the walkway?

(A) 23 m^2
(B) 48 m^2
(C) 52 m^2
(D) 80 m^2

17. Which decimal is closest to 7?

(A) 7.1
(B) 6.98
(C) 6.9
(D) 7.01

18. The perimeter of the rectangle is 28 cm.

What is the length of the rectangle?

(A) 7 cm
(B) 10 cm
(C) 14 cm
(D) 24 cm

Go on to the next page →

19. A bucket is filled with green and pink candies. If a candy is pulled out of the bucket at random, there is a 5 out of 9 chance that the candy is pink. If there are 40 green candies in the bucket, how many pink candies are in the bucket?

   (A) 32
   (B) 36
   (C) 50
   (D) 90

20. Use the regular hexagon below to answer the question.

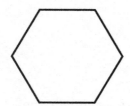

   How many lines of symmetry does the regular hexagon have?

   (A) 3
   (B) 5
   (C) 6
   (D) 9

21. Use the pattern to answer the question.

   $3 + 5 = 2^3$
   $7 + 9 + 11 = 3^3$
   $13 + 15 + 17 + 19 = 4^3$

   Which of the following is equal to 5^3?

   (A) $13 + 15 + 17 + 19 + 21$
   (B) $21 + 23 + 25 + 27$
   (C) $20 + 21 + 22 + 23 + 24$
   (D) $21 + 23 + 25 + 27 + 29$

22. The net below will form which type of shape?

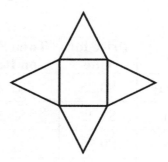

   (A) square pyramid
   (B) triangular prism
   (C) cube
   (D) cone

23. What numbers are represented by A, B, and C on the number line?

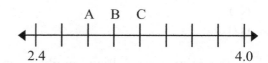

   (A) 2.6, 2.7, 2.8
   (B) 2.7, 2.9, 3.1
   (C) 2.8, 3.0, 3.2
   (D) 3.0, 3.3, 3.6

24. The rectangular prism below is made up of small, equal sized cubes.

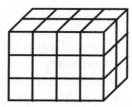

   If the volume of the entire rectangular prism is 48 ft³, what is the volume of each small cube?

   (A) 1 ft³
   (B) 2 ft³
   (C) 3 ft³
   (D) 4 ft³

Go on to the next page →

25. Carol owned x number of cats. Joe owned 5 more cats than Carol. In terms of x, how many cats did Carol and Joe own altogether?

(A) $x + 5$
(B) $x - 5$
(C) $2x - 5$
(D) $2x + 5$

26. A deck of 20 cards has cards labeled 1 through 20. If a card is chosen at random, what is the probability that the number on the card is at least 13?

(A) 7/20
(B) 2/5
(C) 3/5
(D) 13/20

27. J is the average of H and another number. What is the other number?

(A) 24
(B) 26
(C) 30
(D) 36

28. A grocery store receives a shipment of 491 boxes of soup. If each box contains 56 cans of soup, which of the following gives the best estimate for the total number of soup cans in the shipment?

(A) 49×60
(B) 50×60
(C) 400×50
(D) 500×60

29. A bike shop sold 350 bikes. If 2/5 of the bikes that were sold were mountain bikes, how many of the bikes sold were NOT mountain bikes?

(A) 70
(B) 140
(C) 210
(D) 280

30. Both jars below would each hold a cup of liquid if they were filled to the top. The jars are not filled to the top.

If the liquids in the two jars are combined, approximately how much total liquid will there be?

(A) 0.5 cups
(B) 1 cup
(C) 1.5 cups
(D) 2 cups

31. Use the table to determine the rule.

Input ◆	Output □
4	7
7	13
8	15
10	19

What is the rule for the table?

(A) ◆ $+ 3 =$ □
(B) ◆ $+ 5 =$ □
(C) $2($◆ $- 1) =$ □
(D) 2◆ $- 1 =$ □

Go on to the next page →

2

32. Marty biked 2.4 miles on Monday, 5.2 miles on both Tuesday and Wednesday, and 3.6 miles on Thursday. What is the average number of miles that Marty biked over the four days?

(A) 2.8 miles
(B) 3.7 miles
(C) 4.1 miles
(D) 4.4 miles

33. Mrs. Kiernan bought 4 pies for her birthday party. If each pie has 8 slices in it, and there are 20 people coming to the party, approximately how many slices of pie does each person get?

(A) 1 slice
(B) $1\frac{1}{2}$ slices
(C) 2 slices
(D) $2\frac{1}{2}$ slices

34. A potato is taken out of the oven to cool. The table below shows the temperature of the potato over the first 30 minutes.

Time	Temperature
5 min	350° F
10 min	345° F
15 min	335° F
20 min	320° F
25 min	300° F
30 min	275° F

According to the pattern, what will the temperature of the potato be after 40 minutes?

(A) 210° F
(B) 220° F
(C) 225° F
(D) 245° F

35. Use the set of numbers below to answer the question.

1, 4, 2, 4, 6, 8, ___, 6, 5, 6

The set of numbers is incomplete. If the only mode of the data is 6, which of the following could NOT be the missing number in the set?

(A) 4
(B) 6
(C) 7
(D) 9

36. Use the rectangle below to answer the question.

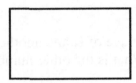

If the midpoints of each side of the rectangle are all connected to each other, meaning each midpoint is connected to each of the other midpoints, how many triangles will be formed?

(A) 4
(B) 6
(C) 8
(D) 10

37. Kurt was thinking of a number in between 12 and 20. He said the number is a multiple of 3 but not a multiple of 2. What is Kurt's number?

(A) 12
(B) 14
(C) 15
(D) 18

Go on to the next page →

38. The graph shows the daily temperature of a city over a 6-day period.

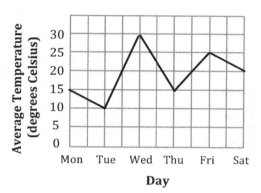

What is the median temperature over the 6 days?

(A) 15° C
(B) 17.5° C
(C) 20° C
(D) 30° C

STOP. Do not go on to
the next section until
you are told to do so.

STOP

Elevate Prep - Practice Test 2   367

ISEE

Reading Comprehension

LOWER LEVEL

Practice Test

Section 3
Reading Comprehension

This section includes five reading passages followed by five questions about that passage. Answer each question based on what is <u>stated</u> or <u>implied</u> in the passage. You may write anywhere in your test booklet. For each answer you select, fill in the corresponding answer choice on your bubble sheet.

Questions 1 – 5

1   I never thought that I would go
2 camping. Growing up in the suburbs of
3 Chicago, there wasn't exactly a lot of
4 nature to be explored. When my brother
5 asked me to accompany him for a long
6 weekend, I was hesitant. "C'mon
7 Margaret, it'll be fun!" he insisted. I finally
8 agreed, and a few hours later we were in
9 his car heading to southern Wisconsin.
10   The whole drive there I was worried
11 we had forgotten something. "Do you have
12 our sleeping bags, Steve?" He looked at
13 me with a sarcastic grin. "I also forgot the
14 tent," Steve quipped. Maybe it wasn't that
15 I was nervous that we had forgotten a vital
16 item, but I was just worried about doing
17 something new.
18   After we arrived at the campsite, we
19 parked the car. I went into the trunk,
20 grabbed the tent, and started to set it up.
21 "Whoa, whoa, whoa!" Steve exclaimed.
22 "What do you think you're doing?" At this
23 point, I was confused. "Well, I would like
24 to sleep somewhere tonight." I insisted.

25 Steve then gave me the worst news of the
26 day, "We're not sleeping here; we have to
27 hike first!"
28   About twenty minutes later, we arrived
29 at a lone picnic table next to a fire ring.
30 "Here's the spot!" Steve said, all too
31 cheerily. We set up the tent, laid our
32 sleeping bags out, and Steve began making
33 a fire. Ten minutes later we were sitting
34 around an admittedly warm fire, enjoying
35 the brisk evening air.
36   In-between the crackles of the fire,
37 Steve and I would talk about anything that
38 came to mind: sports, our friends, the
39 news. Every once in awhile, I would roast
40 a marshmallow or drink some juice. I felt a
41 very odd sense of calm; a calm that I had
42 never quite felt in the city. I decided right
43 there that I really liked camping. "Hey
44 Steve, thanks for bringing me." I said
45 turning towards him. He smiled and
46 laughing said, "At least we didn't forget
47 the sleeping bags!"

Go on to the next page →

1. This main purpose of the passage is to

   (A) describe the bond between a brother and sister.
   (B) tell a story about a new experience.
   (C) express the importance of facing your fears.
   (D) inform the reader about the joys of camping.

2. As used in line 14, the word "quipped" most nearly means

   (A) thought quickly.
   (B) yelled angrily.
   (C) said jokingly.
   (D) whispered nervously.

3. Why did Margaret like camping?

   (A) She enjoyed spending time with her brother.
   (B) She enjoyed sitting around the fire.
   (C) She loved being in nature.
   (D) She felt calmer than she did at home.

4. Based on the last paragraph, we can infer

   (A) Steve is frustrated that his sister is so worried.
   (B) this will likely not be Margaret's last camping trip.
   (C) Steve was actually worried he would forget the sleeping bags.
   (D) Steve and Margaret really enjoy watching the news.

5. Throughout the passage, Margaret's attitude towards camping shifts from

   (A) nervous to optimistic.
   (B) excited to anxious.
   (C) worried to frustrated.
   (D) terrified to excited.

Go on to the next page →

Questions 6 – 10

1   In 1857, it could take over a month to
2 travel from New York to California. Part of
3 the journey was by train, and part of the
4 journey typically took place by wagon. At
5 this time, the trek was still dangerous and
6 required quite a lot of supplies. It was so
7 dangerous that many chose to take a six-
8 month voyage by boat instead. That all
9 changed in 1962 when Congress passed the
10 Pacific Railroad Act.
11   The goal of the Pacific Railroad Act
12 was to connect the east and west coasts of
13 the United States. The bill chartered two
14 different railroad companies to build the
15 new transcontinental railroad. One
16 company, the Central Pacific, started
17 building their railway from Sacramento,
18 California eastward. The other company,
19 Union Pacific, started their construction
20 from Omaha, Nebraska and worked west.
21   The transcontinental railroad was
22 largely built by immigrants. By 1867,
23 Central Pacific employed over 14,000
24 Chinese workers, and Union Pacific
25 employed a similar number of
26 Irish workers. On both sides of the railway,
27 the immigrant workers were often treated
28 much worse than their American associates.
29 Often, Chinese workers were paid less.
30 Sometimes, they were forced to pay for
31 their own food and housing while other
32 workers received these things for free.
33   All workers faced many challenges
34 during construction. First, Central Pacific
35 had to build their railway over the high
36 mountain range on the east side of
37 California: the Sierra Nevada. Secondly,
38 many tunnels needed to be dug through
39 solid rock to make way for the tracks.
40 Lastly, the snow, rain, and extreme cold
41 temperatures often caused delays in the
42 building schedule for both companies.
43 Despite these challenges, the final part of
44 the railway was finished on May 10, 1869.
45 The construction of the transcontinental
46 railroad took seven years. By the end,
47 passengers could travel all the way from
48 New York to California in under a week.

Go on to the next page →

6. The primary purpose of the passage is to

    (A) talk about how immigrant workers are treated poorly in America.
    (B) discuss the building of the transcontinental railroad.
    (C) praise the transcontinental railroad as one of the greatest contributions to America.
    (D) explain why railroads are the best form of transportation.

7. As used in line 13, the word "chartered" most nearly means

    (A) forced.
    (B) recommended.
    (C) destroyed.
    (D) hired.

8. What was the purpose of the Pacific Railroad Act?

    (A) To create a more efficient way to travel across the U.S.
    (B) To establish railroad travel as the only method of transportation in the U.S.
    (C) To create jobs for immigrant workers.
    (D) To create various methods of connecting the east and west coasts of the U.S.

9. The author would most likely agree that

    (A) the transcontinental railroad took too long to build.
    (B) travel by boat is better than travel by railroad.
    (C) only one railroad company should have been responsible for construction.
    (D) the transcontinental changed how Americans were able to travel.

10. As stated in the final paragraph, all of the following were challenges faced when building the railway EXCEPT

    (A) conflicts between the workers.
    (B) the location of the railway.
    (C) the building of tunnels.
    (D) the weather conditions.

Go on to the next page →

Questions 11 – 15

1   With a modern telescope, almost
2 anyone can see the moon in detail.
3 Roughly 500 years ago, this was
4 practically impossible. Magnifying glasses
5 in that day only had a magnification power
6 of 3 - meaning that objects could be seen
7 in detail only 3 times larger. In 1609,
8 Galileo changed that. He was able to take
9 the design of the "modern" telescope of his
10 time and improve it several times over.
11 With these improvements, he likely
12 became the first person to see the craters
13 on the moon in any detail.
14   Born in 1564 in Italy, Galileo is
15 considered to be one of the most gifted
16 astronomers the world has ever seen.
17 While studying at the University of Pisa,
18 he discovered that all objects, regardless of
19 mass, fall at the same rate. He proved this
20 by rolling balls of different weight down a
21 ramp and measuring the time elapsed. This
22 was one of the primary pieces of data that
23 Newton cited when developing his laws of
24 gravitation.
25   Using his newfound telescope
26 technology, Galileo was able to observe

27 the rings of Saturn for the first time,
28 although he didn't know it! All he could
29 make out were blobs around the planet -
30 and they would disappear when viewed at
31 the wrong angle. He next turned his
32 attention to Jupiter. He was the first to
33 discover four massive moons that orbit the
34 planet: Io, Ganymede, Europa and Callisto.
35   In the later years of his career, Galileo
36 was instrumental in confirming a suspicion
37 that astronomers, physicists, and scientists
38 had been holding for years: the Copernican
39 system. In Galileo's time, the prevailing
40 belief was that the Earth was the center of
41 the universe, but his observations proved
42 otherwise. In spite of a ban by the Catholic
43 Church, he published his findings in 1632.
44   The Church did not take kindly to this
45 notion - they called it 'hearsay'. He was
46 found guilty of disobeying the Church and
47 placed on house arrest for the remaining
48 nine years of his life. Although his
49 scientific career was cut short, Galileo will
50 be remembered as one of the most
51 influential astronomists to have ever lived.

Go on to the next page →

11. The passage is primarily concerned with

(A) the history of Italian scientists.
(B) the life and marriages of Galileo.
(C) the inventions and discoveries of Galileo.
(D) the discovery of gravity.

12. In line 9, the word "modern" is in quotation marks because

(A) the author intends for the word to be spoken out loud.
(B) the telescopes would not be considered modern by today's standards.
(C) other countries had much better telescopes than Galileo's.
(D) Galileo's telescope was better than what scientists use today.

13. As used in line 36, the word "instrumental" most nearly means

(A) not helpful.
(B) blamed.
(C) very important.
(D) unsure.

14. It can be inferred that when Galileo did his ball and ramp experiment

(A) the heavier balls rolled a lot faster than the light balls.
(B) he knew his findings would help Newton create his laws of gravitation.
(C) he was completing a project assigned to him by his college professor.
(D) all of the balls rolled at essentially the same speed.

15. According to the passage, Galileo helped prove

(A) that the Earth is not the center of the universe.
(B) that objects of different sizes drop at different rates.
(C) that the sun is the center of the universe.
(D) that Saturn had more rings than people had previously thought.

Go on to the next page →

<u>Questions 16 – 20</u>

1   The novel *The Great Gatsby* follows a
2 brilliant man on a quest for his lost love,
3 set within the extravagant setting of 1920's
4 New York. *Gatsby's* author, F. Scott.
5 Fitzgerald, only wrote three other novels
6 during his lifetime, in addition to many
7 short stories and novellas. Although he
8 may have written less material than other
9 authors, he is widely considered to be one
10 of the best American writers of the 20th
11 century.
12   Fitzgerald was born in 1896 in St. Paul,
13 Minnesota. His family moved frequently,
14 and because of this, Fitzgerald lived in
15 several states as a young boy. After
16 eventually moving back to Minnesota, his
17 first published work was featured in the
18 school newspaper; it was a short story
19 about a detective.
20   At age 18, Fitzgerald enrolled at the
21 prestigious Princeton University. There, he
22 studied literature and honed his writing
23 abilities, often at the expense of his
24 studies. For several semesters in college,
25 he was placed on academic probation and
26 threatened with expulsion. This, in part,

27 caused him to drop out of Princeton and
28 enlist in the military in 1917.
29   After exiting the military, Fitzgerald
30 continued to write, taking odd jobs to
31 support himself along the way. In the fall
32 of 1919, his previously rejected short story
33 was accepted by Scribner's, a publishing
34 agency. His novel, *This Side of Paradise*,
35 was an instant classic and sold over 40,000
36 copies in its first year.
37   Over the next fifteen years, Fitzgerald
38 would go on to write and publish the other
39 three novels for which he is now famously
40 known. The 1930's proved to be quite
41 problematic for Fitzgerald. He encountered
42 marital problems and bouts of tuberculosis.
43   Fitzgerald died from a heart attack in
44 his home in 1940. His funeral was held in
45 Bethesda, Maryland, and it was attended
46 by almost 30 people, most notably his only
47 daughter, Frances. He left behind one
48 unpublished manuscript, *The Last Tycoon*,
49 which was released in 1941. Fitzgerald
50 leaves behind a legacy of great American
51 storytelling that will be remembered for
52 generations to come.

Go on to the next page →

16. What is the main idea of the passage?

(A) American storytelling has changed throughout the 20th century.
(B) F. Scott Fitzgerald does not get the recognition he deserves.
(C) *The Great Gatsby* is one of the greatest novels ever written.
(D) F. Scott Fitzgerald was an influential American author.

17. As used in line 22, the word "honed" most nearly means

(A) demonstrated.
(B) differentiated.
(C) improved.
(D) lost.

18. The passage supplies information to answer which question?

(A) How many novels did F. Scott Fitzgerald write?
(B) How long was F. Scott Fitzgerald in the military?
(C) What was the name of F. Scott Fitzgerald's wife?
(D) How much money did F. Scott Fitzgerald make?

19. Based on the passage, one can infer that

(A) Fitzgerald's daughter will likely publish her own books.
(B) Fitzgerald's first novel was a huge success.
(C) Fitzgerald is likely to be forgotten in the next 20 years or so.
(D) Fitzgerald's tuberculosis contributed to his novel *This Side of Paradise*.

20. The author's tone towards F. Scott Fitzgerald can best be described as

(A) indifferent.
(B) envious.
(C) respectful.
(D) critical.

Go on to the next page →

Questions 21 – 25

1   "Jasmine!" my father yelled, "Stop
2 touching the dang radio or you're going to
3 crash!" I put my hand back on the wheel
4 and stared forward at the empty parking
5 lot. "Now this time, try to go a little
6 slower. The car is easier to control if
7 you're under control." I took my foot off
8 the brake and began to roll forward. I
9 wasn't enjoying this whole process, but if I
10 wanted to get my license, I had to spend
11 time behind the wheel with my dad.
12   Maine's requirements to get a license
13 were clear, and to be honest, they were
14 also pretty relaxed. I had to drive for a total
15 of 50 hours, and 10 of those had to be at
16 night. Every hour, regardless of when it
17 was, had to be with one of my parents.
18 Seeing as my mom had two jobs and
19 practically no time, the driving duty fell
20 mostly to my dad.
21   I was young for my grade, so I had
22 heard countless horror stories from my
23 friends about their actual tests. "I swear the
24 parallel parking spot they give you is only

25 big enough for a tricycle," my friend
26 Jennifer told me. "The guy told me to go
27 through a red light, and when I listened, he
28 failed me," another friend complained.
29 While I wasn't happy to be practicing in
30 this parking lot, I was happy that the
31 chances of me failing my test dropped
32 lower the longer I spent driving.
33   A few weeks later, my dad decided it
34 was finally time to practice parallel
35 parking. "Okay, Jasmine, it's not as bad as
36 everyone says it is. I might be biased,
37 though. I lived in Chicago for a year, so I
38 used to do this all the time." I rolled my
39 eyes and got in the car.
40   "Now, first things first. Pull up next to
41 the car in front of you. You want to line
42 your steering wheel up with theirs." He
43 pulled forward and came to a stop. "Next,
44 turn the wheel and slowly pull back into
45 the space; be extra careful." He backed up
46 towards the curb. *Crunch.* My dad froze.
47 We looked at each other. "Maybe you can
48 give it a shot."

Go on to the next page →

21. The main idea of the passage is to

    (A) describe the preparation Jasmine is undergoing for her driving test.
    (B) prove that Jasmine is a better driver than her father.
    (C) discuss why the driving test was difficult for Jasmine.
    (D) describe the relationship between Jasmine and her father.

22. Jasmine had to practice driving with her father because

    (A) her mother wasn't a good driver and didn't want to help Jasmine.
    (B) her mother was too busy with work.
    (C) Maine required students to drive with their fathers.
    (D) her father thought he was a better driver than her mother.

23. The passage supplies information to answer which question?

    (A) Did Jasmine pass her driving test?
    (B) How many driving hours did Jasmine have left?
    (C) What is one example of how someone can fail the driving test?
    (D) How many of Jasmine's friends failed their driving test?

24. What does Jasmine's father mean when he says, "I might be biased," in line 36?

    (A) He wished his daughter learned how to drive in Chicago.
    (B) He thinks that Chicago drivers are better than other drivers.
    (C) He didn't understand why some people thought parallel parking was difficult.
    (D) He was used to parallel parking, so it seemed easy to him.

25. How did Jasmine feel about learning to drive with her father?

    (A) She didn't enjoy it, but knew it was necessary.
    (B) She was excited to learn from her father.
    (C) She was terrified that her dad wouldn't be proud of her.
    (D) She appreciated her dad's relaxed approach.

STOP. Do not go on to the next section until you are told to do so.

STOP

ISEE

Mathematics Achievement

LOWER LEVEL

Practice Test

Section 4
Mathematics Achievement

30 Questions   **Time: 30 Minutes**

Each question is followed by four answer choices. Read each question and decide which answer choice is correct.

Find the question number on your answer sheet and mark the space having the same letter as the answer choice that you chose. You may show your work in your test booklet.

SAMPLE QUESTION:

Which number is divisible by 5?

Sample Answer

(A) 89
(B) 154
(C) 203
(D) 275

The correct answer is 275, so circle D is darkened.

---

1. Use the figure to answer the question.

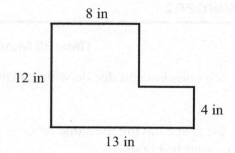

8 in

12 in

4 in

13 in

What is the perimeter of the figure?

(A) 37 in
(B) 45 in
(C) 48 in
(D) 50 in

2. London is in a time zone that is 4 hours ahead of New York. If a plane leaves London at 11:00 P.M. and arrives in New York 9 hours later, what time is it in New York when the plane arrives?

(A) 4:00 A.M.
(B) 8:00 A.M.
(C) 12:00 P.M.
(D) 6:00 P.M

3. Haley had 8 red pencils and 12 blue pencils. She gave half of her red pencils to her brother and a fourth of her blue pencils to her sister. How many pencils does Haley have left?

(A) 7 pencils
(B) 10 pencils
(C) 12 pencils
(D) 13 pencils

4. Which of the following has a remainder of 5 when divided by 9?

(A) 45
(B) 61
(C) 77
(D) 85

5. Which of the following illustrates the distributive property?

(A) $5(9 \times 7) = (5 \times 9) + (5 \times 7)$
(B) $5(9 - 7) = (5 \times 9) - (5 \times 7)$
(C) $5(9 + 7) = (5 + 9) \times (5 + 7)$
(D) $5(9 - 7) = (5 \times 9) + (5 \times 7)$

6. What is the standard form of five hundred six thousand seventy-two?

(A) 506,072
(B) 506,720
(C) 560,072
(D) 567,200

7. The height of a triangle is 10 ft. Which equation can be used to determine the base of the triangle? ($A = \frac{1}{2}bh$, where A = area, b = base, and h = height.)

(A) $b = \frac{2(A)}{10}$

(B) $b = \frac{10(A)}{2}$

(C) $b = 2(A) \times 10$
(D) $b = 2(A) - 10$

Go on to the next page →

8. Use the figure to answer the question.

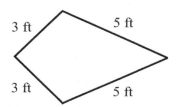

3 ft   5 ft

3 ft   5 ft

What is the name of the quadrilateral above?

(A) rectangle
(B) parallelogram
(C) trapezoid
(D) kite

9. Which of the following is equivalent to 0.06?

(A) 6%
(B) $\dfrac{6}{10}$
(C) 60%
(D) $\dfrac{6}{1000}$

10. Carlton randomly selects four cards from a stack of cards labeled 1 through 9. If none of the cards repeat, what is the probability that the first card picked is labeled with the number 4?

(A) 1/9
(B) 1/4
(C) 4/9
(D) 4/5

11. What is the value of the expression $476 + 2,598$?

(A) 2,964
(B) 3,064
(C) 3,074
(D) 7,358

12. What is the value of the expression $5,106 \div 3$?

(A) 172
(B) 173
(C) 1,702
(D) 1,703

13. Which fraction is in between $\dfrac{1}{4}$ and $\dfrac{2}{5}$?

(A) $\dfrac{1}{2}$
(B) $\dfrac{1}{3}$
(C) $\dfrac{2}{9}$
(D) $\dfrac{4}{7}$

14. What is the prime factorization of 54?

(A) 2×3^3
(B) 3^4
(C) 2×27
(D) $2^3 \times 7$

15. The Burj Khalifa in Dubai is 2,722 feet tall. Which of the following structures has a height closest to $\dfrac{1}{4}$ that of The Burj Khalifa?

(A) The Anaconda Smelter Stack, which has a height of 585 feet
(B) The Hassan II Mosque, which has a height of 698 feet
(C) The Jinping-I Dam, which has a height of 1,001 feet
(D) The Kiev TV Tower, which has a height of 1,263 feet

Go on to the next page →

16. The table below shows the prices at an all you can eat buffet.

	Children	Adults
Breakfast Buffet	$5	$13
Lunch Buffet	$12	$18
Dinner Buffet	$16	$20

How much more does it cost 1 adult and 2 children to eat at the dinner buffet than the breakfast buffet?

(A) $14
(B) $25
(C) $29
(D) $52

17. Use the coordinate grid below to answer the question.

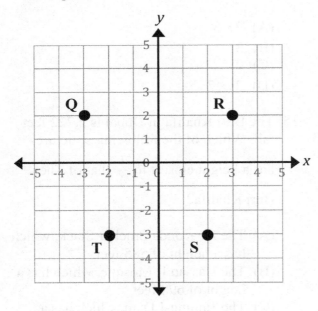

Which point has coordinates (2, –3)?

(A) Point Q
(B) Point S
(C) Point T
(D) Point R

18. What is the value of the expression $5\frac{2}{5}+4.7$?

(A) $9\frac{1}{10}$

(B) $9\frac{9}{10}$

(C) $10\frac{1}{10}$

(D) $10\frac{1}{5}$

19. If $15-\frac{24}{\Delta}=12$, then what does Δ equal?

(A) 3
(B) 6
(C) 8
(D) 9

20. Winston gives away 3/8 of his baseball card collection to his friend Jack and 1/4 of his collection to his friend Heather. What fraction of his collection does he have left?

(A) 1/4
(B) 3/8
(C) 3/4
(D) 5/8

21. George drank 19.75 bottles of water last week. If one bottle holds 2.15 cups of water, which of the following expressions gives the best estimate of the total cups of water George drank?

(A) 19×2
(B) 19×3
(C) 20×2
(D) 20×3

Go on to the next page →

22. The chart below shows the number of donuts sold by four bakeries over the course of a week.

Happy Donuts	◎◎◎◎◎◎
Donut World	◎◎(
Dip and Sip	◎◎
Dunk More	◎◎◎◎◎(

◎ = 50 donuts

How many more donuts did Dunk More sell than Dip and Sip?

(A) 35
(B) 125
(C) 150
(D) 175

23. Use the figure to answer the question.

If the pattern continues, how many circles will be in the seventh column?

(A) 13
(B) 16
(C) 19
(D) 22

24. Use the set of numbers shown to answer the question.

$$\left\{ \frac{5}{4}, \frac{9}{2}, \frac{17}{3}, \frac{25}{6} \right\}$$

Which describes this set of number?

(A) rational numbers
(B) integers
(C) mixed numbers
(D) whole numbers

25. The bar graph shown represents the number of points scored by 7 players on a basketball team last season.

POINTS SCORED LAST SEASON

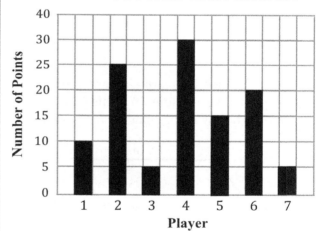

What is the mode of the data?

(A) 5
(B) 10
(C) 15
(D) 25

Go on to the next page →

26. 400 children were asked about their favorite flavor of juice. The results are shown in the circle graph below.

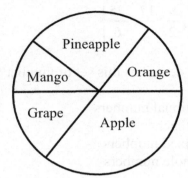

Approximately what percent of children chose pineapple as their favorite type of juice?

(A) 10%
(B) 25%
(C) 40%
(D) 50%

27. Mr. Williams is creating a garden in the shape of a parallelogram in his backyard. Shown below is the plan for his garden.

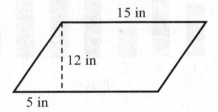

According to Mr. William's plan, what is the area of his garden?

(A) 120 in^2
(B) 180 in^2
(C) 192 in^2
(D) 240 in^2

28. Sheila owns a candle shop. She has 36 candles and wants to package them into boxes of 4 candles. Which equation can be used to determine how many boxes, b, Sheila needs to package her candles?

(A) $b \times 4 = 36$
(B) $b \div 4 = 36$
(C) $b + 4 = 36$
(D) $b \div 36 = 4$

29. Use the figure to answer the question.

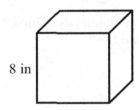

What is the volume of the cube?
(Volume $= s \times s \times s$)

(A) 24 in^3
(B) 64 in^3
(C) 452 in^3
(D) 512 in^3

Go on to the next page →

30. The chart below shows how long Pam exercised each day for two weeks.

	Mon	Tue	Wed	Thurs	Fri	Sat	Sun
Week 1	20 min	20 min	30 min	40 min	30 min	20 min	20 min
Week 2	30 min	30 min	40 min	50 min	40 min	30 min	30 min

Which statement is true based on the table?

(A) Pam worked out more during week 1 than during week 2.
(B) The median and mode for the first week are the same.
(C) The median time Pam worked out during week 2 was 50 minutes.
(D) The range for the entire table is 20 minutes.

STOP. Do not go on to the next section until you are told to do so.

STOP

ISEE

Essay

LOWER LEVEL

Practice Test

Essay Topic Sheet

You will have 30 minutes to plan and write an essay on the topic given on the other side of this page.

The essay is designed to give you the chance to show how well you can write. Be sure to express your thoughts clearly. The quality of your writing is much more important than how much you write, but it is important to write enough for a reader to understand what you mean. You will probably want to write more than a short paragraph.

You are only allowed to write in the appropriate section of the answer sheet. Please write or print neatly; you may write your essay in print or cursive.

You may take notes and plan your essay on the backside of the page. You must copy the essay topic into the box provided on your essay sheet. Please remember to write the final draft of your essay on the two lined sheets provided and to write it in blue or black pen. These are the only sheets that will be sent to the schools.

Directions continue on the next page.

REMINDER: Please write this essay topic in the box provided on your essay sheet.

Essay Topic

If you could choose one superpower, what superpower would you choose? What would you use your superpower for?

- **Only write on this essay question**
- **Only the next two pages will be sent to schools**
- **Only write in blue or black pen**

Notes

_____

_____

_____

_____

_____

_____

_____

_____

_____

_____

_____

_____

_____

STUDENT NAME _____ GRADE APPLYING FOR _____

Use a blue or black ballpoint pen to write the final draft of your essay on this sheet.

You must write your essay topic in this space.

_____

_____

_____

Use specific details and examples in your response.

_____

_____

_____

_____

_____

_____

_____

_____

_____

_____

_____

_____

_____

_____

_____

_____

_____

_____

_____

_____

_____

_____

_____

_____

_____

ISEE LL Practice Test 2 Answer Key

Verbal Reasoning	Quantitative Reasoning	Reading Comprehension	Mathematics Achievement
1. D	1. A	1. B	1. D
2. B	2. A	2. C	2. A
3. C	3. A	3. D	3. D
4. A	4. B	4. B	4. C
5. C	5. C	5. A	5. B
6. D	6. B	6. B	6. A
7. C	7. D	7. D	7. A
8. A	8. B	8. A	8. D
9. B	9. B	9. D	9. A
10. C	10. D	10. A	10. A
11. B	11. D	11. C	11. C
12. D	12. C	12. B	12. C
13. B	13. B	13. C	13. B
14. A	14. A	14. D	14. A
15. A	15. A	15. A	15. B
16. C	16. B	16. D	16. C
17. D	17. D	17. C	17. B
18. D	18. B	18. A	18. C
19. B	19. C	19. B	19. C
20. D	20. C	20. C	20. B
21. A	21. D	21. A	21. C
22. C	22. A	22. B	22. D
23. C	23. C	23. C	23. D
24. A	24. B	24. D	24. A
25. D	25. D	25. A	25. A
26. A	26. B		26. B
27. C	27. A		27. B
28. B	28. D		28. A
29. D	29. C		29. D
30. C	30. B		30. B
31. B	31. D		
32. D	32. C		
33. A	33. B		
34. A	34. A		
	35. A		
	36. C		
	37. C		
	38. B		

Scoring Your Test

On the ISEE you receive one point for every question you answer correctly, and you receive no points for questions you answer incorrectly. The ISEE also includes 3 to 5 experimental questions on each section that do not count towards your score; you will not be told which questions are not scored. This means that it is not possible to determine your exact scores for each section of this practice test, but you can estimate your scores using the tables and charts below.

Calculating Raw Score

To calculate your raw score, add up all of the questions you answered correctly in each section, and then subtract 3 to 5 points for each section to account for the experimental questions. Use the table below to calculate your raw score.

CALCULATING RAW SCORE			
Section	Number of Correct Answers		Raw Score
Verbal Reasoning		− 4 =	
Quantitative Reasoning		− 3 =	
Reading Comprehension		− 5 =	
Mathematics Achievement		− 5 =	

Calculating Scaled Scores and Percentiles

Now that you've found your raw score, you can convert it into approximate scaled scores and percentiles using the tables below. Since these scores are estimates, they may differ slightly from your scaled scores and percentiles when you take your official ISEE exam, depending on the specific scaling for that version of the exam.

Verbal Reasoning Conversion Tables

Raw Score	Scaled Score Range	
30	874	904
29	870	900
28	866	896
27	862	892
26	859	889
25	855	885
24	851	881
23	847	877
22	843	873
21	840	870
20	836	866
19	832	862
18	828	858
17	824	854
16	820	850
15	817	847
14	813	843
13	809	839
12	805	835
11	801	831
10	798	828
9	794	824
8	790	820
7	786	816
6	782	812
5	779	809
4	775	805
3	771	801
2	767	797
1	763	793
0	760	790

Percentiles from Scaled Scores			
Grade Applying To	75th	50th	25th
5	858	841	827
6	867	855	840

Quantitative Reasoning Conversion Tables

Raw Score	Scaled Score Range	
35	877	907
34	874	904
33	870	900
32	867	897
31	864	894
30	861	891
29	858	888
28	854	884
27	851	881
26	848	878
25	845	875
24	841	871
23	838	868
22	835	865
21	832	862
20	829	859
19	826	856
18	822	852
17	819	849
16	816	846
15	813	843
14	810	840
13	806	836
12	803	833
11	800	830
10	797	827
9	793	823
8	790	820
7	787	817
6	784	814
5	780	810
4	777	807
3	774	804
2	771	801
1	768	798
0	764	794

Percentiles from Scaled Scores			
Grade Applying To	75th	50th	25th
5	861	845	829
6	874	858	843

Reading Comprehension Conversion Tables

Raw Score	Scaled Score Range	
20	883	913
19	877	907
18	871	901
17	865	895
16	859	889
15	853	883
14	847	877
13	841	871
12	835	865
11	829	859
10	823	853
9	816	846
8	810	840
7	804	834
6	798	828
5	792	822
4	786	816
3	780	810
2	774	804
1	768	798
0	762	792

Percentiles from Scaled Scores			
Grade Applying To	75th	50th	25th
5	855	832	815
6	868	849	827

Mathematics Achievement Conversion Tables

Raw Score	Scaled Score Range	
25	874	904
24	870	900
23	866	896
22	862	892
21	859	889
20	855	885
19	851	881
18	847	877
17	844	874
16	840	870
15	836	866
14	833	863
13	829	859
12	825	855
11	822	852
10	818	848
9	814	844
8	811	841
7	807	837
6	803	833
5	800	830
4	796	826
3	792	822
2	788	818
1	785	815
0	781	811

Percentiles from Scaled Scores			
Grade Applying To	75th	50th	25th
5	865	850	834
6	876	864	849

Calculating Stanines

Now that you've calculated your scaled scores and percentiles, you can use the table below to calculate your stanine for each section. A stanine is a number from 1-9 obtained by dividing the range percentile scores into 9 segments, as shown in the table below.

Percentile Range	Stanine Score
1-3	1
4-10	2
11-22	3
23-39	4
40-59	5
60-76	6
77-88	7
89-95	8
96-99	9

Although it is not possible to calculate an exact stanine score from this practice test, since the percentiles are ranges rather than exact scores, you can still estimate your stanine using the percentile ranges. For example, if you scored in between the 50th and 75th percentile your stanine score would be in between 5 and 6.

THIS PAGE IS INTENTIONALLY LEFT BLANK

Elevate Prep

PRACTICE TEST

ISEE

LOWER LEVEL TEST 3

Test Instructions

The format of this practice test is the same format as the actual ISEE. The number of questions and the number of minutes allowed for each section are both listed on the instruction page of each section, under the title of the section. The chart below also shows the number of questions and the number of minutes allowed for each section.

Section	Number of Questions	Number of Minutes
Verbal Reasoning	34 Questions	20 Minutes
Quantitative Reasoning	38 Questions	35 Minutes
Reading Comprehension	25 Questions	25 Minutes
Mathematics Achievement	30 Questions	30 Minutes
Essay	-----	30 Minutes

Use the answer sheet provided on the next two pages to record your answers. We suggest tearing the answer sheet out of the book. **You can also download and print a free answer sheet on our website: www.elevateprep.com/isee-lower-level**

When you've finished taking the test, grade your test using the answer key at the end of the test. On the pages following the answer key, you will see information on how to score your test, including how to find your raw score, percentile, and stanine for each section.

*The Independent School Entrance Examination and ISEE are trademarks owned by Educational Records Bureau which is not affiliated with and does not endorse this practice test.

Elevate Prep

ISEE Lower Level

Answer Sheet

SECTION 1: VERBAL REASONING

1 Ⓐ Ⓑ Ⓒ Ⓓ   15 Ⓐ Ⓑ Ⓒ Ⓓ   29 Ⓐ Ⓑ Ⓒ Ⓓ
2 Ⓐ Ⓑ Ⓒ Ⓓ   16 Ⓐ Ⓑ Ⓒ Ⓓ   30 Ⓐ Ⓑ Ⓒ Ⓓ
3 Ⓐ Ⓑ Ⓒ Ⓓ   17 Ⓐ Ⓑ Ⓒ Ⓓ   31 Ⓐ Ⓑ Ⓒ Ⓓ
4 Ⓐ Ⓑ Ⓒ Ⓓ   18 Ⓐ Ⓑ Ⓒ Ⓓ   32 Ⓐ Ⓑ Ⓒ Ⓓ
5 Ⓐ Ⓑ Ⓒ Ⓓ   19 Ⓐ Ⓑ Ⓒ Ⓓ   33 Ⓐ Ⓑ Ⓒ Ⓓ
6 Ⓐ Ⓑ Ⓒ Ⓓ   20 Ⓐ Ⓑ Ⓒ Ⓓ   34 Ⓐ Ⓑ Ⓒ Ⓓ
7 Ⓐ Ⓑ Ⓒ Ⓓ   21 Ⓐ Ⓑ Ⓒ Ⓓ
8 Ⓐ Ⓑ Ⓒ Ⓓ   22 Ⓐ Ⓑ Ⓒ Ⓓ
9 Ⓐ Ⓑ Ⓒ Ⓓ   23 Ⓐ Ⓑ Ⓒ Ⓓ
10 Ⓐ Ⓑ Ⓒ Ⓓ   24 Ⓐ Ⓑ Ⓒ Ⓓ
11 Ⓐ Ⓑ Ⓒ Ⓓ   25 Ⓐ Ⓑ Ⓒ Ⓓ
12 Ⓐ Ⓑ Ⓒ Ⓓ   26 Ⓐ Ⓑ Ⓒ Ⓓ
13 Ⓐ Ⓑ Ⓒ Ⓓ   27 Ⓐ Ⓑ Ⓒ Ⓓ
14 Ⓐ Ⓑ Ⓒ Ⓓ   28 Ⓐ Ⓑ Ⓒ Ⓓ

SECTION 2: QUANTITATIVE REASONING

1 Ⓐ Ⓑ Ⓒ Ⓓ   15 Ⓐ Ⓑ Ⓒ Ⓓ   29 Ⓐ Ⓑ Ⓒ Ⓓ
2 Ⓐ Ⓑ Ⓒ Ⓓ   16 Ⓐ Ⓑ Ⓒ Ⓓ   30 Ⓐ Ⓑ Ⓒ Ⓓ
3 Ⓐ Ⓑ Ⓒ Ⓓ   17 Ⓐ Ⓑ Ⓒ Ⓓ   31 Ⓐ Ⓑ Ⓒ Ⓓ
4 Ⓐ Ⓑ Ⓒ Ⓓ   18 Ⓐ Ⓑ Ⓒ Ⓓ   32 Ⓐ Ⓑ Ⓒ Ⓓ
5 Ⓐ Ⓑ Ⓒ Ⓓ   19 Ⓐ Ⓑ Ⓒ Ⓓ   33 Ⓐ Ⓑ Ⓒ Ⓓ
6 Ⓐ Ⓑ Ⓒ Ⓓ   20 Ⓐ Ⓑ Ⓒ Ⓓ   34 Ⓐ Ⓑ Ⓒ Ⓓ
7 Ⓐ Ⓑ Ⓒ Ⓓ   21 Ⓐ Ⓑ Ⓒ Ⓓ   35 Ⓐ Ⓑ Ⓒ Ⓓ
8 Ⓐ Ⓑ Ⓒ Ⓓ   22 Ⓐ Ⓑ Ⓒ Ⓓ   36 Ⓐ Ⓑ Ⓒ Ⓓ
9 Ⓐ Ⓑ Ⓒ Ⓓ   23 Ⓐ Ⓑ Ⓒ Ⓓ   37 Ⓐ Ⓑ Ⓒ Ⓓ
10 Ⓐ Ⓑ Ⓒ Ⓓ   24 Ⓐ Ⓑ Ⓒ Ⓓ   38 Ⓐ Ⓑ Ⓒ Ⓓ
11 Ⓐ Ⓑ Ⓒ Ⓓ   25 Ⓐ Ⓑ Ⓒ Ⓓ
12 Ⓐ Ⓑ Ⓒ Ⓓ   26 Ⓐ Ⓑ Ⓒ Ⓓ
13 Ⓐ Ⓑ Ⓒ Ⓓ   27 Ⓐ Ⓑ Ⓒ Ⓓ
14 Ⓐ Ⓑ Ⓒ Ⓓ   28 Ⓐ Ⓑ Ⓒ Ⓓ

SECTION 3: READING COMPREHENSION

1 Ⓐ Ⓑ Ⓒ Ⓓ   15 Ⓐ Ⓑ Ⓒ Ⓓ

2 Ⓐ Ⓑ Ⓒ Ⓓ   16 Ⓐ Ⓑ Ⓒ Ⓓ

3 Ⓐ Ⓑ Ⓒ Ⓓ   17 Ⓐ Ⓑ Ⓒ Ⓓ

4 Ⓐ Ⓑ Ⓒ Ⓓ   18 Ⓐ Ⓑ Ⓒ Ⓓ

5 Ⓐ Ⓑ Ⓒ Ⓓ   19 Ⓐ Ⓑ Ⓒ Ⓓ

6 Ⓐ Ⓑ Ⓒ Ⓓ   20 Ⓐ Ⓑ Ⓒ Ⓓ

7 Ⓐ Ⓑ Ⓒ Ⓓ   21 Ⓐ Ⓑ Ⓒ Ⓓ

8 Ⓐ Ⓑ Ⓒ Ⓓ   22 Ⓐ Ⓑ Ⓒ Ⓓ

9 Ⓐ Ⓑ Ⓒ Ⓓ   23 Ⓐ Ⓑ Ⓒ Ⓓ

10 Ⓐ Ⓑ Ⓒ Ⓓ   24 Ⓐ Ⓑ Ⓒ Ⓓ

11 Ⓐ Ⓑ Ⓒ Ⓓ   25 Ⓐ Ⓑ Ⓒ Ⓓ

12 Ⓐ Ⓑ Ⓒ Ⓓ

13 Ⓐ Ⓑ Ⓒ Ⓓ

14 Ⓐ Ⓑ Ⓒ Ⓓ

SECTION 4: MATHEMATICS ACHIEVEMENT

1 Ⓐ Ⓑ Ⓒ Ⓓ   18 Ⓐ Ⓑ Ⓒ Ⓓ

2 Ⓐ Ⓑ Ⓒ Ⓓ   19 Ⓐ Ⓑ Ⓒ Ⓓ

3 Ⓐ Ⓑ Ⓒ Ⓓ   20 Ⓐ Ⓑ Ⓒ Ⓓ

4 Ⓐ Ⓑ Ⓒ Ⓓ   21 Ⓐ Ⓑ Ⓒ Ⓓ

5 Ⓐ Ⓑ Ⓒ Ⓓ   22 Ⓐ Ⓑ Ⓒ Ⓓ

6 Ⓐ Ⓑ Ⓒ Ⓓ   23 Ⓐ Ⓑ Ⓒ Ⓓ

7 Ⓐ Ⓑ Ⓒ Ⓓ   24 Ⓐ Ⓑ Ⓒ Ⓓ

8 Ⓐ Ⓑ Ⓒ Ⓓ   25 Ⓐ Ⓑ Ⓒ Ⓓ

9 Ⓐ Ⓑ Ⓒ Ⓓ   26 Ⓐ Ⓑ Ⓒ Ⓓ

10 Ⓐ Ⓑ Ⓒ Ⓓ   27 Ⓐ Ⓑ Ⓒ Ⓓ

11 Ⓐ Ⓑ Ⓒ Ⓓ   28 Ⓐ Ⓑ Ⓒ Ⓓ

12 Ⓐ Ⓑ Ⓒ Ⓓ   29 Ⓐ Ⓑ Ⓒ Ⓓ

13 Ⓐ Ⓑ Ⓒ Ⓓ   30 Ⓐ Ⓑ Ⓒ Ⓓ

14 Ⓐ Ⓑ Ⓒ Ⓓ

15 Ⓐ Ⓑ Ⓒ Ⓓ

16 Ⓐ Ⓑ Ⓒ Ⓓ

17 Ⓐ Ⓑ Ⓒ Ⓓ

ISEE

Verbal Reasoning

LOWER LEVEL

Practice Test

Section 1
Verbal Reasoning

34 Questions   **Time: 20 Minutes**

This section is split into two parts that contain two different question types. Once you've finished Part One, move on to Part Two. You may write anywhere in your test booklet. For each answer you select, fill in the corresponding answer choice on your bubble sheet.

Part One – Synonyms

Each question in Part One includes a word in capital letters followed by four answer choices. Choose the word that has the closest meaning as the capitalized word.

SAMPLE QUESTION: Sample Answer

    ABANDON: Ⓐ ● Ⓒ Ⓓ

    (A) claim
    (B) desert
    (C) abuse
    (D) neglect

Part Two – Sentence Completion

Each question in Part Two includes a sentence with one blank. The blank indicates that a word or phrase is missing. Each sentence is followed by four answer choices. Choose the answer choice with the word or phrase that best completes the sentence.

SAMPLE QUESTIONS: Sample Answers

    Although she barely studied for her test,   ● Ⓑ Ⓒ Ⓓ
    Andrea felt ----- about her performance.

    (A) confident
    (B) unhappy
    (C) casual
    (D) disappointed

    While Fred usually enjoys live music, he -------   Ⓐ ● Ⓒ Ⓓ

    (A) loved the music festival he attended last week.
    (B) didn't enjoy the concert he saw to tonight.
    (C) really likes playing the guitar.
    (D) attends concerts every month with his friends.

Part 1 – Synonyms

Directions: Select the word that is closest in meaning to the word in capital letters.

1. COURTEOUS

   (A) likeable
   (B) polite
   (C) joyful
   (D) serious

2. COLLEAGUE

   (A) manager
   (B) enemy
   (C) friend
   (D) coworker

3. STUBBORN

   (A) upsetting
   (B) hateful
   (C) willful
   (D) flexible

4. PUZZLE

   (A) confuse
   (B) challenge
   (C) activity
   (D) comprehend

5. FURY

   (A) hairy
   (B) intolerance
   (C) calmness
   (D) rage

6. PERSPECTIVE

   (A) outlook
   (B) recommendation
   (C) clever
   (D) suspicion

7. INCOHERENT

   (A) unstable
   (B) unclear
   (C) unable
   (D) underestimated

8. HOSTILE

   (A) mild
   (B) strange
   (C) aggressive
   (D) unlikeable

9. AMPLIFY

   (A) advise
   (B) decrease
   (C) activate
   (D) intensify

10. PRELIMINARY

    (A) concluding
    (B) expected
    (C) introductory
    (D) logical

11. ACCOMMODATING

    (A) helpful
    (B) engaging
    (C) simple
    (D) selfish

12. DIGNITY

    (A) patience
    (B) generosity
    (C) desire
    (D) pride

Go on to the next page →

13. EMPHASIZE

    (A) animate
    (B) highlight
    (C) question
    (D) declare

14. BIAS

    (A) equality
    (B) dishonesty
    (C) prejudice
    (D) hatred

15. DEFIANT

    (A) resistant
    (B) unbelievable
    (C) apologetic
    (D) forceful

16. INJUSTICE

    (A) rudeness
    (B) unfairness
    (C) revenge
    (D) criminality

17. PACIFY

    (A) agitate
    (B) amplify
    (C) sympathize
    (D) soothe

Go on to the next page →

Part 2 – Sentence Completion

Directions: Select the word or phrase that best completes the sentence.

18. The Roman Empire made many ------- that helped shape the modern world, including newspapers, plumbing, and even surgical tools.

    (A) decisions
    (B) contributions
    (C) dilemmas
    (D) theories

19. Although it seemed to be the longest flight ever, Evan's mother assured him that they would ------- reach their destination.

    (A) never
    (B) immediately
    (C) probably
    (D) eventually

20. Cory had a(n) ------- for fixing things and repaired his mother's kitchen sink, dishwasher and toilet in a few hours.

    (A) knack
    (B) career
    (C) incompetence
    (D) purpose

21. While Kevin was normally cautious and unadventurous, he showed a lot of ------- when he overcome his fear of heights and went cliff jumping.

    (A) uniqueness
    (B) bravery
    (C) cowardice
    (D) insanity

22. As a fan of murder mysteries, Jen wanted to ------- how the neighbor's cat was killed.

    (A) forget
    (B) narrate
    (C) understand
    (D) investigate

23. Martin Luther King Jr. is one of the most ------- civil rights leaders, known around the world for his lasting impact on the lives of African Americans.

    (A) underestimated
    (B) intelligent
    (C) notable
    (D) verified

24. Although many people thought it was ------- that my friend and I showed up to school in the same shirt, we had planned our matching outfits the night before.

    (A) coincidental
    (B) intentional
    (C) humorous
    (D) peculiar

25. While Ashley claimed it was an accident that she threw the ball at Emma's face, the other players thought she had ------- tried to hurt Emma.

    (A) unintentionally
    (B) jokingly
    (C) deliberately
    (D) violently

Go on to the next page →

26. Because of the ------- weather of her travel destination, Ashley had to pack every type of clothing, from warm coats and scarves to sunglasses and sandals.

(A) temperate
(B) humid
(C) harsh
(D) unpredictable

27. After realizing that the police had hard evidence to convict them of the crime, the suspects decided to -------, in an attempt to receive a lesser punishment.

(A) cooperate
(B) flee
(C) argue
(D) weep

28. The family found an ideal location with plenty of land that allowed for the ------- of their already thriving farm business.

(A) reduction
(B) success
(C) expansion
(D) creation

29. Norberto loved eating dessert, although curiously, he -------.

(A) eats two desserts each day.
(B) really did not care for cookies.
(C) never learned to bake.
(D) hated eating vegetables.

30. Excluding the diamond necklace that Chastity received for her 25th birthday, she had never -------.

(A) received gifts for Hanukkah.
(B) had a birthday party.
(C) bought diamonds before.
(D) owned expensive jewelry before.

31. Because she was trying to be more independent, Kris decided that she would -------.

(A) sign up for a hip-hop dance class.
(B) start reading more books and watching less TV.
(C) bike to work instead of having her parents give her a ride.
(D) focus and study more in school.

32. At just 17 years old, Malala Yousafzai made history when she -------.

(A) became the youngest Nobel Peace Prize winner.
(B) learned how to speak three languages.
(C) became interested in fighting for women's rights.
(D) wrote a blog about her life.

33. Although Linda was friendly with her coworkers and enjoyed spending time with them outside of work, she -------.

(A) was the most hard working employee at her company.
(B) did not think that they were responsible employees.
(C) would avoid them whenever possible.
(D) rarely gave presentations at work.

34. Even if it is freezing outside, Dale still -------.

(A) checks the weather forecast.
(B) wears shorts and sandals.
(C) calls his mother before work.
(D) puts on a sweater and scarf.

STOP. Do not go on to the next section until you are told to do so.

STOP

ISEE

Quantitative Reasoning

LOWER LEVEL

Practice Test

Section 2
Quantitative Reasoning

38 Questions   **Time: 35 Minutes**

Each question is followed by four answer choices. Read each question and decide which answer choice is correct.

Find the question number on your answer sheet and mark the space having the same letter as the answer choice that you chose. You may show your work in your test booklet.

EXAMPLE 1:   Sample Answer

    What is the value of the expression $10 - 7 + 2$?   (A)(B)●(D)

    (A) 1
    (B) 3
    (C) 5
    (D) 6

    The correct answer is 5, so circle C is darkened.

EXAMPLE 2:   Sample Answer

    Which could be the dimensions of a triangle with   (A)●(C)(D)
    an area of 12 in^2?

    (A) 1 in × 6 in
    (B) 3 in × 8 in
    (C) 6 in × 2 in
    (D) 10 in × 2 in

    The correct answer is 3 in × 8 in, so circle B is darkened.

---

1. If 12 and 18 can both be divided by x without a remainder, then what other number can be divided by x without leaving a remainder?

   (A) 3
   (B) 4
   (C) 6
   (D) 9

2. The figure below is made up of equal sized triangles.

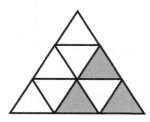

   What is the ratio of the shaded area to the non-shaded area?

   (A) 1:2
   (B) 2:1
   (C) 1:3
   (D) 3:1

3. What number is represented by M on the number line?

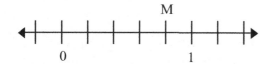

   (A) $\frac{1}{5}$

   (B) $\frac{1}{2}$

   (C) $\frac{3}{4}$

   (D) $\frac{4}{5}$

4. The graph shows the daily temperature of a city over a 6-day period.

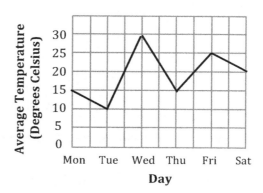

   What is the relationship between the temperature on Tuesday and the temperature on Thursday?

   (A) The temperature on Tuesday was 20° less than the temperature on Thursday.
   (B) The temperature on Thursday was 1.5 times the temperature on Tuesday.
   (C) The temperature on Thursday was 10° higher than the temperature on Tuesday.
   (D) The temperature on Tuesday was half of the temperature on Thursday.

5. At a certain high school, there are 200 seniors in the graduating class. If 90% of the graduating class is attending college next year, how many students from the graduating class are attending college next year?

   (A) 90
   (B) 110
   (C) 160
   (D) 180

Go on to the next page →

6. If 2 gallons is equal to 16 pints, how many gallons are there in 40 pints?

   (A) 3.5 gallons
   (B) 4 gallons
   (C) 4.5 gallons
   (D) 5 gallons

7. Christina has been tracking how much time she has spent doing homework over the last five days. She spent $1\frac{1}{3}$ hours on Monday, $2\frac{1}{3}$ hours on both Tuesday and Wednesday, 1 hour on Thursday and 2 hours on Friday. What is the average number of hours Christina spent on homework each day?

   (A) $1\frac{2}{3}$

   (B) $1\frac{4}{5}$

   (C) $2\frac{1}{5}$

   (D) $2\frac{1}{4}$

8. A spinner is broken up into 20 equal sized sections. If you throw a dart and it hits the board, the probability that you hit a blue section is 2 out of 5. How many sections are blue?

   (A) 2
   (B) 4
   (C) 8
   (D) 10

9. The volume of the small, shaded cube below is 1 cm³.

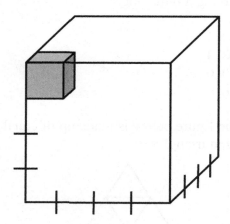

What is the volume of the larger cube?

   (A) 16 cm³
   (B) 27 cm³
   (C) 64 cm³
   (D) 256 cm³

10. Which number below is NOT the product of two prime numbers?

   (A) 6
   (B) 15
   (C) 35
   (D) 42

11. On a coordinate grid, point A is translated 1 unit up and 2 units right. The new coordinates of point A are (5, 8). What were the starting coordinates of point A?

   (A) (3, 7)
   (B) (4, 6)
   (C) (6, 10)
   (D) (7, 9)

Go on to the next page →

12. Use the figure below to answer the question.

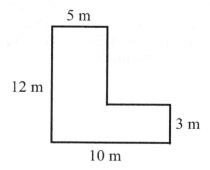

What is the area of the figure?

(A) 60 m^2
(B) 75 m^2
(C) 90 m^2
(D) 120 m^2

13. The probability of choosing a caramel chocolate from a box of chocolates is 3 out of 4. Which of the following could be a possible combination of chocolates?

(A) 6 caramel chocolates and 8 other chocolates
(B) 9 caramel chocolates and 6 other chocolates
(C) 21 caramel chocolates and 7 other chocolates
(D) 30 caramel chocolates and 40 other chocolates

14. Mel took a test with 50 questions. If she answered 10 more questions correctly than she did incorrectly, how many questions did she answer correctly?

(A) 15 questions
(B) 20 questions
(C) 30 questions
(D) 35 questions

15. Use the figure to answer the question.

If the pattern continues, what will be the 27th shape in the pattern?

(A) ▽

(B)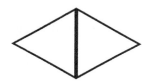

(C) □

(D) ⊗

16. The figure below is made up of two equilateral triangles.

If the perimeter of each triangle is 27 in, what is the perimeter of the entire figure?

(A) 28 in
(B) 36 in
(C) 45 in
(D) 54 in

17. The length of PQ is a and the length of QR is b.

What is the length of PR?

(A) $a + b$
(B) $a - b$
(C) $b - a$
(D) ab

Go on to the next page →

18. Which fraction is in between 0.3 and 0.5?

    (A) $\dfrac{3}{10}$

    (B) $\dfrac{3}{5}$

    (C) $\dfrac{1}{4}$

    (D) $\dfrac{1}{3}$

19. Use the number line to answer the question.

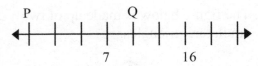

What is the average of P and Q?

    (A) 4
    (B) 5
    (C) 7
    (D) 20

20. Which equation can be read as "five less than a number is equal to three more than four times the number"? Let x represent the unknown number.

    (A) $x - 5 = 4x + 3$
    (B) $x - 5 = 3x + 4$
    (C) $5 - x = 4x + 3$
    (D) $5 - x = 3x + 4$

21. What is the value of y in the math equation $30 = 6 + 3y$?

    (A) 6
    (B) 8
    (C) 9
    (D) 12

22. Gina and Weston are putting gift bags together for a party. They each work at the same rate, and Gina can make 6 gift bags every 30 minutes. At this rate, how many gift bags could they make if they both work for 45 minutes?

    (A) 9
    (B) 12
    (C) 16
    (D) 18

23. The perimeter of the triangle below is 36 m. The lengths of two sides are shown.

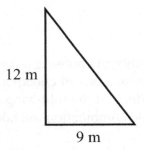

What is the length of the third side of the triangle?

    (A) 15 m
    (B) 21 m
    (C) 47 m
    (D) 57 m

24. Which story best fits the equation $8 \times 12 = 96$?

    (A) I have $96. After spending $8, how much money do I have left?
    (B) I bought 8 shirts and each shirt cost $12. How much total money did I spend?
    (C) I have $8 and my friend has $12. How much money do we have altogether?
    (D) I split $96 into 20 equal piles. How much money is in each pile?

Go on to the next page →

25. Each small square below represents 1 square unit.

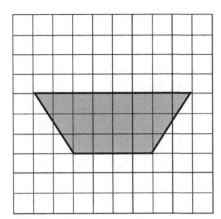

What is the area of the shaded region?

(A) 12 square units
(B) 15 square units
(C) 18 square units
(D) 24 square units

26. A survey of 80 people's favorite month is shown in the circle graph below.

Approximately what fraction of people chose May as their favorite month?

(A) $\frac{1}{8}$

(B) $\frac{1}{5}$

(C) $\frac{1}{4}$

(D) $\frac{1}{3}$

27. Will bought a box of cookies. He split the cookies evenly among his five friends and had 3 cookies leftover for himself. If each friend got 6 cookies, how many cookies were in the box that Will bought?

(A) 27 students
(B) 30 students
(C) 33 students
(D) 39 students

28. Use the pentagon below to answer the question.

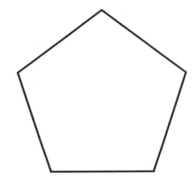

How many lines are needed to connect all of the non-consecutive vertices of the pentagon?

(A) 4
(B) 5
(C) 6
(D) 10

29. If the total area of all of the faces of a cube is 24 square inches, what is the side length of the cube?

(A) 2 in
(B) 4 in
(C) 6 in
(D) 8 in

Go on to the next page →

30. Use the table to answer the question.

Input □	Output Δ
6	x
9	14
y	16
15	26

The rule for the table is $\square = \dfrac{\Delta + 4}{2}$. What does $x + y$ equal?

(A) 15
(B) 18
(C) 21
(D) 36

31. If 0.02 is equal to $\dfrac{x}{100}$, then x is equal to which of the following?

(A) 0.002
(B) 0.2
(C) 2
(D) 20

32. Which of the following could be the dimensions of a rectangle with a perimeter of 48 cm?

(A) 6 cm and 8 cm
(B) 20 cm and 28 cm
(C) 9 cm and 16 cm
(D) 13 cm and 11 cm

33. What is a reasonable estimation for the value of $\dfrac{97 \times 43}{19}$?

(A) between 50 and 100
(B) between 100 and 150
(C) between 150 and 250
(D) between 250 and 350

34. Five college students tracked the number of hours spent working over a period of one week and recorded their data in the graph shown.

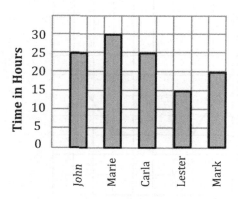

Based on the graph, which of the following statements is true?

(A) John and Mark worked the same number of hours.
(B) The mode of the data is 20 hours.
(C) The range of the data is more than the number of hours Lester worked.
(D) The mean is above 20 hours.

35. The figure below is made up of two overlapping squares.

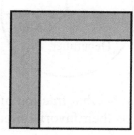

The side length of the larger square is 8 ft, and the area of the shaded region is 28 ft². What is the side length of the smaller square?

(A) 4 ft
(B) 6 ft
(C) 7 ft
(D) 10 ft

Go on to the next page →

36. Angela is training for a race. The table below shows her race time over six months.

Month	Race Time
November	45 min
December	44 min
January	42 min
February	41 min
March	39 min
April	38 min

If the pattern continues, what would Angela's expected race time be in July?

(A) 33 minutes
(B) 34 minutes
(C) 35 minutes
(D) 36 minutes

37. Pam has been working as a part time lifeguard for the past year. She worked a total of 189 days for an average of 4.3 hours each day. Which of the following gives the best estimate for the total number of hours Pam has worked as a lifeguard this year?

(A) 19×4
(B) 19×5
(C) 200×4
(D) 200×5

38. Use the diagram to answer the question.

Which piece would complete the diagram to make a square?

(A)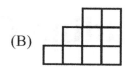

(B)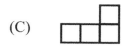

(C)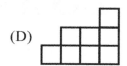

(D)

ISEE

Reading Comprehension

LOWER LEVEL

Practice Test

Section 3
Reading Comprehension

25 Questions   **Time: 25 Minutes**

This section includes five reading passages followed by five questions about that passage. Answer each question based on what is <u>stated</u> or <u>implied</u> in the passage. You may write anywhere in your test booklet. For each answer you select, fill in the corresponding answer choice on your bubble sheet.

Questions 1 – 5

During the last ice age, roughly 2.6 million years ago, almost a third of the globe was covered in glaciers. These vast, dense ice sheets are formed when snow becomes compacted into ice. Over hundreds and thousands of years, continual cycles of snowfall and compaction lead to ice sheets that can be hundreds of feet thick.

Glaciers exist on every continent on earth, but they only form in areas where there is permanent snow. Because these locations need to be below or near-freezing year round, glaciers are found only around the poles and at high elevations.

In the US, glaciers exist in nine states, all of them concentrated in the American West and Pacific Northwest. Although many states can boast glaciers, only one can be considered the king: Alaska. Of the roughly 35,000 glaciers in the United States, over 75% of them exist here; this makes up over 5% of the state's total landmass.

Recently, though, the situation has become dire for the world's glaciers. In some areas of Patagonia, South America, scientists report glaciers have lost almost half of their mass. In Greenland, glaciers on the southern coast have receded by several miles. At the current pace, Glacier National Park, Montana, will have no more glaciers by the year 2050.

The major cause of this meltdown is global climate change, caused primarily by human activity. Processes that burn fossil fuels - like oil, coal, and natural gas - are a major contributor to the earth's temperature rise. Driving cars, manufacturing goods, and heating homes all play a part in this process.

Hope isn't lost, though. Technology that reduces the need for oil and coal are developed every year. Alternative and renewable energy sources like wind and solar make it easier to use energy sustainably. Hopefully these changes are enough to save the giant, beautiful ice sheets around the globe.

Go on to the next page →

1. The author wrote the passage to

   (A) show that glaciers are at risk of melting.
   (B) present the beauty of glaciers.
   (C) explain ways that we can preserve glaciers.
   (D) describe how glaciers are formed.

2. In lines 25 – 26, what is meant by the phrase "the situation has become dire"?

   (A) Animals that depend on the glaciers as a source of water may die.
   (B) Scientists are not concerned about the world's glaciers melting.
   (C) Glaciers are melting at an alarmingly fast pace.
   (D) Glaciers are growing too large in some areas of the world.

3. According to the third paragraph

   (A) 5% of Alaska's glaciers have melted.
   (B) less than 25% of America's glaciers are in states other than Alaska.
   (C) 75% of the world's glaciers are in Alaska.
   (D) there are 35,000 glaciers in Alaska.

4. Based on the 5th paragraph, one can infer that

   (A) climate change is only caused by humans.
   (B) everyone should stop driving cars immediately.
   (C) renewable energy can completely reverse the effects of climate change.
   (D) climate change has become worse since humans discovered oil, coal, and natural gas.

5. The author's tone in the last paragraph could be described as

   (A) sarcastic.
   (B) worried.
   (C) optimistic.
   (D) frustrated.

Go on to the next page →

Questions 6 – 10

1   Piano had always been a part of Juan's
2   life. It was an instrument that practically
3   everyone in his family played, so when he
4   was only four or five, he began to play as
5   well. His parents were relentless. He
6   practiced three times a week with his
7   teacher, and he was expected to practice
8   for at least 45 minutes every other day.
9   Now that he was 13, it was time to start
10 competing.
11   Juan was worried, though. He had a
12 judged piano recital coming up, and it
13 would be his first time playing in front of
14 an audience bigger than his family. *What if*
15 *I mess up?*
16   For the month leading up to the
17 competition, he met with his teacher
18 almost every day. They spent time working
19 on the hardest parts of his piece, checking
20 his tempo, and memorize the ends of each
21 page. Slowly but surely, he was making
22 progress.
23   Finally, competition Saturday had
24 arrived. Juan was sweating even more than
25 normal, and now he was wearing a suit. He
26 peered out from behind the curtain as the
27 crowd took their seats. Stretched out across
28 a whole row Juan saw everyone who was

29 there for him: his mom, dad, sisters,
30 brother, aunt, grandparents, and piano
31 teacher.
32   "And now, performing *Minuet* in G
33 major, Juan Diaz!" boomed the
34 loudspeaker. The crowd began clapping
35 which gave Juan a few moments to sit
36 down at the piano and orient himself.
37 "You've practiced this hundreds of times,"
38 Juan thought to himself. He inhaled,
39 exhaled, and began to play.
40   It was almost like time simultaneously
41 stood still and sped up. Juan felt himself
42 playing the music, but he couldn't
43 remember what he had just played. He felt
44 entirely in the moment. And just like that,
45 he was playing the finishing crescendo.
46 Moments after he played the final G chord,
47 the crowd erupted into applause.
48   After the rest of the musicians had
49 played their pieces, he met his parents in
50 the lobby for the scoring intermission. As
51 he had hoped, they thought he had played
52 beautifully. As they waited for the scores,
53 his parents asked, "Juan, do you think
54 you'll place in the competition?" He
55 thought momentarily, "I think that I'll be
56 happy either way."

Go on to the next page →

6. Which of the following best summarizes the passage?

   (A) Juan realizes how much love and support he has from his family.
   (B) Juan learns that he is not as good at piano as he thought he was.
   (C) Juan confronts his fear and plays in a competition.
   (D) Juan struggles with the pressure his family puts on him.

7. What was the purpose of the line, "and now he was wearing a suit," in line 25?

   (A) To show that Juan dressed nicely for his performance.
   (B) To emphasize how much Juan was sweating.
   (C) To explain that Juan hated to dress up.
   (D) To show how embarrassed Juan was about his outfit.

8. Juan's parents could be described as

   (A) strict but proud of their son.
   (B) unreasonable and impossible to please.
   (C) carefree and supportive of their son.
   (D) critical and solely focused on their son winning.

9. As used in line 50, the word "intermission" most nearly means

   (A) suspense.
   (B) competition.
   (C) reveal.
   (D) break.

10. From the last paragraph, it can be inferred that while waiting for the scoring results Juan felt

   (A) disappointed and insecure.
   (B) relaxed and content.
   (C) terrified but optimistic.
   (D) calm but uninterested.

Go on to the next page →

Questions 11 – 15

1　　As she stepped out of the car, Hui
2　looked up at the bright lights above the
3　glass sliding doors. She had never been to
4　an airport before, let alone been on a flight.
5　Her mother opened the trunk to collect the
6　luggage and turned to say goodbye. "Don't
7　worry Hui! You'll be there in no time."
8　They embraced for a moment before her
9　mom slowly started to drive away.
10　　Hui's parents had recently divorced.
11　Because she was now 16, Canadian
12　regulations meant that she could fly on her
13　own, even if it was her first time. *At least*
14　*the flight is short,* she thought. Her father
15　had moved about 150 kilometers south to
16　Seattle, Washington. The trip from
17　Vancouver was expected to take 65
18　minutes.
19　　Hui approached the security checkpoint
20　and ran through all the pointers her mother
21　had given her: "The nice people at security
22　are just trying to help you, so listen to what
23　they say." She removed the shampoo from
24　her bag, slipped her shoes off, and started
25　to walk towards the metal detector.

26　　Placing her hands above her head, she
27　let out a nervous breath. The machine
28　whirled around her and she stepped out.
29　"You're good!" barked the security
30　attendant. She gathered her bags and
31　rushed towards her plane.
32　　Hui had an hour-wait before her flight
33　took off, but it may as well have been a
34　year. She sat nervously, staring at the door
35　she would walk through to board a plane
36　for the first time ever. *Last call for Seattle,*
37　the loudspeakers chimed above her. Hui
38　bolted up and rushed to find her seat.
39　　*26B, 26B...* locating her seat, Hui
40　settled into the less-than-comfortable chair
41　and finally looked around her. There was a
42　gentle buzz of conversation as the flight
43　attendants demonstrated how to use the
44　seatbelts and emergency exits. Before she
45　knew it, Hui felt the plane start to
46　accelerate and the engine noise drowned
47　everything else out. As the wheels began to
48　leave the ground, she smiled. *Seattle, I'm*
49　*ready for you.*

Go on to the next page →

11. What is the main purpose of this passage?

   (A) To express the fear of flying that many people have.
   (B) To show the feelings of uncertainty with a new experience.
   (C) To explain how children feel when their parents get divorced.
   (D) To show the bravery of teenagers.

12. Hui was most likely nervous about travelling to visit her father because

   (A) she had never been on a plane before.
   (B) she had never been to Vancouver.
   (C) she hadn't seen her father since the divorce.
   (D) she was going to miss her mom.

13. As used in line 29, the word "barked" most nearly means

   (A) motioned.
   (B) whispered.
   (C) insisted.
   (D) yelled.

14. Based on the 5th paragraph, lines 32 – 38, one can infer that

   (A) the airline almost didn't allow Hui on her flight.
   (B) Hui is patient and likes waiting.
   (C) the airport is about to close, forcing Hui to rush to her plane.
   (D) Hui was one of the last people on the plane.

15. The passage supplies information to answer which question?

   (A) Why did Hui's parents get divorced?
   (B) Why did Hui's father move to Seattle?
   (C) What country does Hui's mother live in?
   (D) How long was Hui going to be in Seattle?

Go on to the next page →

Questions 16 – 20

1   After a long day at school, students
2 often feel burned out and exhausted. As the
3 study sessions stretch out and further
4 intensify, stress slowly but inevitably
5 becomes a part of the studying experience.
6 In this generation, students have more
7 responsibility and higher academic
8 standards to live up to, which ultimately
9 leads to many students feeling
10 overwhelmed by the pressure. When left
11 unprocessed, stress can have a negative
12 result on academic performance, ultimately
13 affecting the student's ability to
14 concentrate and retain information.
15   In an age where our culture praises
16 over-working and all-nighters, the line
17 between productivity and mere "busyness"
18 is ultimately blurred, leaving individuals to
19 associate the feeling of accomplishment
20 with stress; the more stressed out you are,
21 the more productive you will feel. There is
22 now a sense of reward with exhaustion,
23 turning exhaustion and burnout into

24 symbols of dedication that students and
25 professionals alike proudly display.
26   Unfortunately, this sense of "reward"
27 that many students feel from overworking
28 themselves comes with some pretty
29 detrimental side effects. Stress can lead to
30 physicals symptoms such as headaches,
31 stomachaches, frequent illness, and sleep
32 issues. It can also be harmful mentally and
33 emotionally, causing irritability, difficulty
34 concentrating, anxiety, and depression. In a
35 recent study, over 50% of students
36 reported feeling depressed or anxious due
37 to the stress of school.
38   As more and more individuals suffer
39 from long-term stress, it is becoming
40 incredibly important for students to
41 unwind after a long study session. This can
42 easily be done by reading a good book,
43 spending a few hours off the Internet, or by
44 working out. These, among many things,
45 can help students relax and reduce stress.

Go on to the next page →

16. What is the author's purpose in writing this passage?

    (A) To explain the science behind what causes stress.
    (B) To explain how stress makes people more productive.
    (C) To argue that studying is harmful to students' health.
    (D) To highlight the importance of students finding ways to reduce their stress.

17. In the first paragraph, the author implies that

    (A) school has become more stressful for students over time.
    (B) school was not stressful for students in past generations.
    (C) students in this generation aren't capable of managing stress.
    (D) parents' high expectations are the main cause of stress for students.

18. The author states that students can relieve stress by

    (A) writing in their journal.
    (B) surfing the internet.
    (C) studying in small chunks.
    (D) exercising.

19. As used in line 29, the word "detrimental" most nearly means

    (A) fatal.
    (B) harmful.
    (C) common.
    (D) beneficial.

20. Based on the second paragraph, lines 15 – 25, which of the following would be praised in our culture?

    (A) Staying up all night to finish an important project for work.
    (B) Not completing your homework because you were too tired.
    (C) Quitting your job because it was making you depressed.
    (D) Choosing a job that allows you to take time off.

Go on to the next page →

Questions 21 – 25

1   In 2019, most of the United States
2 celebrated National Arbor Day on April
3 26th. In the state of Alaska, it was
4 observed on May 20th. Typically, it is
5 celebrated on the first Thursday in May in
6 Canada. Regardless of when Arbor Day is
7 observed, the intention of the holiday is
8 always the same: planting trees.
9   The origins of Arbor Day stretch back
10 much earlier than people may imagine. In
11 1594, the Spanish village of Mondoñedo
12 documented the first arbor plantation
13 festival. Several hundred years later, in
14 1805, the first 'modern' Arbor Day was
15 launched in a different Spanish village:
16 Villanueva de la Sierra.
17   The American tradition of Arbor Day
18 was started in Nebraska by a man named J.
19 Sterling Morton. He and his wife had
20 recently moved from Michigan to
21 Nebraska and wanted to beautify the
22 landscape by improving the environment.
23 On April 10th, 1872, Nebraskans planted
24 over 1 million trees. Partly due to the

25 successful spread of Arbor Day, J. Sterling
26 Morton would go on to serve as the United
27 States secretary of Agriculture under
28 President Grover Cleveland from 1893 to
29 1897.
30   About a decade after the first American
31 Arbor Day, Birdsey Northrop was
32 appointed Chairman of the American
33 Forestry Association. In this role, his duty
34 was to campaign in support of Arbor Day
35 worldwide. Over the next several years, he
36 brought the tree-planting message to all
37 corners of the globe: Japan, Australia, and
38 Europe.
39   Since that time, Arbor Day has spread
40 to dozens of countries. Interestingly, the
41 date varies from place to place. This is due
42 to differences in climate and ideal growing
43 season. Over the last 150 years since the
44 first American Arbor Day, millions of
45 people around the world have planted over
46 one billion trees, and that number rises
47 every year.

Go on to the next page →

21. The primary purpose of this passage is to

   (A) inform the reader on the importance of trees to the environment.
   (B) educate the reader on the necessity of Arbor Day.
   (C) discuss the history of a certain holiday.
   (D) marvel at how many trees have been planted since 1850.

22. As used in line 9, the word "origins" most nearly means

   (A) beginnings.
   (B) festivities.
   (C) importance.
   (D) Spanish history.

23. Based on paragraph 2, lines 9 – 16, we can assume that

   (A) no one knew that Arbor Day started in Spain.
   (B) Arbor day started hundreds of years before 1594.
   (C) some people don't know the full history of Arbor Day.
   (D) Americans stole Arbor Day from the Spanish without giving them credit.

24. Based on the passage one can infer that Arbor Day is celebrated later in Alaska because

   (A) nobody is willing to plant trees in April.
   (B) it is too dangerous to celebrate Arbor Day any earlier.
   (C) the sun doesn't rise until early May in Alaska.
   (D) the ideal growing season starts later.

25. The passage supplies information to answer which of the following questions?

   (A) Exactly how many trees have been planted since the first Arbor Day?
   (B) Who started the tradition of Arbor Day in America?
   (C) How many countries celebrate Arbor Day?
   (D) Who started Arbor Day in Spain?

STOP. Do not go on to the next section until you are told to do so.

STOP

ISEE

Mathematics Achievement

LOWER LEVEL

Practice Test

Section 4
Mathematics Achievement

30 Questions   **Time: 30 Minutes**

Each question is followed by four answer choices. Read each question and decide which answer choice is correct.

Find the question number on your answer sheet and mark the space having the same letter as the answer choice that you chose. You may show your work in your test booklet.

SAMPLE QUESTION: <u>Sample Answer</u>

Which number is divisible by 5?

(A) 89
(B) 154
(C) 203
(D) 275

The correct answer is 275, so circle D is darkened.

---

1. Which mixed number is equivalent to $\frac{29}{7}$?

   (A) $3\frac{1}{7}$

   (B) $3\frac{2}{7}$

   (C) $4\frac{1}{7}$

   (D) $4\frac{2}{7}$

2. What is the greatest common factor of 16 and 24?

   (A) 4
   (B) 8
   (C) 32
   (D) 48

3. A group of 250 people took a survey on their favorite dessert. 27 people chose cake, 103 people chose ice cream, 48 people chose pie, and 72 people chose chocolate. Approximately what fraction of people chose pie?

   (A) 1/10
   (B) 1/6
   (C) 1/5
   (D) 1/4

4. Lorraine wants to estimate 246×52 to see if her answer is reasonable. Which of the following gives Lorraine the best estimate?

   (A) 240×60
   (B) 240×50
   (C) 250×60
   (D) 250×50

5. Use the figure to answer the question.

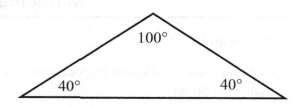

   What type of triangle is shown?

   (A) obtuse isosceles
   (B) obtuse scalene
   (C) acute isosceles
   (D) acute scalene

6. A coordinate grid is shown.

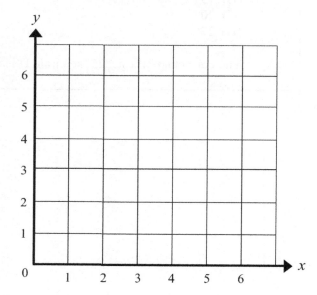

   The following points are plotted on the grid: (0, 1), (6, 1), (3, 4), (6, 4). Which type of polygon is formed by the points?

   (A) rectangle
   (B) square
   (C) parallelogram
   (D) trapezoid

7. Use the figure to answer the question.

    What fraction of the shapes are circles?

    (A) $\dfrac{1}{4}$

    (B) $\dfrac{2}{5}$

    (C) $\dfrac{1}{2}$

    (D) $\dfrac{2}{3}$

8. Which number is divisible by 9 without a remainder?

    (A) 732
    (B) 734
    (C) 736
    (D) 738

9. The number machine performs the same operation on each input number to create an output number. The machine only takes even numbers as inputs.

Input	Output
12	84
10	60
6	24
4	12
2	4

    Which output comes from an input of 18?

    (A) 126
    (B) 144
    (C) 162
    (D) 180

10. In a certain town, 53% of adults have at least 2 children, 38% of adults have 1 child, and the rest of the adults have no children. What percent of adults in the town have no children?

    (A) 9%
    (B) 11%
    (C) 15%
    (D) 91%

11. Use the number sequence to answer the question.

    100, 80, 62, 46, 32, ____

    What is the next number in the sequence?

    (A) 12
    (B) 18
    (C) 20
    (D) 22

12. If the perimeter of a rectangle is 30, which equation can be used to find the length of the rectangle? ($P = 2l + 2w$, where P = perimeter, l = length, and w = width.)

    (A) $l = 15 - w$
    (B) $l = 15 + w$
    (C) $l = 30 - 2w$
    (D) $l = 30 + 2w$

13. If $4(\square - 3) = 28$, then what does $\square$ equal?

    (A) 4
    (B) 7
    (C) 9
    (D) 10

Go on to the next page →

14. Use the number line to answer the question.

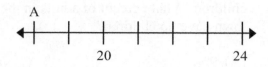

What number is represented by A on the number line?

(A) 16
(B) 18
(C) 19
(D) 22

15. The table below shows the ages of 1,000 residents of Pleasantville.

Age in Years	Number of Residents
0 to 9	130
10 to 19	180
20 to 29	250
30 to 39	280
40 to 49	160

If one person from Pleasantville is chosen at random, what is the probability that he/she will be in between 20 and 29 years old?

(A) $\frac{1}{25}$

(B) $\frac{9}{50}$

(C) $\frac{1}{5}$

(D) $\frac{1}{4}$

16. Which of the following properties is illustrated by: $\square + (\bigcirc + \Delta) = (\square + \bigcirc) + \Delta$?

(A) associative property
(B) distributive property
(C) identity property of addition
(D) commutative property

17. What value does the digit 8 represent in the number 68,035?

(A) 80
(B) 800
(C) 8,000
(D) 80,000

18. Which fraction below is the greatest?

(A) $\frac{7}{9}$

(B) $\frac{3}{7}$

(C) $\frac{8}{11}$

(D) $\frac{2}{5}$

19. What is the value of the expression $10 - 2 \times (5 - 3) + 8 \div 2$?

(A) 5
(B) 10
(C) 12
(D) 20

20. How many millimeters are in 40 centimeters?

(A) 0.4
(B) 4
(C) 400
(D) 4,000

Go on to the next page →

21. Bridget is 4.9 ft tall. Her older brother, Nick, is $5\frac{3}{4}$ ft tall. How much taller is Nick than Bridget?

(A) 0.44 ft
(B) 0.85 ft
(C) 0.95 ft
(D) 1.05 ft

22. What is the value of the expression $453.6 + 38.94$?

(A) 481.54
(B) 492.5
(C) 492.54
(D) 843

23. What is the value of the expression $2,568 \div 12$?

(A) 214
(B) 216
(C) 230
(D) 246

24. What is the value of the expression $7\frac{2}{5} - 4\frac{7}{10}$?

(A) $2\frac{3}{10}$

(B) $2\frac{7}{10}$

(C) $3\frac{3}{10}$

(D) $3\frac{7}{10}$

25. The width of a rectangle is 8 inches. If the length of the rectangle is twice the width, what is the area of the rectangle?

(A) 16 in^2
(B) 48 in^2
(C) 122 in^2
(D) 128 in^2

26. Use the figure to answer the question.

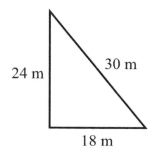

What is the perimeter of the triangle?

(A) 42 m
(B) 72 m
(C) 144 m
(D) 216 m

27. In which pair of shapes do both shapes have an equal number of lines of symmetry?

(A)

(B)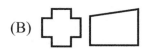

(C)

(D)

Go on to the next page →

28. Amber is buying colored paper for her 3rd grade class. She buys 20 packs of paper, and each pack has 12 sheets in it. If she splits the paper evenly between the 30 students in her class, how many sheets of colored paper does each student get?

(A) 6
(B) 8
(C) 210
(D) 240

29. The bar graph shown represents the number of miles ran last week by 7 members of the cross-country team.

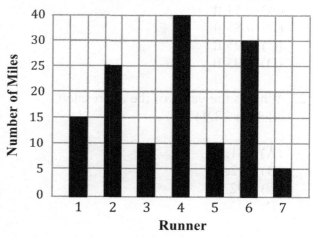

MILES RAN LAST WEEK

What is the median of the data?

(A) 10
(B) 15
(C) 25
(D) 40

30. Olga is growing three plants in her backyard. The table below shows the heights of each plant over the period of 5 days.

	Plant 1	Plant 2	Plant 3
Start	5 cm	10 cm	1 cm
Day 1	6 cm	12 cm	2 cm
Day 2	8 cm	14 cm	4 cm
Day 3	11 cm	16 cm	8 cm
Day 4	15 cm	18 cm	16 cm
Day 5	20 cm	20 cm	32 cm

What is the difference between the height of Plant 3 and the height of Plant 1 on Day 2?

(A) 4 cm
(B) 5 cm
(C) 6 cm
(D) 10 cm

ISEE

Essay

LOWER LEVEL

Practice Test

Essay Topic Sheet

You will have 30 minutes to plan and write an essay on the topic given on the other side of this page.

The essay is designed to give you the chance to show how well you can write. Be sure to express your thoughts clearly. The quality of your writing is much more important than how much you write, but it is important to write enough for a reader to understand what you mean. You will probably want to write more than a short paragraph.

You are only allowed to write in the appropriate section of the answer sheet. Please write or print neatly; you may write your essay in print or cursive.

You may take notes and plan your essay on the backside of the page. You must copy the essay topic into the box provided on your essay sheet. Please remember to write the final draft of your essay on the two lined sheets provided and to write it in blue or black pen. These are the only sheets that will be sent to the schools.

Directions continue on the next page.

Essay Topic

What is something new that you've always wanted to learn or try?

- **Only write on this essay question**
- **Only the next two pages will be sent to schools**
- **Only write in blue or black pen**

Notes

_____

_____

_____

_____

_____

_____

_____

_____

_____

_____

_____

_____

_____

_____

STUDENT NAME _____**GRADE APPLYING FOR** _____

Use a blue or black ballpoint pen to write the final draft of your essay on this sheet.

You must write your essay topic in this space.

_____

_____

_____

Use specific details and examples in your response.

_____

_____

_____

_____

_____

_____

_____

_____

_____

_____

_____

_____

_____

_____

_____

_____

_____

_____

_____

_____

_____

_____

_____

_____

ISEE LL Practice Test 3 Answer Key

Verbal Reasoning	Quantitative Reasoning	Reading Comprehension	Mathematics Achievement
1. B	1. C	1. A	1. C
2. D	2. A	2. C	2. B
3. C	3. D	3. B	3. C
4. A	4. B	4. D	4. D
5. D	5. D	5. C	5. A
6. A	6. D	6. C	6. D
7. B	7. B	7. B	7. B
8. C	8. C	8. A	8. D
9. D	9. C	9. D	9. D
10. C	10. D	10. B	10. A
11. A	11. A	11. B	11. C
12. D	12. B	12. A	12. A
13. B	13. C	13. D	13. D
14. C	14. C	14. D	14. B
15. A	15. C	15. C	15. D
16. B	16. B	16. D	16. A
17. D	17. A	17. A	17. C
18. B	18. D	18. D	18. A
19. D	19. A	19. B	19. B
20. A	20. A	20. A	20. C
21. B	21. B	21. C	21. B
22. D	22. D	22. A	22. C
23. C	23. A	23. C	23. A
24. A	24. B	24. D	24. B
25. C	25. C	25. B	25. D
26. D	26. A		26. B
27. A	27. C		27. C
28. C	28. B		28. B
29. B	29. A		29. B
30. D	30. B		30. A
31. C	31. C		
32. A	32. D		
33. B	33. C		
34. B	34. D		
	35. B		
	36. A		
	37. C		
	38. D		

Scoring Your Test

On the ISEE you receive one point for every question you answer correctly, and you receive no points for questions you answer incorrectly. The ISEE also includes 3 to 5 experimental questions on each section that do not count towards your score; you will not be told which questions are not scored. This means that it is not possible to determine your exact scores for each section of this practice test, but you can estimate your scores using the tables and charts below.

Calculating Raw Score

To calculate your raw score, add up all of the questions you answered correctly in each section, and then subtract 3 to 5 points for each section to account for the experimental questions. Use the table below to calculate your raw score.

CALCULATING RAW SCORE			
Section	Number of Correct Answers		Raw Score
Verbal Reasoning		− 4 =	
Quantitative Reasoning		− 3 =	
Reading Comprehension		− 5 =	
Mathematics Achievement		− 5 =	

Calculating Scaled Scores and Percentiles

Now that you've found your raw score, you can convert it into approximate scaled scores and percentiles using the tables below. Since these scores are estimates, they may differ slightly from your scaled scores and percentiles when you take your official ISEE exam, depending on the specific scaling for that version of the exam.

Verbal Reasoning Conversion Tables

Raw Score	Scaled Score Range	
30	874	904
29	870	900
28	866	896
27	862	892
26	859	889
25	855	885
24	851	881
23	847	877
22	843	873
21	840	870
20	836	866
19	832	862
18	828	858
17	824	854
16	820	850
15	817	847
14	813	843
13	809	839
12	805	835
11	801	831
10	798	828
9	794	824
8	790	820
7	786	816
6	782	812
5	779	809
4	775	805
3	771	801
2	767	797
1	763	793
0	760	790

Percentiles from Scaled Scores			
Grade Applying To	75th	50th	25th
5	858	841	827
6	867	855	840

Quantitative Reasoning Conversion Tables

Raw Score	Scaled Score Range	
35	877	907
34	874	904
33	870	900
32	867	897
31	864	894
30	861	891
29	858	888
28	854	884
27	851	881
26	848	878
25	845	875
24	841	871
23	838	868
22	835	865
21	832	862
20	829	859
19	826	856
18	822	852
17	819	849
16	816	846
15	813	843
14	810	840
13	806	836
12	803	833
11	800	830
10	797	827
9	793	823
8	790	820
7	787	817
6	784	814
5	780	810
4	777	807
3	774	804
2	771	801
1	768	798
0	764	794

Percentiles from Scaled Scores			
Grade Applying To	75th	50th	25th
5	861	845	829
6	874	858	843

Reading Comprehension Conversion Tables

Raw Score	Scaled Score Range	
20	883	913
19	877	907
18	871	901
17	865	895
16	859	889
15	853	883
14	847	877
13	841	871
12	835	865
11	829	859
10	823	853
9	816	846
8	810	840
7	804	834
6	798	828
5	792	822
4	786	816
3	780	810
2	774	804
1	768	798
0	762	792

Percentiles from Scaled Scores			
Grade Applying To	75th	50th	25th
5	855	832	815
6	868	849	827

Mathematics Achievement Conversion Tables

Raw Score	Scaled Score Range	
25	874	904
24	870	900
23	866	896
22	862	892
21	859	889
20	855	885
19	851	881
18	847	877
17	844	874
16	840	870
15	836	866
14	833	863
13	829	859
12	825	855
11	822	852
10	818	848
9	814	844
8	811	841
7	807	837
6	803	833
5	800	830
4	796	826
3	792	822
2	788	818
1	785	815
0	781	811

Percentiles from Scaled Scores			
Grade Applying To	75th	50th	25th
5	865	850	834
6	876	864	849

Calculating Stanines

Now that you've calculated your scaled scores and percentiles, you can use the table below to calculate your stanine for each section. A stanine is a number from 1-9 obtained by dividing the range percentile scores into 9 segments, as shown in the table below.

Percentile Range	Stanine Score
1-3	1
4-10	2
11-22	3
23-39	4
40-59	5
60-76	6
77-88	7
89-95	8
96-99	9

Although it is not possible to calculate an exact stanine score from this practice test, since the percentiles are ranges rather than exact scores, you can still estimate your stanine using the percentile ranges. For example, if you scored in between the 50th and 75th percentile your stanine score would be in between 5 and 6.

Made in the USA
Monee, IL
20 September 2023

43041124R10247